Christian Humanism

American University Studies

Series VII
Theology and Religion

Vol. 156

PETER LANG
New York • Washington, D.C./Baltimore • San Francisco
Bern • Frankfurt am Main • Berlin • Vienna • Paris

Christian Humanism

International Perspectives

Edited by
Richard P. Francis
and Jane E. Francis

PETER LANG
New York • Washington, D.C./Baltimore • San Francisco
Bern • Frankfurt am Main • Berlin • Vienna • Paris

Library of Congress Cataloging-in-Publication Data

Christian humanism: international perspectives /
edited by Richard P. Francis and Jane E. Francis.
p. cm. — (American university studies. Series VII,
Theology and religion; vol. 156)
Papers presented at the Second World Congress of Christian Philosophy,
held in Monterrey, Nuevo Leon, Mexico in October 1986.
Includes bibliographical references.
1. Christianity and religious humanism—Congresses. I. Francis, Richard P.
II. Francis, Jane E. III. Series.
BR128.H8C48   144—dc20   93-6955
ISBN 0-8204-2165-0
ISSN 0740-0446

Die Deutsche Bibliothek-CIP-Einheitsaufnahme

Christian humanism: international perspectives/
edited by Richard P. Francis and Jane E. Francis. - New York;
Berlin; Bern; Frankfurt/M.; Paris; Wien: Lang.
(American university studies : Ser. 7, Theology and religion; Vol. 156)
ISBN 0-8204-2165-0
NE: Francis, Richard P. [Hrsg.]; American university studies/07

The paper in this book meets the guidelines for permanence and durability
of the Committee on Production Guidelines for Book Longevity
of the Council of Library Resources.

© 1995 Peter Lang Publishing, Inc., New York

Printed in the United States of America.

Acknowledgments

Since this is an anthology, we wish to thank all of the scholars who have contributed their writings to make this book possible. Without them, it simply would not be.

The editors, as well as the contributors, are grateful to Dr. James A. Null, Dean of the College of Letters, Arts and Sciences, University of Colorado, Colorado Springs, for his encouragement and funding of technical assistance.

Our heartfelt appreciation goes to Elaine Schantz, whose professional expertise and friendly enthusiasm brought a sense of excitement and confidence to the editing of this book. Her quiet, careful sense of excellence we gratefully admire.

Dr. Thomas Napierkowski, Chairman of the English Department, University of Colorado, Colorado Springs, deserves our gratitude for reading the final version with knowledge and meticulous care.

Finally, we commend our son Mark whose diligence, computer skills and perseverance carried us through from start to finish. He and his wife Debbie brought this manuscript to its final completion for publication.

CHRISTIAN HUMANISM: INTERNATIONAL PERSPECTIVES

Table of Contents

Part III: Humanism and the Person

Part IV: Metaphysics of the Person

Part V: Theological Dimensions of Humanism

Part VI: Humanistic Social Philosophy

CHRISTIAN HUMANISM: INTERNATIONAL PERSPECTIVES

Preface

A group of international scholars, meeting at the Second World Congress of Christian Philosophy in Monterrey, Nuevo Leon, Mexico, in October, 1986, discovered a common bond of language, creed and philosophy of life in the Congress theme of "Humanism and Christian Metaphysics in Our Times." It was decided that the writings of the English speaking professors should be combined and published for a wider audience. And so this book has come into being.

Many backgrounds, varied cultural perspectives and unique approaches add color and insight to the important theme of Christian Humanism. While coming from different countries, such as South Africa, China, India, Germany, Liechtenstein, Canada, Greece, Ireland, and the United States, including Puerto Rico, and thereby adding a cosmopolitan outlook, all of these scholars share a commitment to a Christian view of life. This mixture of people, although predominantly philosophers, includes those of other disciplines including sociology, political science and theology. Some are ordained clergy or members of religious orders. Most are lay persons, and all are teachers and Doctors of Philosophy. To keep alert spiritually, intellectually and otherwise, these scholars have formed a new society called the International Association for Christian Thought which meets regularly with other Associations and Congresses worldwide. Through an exchange of ideas and scholarly research, this group encourages the participation of members in the exciting arena of Philosophical debate. Using a common theme, two separate but compatible papers are presented at these meetings allowing for discussion and encouragement of new concepts.

We hear so much about secular humanism in today's society. The moral dilemma, the breakdown of the family, drug use, guns, gangs, violence of all kinds on our streets, in our neighborhoods, even in our homes and schools, all vie for the daily news coverage. What has happened to us? Have we become so deluded that we have lost sight of the meaning of values? Have we stressed our humanism so much that we can no longer look beyond it? Are we concentrating so much on our beginnings, our purely scientific rise from some kind of so-called primordial protoplasm that we refuse to acknowledge the divine spark that once motivated the creation of great art and music, magnificent cathedrals, the haunting simplicity of Gregorian plain chant, the founding of religious orders? Are we so concerned with secularism that we are no longer excited by the richness of the marvelous tapestry not only of this life but of what lies beyond? Have we moved too far to the left? Are we so engrossed with the scientific aspect of our being that we neglect the moral, intellectual, religious, and philosophical questions that lift us beyond the mere physical? Have we abandoned the golden mean and the religious heritage that was once a guiding light?

Humanism comes in many forms, from that of the Greek sophists, Socrates, Plato and Aristotle, to that of the pragmatic Romans, Aulus Gellius and Cicero. The philanthropic Greeks gave us the doctrine of the golden mean and the notion that man is the measure of all things. Roman practicality and pragmatism gave us Stoicism and the basis for education and law. Roman oratory grew from Greek rhetoric. From Greco-Roman humanism came a Patristic prophetic message of social justice which was based on doing the will of God as revealed in the Torah. Through Jesus the law and the prophets were fulfilled in His teaching of love of God and neighbor, now interpreted as the ultimate principle of order. In other words, the fulfillment of the law is love.

Christian Scholasticism brought stability to humanism. Renaissance humanism fostered free inquiry and aesthetic growth. Enlightenment humanism spurred revolutions that continue even now as a means for philanthropic renewal of social justice. Kant saw the danger in limiting humanism to reason alone and even he saw the necessity for a theism which could make humanism worthwhile. Nietzsche, Heidegger and Derrida challenge humanism. Kierkegaard believed that genuine ethics must be based on faith.

In general, humanism is a system of thought which gives predominant interest to the affairs of men as compared with the supernatural or abstract. The term is specifically applied to the movement of thought in western Europe in the 15th century which broke through mediaeval traditions of scholastic theology and philosophy to study and stress the ancient classics. Essentially a revolt against intellectual, and especially ecclesiastical authority, humanism is the parent of all modern developments, intellectual, scientific or social. This revival of classical letters, individual and critical spirit, and emphasis on secular concerns was characteristic of the Renaissance. As a philosophy that asserts the dignity and worth of man and his capacity for self-realization through reason, humanism rejects supernaturalism. Christian humanism seeks to restore that spark of the divine. This volume is meant to reveal God in man's modern world.

How Christianity fits into the scheme of things in our busy world, how it has shaped our existence in this computer-age society and how Christian philosophy comes to terms with modern humanism is a legitimate concern for everyone. "Man does not live by bread alone," and over the ages, when other disciplines such as science, literature, the arts, etc. have fallen short and have been found lacking, philosophy has provided the spark, the food for thought, the impetus, the leaven. Because of the role of philosophy, its range and "back-to-basics" nature, it is natural that this book be philosophical in nature. Because Christianity gives vitality to our humanistic society, it is natural that this be a common theme with an international flair. It is hoped that these writings will bring about a deeper understanding of what it means to be a Christian in today's technological world.

Jane E. Francis

CHRISTIAN HUMANISM: INTERNATIONAL PERSPECTIVES

Introduction

Because of the transcendent other-worldliness of Christianity, the concept of Christian humanism seems to be misplaced or even self-contradictory. On the other hand, Christ came to our very own human world, this same twentieth century world in fact, to redeem it, to sanctify it, to improve it, and to establish and sustain his community of believers until the end of time. Civilizations come and go, but Christianity overall endures generation after generation with remarkable perseverance.

Certainly, the Christian experience at times tends more toward a purely sacred, even contemplative condition, calling its faithful to mortification of the things of this world, demanding detachment from material possessiveness and setting our affection on things above. At other times, the Christian experience tends more toward the secular, toward this world, energizing the faithful to immerse themselves in our worldly problems and affairs, to become practitioners of salvation and holiness, somehow being in the world, yet not of it.

At least superficially, the term "humanism" better serves the secular world. In fact, "secular humanism" is used as a rallying cry for those forces which contend against Christianity. It inherently rejects anything holy or religious, and restricts our experience to satisfying only our human potentiality in strictly human terms. It is the business of religious humanism to break through the barriers of the purely secular world in order to call it to holiness, to convert it, to teach the gospel message to all nations including the more secular kind. Thereby, the case for Christian humanism can be made.

Certainly Christian humanism inherently cannot reject God. Instead it must celebrate God within the human sphere of interests, needs, and activities as divine concurrence and regular creation. It celebrates life in the Spirit, as the continuous, unbroken dimension of the Pentecost of nearly two thousand years ago. It reveres and submits to the boundless power of the Holy Spirit to dwell within the human individual and community, to sanctify it, to enable the faithful to progress with a strong abiding sense of hope and love. It acknowledges Christ as Lord and brother, who as lord accomplished our salvation in the terrible drama of Calvary, now dwells in Heaven, and will come to judge this world at the end of time. As brother, Jesus possessed all of our human attributes, except sin. In some mystical way, Christ still remains in this world, in the final covenantal partnership with human beings. This then fundamentally is Christian humanism, the way of Christ in this world, in a shared creation, redemption and sanctification. It blends the sacred and the secular, always giving prominence to the sacred.

Containing thirty-four essays, this volume represents the latest thinking of a special group of internationally active scholar-professors in the field of Christian humanism. It revolves around six main themes: The Conceptual Basis for Christian Humanism; Scientific Aspects of Christian Humanism; Humanism and the Person; Metaphysics of the Person; Theological Dimensions of Humanism; and Humanistic Social Philosophy.

The conclusion recaptures the main ideas of each contributor for a quick review and to gain the overall direction of the thinking of these internationalists. With the world being ever more accessible to ever more people by rapid communication and transit, this compilation opens avenues for discussion and understanding. To some degree, the material presented here can serve as a reinforcement of traditional ideas refurbished for today's world. That can be satisfying. But there are occasional disjunctions as these professionals struggle with today's collapse of values in some areas. In some essays correctives are offered and, because they are Christian, the virtue of hope puts their trust in God's hands. They remain faithful to Christian philosophy, as diverse as that can be, reflecting where indicated the theology of believers, even as they profess and practice the abiding love for God and neighbor.

Some encouragement and even inspiration can be found regarding the importance of this collection as Karol Wojtyla's (Pope John Paul II) recent teachings about *Christian Humanism* are found published under that very title. His work originated at Lublin, Poland, under the Communist regime in an ideological confrontation of over forty years. He teaches that a true, authentic humanism always deals with human dignity, destiny, transcendence, love and topics fairly correlative with our own collection.

Richard P. Francis

PART I

THE CONCEPTUAL BASIS
FOR CHRISTIAN HUMANISM

CHRISTIAN HUMANISM: SOLID BASIS AND ANTECEDENTS

Walter W. Artus

Given that the term "humanism" has a number of "more or less distinct meanings"[1] it is well to bring out its meaning at the outset of this communication. In its first and strict meaning the term names "a literary and intellectual movement, the 'new learning,' running from 14th-century Italy through Western culture generally into the 17th century . . . marked by devotion to Greek and Latin classics as the central and highest expression of human values."[2] Essentially retaining that meaning, the term has been extended to comparable developments in the Middle Ages and other periods. About those instances of humanism I do not intend to speak here. My concern will be rather with a broader humanism, with humanism as more recently understood and as signifying certain 20th-century philosophical, cultural and political movements which deservedly focus on and stress the dignity and central importance of man within the known universe, or even the whole of reality.[3] This second meaning comes to mind readily when one reads or hears about the several movements which today are given or take to themselves the name "humanism." As a matter of fact, inspection soon discloses that these humanisms are sometimes mutually exclusive, undoubtedly the result of different, and at times contrary, understandings of the essential nature and destiny of human beings,[4] as well as of the rest of reality at least implicitly. Thus in books and in newspapers, we come across different types or species of humanism. In their discussions and in their articles, we find references to classical humanism, Marxist humanism, existential humanism, atheistic humanism, civic humanism, secular humanism, integral humanism, religious humanism, Christian humanism, etc.[5]

In order to determine which, if any, of the intellectual and cultural movements that arrogate to themselves the name "humanism" are in essence compatible with orthodox Christian thought, there is no choice but to ascertain first, before anything else, which of them provide us with a philosophically sound humanism. They will do so only if based on a proper and correct understanding of the human person, since it is on its account that they are supposedly designated by that name. That understanding must entail, of course, the rational grasp of the fundamental character or nature of human beings. At the very least, it must unequivocally determine rationally whether man is or is not just a part, albeit the highest one, of a purely physical or natural universe, a universe that might perhaps at least practically exclude the reality of the Transcendent Being known as God in religious language.[6] In other words, we must first be rationally satisfied about whether or not the proper understanding of man's basic nature necessitates at the same time the recognition of the truth of the existence of the Supreme Existent who, as such, is entitatively distinct from the totality of finite things which includes the world and man.

Now simply on the basis of their conception of man, as implying or as excluding the reality of the Transcendent Being, the many instances of humanism named above and others can be reduced to one or the other of two contrary forms of humanism. They are: a) a spiritualistic, theist, or, preferably and more simply, theocentric humanism and b) a naturalistic, non-theist (whether atheistic, agnostic or neutral) or, preferably, anthropocentric humanism.[7] Within the latter we include all those instances of humanism which, though in different ways and not always for the same reasons, in theory or practice, declare that man or the human species is the absolute and unconditional metaphysical center or point of reference of the whole of reality.[8] Every man-centered humanism looks upon man as the highest reality, possessed therefore of a supreme value and dignity, above that of everything else, including God whose existence might be even denied or ignored completely. Man is accordingly enthroned as the highest being and good, with a consequent understanding that the energies and operations of every other thing in existence should logically and totally be directed to the well-being of man. After all, he is then the supreme being and consequently their ultimate good and purpose. As for himself, he has no higher reality and purpose toward which he ought to direct the whole of his existence and life. Within all man-centered humanism therefore, the totality of reality is beholden to man as to its supreme center and goal. Should it be asserted moreover explicitly, as is done by many who embrace this type of humanism, that man's destiny does not individually extend beyond the grave, then obviously the only meaningful and pressing task of each and every right-thinking person can only be this: to secure for himself by all possible means the utmost in physical and psychological well-being during the years of earthly existence allotted to each on this or another planet. Such is and will always be, according to anthropocentric humanism, the foremost or paramount objective of every right-thinking person without exception. Consequently all that may in the least contribute effectively to the supposed enhancement and advancement of the human family during its earthly sojourn is thereby legitimized and may even be said to be morally obligatory on the members of the species.[9]

Notwithstanding the recent vintage of most of the instances of humanism, it is easy to discover its ancestral antecedents in the days of man's earliest philosophical speculations in Ancient Greece. More accurately, however, their basic thought was already succinctly expressed in the well-known dictum of Protagoras of Abdera: "Man is the measure of all things, of the things that are that they are, and of things that are not that they are not."[10] Generally both proponents and opponents look upon the dictum as the fountainhead and first explicit formulation of what often unfortunately simply goes by the name "humanism," without further qualifications. Its basic tenets were clearly stated in a "Humanist Manifesto" published in *The Humanist* in 1933. They read: a) the universe is self-existing and not created; b) man is simply a part of nature and has evolved as part of a continuous process; c) modern science provides the only acceptable explanation of the universe or of human values; and d) the end of man's life is the complete realization of the human personality in this world.[11]

Though not always explicitly nor necessarily atheistic or agnostic,[12] anthropocentric humanism, particularly when it characterizes itself as "secular," may be defined as any "philosophical, political or cultural affirmation of man as the principal object of concern, to the exclusion of all religious or theological theses about the origin and destiny of human beings."[13] The definition does not ignore the fact that some secular humanists speak of their philosophy as religious.[14] They speak thus because their doctrine claims "the ultimacy of religious truth."[15] Indeed a few "religious humanists" are willing to permit the term "God" provided it only means "whatever humans cherish as their highest ideal."[16] But if the term names "a transcendent being or reality who created man and influences and controls his destiny then the answer (to 'Does God exist?') is 'No' for there is insufficient evidence."[17] If consistent, the defenders of secular humanism "should unabashedly defend atheism, agnosticism, or skepticism on intellectual and moral grounds."[18] No wonder then that to people who acknowledge a supreme and supernatural being, secular humanism often seems and is not only agnostic and atheistic, but also aggressively anti-theist. Definitely such has been the case of leading exponents of Marxist humanism, as well of a number of the signers and defenders of "The Humanist Manifesto," both on this and on the other side of the Atlantic.

Distinct from and contrary to the various sorts of anthropocentric humanism, there have developed in our century a few types of what by contrast is correctly identified as a God-centered or theocentric humanism. These types are designated thus on account of mainly two reasons: first, in partial agreement with their opposites, they rightly insist on man's unique dignity, as well as on his centrality in the universe.[19] More importantly and secondly, however, their understanding of man's basic nature and indeed of the entire realm of reality requires their unequivocal affirmation of the existence of a Supernatural Being,[20] one who is transcendent and infinitely superior to humans and whatever else might be given in reality. Indeed all existing things owe to Him their existence and life. Hence God is fittingly declared the primeval source and the supreme good and goal of all that is not Himself actually. Obviously what is at issue here is nothing more than the understanding of the First Being according to classical theism.[21]

Within any genuine theocentric humanism, man cannot be regarded as the absolute metaphysical center of the totality of reality. Legitimately, however, he is well deemed and declared a *secundum quid* or relative center in a very meaningful way. The noblest and most perfect of all earthly creatures, man is indeed the metaphysically most important and central figure of the natural or physical world. Accordingly, he must be regarded as its proper entitative center, if not that of the entire created universe, but only in a relative way which allows one to speak of God as its absolute center. As the most significant and valuable entity of the natural world, man is entitled to utilize and to direct to his appropriate well-being the resources and energies that belong to beings lesser than himself, particularly when there is question of his attaining to his fulfillment and perfect happiness in the intellectual and immaterial possession of the Highest Good. Nevertheless after all is said and done, the human person can never be more than the world's relative center, its center therefore in a rationally limited way. The requirements of his own nature, and even more so those of the perfect nature of the ontologically First Being, make it obligatory that men and women recognize Him as the world's absolute center. Why? Simply because he is the Supreme Existent, as well as their creative source and intended end. This means that only with and in God will each of them be able to realize fully some day all his or her entitative and moral possibilities.[22]

In examining the examples of humanism developed by leading Christian thinkers in our century, we need distinguish two distinct types of theocentric humanism: a) the philosophically sound Christian humanism developed within the Aristotelico-Thomist tradition,[23] thoughtfully sketched out by Jacques Maritain fifty years ago in his *Integral Humanism* and more recently by other Christian thinkers, such as our present Pope John Paul II;[24] b) the philosophically less appealing hyper-Christian humanism of a few Protestant theologians, with Karl Barth at the head of them.[25] The Barthian Christian humanism is characterized by the assumption that "humanity has no meaning other than the meaning it receives from the divine history of redemption and that even with redemption humanity remains without inherent value."[26] This assumption seems to be a logical consequence of the Lutheran interpretation of the character and of the results of original sin, with apparently totally corrupting consequences on human nature.[27] Contrariwise the sounder and philosophically more meaningful Christian humanism present in the writings of Maritain and John Paul II, in a different vein and in accord with Catholic thought, holds that "humanity, even damaged with sin, retains an essential meaning and value."[28]

Not much effort is needed to show that, from the vantage point of rationally sound philosophy, the balanced Christian humanism of the just mentioned Catholic thinkers is both more meaningful and fruitful. Its philosophical validity and superiority are assured when measured against the traditional and correct understanding of God and of man upheld by Christian philosophers who continue the task of philosophy in the spirit of Plato and Aristotle. There is no serious reason to think that the theocentric humanism of much of Christian thought today is just a 20th century development and a reaction to the fast-spreading non-theist, and at times aggressive, atheistic, humanism of much of our modern age. It is of course a fact that the term "humanism" in much of its present day meaning has only lately come into widespread use. It is also a fact that the sustained and explicitly conscious efforts to develop a well-thought-out Christian humanism relevant for our days have been occasioned by the spread of various sorts of atheistic humanism since the last century,[29] with a consequent earnest acceptance by many in both East and West of the goals and programs of that humanism.[30] On the other hand, however, it is likewise true that since the earliest days when Christian thought began to develop dialectically with often the beneficial assistance of philosophy and with regard, of course, for the demands of an authentic faith and the limits of human reason, Christian thinkers have well-nigh unanimously insisted on the lofty worth, dignity and destiny of each and every human person. The basis for such an attitude in each instance has been the constant recognition of the spiritual character of the rational life principle within humans and of their legitimate claim to a destiny beyond the years of their earthly existence.[31]

The implications of these truths gave Christian thinkers very early no choice but to look upon humanity as practically the entitative high point and center of the visible universe certainly — and possibly of the entire created world — with the proviso dictated by sound classical theism wherein God is established as the absolute center of the whole of reality. This has to be so by reason of His infinite perfection, infinity and transcendence since He is the First Being, the creative source and the ultimate completion of all beings.[32] How could reflective Christian thinkers ever think correctly otherwise? In a realistic fashion they have recognized in nearly all cases not just man's real kinship with all physical reality, but also they have always been keenly aware of his entitative superiority over all other physical entities, due to the presence within him of a spiritual soul with its lofty powers of understanding, reason and will. With the earlier non-Christian philosopher, Aristotle, Christian thinkers have understood that, with and because of his intellectual soul, man not only becomes but rises above all things in our universe and that, particularly through his power of rational and free choices, he is within ineluctable limits a real master of his destiny for good or evil. Moreover and very importantly their Christian faith has continued for them the inspired thought of the Hebrew Scriptures, with its understanding of the creation of human beings in the likeness and image of their Creator.[33] Each human person carries within itself the imprint of its Maker from the moment when He breathed into the bodies of the first man and woman a life-giving soul endowed with the spiritual powers of intellect and will. For that precise reason, humans have been, since their initial creation, more than microcosms which, in the rich perfection, complexity and beauty of their bodies, encompass and bring to its highest point of perfection the world of physical reality and life. By reason of the spiritual soul which animates their material bodies, they are full participants also in the reality and life of spiritual entities.[34] Indeed through that same rational soul men are somewhat akin to even the divine reality, as already intimated in Plato's pre-Christian philosophy.[35] Noble as a human body is, it is actually because of the spiritual part of its being that each person is truly a center of created reality, a center wherein, as in a bridge, unite the physical and the spiritual realms.[36] At the midway point between these two realms, human beings cannot but count as the most valuable kind of entities in the natural world. Indeed, through and in each person, humanity stands in a meaningful manner at the center of that world and of all creation possibly. It is a center truly with the previously stated proviso that man at the same time acknowledge that his own center, as well as the absolute center of all reality, is none but the First and Supreme Being, the source of his own life. Only with the earnest acceptance of the intrinsic worth of the human person and nature have Christian believers and thinkers been able to speak down through the centuries of an Incarnate God and Redeemer. Countless heinous sins since the first act of disobedience have without a doubt wounded man's nature gravely. But they have not corrupted it so completely that its dignity as God's noblest visible creation has been irretrievably lost. Were that the case, how would Christians understand the truth that grace builds upon nature?

Above it was noted that sustained efforts to develop an explicit and consciously authentic humanism have been made by Christian thinkers only during our century. It does not mean, however, that the necessitating premises of such a humanism had not been explicitly formulated before with sufficient clarity. Its antecedents, not to say an implicit humanism, can without much difficulty be gathered from the writings of earlier Christians who have, since the inception of Christianity practically, investigated matters in the philosophical spirit and manner. Time permits no more than to recall briefly the names and thought of a few acknowledged exponents of Christian philosophical thought who noted down in their writings the solid bases of a rationally sound Christian humanism. Already well into the second century the Greek apologist Marcianus Aristides, "a philosopher of Athens," concluded his proofs for the existence of the Mover of the world with the declaration that He is "the God of all, who made all for the sake of man."[37] Not more than two centuries later St. Gregory of Nizza composed the perhaps first Christian anthropological treatise, a *De Hominis Opificio* or *On The Formation of Man*.[38] On its pages the author portrayed man, a composite substance made up of body and soul, as a microcosm governed by its soul much like the macrocosm is ruled by God.[39] Made in the image of God, man is on that account a king with respect to the whole world, as well as a "mean and medium between the sensible and the spiritual worlds."[40] At the apex of sensible nature, man contains within the entitative make-up of his body all the lower degrees of being. But yet again, it is by reason of the spiritual life proper to his rational soul that he is a bridge between the kingdoms of matter and spirit.[41] Moreover, if man's creation followed that of all other things, it was so because they were all created for man.[42]

Not differently wrote the great Latin St. Augustine. The human composite that is man owes his unique and great dignity to being, particularly through the soul's capacity for God, a divine image in a manner unmatched by anything else in the visible world.[43] As if to warn us that we commit no wrong through being rightly concerned with earthly things, Augustine reminds the reader of the basic ontic value and goodness of all created things.[44] All of them are metaphysically good because they have been all created by a Perfect Being out of love for intellectual creatures like ourselves.[45]

A similar high esteem of man's exalted dignity and of his importance in a universe that is basically good — with at the same time the proper recognition that man's nobility and glory have their basis in his relation to the Supreme Being — is also readily noticeable in the writings of the mediaevals. According to St. Bonaventure, for example, God created the totality of things we call the world, first of all to manifest His power and goodness. Yet it has been brought into existence with man as truly its secondary but real end. "Without a doubt it is true that we are the end of all things and that corporeal things have been made a gift to man . . . . "[46] Hence this world is a perfect house for man until he arrives at a higher and heavenly dwelling after his life on earth.[47] St. Bonaventure's great contemporary, St. Thomas Aquinas, had equal thoughts on this matter. They are well captured and expressed in a discourse of John Paul II wherein he lists various reasons to demonstrate the timeliness of the Angelic Doctor's philosophy for our times. After extolling Aquinas' deep sense of man, "tam nobilis creatura,"[48] the Pope says:

> The idea he has of this "nobilis creatura," the image of God, is so easy to observe every time he begins to talk of the Incarnation. . . . he does not hesitate to compare man to the "sea," in that he collects, unifies and elevates in himself the less than human world, as the sea collects all the waters of the

rivers which flow into it. . . . He defines man as the horizon of creation in which sky and land join, like a link between time and eternity, like a synthesis of creation. . . . Inspired by St. Augustine he affirms that by merely taking human nature, the Word could show "quanta sit dignitas humanae naturae . . . quam excelsum locum inter creaturas habeat humana natura."[49]

Another contemporary of the last two Doctors but one who outlived them by about forty years, the Illuminated Doctor Ramon Llull, likewise expressed clearly and repeatedly the basic ideas underlying a sound humanism much along the same lines.[50] The proximate or immediate end and fulfillment of all corporeal beings is man, he tells us, for it is for his benefit and service that they have been created.[51] Though made for God as their highest and ultimate end, physical things can and will achieve the high purpose of their existence but only indirectly or vicariously by means of, or through, the glorified bodies of the happy rational creatures that will directly attain to the possession of the highest good in heaven.[52] The multifaceted structure and character of man's composite nature reveals him a microcosm that in his body has a real share or participation in all the perfections of the non-spiritual or physical realm of reality. Yet above all it is by reason of and in his spiritual soul — which renders the body and whole composite truly human — that man has become and been appropriately appointed as the "means and instrument" whereby all physical beings will attain to their highest end in God.[53]

St. John's University
New York, New York USA

NOTES

1. S. J. Ong, "Humanism," The New Catholic Encyclopedia, ed. The Catholic University of America (New York: McGraw Hill Co., 1967), Vol. 7, p. 215.

12

2. Loc. cit.

3. Loc. cit.

4. Andrew N. Woznicki, "The Christian Humanism and Adequate Personalism of Karol Wojtyla," *Pope John Paul II Lecture Series* (St. Paul, Minnesota: College of St. Thomas, 1985), p. 36.

5. W. P. Haas, "Secular Humanism," *The New Catholic Encyclopedia*, ed. The Catholic University of America (New York: McGraw Hill Co., 1967), Vol. 7, pp. 226-28. Also Vernon J. Bourke, "Humanism as a Basis for Moral Philosophy," in *God, Man and Philosophy: Symposium*, ed. Carl Grindel (New York: St. John's University, 1971), pp. 75-6. Also Jean Paul Sartre, *Existentialism and Humanism*, tr. Philip Mairet (Brooklyn: Haskell House Publishers, 1977), p. 55. Also Anonymous, "Secular Humanism: Meaning and Various Political Stances," *The New York Times*, A 19, Feb. 28, 1986.

6. Woznicki, p. 36.

7. Jacques Maritain, *Integral Humanism*, tr. Joseph W. Evans (New York: Charles Scribner's Sons, 1968), pp. 27-28. Also Woznicki, op. cit., p. 36.

8. J. A. Fagginger Auer, "The Case of Humanism," in J. A. Fagginger Auer and Julian Hart, *Humanism versus Theism* (Ames, Iowa: Iowa University Press, 1971), pp. 3-5. Also Maritain, op. cit., p. 28.

9. Paul Kurtz, "Humanism and Religion: A Reply to Critics of Humanist Manifesto II," *The Humanist*, Vol. 34 (1974), pp. 4-5.

10. Charles M. Bakewell, *Source Book in Ancient Philosophy* (New York: Charles Scribner's Sons, 1939), p. 67.

11. Haas, op. cit., p. 226.

12. Kurtz, op. cit., p. 4.

13. Haas, op. cit., p. 226.

14. Auer, 14. op. cit., pp. 24-5.

15. Haas, op. cit., p. 226.

16. Kurtz, op. cit., p. 4.

17. Ibid., p. 5.

18. Ibid., p. 4.

19. Woznicki, op. cit., p. 36. Also Julian Hart, "The Central Elements of Theism," in J. A. Fagginger Auer and Julian Hart, *Humanism versus Theism* (Ames, Iowa: Iowa University Press, 1971), pp. 95-6.

20. Maritain, op. cit., p. 2.

21. On the understanding of God in Classical Theism see Hart, op. cit., pp. 87-92.

22. Julian Hart, "Theism and the Christian Faith," in J. A. Fagginger Auer and Julian Hart, *Humanism versus Theism* (Ames, Iowa: Iowa University Press, 1971), pp. 135-6.

23. Haas, op. cit., p. 229.

24. For an introduction to Pope John Paul II's Christian humanism see Woznicki, op. cit., pp. 35-40. A more extended treatment is Andrew N. Woznicki, *A Christian Humanism: Karol Wojtyla's Existential Personalism* (New Britain, CT: Mariel Publications, 1980).

25. Haas, op. cit., p. 229.

26. Loc. cit.

27. Maritain, op. cit., pp. 16-7.

28. Haas, op. cit., p. 229. Also Maritain, op. cit., pp. 9, 13, 16. At a general audience on April 9, 1986, Pope John Paul II made this point also. Report of it under "Pope John Paul II: Man is Created in the Image of God," in *The Wanderer*, p. 2, May 1, 1986.

14

29. D. J. Forbes, "Christian Humanism," *The New Catholic Encyclopedia,* ed. The Catholic University of America (New York: McGraw Hill Co., 1967), Vol. 7, p. 224. Also Maritain, op. cit., pp. 9-10.

30. Maritain, op. cit., pp. 28-34.

31. Ibid., p. 9.

32. What other meaning are we to place on the early Greek apologist Marcianus Aristides' declaration to the effect that the Mover of the world is none other than "the God of all, who made all for the sake of man"? Frederick Copleston, *A History of Philosophy* (Westminster, Maryland: The Newman Press, 1962), Vol. 2, p. 18.

33. Genesis 1:26, in *The Old Testament,* tr. Ronald Knox (New York: Sheed and Ward, 1968), Vol. 1, p. 2.

34. Martin Vaske, *A Philosophy of Morality* (Omaha, Nebraska: Creighton University, 1980), pp. 6-7.

35. Plato, *Timaeus,* 41, c-7, in *The Collected Dialogues of Plato,* ed. Edith Hamilton and Huntington Cairns (Princeton: Princeton University Press, 1971), p. 1170.

36. The point has already been made by St. Gregory of Nizza late in the fourth century.

37. Copleston, op. cit., Vol. 2, p. 16. Also Etienne Gilson, *History of Christian Philosophy in the Middle Ages* (New York: Random House, 1955), pp. 10, 554.

38. Op. cit., p. 56.

39. Ibid., pp. 56-7.

40. Ignatius Brady, *History of Philosophy,* Mimeo Notes (Detroit: Duns Scotus College, 1950), Vol. 1, 170.

41. Loc. cit.

15

42. Gilson, op. cit., p. 56.

43. Brady, op. cit., Vol. 1, p. 205.

44. Recently this point was brought out clearly in one of Pope John Paul II's general audiences on April 22, 1986. See report of it under the title "Pope John Paul II: Created Things Have a Legitimate Autonomy" in *The Wanderer*, p. 1, April 24, 1986.

45. Gilson, op. cit., p. 72.

46. St. Bonaventure, *Breviloquium*, II, 4, in *Opera Omnia* (Quaracchi: Typographia Collegii S. Bonaventurae, 1891), Vol. 5, p. 222.

47. St. Thomas Aquinas, *De Veritate Catholicae Fidei*, IV, 1 (Paris: Apud Bloud et Barral Bibliopolas, 1986), p. 486.

48. Pope John Paul II, "Method and Doctrine of St. Thomas in Dialogue with Modern Culture," *The Whole Truth About Man*, ed. James V. Schall (Boston: St. Paul Editions, 1981), p. 274.

49. Loc. cit.

50. For a more extended treatment see Walter Artus, "Man's Cosmic Ties Within the Thought of Ramon Llull," *Estudios Lulianos*, Vol. 27 (1981), pp. 25-46.

51. Ramon Llull, *Liber de Homine*, p. 2, in *Beati Raymundi Lulli Opera* (Mainz: John Henry Haeffner, 1737), Vol. 6, p. 481.

52. Llull, *Liber de Anima Rationali*, op cit. p. 1, p. 416.

53. Ibid.

THE CHRISTIAN RENEWAL OF ART

Richard P. Francis

The purpose of this writing is to show that aesthetic and religious experience are at least equivalent and that they both serve as a continuous renewal of the divine-human encounter. Art and religion are usually distinct except in the final acquisition of the beautiful. Further, we show that religious conversion is a constant renewing of the willful act of attaining the aesthetic object, God.

Although Hans Urs von Balthazar gave us the first Christian theology of aesthetics, the philosophical role in aesthetics, claims Arthur Berndtson, is the typical philosophical role in anything, namely to seek a high degree of unity of the subject.[1] The same role operates in religion, to seek a high unity in religious matters. As in any work of art, so too in religious experience and expression, there needs to be a unity of parts, a vital organic whole, a unity of different parts distinct in themselves. Both in art and religion, the involved parts have the quality, to some extent, of blending together as do the colors, shapes, forms and design of a painting. The various parts and aspects of religion and art blend or merge into a unity, a whole. This vital organization or unity involves the quality of "intensive magnitude" which solicits and admits those things that belong to that particular whole. Once unity is achieved, the parts fit together almost naturally with an affinity that cannot be otherwise. Integration or integrity is achieved. Any integrated part that thereafter should be missing challenges and distorts the whole, and it usually cannot be substituted for by anything else without distressing the unity already gained.

Thus, both religious and aesthetic experience achieve a living unity of distinct parts that unite with intensive magnitude. This is the *integrity* that St. Thomas Aquinas assigns to the nature of beauty.[2] St. Augustine also explains that "unity is the form of all beauty,"[3] which is the same as integrity. Religious and aesthetic integrity operate ontologically to make a being complete and undivided in itself and divided from others. This separation from others is called "extensive magnitude," which serves as a barrier to block or inhibit what does not belong to the unity. "The more divided a thing is the less beauty it has."[4] Both religious and artistic integrity can be composed of many things but always requires unity. A conglomeration of things without unity or integrity has no beauty.[5] Jacques Maritain asserts that the integrity of beauty acquires the fullness of being which metaphysically attracts the human intellect. Beauty thus unlocks the ontological secret, the operating mystery, the actualizing form within that unity which makes beauty real.

Modern scholars such as Jessop, Ducasse, and Beardsley respectively argue whether or not aesthetic experience, beauty, is exclusively objective or subjective or instrumental.[6] These properties need not be so exclusive, for Thomistically beauty is pervasively, ontologically real, and emotionally desirable and creatively productive. To deny any such property badly impoverishes and distorts the nature of beauty.

Primarily, beauty essentially creates a joyful condition.[7] St. Thomas gives a short, direct statement about beauty as "that which when seen gives pleasure." It is something real that relates to us in pleasurable ways. This is not so much a definition as a statement of fact about our condition relating to beauty. The term "seen" can be visual, mental, emotional, etc. He adds three conditions for beauty, namely integrity or perfection, proportion or harmony, and brightness or clarity.[8] Integrity is the unity or wholeness explained throughout this writing. Harmony means balance, a proper proportionality. And clarity exposes the form of beauty with intellectual and sensory brilliance.

Maritain insists that the beautiful is "connatural to man" and is expressed in art.[9] Beauty captured in art is at first not so much intellectual as it is delectable, appetitive or emotional. Only later is beauty subject to intellectual reflection. The beautiful is not a kind of intellectual truth but rather a kind of good that we desire and basically find delightful. Truth enlightens intelligence, but beauty stirs desire and produces love. Indeed, it is by the rapturous absorbing beauty of a work of art that we are delightfully seized. Our love then is caused by the beauty of what we love. In religion this is God's beauty. We delight in anything truly beautiful, including beautiful people, works of art, manner of living, and so forth. But when God enters in, art and religion begin to lose their distinctiveness, because the beloved object of both art and religion is the same, God. In the religious aesthetic our love of God only intensifies.

What distinguishes artistic value from religious value is that the latter inherently includes the sense of the sacred. Usually we do not ascribe the sacred to art as such, but history affirms that the greatest works of art in literature, music, painting, poetry, sculpture, architecture, etc. contain religious themes. We note for music the Berlioz Requiem, Bach's St. Matthew Passion, Handel's Messiah, and for painting the celebrated creativity of Raphael, Michelangelo, Giotto, Tintoretto and others. Art is regularly energized by the beauty of religion so that across the ages there persists a preponderance of religious themes. Religious aesthetics achieves and classically sustains the vital, organic unity or integrity of beauty. Religious aesthetics comes into play with the capture and release of both beauty and holiness. The capture holds our interest and essentially controls the proper arrangements of whatever contributes to beauty and holiness. The release essentially frees both beauty and holiness to stimulate and exhilarate the artist and other beneficiaries further along similar creative paths. The integrity of beauty and sacredness both captures and releases creative power to be enjoyed and desired. Everyone involved experiences a kind of love caused by beauty. Any abuse of that integrity, such as disorder or bad taste, is glaringly disruptive and injurious to our aesthetic and religious sensitivity.

Of course, holiness comes only from God. Hence, in some mysterious way, God participates freely in the arrangement of things beautiful. This adds the quality of the divine to the integrity of beauty. God's creative power is part of the beautiful. Certainly there is no good reason why any artistic creation or production must have few or many parts, or that God should enter in. A simple line drawing can be as beautiful as a brilliantly color-flushed canvas. Plain chant can be as beautiful as multi-layered polyphony. The vital unity of beauty with God's participation must be qualitatively enhanced in countless ways. The interplay of sacred value and power in the beautiful can hardly be imagined.

There is no way to know exactly how many ingredients are required to achieve unity, or beauty. Skilled artists, of course, know the rules for correct arrangements to capture beauty. Sometimes they succeed, sometimes not. Once beauty is achieved, however, then everything that caused that integrity is essential to its beauty. The essentials hold. Anything less is deficient; anything more is superfluous. Creative freedom dictates that something else might well have been included or omitted. But we do not know what. The act of creating beauty is free and may not provide all that is possible. What attracts us as desirable and lovable is not only what essentially organizes to form the integrity or beauty of the whole, but also mysteriously what might have been included or omitted. Hence we admire and desire the beautiful in what is actually present but also in the mysterious potentiality of what it might be. We capture the beautiful, but then are released by some mystery, some energizing and stimulating power. Again, the sacred is always mysterious and imbues art with enormous power otherwise absent.

The sacred adds transcendence to aesthetics. For example, music is beautiful, but sacred music is enchantingly beautiful because God participates. A chalice and a basilica are as nice to a believer as to a skeptic. But they can be endowed and configured with holiness, one as the vessel of salvation, the other as the temple of God. They are then no longer art objects for their own sake, but are imbued with new consecrated value for the sake of salvation and sanctification. Such transcendence emits a joy and delight, a divine tinkering with things, and a supernatural beckoning. Albert Einstein puts it this way: "The most beautiful thing we can experience is the mysterious side of life. It is the deep feeling which is the cradle of all true art and science. In this sense . . . I count myself among the most deeply religious people."[10] Arnold Toynbee agrees: "Every human being finds that he has been born into a world which is mysterious," because the accessible part is not self-contained, and is a fragment of some partly inaccessible larger whole.[11]

Some thinkers like R. G. Collingwood teach that the holy is indeed the beautiful which is asserted as real.[12] He grounds holiness and beauty in some ontological way to assure that they are real. Our involvement with sacred and aesthetic realities is intransitive because of the sufficiency of these realities. We really capture the sacred or aesthetic objects and are fulfilled no matter how brief or prolonged the experience. Their reality serves as consummatory value and not as transitive or instrumental value towards something else. Another thinker calls this reality "a rapt and intransitive fascination with the object for its own sake."[13] What all this means is that God and beauty are real and compellingly fulfill our interests and desires. If beauty and holiness are connatural to us, then the acquisition of their objects is extremely satisfying. Our own natural conversion towards everything holy and beautiful carries ontological meaning. It is thoroughly real.

A serious problem occurs whenever art objects or allied matters are taken to be themselves intransitive, when they are meant to be transitive. Because anything beautiful, like a person, poem, landscape, symphony, or the like is aesthetically gratifying, we may confuse that value as intransitive, when it is meant to be transitive to a higher and more satisfying beauty, God. As owners of a passing kind of beauty, we may be unwilling to trade temporary satisfaction for the more transcendent, irrevocable, mysterious kind of beauty. In fact, beautiful experiences with people and things can be idolatrous when they displace the real, ultimate intransitive beauty of God.

Art can certainly reach for transcendence. In this way the artist and the aesthetic person traverse the sacred precincts of God. Thus we are motivated by God's beauty not only to create beautiful things, as important as that is, but also to create a beautiful and holy life style. Indeed, transcendence becomes an enduring meaningful component of our lives. The sacred and the beautiful are blended into our lives as a regular, consistent and real conversion. The rewards are high because God, in all of his mystery, resonates in the lives of his holy and beautiful people. Even while transcendent, God works through the configuration of the whole, helping to effect that aesthetic integrity or unity. God graciously and generously exudes beauty, and serves as an irrevocable unlimited resource. Artists and aesthetic people can share in God's bounty by their products, performances and life styles. The potential is enormous, if we are willing to cooperate.

Maritain recalls that beauty is a metaphysical transcendental. He continues: "The moment one touches a transcendental, one touches being itself, a likeness of God, an absolute, that which ennobles and delights our life; one enters the domain of the spirit."[14] Given the problems, disturbances and dislocations of ordinary life, we can still enter the life of the spirit. We then approach goodness or love, and truth, and beauty, which are the names of God.[15] Beauty is God's likeness.

We naturally love beauty, and God is beauty itself. He gives beauty to all created things. Importantly, his beauty causes everything.[16] The beauty of anything is a similitude of divine beauty participated in by things. Therefore, high honor is given to aesthetics and to artistic creation and experience. They share God's beauty. Unfortunately, sometimes our receptiveness to this is clouded by our own human limitations.

While everything said so far applies to Christian art, there is a very special way to understand and to appreciate Jesus' role. Very much of Western religious art, in whatever form, portrays the themes of Jesus' life and teachings. Art captures creation, redemption, and sanctification often from biblical sources. Beauty reverberates in the divine-human encounter. We are encouraged to love the beauty of God, who is love, and to love his son Jesus, not in the abstract so much, but in the real world in aesthetic-religious ways. St. Thomas declares that the name beauty is most fittingly attributed to God's son, Jesus. Aquinas draws from St. Augustine who proclaims that Jesus is the perfect Word, to whom nothing is lacking, and so to speak, is "the art of almighty God."[17] Jesus is the art of God.

The art of God is portrayed in creating the universe out of beauty and redeeming its fallen nature by Jesus' action. The beauty of his mighty mission, as tragic as the details are, destroyed everlasting death and re-claimed eternal life. Our salvation is beautiful, and Jesus is that instrument. The divine integrity, beauty, persists throughout the drama of the Gospels and remains today vibrantly in the indwelling of the Holy Spirit. Life in the Spirit is forever renewing and refreshing, and gives inspiration and impetus to the creative power of art. It provides a sense of vision, of hope, of benefit, of exhilaration even when the game of life seems desperately cruel and hopeless. Endless opportunities for aesthetic delight are generated in religious matters. This suggests continuous conversion and self-propagating renewal. The forms of portrayal are up to the artist and anyone who loves beauty. A world devoid of beauty mimics hell.

Religion is always a factor for cultural renewal and re-creation. Berndtson claims that religion supplies a good that is unique, "a fresh dimension or perspective in life."[18] This includes "the ideal of perfect value as the object of perfect love." He adds that thereby we can identify and have companionship with being and gain a sense of general purposiveness. Such attraction for the ideal can effect tremendous grounds for creativity. Similarly, Whitehead calls religion "a force of belief cleansing the inward parts."[19] So we can always begin afresh.

Participation in the religious aesthetic is not automatic. Whitehead recounts that "the primary religious virtue is sincerity, a penetrating sincerity."[20] While sincerity may not be the commanding Christian virtue, it does show the importance of conviction and perseverance in religion. Even so, there must be a beginning. Benedetto Croce insists that we must "will" to stretch out our hands on the piano and to take up brush and chisel.[21] Artistic talent is always latent until someone wills to do something about it.

Creativity cannot be forced and best operates in freedom. But with Christ-in-God as our partner, what beauty, what poetry, what music, what architecture, what life-style can we create! Christ is God's art, and we can share God's art. Mindful of the theological and spiritual quality of beauty, one writer celebrates our "immortal instinct for the beautiful which makes us consider the earth and its various spectacles as a sketch of or a correspondence with Heaven." He correctly adds that it is through music, poetry and other artistic expressions and experiences that our souls glimpse the splendors beyond the grave. Our accompanying exquisite, joyful and tearful moments are the testimony of a nature exiled in this imperfect world and desiring to take possession immediately, even on this earth, of a revealed paradise.[22]

In conclusion, we have shown that aesthetic and religious experiences are at least equivalent and regularly renew the divine-human encounter. Religion and art become less distinctive in the final acquisition of the beautiful. Both philosophy and religion seek a high degree of unity, a vital integrity, beauty, that is essentially ontological. Religion brings holiness, and the sacred imbues art with transcendent mystery. The combination of the sacred and the beautiful provides unlimited potential for artistic expression and life style. God is beauty, and Jesus is the art of God. Beauty persists and provides vision, exhilaration, hope and renewal in a world often cruel, drab, despairing and needing such special beauty.

University of Colorado
Colorado Springs, Colorado USA

NOTES

1. Arthur Berndtson, *Art, Expression, and Beauty* (New York: Holt, Rinehart and Winston, Inc., 1969), p. 5.

2. St. Thomas Aquinas, *Summa Theologica*, I, 39, 8, trans. Anton C. Pegis, *Basic Writings of St. Thomas Aquinas* (New York: Random House, 1945).

3. St. Augustine, *De vera Religione*, cap. 41, in Jacques Maritain, "Art and Beauty," *A Maritain Reader*, Donald and Idella Gallagher, eds. (Garden City, NY: Doubleday (Image Books), 1966), p. 357.

24

4. Herman Reith, *The Metaphysics of St. Thomas Aquinas* (Milwaukee: The Bruce Publishing Co., 1962), p. 139.

5. Ibid.

6. John Hospers (ed.), *Introductory Readings in Aesthetics* (New York: Macmillan, 1969), pp. 271-317.

7. Berndtson, p. 86.

8. St. Thomas, *Summa Theologica*, II-II, 47, 10, 2 and I, 39, 8.

9. Maritain, p. 357.

10. Albert Einstein, in F. David Martin, *Art and Religious Experience* (Lewisburg: Buckness University Press, 1972), p. 52.

11. Arnold Toynbee, *Preface*, John Cogley, *Religion in a Secular Age* (New York: Frederick A. Praeger Publishers, 1968), p. v.

12. Robin G. Collingwood, *The Principles of Art*, (Oxford: Clarendon Press, 1938).

13. Melvin Rader, *Art and Human Values* (Englewood Cliffs, NJ: Prentice-Hall Inc., 1976), p. 190.

14. Maritain, p. 362.

15. St. Thomas, *Exposition of Dionysius on the Divine Names*, ch. 4, Lectures 5, 6, tr. Vernon J. Bourke, *The Pocket Aquinas*, (New York: Simon and Schuster, 1960), pp. 269-278.

16. St. Thomas, *Summa Theologica*, I, 39, 8; and Maritain, p. 363.

17. St. Augustine, *De Doctrina Christiana*, I, 5, in Maritain, p. 362.

18. Berndtson, p. 270.

19. Alfred North Whitehead, *Religion in the Making* (New York: The Macmillan Co., 1926), p. 15.

20. Ibid.

21. Benedetto Croce, *Aesthetic*, trans. D. Ainslee (Boston: Nonpareil Books, 1978), p. 50.

22. Baudelaire, *L'Art romantique* (Paris, 1885), p. 167, in Maritain, p. 362.

KAROL WOJTYLA ON THE OBJECTIVITY
AND THE SUBJECTIVITY OF MORAL OBLIGATION

John Crosby

Since one of the secondary themes of my paper is the deep affinities of the thought of Karol Wojtyla with that of Dietrich von Hildebrand, I begin with the following passage from von Hildebrand, which expresses what might be called the paradoxical structure of the experience of moral obligation. He writes:

> Someone discerns a call to intervene in a certain situation. . . .
> He grasps the morally relevant value, he understands its call, he
> is aware of the moral obligation, which appeals to his conscience.
> On the one hand, we find here, in the pure commitment of the
> morally relevant value in itself, a high point of transcendence; on
> the other hand, this call contains in an eminent way the element
> of "tua res agitur" ("it is your personal affair which is at stake").
> This moral call or demand is in a certain sense my most intimate
> and my most personal affair, in which I experience the
> uniqueness of my self. Supreme objectivity and supreme subjec-
> tivity interpenetrate here.[1]

This paradoxical structure of moral obligation has also been seen by Karol Wojtyla, even if it has not yet been thematized by him as precisely a paradoxical structure. He says in *The Acting Person*, "that the assertion 'X is truly good' activates the conscience and thus sets off what is like an inner obligation or command to perform the action . . . ." Thus exists the objective side of a paradoxical structure. In the very same sentence Wojtyla speaks also of the subjective side, for he goes on to say of this command which we discern in conscience that it "is most strictly related with the specific dynamism of the fulfillment of the personal ego in and through the action." And a few pages later Wojtyla expresses the idea of a certain paradoxical structure still more directly: "Being a specific structure of self-governance and self-possession the person realizes himself most adequately in his obligations."[2]

We propose to explore Wojtyla's thought on this marvelous unity of objectivity and subjectivity in the experience of moral obligation, and we will begin with objectivity.

I

Wojtyla sharply distinguishes between the experience of some value, and the experience of that value as the source of a moral duty. He writes: "If a value is to give birth to obligation, it has to elicit the action of the person in a particular way, that is, it has to issue a specific call to the person." It is the task of man's conscience to apprehend values in such a way that they give rise to moral demands. Wojtyla says: "The content and the attractiveness of a value linger, so to speak, at the threshold of the person — this is the threshold of conscience, that is the threshold of the truthfulness of the good; it is here that obligation begins."[3]

This seems to answer well to our moral experience. Even if we take value in the sense of von Hildebrand, that is, as the importance or preciousness which a being has in itself and not just for someone, it is one thing to experience such value, and quite something else to discern, in one's conscience, a duty towards that being. It is one thing to be drawn to a person in virtue of his value, to have awakened in us a value-responding love towards him, and to act towards him on the basis of this value-responding attraction, and it is quite something else to discern a moral demand or imperative to act in behalf of the person. Even though in being drawn to the other in virtue of his value, we experience the other as worthy of our love, and not just as a being which happens to receive our love, and even though our actions in behalf of the other are formed by this consciousness that the other is worthy of them, still it is something quite over and above the value of the other which binds us, when we discern a duty to perform some action of helping the other or of respecting him. This duty has an imperative force, which is not at all the same as the attractive power of the value, of the lovableness of the other. It appeals to our conscience, in a way in which the other considered simply as loveable, does not. And our response to the duty has an element of submission and obedience which would be idolatrous if directed towards another human being, however great the value of that person is, however loveable he is.

We understand why Wojtyla in his Habilitation study was led to criticize Max Scheler for constructing an ethics without duties, an ethics which plays off values against duties.[4] Wojtyla emphatically asserts that there really are those duties which Scheler denied. On this point Wojtyla is close to Kant, and at odds with Scheler. He also criticizes very effectively Scheler's main reason for wanting to eliminate duty from ethics. Scheler thought that a moral duty, a moral imperative could only be appre- hended blindly, without understanding its foundation in goods and values, and thus could be obeyed only blindly. In this Scheler showed himself to be too dependent on Kant; he was able to conceive of duty only as it turns out to be in Kant's formalistic ethics, and was unable to consider other possible conceptions of duty. Wojtyla shows that one can recognize with Kant the phenomenon of moral duty, and can at the same time give an account of our insight into the value foundation of duty. Wojtyla holds, as against Kant, that moral imperatives, though not identical with the intrinsic attractiveness of goods and values, are nevertheless grounded in such goods and values, and are made intelligible to us by them. Wojtyla speaks of the "truthfulness" of moral norms, which is for him nothing other than the fact that they have a foundation in goods and values, and are mediated to our knowledge by such goods and values. We have only to go back to the same experiences in which we discerned moral duties as irreducible to the intrinsic attractiveness of goods and values, and we will find these duties emerging from, being mediated to us, by such goods and values. If I find myself morally obliged to help someone in need, then my moral duty, for all its imperative force, is clearly grounded in the dignity of the other as person, and in the good for the other which I am in a position to provide for him. The apprehension of this duty is not blind but seeing, and the same holds for my obedience to the duty.

Wojtyla thinks very deeply about how we have to experience value so as to experience its moral relevancy, that is, its power to generate moral duties. He says that we have to experience not just goods and values, but the truth about them. We can perhaps gather his meaning from something he says in explaining what it is to know the truth about a being. He makes the profound observation that in knowing the truth about a being, man does not just passively reflect it, but gains a certain distance towards it, or ascendancy over it, which is an expression of the spirituality of the human person. Since Wojtyla so stresses not just the good but the *truth* about the good as the basis for the apprehension of moral duties, he seems to want to say that only when man takes a certain spiritual distance towards goods and values, only when he awakens to them in a specifically personal way, does he become alive to their moral relevance. His thought reminds one of von Hildebrand's concept of "moral consciousness."[5] Only the morally unconscious man may indeed experience values and be moved by them, but he is not sufficiently awakened so as to perceive the duties which they can generate.

Moreover, there is one way in which many philosophers in the Aristotelian tradition have failed to do justice to moral duty with its imperative force, but Wojtyla is not guilty of this failing. In the Aristotelian tradition it is usual to posit a dynamism in man to seek his well-being or happiness, a dynamism which is not a work of man's freedom but which is prior to the exercise of his freedom. It is a dynamism which, to speak in the terms of Wojtyla, happens in man; it is not performed by him as his own free act. In this eudaemonistic scheme of things, man inevitably desires whatever he desires under the aspect of its leading to or constituting a part of his complete well-being. Thus the strongest imperative to which man is subject is only a hypothetical imperative: since you inevitably want to attain your complete well-being, and since this course of action promises to lead you to your well-being, you should commit yourself to this course of action. But moral duty is categorical, as Kant saw for the first time, to his everlasting credit; it is unconditioned by ends that we will, even by those that we inevitably will. This categorical force of moral duty is implied in the imperative force which Wojtyla finds in moral duty. Something has gone fundamentally wrong in a moral theory when this categorical force can no longer be accounted for.

The reason why Wojtyla is free to do justice to the fact that moral obligation binds not hypothetically but categorically is that there is for Wojtyla no inevitable dynamism to will one's full well-being. Wojtyla rather finds that the very ability of man to be appealed to by objective values is an ability which itself rests on a free decision of the person. Man's most fundamental relation to good is, for Wojtyla, not established by an *appetitus*. It is not something which *happens* in man; it is established by *man himself*, who opens himself towards the good by taking a free stance towards it.

The crucial factor in determining the maturity and the perfection of the person is his *consent* to be attracted by positive, authentic values, his unreserved consent to be drawn in and absorbed by them. But this makes it all the more necessary to stress that all the forms and degrees of such absorption or engagement of the will are made personal by the moment of decision. Decision may be viewed as a threshold that the person as a person has to pass on his way toward the good.[6]

The eudaemonist, of course, knows nothing of any decision to let oneself be attracted by one's happiness, by one's objective well-being. Since Wojtyla *does* recognize just such a decision, and since there is as a result no inevitable dynamism in us by which we will our well-being, or other things of objective value, a "space" is opened in the moral existence of man where imperatives can be fully categorical and not just hypothetical. In Wojtyla's view it makes good sense to speak of being categorically bound to seek one's ultimate well-being, and of being categorically bound to respect and protect other goods and values (which are not sought under the aspect of leading to or constituting a part of one's ultimate well-being).

And so Wojtyla not only recognizes the phenomenon of categorical force in moral obligation, he can also explain how it is that the human person is susceptible at all of being bound categorically.

It might be thought that in recognizing the existence of moral duties and in stressing their command-like character, we run the danger of conceiving of moral duty in such a way that it becomes a source of harmful heteronomy for man. So we turn now to Wojtyla's thought on the subjectivity of moral action. Since the focus of *The Acting Person* is more anthropological than ethical, Wojtyla has more to say in it about this subjectivity than about moral imperatives themselves.

II

There is one consideration which has already come up in discussing Wojtyla's understanding of moral duty, and which helps us to understand the congeniality of moral duty with the personhood of the person who is bound by the duty. I refer to the fact that for Wojtyla, in contrast to Kant, a moral duty is grounded in goods and values, and is thus intelligible to us. If moral duty were like a command claiming completely blind submission, if it bound us without revealing anything to us about its justification, then it would indeed be a kind of violence inflicted on us from without, and the dignity which we have as persons would require us to reject it. But everything is different as a result of the fact that moral duties emerge in and through our understanding of the truth about the good. This moment of understanding lets moral duties be introduced into our innermost personal selves, and binds us from within. Wojtyla expresses it this way: "The tension arising between the objective order of norms and the inner freedom of the subject-person is relieved by truth, by the conviction of the authenticity of good."[7]

But we want rather to focus on another thought in Wojtyla in order to show how moral imperatives respect man as person and do not do violence to him. This other thought grows out of Wojtyla's whole conception of what it is to be a person, and to understand it, we have to begin by reminding ourselves of the most basic structure of personal being according to Wojtyla.

He finds this structure in the *self-possession* of the person.[8] Man as person belongs to himself, is his own. This is why a person seems to come to himself as person when he takes possession of himself, when he stands in himself, when his life as person flows out of himself. And this is why a person seems to be immature as a person when he is possessed by other things, as by circumstances, external influences, or by the dynamisms of his nature. But this self-possession is not really understood in Wojtyla's sense if we fail to understand the *reflexive* dimension of it, a dimension which is expressed by the very term which Wojtyla uses, self-possession, and which would not have been equally well expressed by other available terms, such as "autonomy." Wojtyla's idea is that man's self-possession is not just actualized in freely relating himself to objects, but in consciously encountering himself and determining himself. It is not enough for man to affirm some good with an act which completely originates in himself; in respecting the good he must come to himself and determine himself.

In fact Wojtyla says repeatedly that in a certain sense the primary object of every act directed towards some good is the acting person himself and not the good towards which the person acts. This does not mean that the person is an intentional object for himself in the way in which the good which the person affirms is an intentional object, and that the person's concern with himself can distract him from the good towards which he acts. It is of course possible for the person to make himself an object among other objects, and then his concern with himself may well stand in conflict with his concern for another person. But Wojtyla has in mind something very different, a certain presence of the person to himself, which the person can have only to himself and never to another, and which is such that it could never compete with or distract from the intentional object of the act. It is this self-presence which lets the person determine himself and take possession of himself in and through the act of deciding for the good to which he is intentionally related.

Now how does the person actualize his self-possession as person? Wojtyla teaches that the human person must get free from all dynamisms of his nature, as well as from all objects which stimulate such dynamisms. Otherwise, he is more a subject *in which* things happen, than a person *who acts himself*. But in order to achieve this independence, man has paradoxically to enter into a relation of dependence on the "truth about good." "It seems to be this 'dependency in the truth' which ultimately accounts for the person's transcendence in action and his ascendancy over his own dynamism."[9]

Surprising as this may seem in the abstract, it answers well to our experience, as we can show by considering von Hildebrand's concept of "the importance of the merely subjectively satisfying." This is a kind of good which is precisely not sought "in the truth"; our only consideration in pursuing it, is what gratifies some bodily want or some spiritual craving, as when we find something desirable because it gratifies our envy. The pursuit of this kind of good tends to dethrone us as persons. Needs and cravings rise up in us, and seek their object; they often carry us away with their dynamism, bypassing us as persons. They do not confront us with ourselves, and challenge us to determine ourselves. In fact, a person who is used to living for such merely subjective goods even falls to some extent under the influence of causal laws, and in this way tends to lose his personal self-possession. If he tries to assert himself, and to recover himself, he may find that he is almost impotent in dealing with the forces which have been unleashed in him as a result of living only for the merely subjectively satisfying. Such a person might appropriate to himself the words of Oscar Wilde, who, when looking back on his life of unbridled pleasure-seeking, said, "I ceased to be captain of my soul." Only the good which is pursued "in the truth" respects us as persons, and appeals to our freedom, so that when we take an interest in it, we can transcend all that happens in us, and can act out of ourselves.

Let us now suppose that in apprehending the truth about the good, I go on to apprehend the good in its moral relevance, that I discover in my conscience some moral imperative to act to respect or protect the good. It is then that I am really taken seriously as person. It is then that I, I myself, am challenged to act, and am enabled to transcend all the dynamisms of my nature. The demand of duty does not just create another dependence which restrains the full development of my person-hood just like the dependence on all that happens in me. Here we rather have a dependence which enables me to actualize my subjectivity as person. To understand this we have above all to remember what was just said about the reflexive structure of the person, about the person as a being who possesses himself.

When I discern in my conscience that I morally ought to do some-thing, I am not only confronted with this "ought," but I also "quicken" in my innermost being, and am aware of having to do with myself in a unique way, though not exactly as an intentional object. I come power-fully to myself as person, and am aware that I will determine myself in a fateful way by the response which I give to the moral imperative. I am aware that my ultimate worth as a human being has been put at issue, and that I will become sound and true in my innermost self by submitting to my duty. I cannot will to perform the action required of me without willing this ultimate soundness and truth in myself. But in willing this soundness and truth in myself, I determine myself, take possession of myself. This is why Wojtyla says that the awareness of my fulfillment as person is integral to the experience of being bound in conscience. And this is why he can say, echoing the idea of von Hildebrand with which we began, "Being a specific structure of self-governance and self-possession the person realizes himself most adequately in his obligations."[10]

Here then we have the answer to the question posed above. A moral imperative does not do violence to me as person. Just the contrary, it sets me in a unique relation to myself, and creates the possibility of my deter-mining myself. It calls for a response in which, if I give it, I not only respond to some value, but also actualize myself as person, my personal self-possession. If it were not for this relation of me to myself in the moral action, if my action existed exclusively for the sake of some good which my action tries to promote, then the moral imperative really would be harmful for me as person. This harm would become all the greater if one were to conceive of my action in consequentialist terms, and were to think that it exists exclusively for the sake of producing some good result. In this conception moral action would be radically depersonalized, and the moral agent would become the victim of a degrading heteronomy. But no such heteronomy follows in Wojtyla's view of moral action; his understanding of the person as a being who possesses himself enables him to explain in an original way the drama of personal subjectivity which is enacted in relation to moral obligation.

There is a possible misunderstanding of this "having to do with myself" in responding to a moral duty. Wojtyla does not warn as explicitly against this misunderstanding as does von Hildebrand, but if we consider Wojtyla's thought as a whole, we can be quite certain that he is just as concerned as von Hildebrand to avoid it. Von Hildebrand insists that the moral duty is not a mere *occasion* for actualizing myself as person. The moral duty is not rightly responded to unless I submit to it for its own sake and unless I take a real interest in the value which grounds it. But no one insists more than Wojtyla that persons are to be respected for their own sakes. It would be completely opposed to his "personalist" thought to say that the main thing about my respecting other persons is that I actualize my personal self-possession in showing them respect. Wojtyla, then, does not fall prey to the misunderstanding just mentioned when he lays special stress on the fact that in being bound to respect other persons, I not only have to do with them; I also, if in a very different way, have to do with myself.

We might conclude with a thought on the image of man which emerges from our attempt to understand Wojtyla on the paradoxical structure of the experience of moral duty. It seems to be a certain creaturehood of man which emerges. It takes an encounter with that which calls for submission and obedience, for man to come to himself as person and to actualize himself in a unique way. This suggests, as Wojtyla himself clearly recognizes, that man's self-possession is not the whole truth about him. His self-possession seems to be a creaturely self-possession, for which imperative moral demands are not a source of heteronomy but rather, paradoxically, a source of that autonomy which is proper to the human person.

University of Dallas
Irving, Texas USA

36

NOTES

1. Dietrich von Hildebrand, *Das Wesen der Liebe*, (Regensburg, Germany: J. Habbel Press, 1971), pp. 244-76.

2. Karol Wojtyla, *The Acting Person*, (Holland: Riedel-Kluwer Academic Press, 1979), IV, 4, pp. 163, 168-69.

3. Ibid., p. 167.

4. Wojtyla, "Uber die Moeglichkeit, eine christliche Ethik in Anlehnung an Max Scheler zu schaffen," in *Primat des geistes* (Stuttgart, 1980), pp. 134-49.

5. von Hildebrand, *Ethics* (Chicago: Franciscan Herald Press, 1953), Ch. 19, 25.

6. Wojtyla, *The Acting Person*, p. 127, 158.

7. Ibid., p. 166.

8. Ibid., Ch. 3, sections 1, 2.

9. Ibid., p. 138.

10. Ibid., pp. 168-69, 74.

CHRISTIANS AND HUMAN RIGHTS TODAY: A CONTRIBUTION TO THE PHILOSOPHICAL DISCUSSION

Alexius J. Bucher

Philosophy as a reflective science does not invent its problems; it just uncovers them. Philosophy finds fundamental reflection in the area of profound questions concerning the foundation of human rights. Jurisprudence as the study of the rights and duties of man and theology as the study of man's faith try to find an interpretation of mankind. This interpretation owes itself to the significance of man. It is easy for the aforementioned reflective sciences to come to an agreement on the historical position of human rights. But the explosiveness of the subject of human rights is distinguished not by historical entanglement but by actual disagreement. It seems that an interdisciplinary dialogue is necessary if new preconditions for a worthy life for everyone can be found by discussing the hopeless situation of people without rights. The required dialogue is burdened, on the one hand, by the fact that Christian theology, entangled with moral appeals, lacks a theoretical basis and, on the other hand, by jurisprudence entangled by legalistic axioms.

The Contribution of Christian Self-Concept

Christian theology regards itself as a systematically guided reflection of truth accepted by faith. In the institutional and spiritual community of their churches, Christians regard themselves as being called by God "to work for men and man's salvation." If Christians want to submit their specific Christian contribution to human happiness/salvation, they have to know the basis of human happiness and they must help to make it possible. For Christians, the problem of human rights is part of the question of the basis of perfect happiness.

The Christian self-concept leads up to the need for action. Therefore, in the dialogue on human rights, Christians are most affected where man's dignity seems to be endangered. Christians do not want to enlarge the catalogue of human rights by special rights for Christians as a kind of privilege. Instead they want to discover general improvements for mankind in a genuinely Christian perspective.

With regard to the Christians' long historical and painful road to a positive understanding of human rights, access to these has to be opened up carefully. Many Christians saw human rights only as rights of defense against an authority, which was thought to be legitimate, because of the anti-Christian mask of human rights within the framework of the constitution of the French Revolution in 1791. Only the bitter experience of fascistic and ideological regimes has forced the churches to think about the subject anew and led to a breakthrough in human rights in Christian communities. Specific Christian grounds for the general validity of human rights must be recognizable in consequences in the Christian sphere of influence. Every human being and every social, political, cultural or economical power quoting Christian norms could be referred to the binding character of human rights as part of Christian ethics. The journeys of Pope John Paul II to South America and Africa served this immanently Christian logic.

The Removal of the Deficit in The Execution of Human Rights

Because of their self-concept, Christians see their duty first of all in removing the alarming gap between the concept of human rights and their realization. Christians should allow their new and specific perspective of human happiness to become convincingly manifest in their fight against unjust structures. Otherwise all Christian talk about human salvation and happiness will remain simple theory (which very often helps to reproduce inhumane conditions). This can be achieved by an up-to-date interpretation of the Christian supertemporal responsibility for the world and a new line of action for a world which is changing rapidly.

Missionary work, for example, is no longer regarded as a way to superimpose European structures and values. But owing to a radical love for mankind, it aims to make it possible to live self-determinedly and with a personal responsibility to offer to shape consciousness as a practical means leading to self-help. Mother Teresa in her hospices in India and Ernesto Cardenal in the centers for alphabetization in Nicaragua are an example of the thousands who help to realize human rights. Bishop Romero's fatal struggle for the rights of the oppressed and impoverished is another name among many who testify for the struggle fundamentally based on Christian faith.

The work of Christians in the Third World manifests itself in a new consideration of the Christian responsibility for the worldwide service of advancing human rights. Theology of liberation, emancipated from Occidental categories of thought, defines being a Christian as a chance to live really as a human being (also because Christianity claims and discloses the right to live even beyond death).

A Contribution to a Pluralistic Dialogue

Concerning human rights, it is impossible to have an exclusive round of talks with self-appointed competence. As one who is concerned, every human being has to claim his right and give an answer. Christians as well find themselves being under this general obligation. They cannot just think about it among themselves, but they must take part in a pluralistic dialogue where there are different viewpoints. There must be a frankness which neither renounces one's own doctrine of faith nor forces answers upon others dogmatically. On that condition one can discern two basic tendencies of a Christian contribution to the dialogue on human rights:

(1) Radicalization of the question of the foundation. Human rights as part of a general human ethos are not at all unquestionably self-evident. Human rights cannot be accepted either with a philosophically naive presumption or with a legally arbitrary foundation. A critical mind is not content with this alternative. Critical Christian theology asks if it is also possible and how to find a general and necessarily binding justification for human rights, independent of arguments presupposing certain conditions and positions. If specifically Christian reasons are not declared as a generally binding position, the human rights claim to be normative will be questioned. Are there critical fundamental ethics of human rights? This question must be the main point of a discussion about human rights which is binding on everyone.

(2) The development of the concept of human rights. Since the French Revolution when, in the shape of its constitution, the concept of human rights became a secular theme, the content of this concept has been enlarged considerably. When Karl Marx criticized the human rights of the French Revolution as "a product of an egoistic and bourgeois individual," he, too, shared the skeptical attitude of Christians. The concept of human rights in 1791 declared the right of the individual in contrast to society. Nothing was said about the interests of society in

contrast to the individual and the following release from this confrontation. Only the Roman synod in 1963 and the assembly of the World Council of Churches after the War abandoned this limited orientation of human rights to the individual in their documents. Even if, with regard to totalitarian social systems in our time, this keystone of the concept of human rights oriented to the individual must be defended, the whole concept cannot be restricted to the individual's rights of defense. Man as created and endowed "with reason and freedom" is "a social being." This essential dignity not only corresponds to rights *in contrast* to society but also to rights *in* society and to rights *of both* individual *and* society.

Christians require that the concept of human rights should be enlarged by the concept of rights to cooperate. Men must have a say and participate in all political, cultural and economic forms of society. As never before, Christians, therefore, feel it especially painful that these rights to cooperate, which also correspond to the dignity of a Christian, have still been withheld from them.

When we mention the enlargement of the concept of human rights, there still remains something to be said about the drastic change in meaning of human rights in our time. Christian decisions of general principle in the seventies (Roman Synod 74f, World Council of Churches, Evian, Nairobi etc.) indicated vigorously that both rights of defense and rights to cooperate must be embedded in the socio-economic and worldwide ecologic framework. The existing inadequate situation with regard to nearly all basic demands of man indicates the material preconditions of every right formally claimed and granted. The right to execute human rights concretely, their realization in a concrete situation, presupposes the right to preconditions which make human rights possible.

Therefore, the Roman bishops' conference mentions material conditions as everyone's rights to claim. The right to live combined with the fight against war and torture, the right to have something to eat combined with the fight against hunger and a monopolistic economy of resources, the right to education, the right to socio-economic and political-cultural participation combined with the right against multinational exploitation and racial discrimination are all human rights. The inclusion of rights to claim in the concept of human rights means to think about it on conditions of the present world situation.

Without regard to a worldwide inadequate situation, the reflection on human rights remains the typical product of a bourgeois-occidental affluent society. Therefore, Christians ask if there are degrees of priority concerning human rights, if there are standards of human rights, if there is a hierarchy within the plan to execute human rights for everyone. The dialogue on human rights has changed into a catalogue of claims.

It is also no longer a discussion between East and West primarily. Helsinki is a rearguard action: Should the main stress rather be put on the rights of the individual (West) or on social (East) rights. The present dialogue on human rights takes place between South and North, between people who rightly claim their rights (South) and others who wrongly refuse rights because they can no longer provide for the material basis to make them possible.

Catholic University of Eichstatt
Germany

THE ESSENCE OF CHRISTIAN RENEWAL IN OUR SCHOOLS

John F. Fitzgibbon

The theme of this study is Christian renewing. Among the many definitions of renew in the dictionary, the first is: "to restore to freshness, vigor, or perfection; to better the existing." Does our present, Christian education need to be renewed? If so, why? And how can this be accomplished? Christian education, in the sense of education taken formally in the schools (and I limit my remarks to college education), needs to be renewed because it has so lost its vigor that it is questionable as to whether or not it still exists. The reason for this current condition is that our educators have lost sight of the end or goal of Christian education. Since education is an art it must be directed towards an end. If means are cultivated for their own sake they cease to lead to the end. The resulting collapse of a definite goal to be achieved is not only destructive of Christian education but ruinous of any true education.

I wish to point out that there is nothing wrong with many of the means of modern education. As a matter of fact, many of them are excellent and far surpass what we had in the past. It might very well be that because the means are so good we have lost sight of the end of education. It is quite possible that we have thrown the baby out with the bath.

Hence, it would seem that in order to renew our Christian education we must once again establish precisely what our end or goal is. Only then can we investigate the means and determine which of them are most likely to help us reach our end.

The aim of education is to guide the student in his/her self development as a human person, that is, to arm the student with knowledge, good judgment and moral virtue. This is not to deny the legitimate aim of preparing youth to get a job and make a living. However, our education must be so ordered that this utilitarian aspect becomes properly subordinated to the primary aim of perfecting the human person. But how is a human person perfected?

The essential desire of a human person is the desire for freedom, by which I mean creative spontaneity, true spiritual freedom. We gain this freedom by our own efforts through the acquisition of knowledge, wisdom and love. The object of this knowledge and love is truth, not a static thing nor a ready-made formula, but a vital, growing manifestation of being, grasped in an internal activity. It is this truth that sets us free. Here, too, we can see the part played by faith, for the object of faith is also truth. Thus, faith is not to be conceived in a moralistic or legalistic manner, for what intellectual challenge would that offer! What intellectual curiosity is aroused by faith viewed as a set of dogmatic formulas? "Faith seeking understanding" remains the best description of the intellect's search when, informed and challenged by faith, it seeks to understand what God has revealed to it. Such knowledge is the product of the effort man makes to penetrate the deposit of truth which God has graciously given his intellect.

Over forty years ago Robert Hutchins warned us of pragmatism's domination over education but his warning went unheeded. Pragmatism is more dominant now than ever and our Christian education is no exception. The worse result of this domination is the mind's distrust of the very idea of truth. Truth is as infinite as being and it is our progressive attainment of truth that opens and enlarges our mind and sets us free. When pragmatism causes us to reject truth as the proper object of knowledge, we suffer the loss of any true, human perfection. Education is perverted and we end up producing cogs to fit into the giant wheel of industry. We teach students how to make a living but not how to live. We sell our rich, cultural heritage for a mess of pragmatic pottage.

Many may argue that in today's world the time allotted to formal education is too short for us to do more than specialize in some science or technology. In fact, the most rapidly growing specialization is computer science which, together with training in business administration, now constitutes about three-fourths of the student's entire college education. Over the past few years a number of studies have been published stressing the need for us to return to a curriculum with greater emphasis on liberal education. But so far these studies have produced mostly words and very few actions, a great deal of smoke but not much fire. And when the smoke has cleared away the same old business-oriented curriculum still dominates. It seems to be the easiest thing in the world to pay lip service to the liberal arts but the hardest thing in the world to effect it. Have we forgotten that it is through the liberal arts that we attain the creative, spiritual freedom which is the essence of our human perfection? The ever continuing inroads on the liberal arts curriculum can only result in the destruction of all true education.

Liberal education is directed toward truth to be apprehended and wisdom to be acquired. We may not all agree on what constitutes the liberal arts, but, I am sure, no one would exclude literature and poetry, music and art, mathematics and the natural sciences. The crowning point would be the study of philosophy, and, since we are discussing Christian education, the study of theology.

A liberal education is for everyone, and, contrary to popular belief, it is not only for the rich and the elite. If we do so limit it, then we are not only cheating the majority of our youth, we are also eroding our free society. In the United States our most prestigious colleges shun business training and concentrate on the liberal arts in the undergraduate program. Specialization is reserved for the graduate and professional schools. But most of our other colleges, including our Christian schools, follow the program of trying to combine liberal arts with occupational training. As I mentioned before, it is a losing proposition for the liberal arts. Again, our most prestigious colleges are attended, for the most part, by the rich and the intellectual elite, which means that we have relegated the vast majority of our youth to a life of boredom and drudgery because they have had little or no opportunity to develop as true, Christian, human persons. They may make a lot of money but they will probably live dull, uninspiring lives. All students have a right to be liberally educated and not be shunted into vocational or technological training. If this condition prevails for all the liberal arts or humanities, it is even worse for philosophy, the study of which is an occasion for contempt and contumely rather than honor and glory. It is generally contended that philosophy ought not to be studied at all, or, at best, by very few people. As Pico once said, chaste Pallas is rejected, hooted and whistled at in scorn.

One thing that baffles me, as it has so many others in the past, is why liberal education is not seen as being truly practical. After all, in order to live well, indeed, even to earn a living, one is required to think, and, liberal education does just that, it teaches one to think. It is, without exaggeration, the basic preparation for life. Could it be that today's curriculum makers are looking for a shortcut? Is it possible that they believe that occupational training does what liberal education does and more? Or is it that our schools, even our Christian schools, have sold out to mammon, have become subservient to business on the grounds that they cannot otherwise exist? If this is the case, if we cannot exist without such subservience (and I do not accept that such is the case), then perhaps we should inquire as to whether or not our existence is justified!

Let us turn now to considering philosophy and theology in greater detail. Can we truly speak of a Christian philosophy, and, if so, just what is it? I do not wish to go back to the debates of the nineteen-thirties begun by Emile Brehier and so eloquently responded to by Gilson and Maritain. However, I do find it most difficult to deny the existence of a Christian philosophy in the light of all that has been written on the subject in the past fifty years. Let me simply quote Gilson to show that such a denial is nigh unto impossible.

> If pure philosophy took any of its ideas from Christian revelation, if anything of the Bible and the Gospel has passed into metaphysics, if, in short, it is inconceivable that the systems of Descartes, Malebranche and Leibniz would be in fact what they are had they been altogether withdrawn from Christian influence, then it becomes highly probable that since the influence of Christianity on philosophy was a reality, the concept of Christian philosophy is not without a real meaning.[1]

The least we can say is that any time a philosophical doctrine contains, as a basic element of it, a factor of Christian faith, then it is not incorrect to speak of it as a Christian philosophy. For example, modern scientists and philosophers alike admit the intelligibility of the universe and this can be traced to the influence of Christianity in its belief in God as intelligent creator. As a Thomist, I would go further and state that the medieval understanding of *Exodus* as revealing that the essence of God is his very existence profoundly influences metaphysics and is, therefore, the basis of a Christian philosophy, including a philosophy of human nature and an ethics.

It is necessary to return Christian philosophy to its pivotal position in our curriculum. By this I mean the study of metaphysics, philosophy of human nature and ethics. Our curriculum has become so eclectic that it is not only possible but even likely for a student to complete four years in a Christian college and never take a single course in Christian philosophy. The philosophy requirements in many of our Christian colleges are no different from those found in non-sectarian colleges or even public colleges. Sometimes it would appear as though we are afraid to declare ourselves a Christian college lest we antagonize some students and suffer a loss of revenue. Let me assure you that I am not opting for the rigid philosophy curriculum of the past, but, I do believe that the pendulum has swung too far in the opposite direction. The core of Christian philosophy can be required in a college curriculum while still allowing a great measure of freedom of choice of courses. It is necessary for us to find a proper middle ground between the far too rigid program of the past and the total eclecticism of the present.

If Christian philosophy is a necessary part of the curriculum of a Christian college, then, *a fortiori*, theology must be required. Here, again, I would opt for the greatest amount of freedom of choice. However, it would seem as though a course or two covering the Old and New Testament would be a *sine qua non* along with some study of moral theology. But the important point is that theology should hold the central position in the curriculum, tying together all the other courses. As Maritain in his *Education at the Crossroads* so beautifully pointed out, one would be unable to understand his own time if he were unaware of his theological heritage. To quote him precisely:

> The intellectual and political history of the sixteenth, seventeenth, and eighteenth centuries, the Reformation and the Counter Reformation, the internal state of British society after the Revolution in England, the achievements of the Pilgrim Fathers, the Rights of Man, and the further events in world history have their starting point in the great disputes on nature and grace of our classical age.[2]

He goes on to say that neither Dante nor Shakespeare, nor Nietzsche nor Marx, nor many others are understandable without a serious theological background. No one can do without theology and no liberal education worthy of the name can leave it out of the required curriculum.

For theology to be the focal point of the curriculum in a Christian college means that it must be the guiding spirit in producing the universality which is the essential characteristic of any school of higher learning. All courses would be ordered in accordance with their value for producing the fully developed Christian, human person. Interdepartmental courses involving theology could be taught, such as bioethical problems, moral issues in business or government, etc. Thus theology would not be just a number of courses offered; rather, it would be the very *elan vital* of the entire curriculum. A true, integral humanism must make the effort to sanctify the profane, to awaken in the students the need and the joy of the spiritual life, to cultivate an appreciation of knowledge and beauty for themselves.

Rugged individualism must be replaced by a Christian socialism, and by this I mean the idea of a communal society grounded upon human rights and aiming to satisfy the social aspirations and needs of humans. In my many years of teaching I have found that students generally object to the notion of social claims being in any way prior to individual claims. Their sense of social responsibility and human obligations take a back seat to what they view as their individual rights. Note that I said generally, for I am quite cognizant of the great social concern exemplified by many students. But this concern waxes and wanes in accordance with world conditions and, especially, of economic conditions. Moreover, while many students can see the injustice of racism and sexism, they fail to see their own individual obligations to help a person in distress if the rendering of such aid causes them any grave inconvenience. The common good and the general welfare never loom so large as their own personal rights.

It is not enough to teach theology, including Christian social theology. We must encourage our students to participate in the Christian community of the college as well as in the larger surrounding community. But this, of course, presupposes that we establish such a Christian community. It should be obvious that I do not wish in any way to disparage the teaching of theology, but, we could require a dozen courses in theology and still not be a Christian college. What we teach must be put into practice on the college campus itself.

An annual contest with appropriate prizes for Christian art, music, poetry, and literature could be much more effective in developing a young Christian than any number of theology courses. A participation by students and faculty alike in a demonstration for peace or for the sanctity of life could far outweigh the value of courses in Christian philosophy. The actual development of liturgical forms of worship could mean a great deal more than courses in the humanities. In other words, the daily practice of our Christian belief is far more instructive than any number of classroom lectures. If our students lack the sense of social responsibility which we would like to see in them, perhaps the reason is that we have done nothing to encourage this by our own practicing what we teach.

I am not suggesting any kind of dichotomy between teaching and doing, but, rather, I am saying that if teaching does not overflow into doing, then there is something wrong with our teaching. If I might paraphrase St. Anselm by adding to his famous dictum I would say: *Credo ut intelligam et agam.* Naturally, this action is not to be confined to the campus. The college is only the training ground for life in the outside community, the microcosm used to prepare the student for the macrocosm. The whole purpose of a college education is to prepare the student for life. That is why his college education ends with a commencement exercise.

The aim of Christian education is not to produce some kind of typical Christian. Rather, our aim must be to liberate the human person. This freedom, in all likelihood, will not be a quiet freedom, but, rather, a fighting one. Christian education must reaffirm its principles, stress anew its intellectual and moral roots. The very essence of our education is the formation of free persons in a free society. If we lose sight of this, then renewal will be impossible, for with the loss of our goal will come our demise.

Let me close by stressing that I am not denying the great need for technology today. But we must know what the true significance of this technology is and not make it the supreme rule of our lives. We must not allow the means to become the end. Freedom, justice, equality — these are all spiritual values and they are the ones that a Christian education must promote. We must not allow technology, which can be used for so much human good, to turn into technocracy, wherein human life is devalued and the spirit is destroyed.

St. Ambrose College
Davenport, Iowa USA

NOTES

1. Etienne Gilson, *The Spirit of Mediaeval Philosophy* (New York: Scribner's, 1936), p. 18.

2. Jacques Maritain, *Education at the Crossroads* (New Haven, CT: Yale University Press, 1966), p. 74.

BEING HUMAN AND CONTEMPORARY AMBIGUITY

James F. O'Leary

In *The Technological Society*, Jacques Ellul argued that technique requires "a complete reconstitution of the human being so that he can at last become the objective and also the total object of technique."[1] This "reconstitution" requires that one assume the identity of a technological person in order to belong to the everyday modern world. As Ellul describes the character of a technological civilization, he argues that individuals must assume their technological identities at the expense of, if not in spite of, traditional values and conceptions of human achievement. I believe that one can argue, with justification, that Robert Bellah has recently uncovered a phenomenon similar to that Ellul predicted a quarter century ago.

From the interviews and conversations which he and his research group conducted, Bellah noted that people feel that their lives are uncomfortably divided into public and private concerns.[2] Individuals, his research revealed, find themselves publicly successful, but privately troubled. The private lives of people seem to Bellah to be dominated and directed by "traditional values;" while their public lives are dominated by values at odds with these private values. In their private lives, people say they prize nurturing, caring, compassion, and friendship; their public world, in contrast, is dominated by success, achievement, utility, and efficiency. Publicly, individuals find themselves busy remaking, refining, and attempting to control a world which has become harsh, inhospitable, and ultimately the death of individuality and personal fulfillment. Individuals feel that they have lost control of their lives and sense that they are now subservient to the very world they have created by their own participation.

In a fundamental way, the experience Bellah has identified as the conflict between the public and private experience of people is what Ellul characterized as the emerging dominance of technique over the non-technical. Technique makes obsolete and inconsequential value systems that are incompatible with the exigencies of necessity, efficiency, and accommodation. Born of the human desire for control, technique takes on a life and rule of its own which destroys all other civilizations as well as the ultimate value of the Western political and religious tradition. The reality of technique is such that technique, Ellul argues, will undermine the noble ideal of individual achievement and worth. Technique will ultimately limit the aspirations and achievements of the individual. Human excellence and virtue will be reduced to a minimum. Although human beings are necessary, Ellul writes:

> But literally anyone can do the job, provided he is trained to do it. Henceforth, men will be able to act only in virtue of their commonest and lowest nature, and not in virtue of what they possess of superiority and individuality. The qualities which technique requires for its advance are precisely those characteristics of a technical order which do not represent individual intelligence. . . . Technical elements combine among themselves, and they do so more and more spontaneously. In the future, man will apparently be confined to the role of a recording device; he will note the effects of techniques upon one another, and register the results.[3]

This means that individuals are caught in the stifling grip of technique as technique becomes the dominant experience of a culture or civilization. According to Ellul, there is an inevitability bound up in the process of technique that requires the assumption of the disguise of being human as demanded by technique. Bellah's investigations underscore Ellul's claims about the necessity of adaptation and accommodation. The necessity of adaptation has become the common experience of all of us in our everyday world. There are few of us who can convince ourselves that we are essential to and indispensable in this world. We are just like the machines and the tools used in the past. It has been customary to throw away the obsolete and the inefficient. In the post-modern experience, individuals experience themselves as indispensable and incidental. The reality that is now the dominant experience of the everyday world for all individuals is precisely the experience of "being incidental" and "being dispensable." In the public domain of the post-modern world, there now exists a meaning of being human which requires individuals to be the one-dimensional being of efficiency and adaptation. There is very little doubt that human beings feel uncomfortable with the disguise of post-modernity.

It might be said that the conflict identified by Bellah and Ellul is little more than the alienation identified by both Marxists and Existentialists long before Bellah and Ellul. Both Marxists and Existentialists, of course, on the basis of very different analysis, have exercised themselves against the bludgeoning effect of modern industrial commitment and values of bourgeois existence. This alienation has far more reaching consequences than the alienation identified up to this point in our philosophical and religious interpretation of human experience. Ellul's account of human experience is, it seems, more essential than either of these traditions. Ellul sees in technique itself the very grounds for the conflict that has emerged in the industrial society and in the persistent presence of liberal political social orders or bourgeois society. Both the industrial society and liberal, bourgeois state arise out of the demands of efficiency, participation, and accommodation.

Following Ellul, we are witnessing a conflict between the value systems of the non-technical order and the value system required by technique itself. Ellul believes that the wisdom of a non-technical civilization cannot compete with the understanding of being human that is embedded in the technique of the modern, liberal industrial age. Ellul writes: "The civilizations threatened today by our own technical civilization can offer no effective resistance because they are nontechnical."[4]

Technique is such that it crystallizes, or actually fossilizes, what non-technical civilizations value and define as the nature of the human. Any hope of accommodating "traditional values" to the exigencies of "technique" is groundless, if it is believed that the values of technical rationality can exist alongside of and as an alternative value structure to the values of compassion and nurturing. Technique demands, if not creates, a new being for humans. Humans either adapt to the necessity of technique or live out of the interim experience that technique overcomes.

We ask whether or not this leaves us in a complete state of hopelessness and despair. The inevitability and necessity that Ellul has identified in technique would seem to leave us very much adrift and helplessly wandering into the future that technique holds for us. To this we respond that it seems that, if there is any hope, it is being able to break through the mythological grip that technique creates as human reality becomes defined in the terms and according to the conditions of technical existence.

The first order of business is to recognize the exigency of technique and to understand the presence that such an order creates for the personal life of individuals. To break the hold that the technological understanding has on our public, everyday world, an alternative understanding of the human condition has to be cultivated. It is as if the repressiveness and callousness of the technological understanding of human reality is an exaggerated statement of male consciousness and the response required is that of feminine consciousness. It would be readily accepted that both are fundamental to human experience. Equally, most would acknowledge that, while complementary, the two are often at conflict. The dominance of experience by male consciousness, with its assertion of power and control, forces the submissive and cooperative necessity of an equally required dimension of the human reality to assert itself.

But this is an ironic cause for hope. We have yet to see clearly what it means for humans to be rooted in a dialectical reality, which creatively processes itself, and does not depend upon either human will or human understanding for its own effectiveness. Whatever privilege humans enjoy in this drama of existence should not be identified with the class consciousness and limited expression of reality which had been dominant in the liberal, bourgeois society and its industrial and commercial state. And what is ironical about this situation is that there is a moment to our experience which may very well escape the very power we would will to exercise. Perhaps, what is required is the transformation of our culture and our society at a number of different levels. More than anything else the nature of technique can teach us that this transformation can and must take place in an order that is much more fundamental than a private and personal transformation of individual consciousness.

Of course, it is at this point that we encounter the greatest difficulty in trying to assess and to give a response to Ellul's account of the control technique has on the human condition. This is particularly true, for to think in terms of exercising control and influence, is to think in the very terms of technique which Ellul has identified as the source of the problematic for human beings. It almost appears that the human community has to rescue itself from the grip of technique by becoming attuned to the meaning called for by the acknowledgement of helplessness and submission. Tentatively, what seems required by the exigencies and the extremity of our condition is to break with the myth of powerfulness and of control that is central to the dominance of technique.

As with all mythologies, there is a spell that is cast by the presence of myth. It is essential to break the spell of the "myth of technique" by the assertion of a historical consciousness. In its religious and philosophical consciousness, the human community has, often and in its most illuminating moments, acknowledged the vulnerability of persons as they live out their lives both privately and publicly. One could make the case that in their most profound moments, the religious traditions of the human community have understood the vulnerability of the human. To the extent that a response to the dominance of technique can be mounted out of what is, thus, substantive in our philosophic and religious thought, it seems to me, we can hope to overcome the alienation which arises out of the dominance of technique which, presently, appears so formidable. The resolution of the conflict between public and private values is not to be accomplished by a retreat into privatized, solitary, or family experience. Nor does it seem acceptable to have recourse to the values ascribed to by doctrinaire and male dominated formal religious institutions which seem, in some respects, to be extensions of technical rationality.

Technique must be addressed socially. We must make clear a public order which accepts the dispensability of the individual but, also, places that dispensable individual back into the context of a community of relatedness and care. What is, thus, required is a social order that sustains the entire community of persons rather than those who momentarily and occasionally fit into the productivity and maintenance requirements of the dominant and affluent job holders or the property title holders. A major improvement upon Ellul's insight might occur, if we were able to understand and to appreciate the fact that a technological society exists and creates an everyday world of relatedness, precisely to the extent that such a relatedness sustains that technological society. Essentially, the will that is needed, the moral imperative, so to speak, is the will to recognize the nature of the participation which allows the technological society to hold itself together and to extend the advantages and security of the technological society to all persons. Those who participate as either employed or as property title holders do not do so by reason of their will, wit, creative intelligence, and imagination, so much as by the historical fortunes of their private privilege.

In conclusion, we need to be sensitive to an approach to "being human" that is more compatible with and alert to our historical experience of vulnerability. This does not condemn us to romanticizing historical experience and, hence, to escape into the ritual of past social orders or to require the abandonment of technological enterprise. We need to come to terms with the conditions and exigencies of technique. We need to do so in terms that see technique as but a moment or dimension of human experience. Ellul is correct when he links technique to human will and powerfulness. What is now required as well is to understand the caring and sustaining dimensions of human experience that can resist the dominance of will.

The post-modern world cannot be allowed to exist in such a way as to force individuals to be narrowly defined by the limits of will and power and, hence, be cut off from their sensitive experience. The inauthentic moment of technique, which is very much required, cannot be allowed to squeeze from humans their authentic, philosophic or religious life. Humans need to know that there is a meaning to technology that requires human participation and relatedness. To the extent that "to participate in the technological age" has come to mean an abdication of and discount of the relatedness of our sensitive and compassionate experience of being human, to that extent the nature of participation in technique is not yet understood.

From the historical point of view, we are at the dawn of the technological age. We have to fathom the meaning that sustains the restrictive mechanisms of technique so that the meaning of human relatedness is not driven into an unfortunate and unsustainable privacy. To the extent that the present technological configuration functions as if such a meaning of "being human" is not real, our situation is dreadful. Without a breakthrough both politically and socially into the foundation of technique, the question, "what is it to be human," might cease to be asked. Such is the ominous prospect of a technological understanding of "being human."

Daemen College
Amherst, New York USA

NOTES

1. Jacques Ellul, *The Technological Society*, tr. J. Wilkinson (New York: Alfred A. Knopf, Inc., 1964), p. 431.

2. Robert Bellah, *Habits of the Heart* (Berkeley: University of California Press, 1985); see "Conclusion: Transforming American Culture," especially, pp. 275-285.

3. Ellul, pp. 92-93.

4. Ibid., p. 125.

PART II

SCIENTIFIC ASPECTS
OF CHRISTIAN HUMANISM

MODELS, INTERPRETATION AND REALITY: PROSPECTS FOR THE REINTEGRATION OF THE SCIENTIFIC AND HUMANISTIC CULTURES

Charles R. Dechert

It is increasingly recognized that all human knowledge and man's capacity to operate on and in his environment (natural and social) are in considerable part based on his cognitive capacities, and most especially the ability to compress information, to extract from the vast amount of input sensory information, significant *gestalten*, forms, pictures, maps, models — call them what you will. These are reflections (and simplifications) of external reality that order and organize our understanding and permit effective action on the world around us. To a considerable degree they are relational, linking percepts with abstractions, emotions, will and awareness, with notions of process, time, place and form.

In man these "models" are only in part a product of the sensoria and central nervous system operating autonomically; at a more complex level of perceptual integration, the attribution of meaning and significance, these "models" are a product of a complex pattern of associations of percepts and of their association with a symbolic universe, a culture initially imparted by the human group, but itself subject to the action of the individual and collective intellect and will sorting out and selecting from a vast variety of alternative models of the "real world." This process is not entirely at the conscious level; indeed the intellectual and cognitive growth of individual persons and of the civilized human collectivity may be viewed as a process of *conscientization*, a developing awareness of the quasi-artifactual nature of human culture and of the significance of human interventions in the very process of knowing.

Modern science has achieved extraordinary and universal prestige in its acutely self-aware pursuit of the patterns of order revealed by the objective universe. This truth-seeking methodology has social criteria of verification and falsification. Its prestige is testimony to the values, the underlying ethical commitments essential to it: objectivity, honesty,

62

avoidance of the idiosyncratic, a refusal to subordinate inquiry to policy. Granted that public support of science is based largely on a vulgar apprehension of its utility, the subordination of institutionalized science to commercial, political, or ideological goals would destroy the very foundation of this extraordinary cultural achievement.

In our earlier treatment of "information compression," it is clear that we are dealing with one aspect of a perennial concern of the philosopher, the problem of "universals," those abstracted forms that characterize the commonalities of individual elements in classes of entities. Kant, with little knowledge of the mechanisms of perception, recognized that human knowledge is categorized *a priori*. Today we might say that the very physiological, neurological mechanism of knowing inherently "creates" (as it were) the structure of the common-sense universe in which each man exists. (Indeed every sentient entity lives in a universe whose spatial and temporal dimensions and range of "the significant" are products of its perceptual and data processing "machinery.") The spectra of visual and auditory perceptions, the extent and limits of proprioception, the sense of time (varying through life) create an underlying and shared, albeit limited, human cognitive experience. Only by instrumentation (and, in some cases, imagination) can we apprehend a world of radio and infrared radiations, of ultra high audio frequencies and x-rays, of electron beams, binary stars, quasars and black holes, of time-standing-still at the speed of light, of chemical exchanges and double helixes, of the very mechanisms of cognitive activity itself. Our eyes and ears apprehend formal patterns, information conveyed by photons and the compression and rarefaction of air, information that retains its formal structure as it is conveyed inward to the core of the cognitive personality by a process of transduction through various media, mechanical vibration of bony structures, the movement of fluids, chemical/ electrical changes. The *species sensibilis* of the Aristotelian-Thomistic tradition has empirical content.

In the physical sciences, the terms and relationships of the *model* have existential correlates more or less directly observable, more or less directly measurable. On occasion the mathematical elaboration of a model or the deductive extension of its implications may involve logical processes that cannot find parallel in the order of reality — as when $\sqrt{-1}$ enters an equation and is subsequently cancelled out. The fecundity of such models and the broader paradigmatic structure (itself characteristically model and method and mindset) of which they form part lie in their integrative and predictive nature. Their capacity to raise questions and to point the way both to further significant inquiry and to focussed observations and/or experiments that will test their validity and their adequacy to the "real world" they purport to describe or explain and hence their potential for guiding effective action and instrumental applications to the satisfaction of human wants and needs — not least the human need to know and to act — are all enhanced by the technological applications of scientific knowledge.

In the multi-paradigmatic universe of the social and behavioral sciences the situation is far more complex. The perspective of the practitioner may provide a clear focus on only a very limited part of the world he would understand, and these various perspectives and the models they propose do not necessarily cohere. The economic worlds of institutionalists, monetarists, Keynesians, and "supply-siders" — and their policy prescriptions — are quite diverse. The worlds of power-politics oriented "realists," political systems theorists, and interest group analysts validly reflect diverse aspects of an incredibly complex political reality in which social facts interact with will and emotion, dreams and fantasies, cultural commitments and the hardware of civilization.

Indeed the very models of social reality are a significant aspect of the social universe being described, analyzed, explained. It is the distinctive genius of Marxism to insist on this reflexive relation: "Hitherto philosophers have sought to explain the world; our objective is to change it." The model of social reality (in this case a model emphasizing the notion of economic relations, class conflict, dialectical movement) becomes operative as ideology and by defining "the relevant" makes it relevant.

The intellectual and epistemological revolution of the twentieth century is in some sense a result of the perceived failure, or better, inadequacy, of the analytic paradigm which has dominated Western thought since the end of the sixteenth century. Descartes' emphasis on clear and simple ideas, the mathematicians' simplification of the extended universe to coordinates in three dimensions, the Galilean simplifications and definitions that produced modern Mechanics, culminating in Newton's Laws and the consummate achievement of his *Principia* — all of these produced a nearly immediate and substantial enhancement of the human capacity to understand and operate upon nature.

Machiavelli's great simplification, his emphasis on instrumental rationality in the spheres of social and interpersonal relations, produced an immediate and profound effect on emergent modern statecraft. Many view him as the founder of the *science* of politics. In Biology systematic observation and such discoveries as the circulation of the blood, the mechanisms of muscle and bone, and later of reflexes and the electrical nature of neural communication produced a corresponding and justified conviction of the potency of analytic methods.

But by the end of the nineteenth century there was a re-realization that the whole is most often rather more than the sum of its parts; that there exist ordered hierarchies of forms and functions in the material universe, in living things, and in societies; that entities exist in environments and that ecological systems demonstrate structural and processual regularities and order. The French physiologist Claude Bernard spoke of a *milieu interne*. Electromagnetism, radioactivity, and the anomalies relating to the velocity and wave/particle nature of light forced reflection regarding the field(s) in which physical events occur and within which they are linked. Psychological, cultural, and social realities, as they became better known and better understood during the twentieth century, also forced a reconsideration of the analytic paradigm; things and events *in context* increasingly became the basis of understanding.

But if everything is related to everything else, and "everything" is so vast as to escape the possibility of human understanding, how in fact can we effectively comprehend and act on reality? Only by abstracting, simplifying, hierarchically organizing knowledge — by modelling. And the model is tested by its adequacy in representation (subject to falsification) and by its capacity to guide effective action on reality, its adequacy to adjustive and adaptive response (the pragmatic test).

I have attempted to suggest a concept of model which carries us considerably beyond the notion of a scientific model with its operational definition of variables and their relations subject to empirical verification and even measurement. The conceptual structures of the humanist, philosopher, and theologian, though not subject to direct empirical verification, and principally judged on the basis of internal coherence and non-contradiction, nonetheless model reality more abstractly, one or more removes from the flux of empirical reality. How *significant* are the conceptions and categories employed? To what extent do they evoke constructive, ordering, life-enhancing activities, more adequate adjustive and adaptive responses in those who affirm them as individuals or in groups? In many cases, their adequacy is only tested socially by their effect on individuals and groups who cannot themselves, in their lifetimes, benefit from the social learning experience in which they participate. Just as the participants in a field test of a new pharmaceutical product may be benefitted or damaged in the test to the welfare of those who come later, so the adherents of alternative cultures and lifestyles, of diverse philosophical, ideological, theological and behavioral models, have involved themselves in a social learning process from which they, as individuals or groups, may or may not benefit. Society as we know it, in its various manifestations around the world, consists of "survivors." The conceptual, behavioral, and cultural models on which they base themselves have demonstrated a certain adequacy.

Contemporary social scientists often use the terms "functional" and "dysfunctional" to characterize institutions and behaviors conducive to the survival and affirmation of the group or to its failure. So much of human history is the record of failed institutions, inadequate values and cultural adaptations, maladaptive cognitive structures. Strictures against magic and witchcraft, incantation and superstition, institutionalized paranoia, fear and enmity, vendetta and cruelty are, in fact, reflections of a hard-acquired human knowledge of the dysfunctional consequences of certain patterns of behavior and the models of reality, the visions from which they flow. Such social failures and the misconceptions underlying them simply disappear — although, of course, the human beings composing them may survive as part of a successor social grouping that may even include substantial elements of the vanished culture.

It is tempting to think of "models" only in the abstract terms of mathematical and verbal symbols, but the term itself conjures up the notion of a physical object that reflects the physical form of what is represented or is a physical analog of a process. The term "model" is applicable to the whole range of cultural artifacts that "represent" reality, simplify and make intelligible the world.

The representative arts themselves model reality, often expressing the universal, an ideal, in concrete form. This is clear, for example, in classic or medieval European sculpture or in the paintings of the old masters. In those single forms and assemblies there is represented a simplified and abstracted view of reality that can form the vision of the observer. Similarly in literature, each author in concrete form, by selection and emphasis and the delineation of what he conceives to be significant relations, models a universe. The world of Dostoyevsky differs greatly from that of Dickens or Jane Austin or Stendhal or Manzoni — and each represents a *weltanschauung* of greater or lesser validity, of greater or lesser utility to the reader in the conduct of his own life. As a bookish young man I recall receiving the good advice: "read the great authors and learn vicariously something of life and human behavior from those whom the critical judgment of mankind has deemed useful and perceptive guides."

History, though presumably and ideally an objective account of events and their interrelationships, treating of the specific and concrete, must select from the infinitude of objects and events that which the historian deems significant. He is usually guided by the traditions and accepted wisdom of his profession as reflected in the pro-seminar or methodologies course of the history departments of the great universities around the world. Alternative schools of history may present subtly or radically different versions of the past, the Whig account of the history of England as opposed to Lingard's, for example. Revisionist histories of the Japanese attack on Pearl Harbor, or the Cold War, or American social movements in the 1920s and '30s often select quite different persons, events, documentary sources, and relationships as significant. There is some degree of truth in the statement that history is written by winners, and that failed social movements end up in the dustbin of history. What do Adolf Hitler, Benito Mussolini, Smedley Butler, or Oswald Mosley have in common? With what widely differing outcomes did similar events occur in St. Petersburg in October of 1917, in Prague in the Spring of 1968, in Paris in May of 1968? In brief, history, too, is a simplified vision, a model of the past which reflects and forms the human perceptions on which decision and action will be based.

Even abstract art may in some sense be thought to model, reflecting an image of reality, not of a reality perceived by the reality of the internal perceptual mechanisms of the aesthetically stimulated perceiver. Why do indigenous Amazonian tribesmen, untouched by civilization, enjoy Mozart? Do the rules of harmony reflect some inner perceptual mechanisms in man? Do the color harmonies of the great abstract artists reflect neurological mechanisms whose nature and inner dynamics derive some profound satisfaction from them?

In this paper I have suggested that more recent approaches to knowledge in terms of contextual thinking and a recognition of the hierarchical and systemic structure of external reality, non-living, living, and social as reflected in contextual thinking, is beginning to replace the analytic paradigm which has dominated Western thought for four centuries. In recognizing that most of *human* knowledge requires the information compression and simplification involved in modelling, we may have one key to a reconciliation of the "Two Cultures," scientific and humanistic, whose separateness is emphasized by C. P. Snow. We can legitimately regard the products of the humanistic and scientific cultures as equally relevant to the fullness of the human condition, to men's knowledge of themselves and of the natural, social, and cultural universe in which they live. When true and good, such models produced by the humanistic culture are life-enhancing in a manner otherwise impossible while possessing a validity akin to the truth of scientific models. Perhaps thus we may again begin to reaffirm the unity both of knowledge and of man, whose cognitive processes do more than merely reflect a given "real world." They participate with increasing self-awareness in the creative processes by which the world is made.

The Catholic University of America
Washington, D.C., USA

HUMANISM, PHILOSOPHY, AND THE HUMAN SCIENCES

Feodor F. Cruz

There are many reasons why we are interested in the problem of man. But our interest is not and cannot be merely one of curiosity, even of the kind entertained by serious scientists. It is deeper than that. It is actually genuine concern; we are concerned about his survival because we are involved in humanity. Our concern is, therefore, an expression of a more fundamental instinct.

Humanism is, at the very least, this concern for understanding man. At its best, it is a commitment to identify and promote the truly human in man and the good or goods that befit man as man. The main question here is how this concern and commitment can be attended to in the most appropriate manner. Whatever route or routes may come to view, philosophy will be an indispensable part of discovering and exploring them, but philosophy not in isolation but as complemented by the human sciences.

If we are, then, to articulate the problem of man from such a vantage point, we may come up with some description of the philosophical task as aimed:

> . . . to formulate a synthesis of the philosophical implications of common experience and selected findings of natural, social, and behavioral studies in the understanding of the uniqueness of the human species within the natural order, focusing on the issues of life's origin and end, knowledge and language, emotions and choice, personhood and personality, spirituality and immortality.[1]

To validate this conception, it is necessary to elaborate on two points: 1) the distinctive concern of and need for philosophy in the study of the problem of man and 2) the relationship between philosophy and science in general and in the treatment of the problem of man in particular. But first the far-reaching contributions of the sciences must be acknowledged.

The Contributions of Natural and Behavioral Sciences

Before examining the kind of and the need for a knowledge of man that only philosophy can provide, tribute must be paid to the efforts of the sciences, which contributed to this area. It is hardly necessary to describe the intense work and enumerate the outstanding results achieved by scientists, individually and collectively, in the timeless project of understanding man. Inquirers in the area of physical and biological sciences deserve praise just as much as those engaged in behavioral studies. Researches conducted on those seemingly unrelated matters of nature and life are proving to be highly significant to those done on human nature and conduct[2]. As a consequence, the present is witnessing the unification of various fields of inquiry previously pursued independently. To cite some instances, there are now mixed sciences, such as molecular biology, genetic engineering, biochemistry, cybernetics, ecology, etc. Even in the so-called behavioral studies, overlapping is not uncommon. The Behavioral Research Council reported:

> Within these older fields the overlapping and duplication of effort at times borders on chaos, and the interdependences and similarities seem even more pronounced recently. For example, both anthropology and sociology sometimes are claimed to be "integrating" sciences, the one taking "culture" as the basic integrating idea, and the other, "social group" or "society." Economic and political science continually interrelated economic and political behavior, and both employ psychological hypotheses (and recently hypotheses from game theory and decision theory). Psychology stands between biology on the one side and sociology and anthropology on the other.[3]

What is happening is neither surprising nor unfortunate. Instances of overlap and duplication are indicative of the continuity of objective knowledge and, hence, of the sciences aim of determining and expressing the laws of natural phenomena. Principles and approaches to discovery, intent and concerns of individual scientists, may vary; but they are all directed to capturing the features of one and the same reality.

However, for reasons of necessity and economy, trends toward division of labor and some degree of specialization have and will continue. The necessity comes from the fact that our understanding is not intuitive but rational. From the raw materials gathered by the various senses, the mind abstracts, i.e., forms ideas, to refer to all objects having certain characteristics in common; it labels and classifies (or vice versa), it proceeds discursively by identifying or separating ideas. In effect, the processes involved reveal the imperfect nature of human knowing. It has to cut reality into bits: seconds, minutes, hours, days, weeks, years, etc., to make things intelligible. We put lines across the globe to locate places, but a grid in the heavens to make sense of the multitude of stars and planets.

Economy is required by the fact that the number of data to be gathered, selected, and organized is indefinite. Concentration of efforts on a specific area is both time-saving and productive. But economy is not an end-in-itself. Specialization is only a broader type of analysis. And just as the analytic phase of inquiry has to be supplemented or completed by synthesis, so also specific fields of study must be, at least, compared, if not integrated. The final aim of knowledge is, after all, metaphysics, that is, not only *seeing everything together* but *seeing everything as one.*

But whether considered compositively or distributively, the results of the scientific enterprise are praiseworthy. Sciences like anthropology, ecology, economics, genetics, geography, history, paleontology, linguistics, neurology, physiology, psychiatry, sociology, psychology, etc., have already cast ample light on man's becoming, makeup, behavior, individuality and inter-relatedness. In every area, new bits of knowledge are constantly surfacing as old ones are either being discarded or being confirmed.[4] It is hardly necessary to mention examples here. Scientific statements on selected topics will be mentioned below in the treatment of various questions.

Similarly, joint concerns produced *field* theories, like Darwin's biological *evolution,* Freud's conception of the *unconscious, Einstein's relativity,* and Planck's *quantum.* These are called *field theories* precisely because their implications extend outside the discipline within which they were originally conceived and proposed. This only indicates that communication among scholars from diverse lines of expertise is not only possible but desirable in gaining deeper and more integrative knowledge. The awakening in this century of appreciation for the value of cooperative efforts has transformed interdisciplinary inquiries from a luxury to a necessity. Some recommendations offered by the Behavioral Research Council are worth noting:

The first problem of the behavioral sciences is adequately to describe, account for, and predict human transactions (in full if-then form of scientifically warranted assertions), and to provide some basis for policy decisions. But the most efficient organization of behavioral research is not necessarily in terms of existing academic departmentalization or specialization, especially of the older fields. Rather, the lines between the sciences are at times arbitrary and need to be overcome whenever such boundaries restrict inquiry.... This need for more problem-centered inquiry suggests that a mutual and cooperative investigation by many different behavioral scientists and teams having different vantage points, and drawing upon the experience and literature of the various disciplines and specialties should be increasingly developed. One way to enrich behavioral inquiry is to have many different specialists contribute jointly to specific problems.[5]

Considering the achievements of both natural and behavioral sciences, why then call upon a different approach? Why precisely philosophy? What is distinctive about its method? What kind of knowledge can be attained through it? Does not the need for philosophy suggest limitation on the part of scientific knowledge?

The Need for a Philosophy of Man

In order to answer the crucial questions just raised in a satisfactory manner, it is necessary to I) discuss the nature of the scientific method, II) recall the characteristics of philosophical questions and method(s), particularly those concerning the topic of *man*, III) determine points of comparison (differences and relations) between science and philosophy.

I. The Scientific Method

It would be presumptuous to even merely suggest that the topic of this section can be adequately treated in a few paragraphs. The controversy over the nature of science has a long history and is, by no means, ended. It would also be hasty to make the claim that the issue can be dealt with independent of any bias. (Some notional preferences are made to initiate discussion and identify methodological framework for subsequent discussions.) The history of philosophy amply shows that, in any discussion, some presuppositions must be taken for granted. Otherwise, no deliberation can begin. What can be done to approximate objectivity is to start from what scientists themselves say about their method.[6]

In simpler terms, the scientific method can be summed up according to the usual sequence of observation (which includes selection), formulation of a hypothesis, and verification. These phases may be explained as follows:

A. Observation. Upon perception of a certain problem and entertainment of apparent explanations (tentative hypotheses), more intense observation is conducted and additional facts are collected and selected to a point of sufficiency.

B. Formulation of a Hypothesis. At some juncture, the inquirer reaches the conclusion that he or she has all the facts needed and, therefore, feels warranted to assert a conclusion. Irving Copi describes this phase as follows:

The result or end product of such thinking, if it is successful, is a hypothesis which accounts for all the data, both the original set of facts which constituted the problem and the additional facts to which the preliminary hypotheses pointed. The actual discovery of such an explanatory hypothesis is a process of creation, in which imagination as well as knowledge is involved.[7]

It must be observed that during the processes of observation and formulation of hypothesis, quantification is utilized. Thus, physics uses calculus, sociology employs statistics, etc. The worth of this aspect of scientific inquiry is very much debated. The limitation of direct experience and inability of (conceptual) language to express exact specifications bring about the need for precise measurements. The two extreme positions on the merit of mathematization can be represented briefly as follows:

1. Negative Appraisal — It is characteristic of our knowledge of material things that we have not reached — and perhaps never will reach — such a knowledge of their accidents that we can form a proper notion

of their specific essence. For example, we know very few qualitative properties of things insofar as they are material substances, and the qualities we do not know are not, strictly speaking, proper. But without a specific knowledge of specifically proper qualities we cannot attain a knowledge of a specific formal essence. In the face of this difficulty, modern science neglects those parts of direct experience which are not capable of exact specification, and *selects* for its study those common traits (such as weight, boiling point, valence) which are capable of exact quantitative determination. The product of this selective abstraction is no longer the existing thing according to its whole reality. But we *consider* it as if it were or revealed an essence. Now, this consideration of a "part" as if it were a whole is a contribution of the mind, helping to constitute the object in its *formal character of being an object*.[8] The author refers to this definition-by-selected-accidents as taxonomic. It is, he says *constructural*, in the sense of being the product of deliberate mental activity. He adds, however, that *they are not fictional, and are by no means false unless someone should assert them of the thing in the real order*.[9]

2. Positive Appraisal — Quantitative methods have been developed chiefly for two reasons: to make possible a finer discrimination and a more precise codification of qualitative differences; and to permit the use of the extensive resources of mathematical analysis for exploring the implications of assumed relations of dependence between variable properties. For example, a quantitative temperature scale enables us to make a larger number of precise discriminations between heat levels than we could possibly indicate by such familiar but vague words as cold, cool, lukewarm, warm, and hot. A similar comment can be relevantly made about attitude scales in psychology, measures of social stratus in sociology, and so on. The introduction of a temperature scale, or any other numerical scale, does not ignore qualitative difference. On the contrary, the numerical measures of temperature represent more accurate distinctions within a qualitative continuum.[10]

C. Verification. This phase may take many forms — deducing further consequences, repeating successful experiments, prediction, testing of consequences, application, etc.[11]

It may now be asked, what kind of knowledge is attained by science? The answer can be found in the determination of the aspect under which a subject-matter is studied by a particular science. For instance, sociology and biochemistry may study the same subject-matter, e.g., man. But the aspect under which that subject-matter is studied varies from one science to another. In the example, sociology studies man-in-a-group, while biochemistry studies man as an organism composed of chemical elements.

In a nutshell, scientific knowledge is essentially characterized as objective, in the sense of being publicly verifiable; descriptive, as opposed to essentialistic; contingent, not necessary or certain; proximate, not ultimate; and partial, not holistic. (The meanings of these technical notions will be discussed later in the section on the comparison of science with philosophy. In the meantime, the characteristics of philosophical questions, aims, and approaches may be recalled to determine the need for a suitable methodology to deal with the matter at hand.)

II. Philosophy and the Question of Man

The topic *man* is central to philosophical inquiry. The main concerns of philosophy, says I. Kant, are: What can I know? What should I do? What may I hope? What is man? And all can be reduced to the last.[12] Indeed, the scope of what is knowable to man is not unlimited. The determination of that scope (in epistemology) is simultaneously the identification of man's cognitive capacities. What should I do (studied in ethics) is a question that is and can be raised and answered only by man. It concerns the matter of *good-as-befitting-man* and of *evil-as-unbecoming-of-man*. What should I hope for? is a quest meaningful only upon discovery of man's inherent potentialities and operative powers within the purview of a metaphysics where man can gainfully employ those capacities.

If all philosophy is reducible to the question of man, can it also be said that all knowledge (including the contents of the sciences) is, in the final analysis, man-centered? An affirmative answer is warranted. For, behavioral sciences are obviously interested in human achievements, actions, conduct, habits, etc., collectively or individually considered. The natural sciences, it can be argued, are directed to the same concern. It can be shown that physics and astronomy ultimately seek for the place of man in the universal scheme of things and for instrumentalities and resources that would satisfy human needs and wants. Biology and chemistry study organisms and substances with eventual applications to human conditions (as indicated by having them required in medical programs).

It may, then, be suggested that the need for a philosophical study of man is identical with the need to find a locus of synthesis, interpretation, and application not only for various philosophical studies but also for the assorted findings of the sciences.

On another score, the kind of knowledge being sought here is one that requires a specifically proportionate approach. *"What is man?"* asks Francis J. Collingwood,

> Is he a mass of protoplasm, a sac of water with an interesting variety of chemicals reacting with one another therein; is he a fantastic piece of workmanship in bone, muscle, and nerve — a highpoint of evolution in the animal kingdom; is he a busy hedonist pursuing thrills until he is overtaken by disillusionment about the joyfulness of pleasure or by the exhaustion of the grave — a lonely battler against cruel fate; or is he a displaced person longing for his home but having an unsure sense of direction toward it, a man immersed in the exigency of reasoning out its own nature and proper end?[13]

The answer, he continues to say, can, true enough, be partially provided by biology and physiology (not to mention other sciences). But since the aim is to look over the nature of man in order to show that from it some conclusions can be drawn that are necessarily true assessments of what the possession of life by men encompasses (i.e., why man acts at all, and why he acts in the ways that are characteristic of man as distinct from other agents, both living and non-living), these sciences need to be supplemented by an analysis of the contents of man's consciousness.[14] Collingwood is evidently referring here to the use of introspection (mentioned above), which is a truly philosophical method.

The limitations of external observations and measuring tools cannot be over-emphasized. These do not have as much authority in providing answers in the sphere of man as they have in their application to appropriate objects. For "how can such subjective aspects of man's being as his feeling when kissed by his child, or being drenched in a warm summer rain, be expressed in quantitative terms?"[15] Physiological processes are manifestations or reactions and do not constitute the internal experience of the subject (man). The redness on the skin is not the pain;

the pale color and fast heartbeats do not make a lie. The water that is drunk and its immediate physical effects are observable and measurable. But the change, as it enters the constitution of an organic being, is beyond the power of senses and gauges to determine.

> To consider the drop of water as part of a living organism is to see it as caught up in an organization that dominates its activities and uses the water to carry on its own proper life. Thus the water is moved about not only according to the laws of gravitation and chemical combination, but also according to the regular order of organic processes.[16]

The same can be said of other questions raised concerning man — how does man cognitively and appetitively differ from other organisms? What holds man to be substantially one and self-identical in the duration of a lifetime? What happens, given his present mode of consciousness, when man dies? Is there evidence for personal survival after death? These are questions on which scientists would neither have nor want much to say.

The conclusion needs no articulation. The need for philosophy is based on the requirement for an appropriate methodology that can address the kind of ultimate questions man seeks about man — what is his nature and what is the human good that befits that nature?

The last statement hinted at the third and final point to be made here concerning the need for philosophy. The kind of knowledge sought in philosophy and the distinct method it employs indicate that only philosophical reflections can provide directions to the human quest for self-understanding and for a purpose based on that understanding. That these quests are inherent in simply being human is borne by the evidence of personal experience. Man's interest in self-knowledge renders the ancient prescription *know thyself* superfluous. To seek self-knowledge is man's inescapable predicament. What Ralph Barton Perry called the *egocentric predicament*[17] applies not only in epistemology but in all human endeavors. But the search of self-knowledge is merely a means. It is sought for what light it can throw on the nature of human finality, i.e., in what consists man's highest good (*summum bonum*).

The relation between what man is and what he ought to be is clearly intimate. The history of mankind is an uninterrupted series of attempts to define what constitutes human purpose, which, in turn, determines moral values. Each attempt is incontrovertibly based on some antecedent conception of human nature. This is why any social, political, religious, or educational theory implies or presupposes an idea or set of ideas about what it means to be human. This is the case even in a view that rejects the notion of human nature. Sartre's denial of human purpose is an apt example. In denying of man an antecedent nature, Sartre describes him as infinitely malleable. In so describing him, Sartre is providing a different view of human nature but of human nature nonetheless.

Significantly, the relation between human nature and human finality cannot be arbitrarily set. Indeed (it may be suggested), the root of many social and psychological ills that modern man suffers from lies in the failure to either understand or accept the objectivity of that relation. This is illustrated by the persistent effort of social and psychological engineers to make individuals adjust to their society rather than to create a society adjusted to the uniquely human needs of the individuals constituting it. Rapid change in all phases of life brought about by technological innovations carries with it much of the disillusionment and identity crises modern man experiences. It is not yet well recognized that fast and continuous productivity is a sign of genuine human progress only if it is directed toward some valid human purpose. In itself, it is as circuitous as the pursuit of a cat after its own tail.

But why cannot science itself be made the basis or guide of the moral life? Has not science, especially more recently, provided mankind instruments of progress and means of developing *lasting cities* on earth? True enough, but science has, in the language of C. J. Ducasse, a debit and a credit. While he admits that it has made possible the cure and prevention of many diseases, the manufacture of highly efficient means of production, communication, and transportation, he is convinced that it has also "complicated man's life, robbed it in large measure of the joy of craftmanship, multiplied his needs, and brought it new diseases and ghastly perils."[18] These consequences manifest the neutrality of science. On its own, it is a two-edged sword; it could, sometimes, render humane service, but at other times create havoc. This is because it is incapable, of itself, to define the human good. Scientists have to move away from their discipline to appraise the moral quality of a given task.

Religion is definitely a guide to the moral life. To a believer it is well ordered to provide secure directions. Unfortunately, the variety of religions in the world exposes him to different religious views some of which may run into conflict with his own. In this predicament, he could find that his own religion is incapable of offering resolution. Also, some religions that have endured through time may not have kept pace with changes and innovations and, therefore, give no more than a modicum of moral guidance in meeting new problems.

What, then, remains is to turn to philosophy. But how can philosophy serve as foundation for moral directives? How can it make a purpose be known to be validly human and, hence, moral? Erick Fromm responds by identifying *a valid human purpose* with a uniquely human need. Man's most intensive passions, he says, are those rooted not in his body but in the very peculiarity of his existence.[19] Aristotle refers to the same as a truly human good. Concretely, goods that perfect inherent human capacities are truly human goods. Understandably, identifying distinctively human capacities is a necessary condition in establishing what precisely constitutes *a valid human purpose.* This briefly means that the problem of *what man is meant for* is irrevocably linked with the issue of *what it means to be human* regardless of time and condition.

The point may thus be restated: only philosophical reflection can provide an understanding of what man is, that kind of knowledge needed to serve as basis and framework of a moral theory.

In summary, this section has attempted to show that philosophy is the only study that provides a) a locus of synthesis, interpretation, and application not only for the reflections in other areas of philosophy but also for the findings of the sciences; b) an appropriate methodology that can address the kind of ultimate questions man seeks about man — what is his nature and what is the human good that befits that nature; c) a necessary basis and framework for axiology and ethics which science cannot provide.

III. Science and Philosophy, Comparison and Relation

An essential distinction exists between science and philosophy while simultaneously asserting an intimate complementarity of the two orders of inquiry particularly in cases of what Mortimer Adler calls *mixed questions.*[20] Much has already been said concerning the distinction. It suffices to explain the distinguishing qualifications of science and philosophy mentioned above and then to proceed to the justification for adopting the view just cited.

Scientific knowledge is objective, in the sense of it having its data externally analyzable (unlike the data of consciousness). The observation

80

phase of the scientific method does not and cannot presume to capture essential being (i.e., the *whatness* of a thing). For, "in science the subject-matter is defined in terms of observed constancy in behavior; its defining elements, therefore, are of the observable order, but taken as pointers to 'some un-get-at-able essence.'"[21] Philosophy, in contrast, seeks to define its subject-matter in terms of its intelligible being.[22] Scientific definitions use indirect external notions (intelligibilities that are taxonomic or accidental and operational)[23] instead of intrinsic formal essence, in the Aristotelian sense, which philosophy largely employs.

Because science proceeds by observing constancy, regularity or uniformity, its statements are descriptive; they tell how things are or appear to be or how things can be expected to appear given the same set of circumstances. This is not, of course, saying that scientific statements are wholly descriptive and are merely expressive of correlations of data. The use of theoretical, often highly abstract and speculative, constructs are involved in their formulation.[24] But being constructs, they are beyond the limits of observation. It is, therefore, difficult to determine where correspondence ends and imagination begins. There are also universal principles in science. For the scientist, at some point, employs deductive reasoning after experimental induction reaches its limit. Klubertanz explains:

> When we try to discover the proper principles, or laws, of natural things, we find again that this is not a simple induction by way of natural abstraction. We must use a different kind of induction, one which employs formal logical processes. We need to make repeated experiments, or at least one experiment under exactly controlled conditions, to reason on the results of these experiments, and to reach a generalization by more or less formal use of statistical methods. At the very least, we "correct" the experimental results according to the norms established by a theory of experimental error. Because of the employment of logical principles in such inductions, we may well call this process one of "rational induction," which means "an induction using reasoned (logical) processes and principles." Principles (laws) established on such a basis are no longer strictly universal, and cannot be used simply without qualification. Thus, for example, Boyle's laws of gases work well within certain limits, but at extremes there is no longer a simple correlation between volume,

pressure, and temperature. Obviously, not only the "extension" but even the *meaning* of conclusions depends on the kind of intelligibility found in the principles.[25]

The reliance on empirical data (availability, collection, selection, repetition) is paramount in the scientific investigation. Verification itself is a process of going back to the original data. Checking and rechecking the conditions that influence the conclusion are a commonplace. This is why no hypothesis is ever closed. The activity is self-corrective. It is also communal, in the sense that a theory of one scientist may be found wanting by another and is, therefore, subject to modification, correction, or rejection. The quest is never for absolute certitude but for the highest degree of probability possible. Thus, the conclusions of science are said to be tentative or contingent (conditional), as opposed to necessary or absolute (universal).

Implied in the concept *contingency* is the understanding that science is not ordained, by reasons of subject-matter and method, to yield knowledge of things "by their first causes and their highest reasons of being."[26] It provides, therefore, not first, in the sense of highest or ultimate, but proximate or circumferential, knowledge of causes and reasons of being.[27] Finally, the concept *partial*, as opposed to *holistic*, indicates the analytic (vs. synthetic) character of scientific knowledge. A particular science concerns itself with a specific aspect of a given reality. To exemplify from the behavioral sciences, anatomy studies the structural parts of man, biochemistry studies the chemical composition of man as an organism, physiology studies the internal functions of the body parts (e.g., receptors, neurons, nerves, etc.). For sharpness of focus, compare this approach with the synoptic intent of philosophical studies (discussed above).

At this point, the claim that science and philosophy are intimately complementary needs to be argued. One good reason for doing so is the fact that the idea of alliance is not a popular one, particularly among traditionalists who sustain not only a rigid distinction of philosophy from science but also the absolute autonomy of the former from the latter (as well as from other disciplines such as theology).[28] The preceding sections have already pointed to some differentiating characteristics. Logically, the position being supported here is against philosophers who reduce science to philosophy and against philosophers (like positivists and empiricists) and scientists who reduce philosophy to science.[29]

There are two significant facts worth considering that bear upon the point at issue. The first is the origin of science, in general, and of scientific psychology, in particular, from philosophy. While this is an external consideration, the genealogy of the sciences casts some light on interests common to the two studies.[30] The second is the development of particular philosophical systems concerning nature ushered in by scientific revolutions. This is not entirely an external matter. For, if it can be shown that an original philosophy was essentially affected by a scientific theory, then it can be said that the two perspectives are not really parallel and completely autonomous from each other.

Regarding the first of these two facts, it cannot be denied that the emancipation of science from philosophy was born of need. The discoveries in neuroanatomy and physiology shed new light on the human mind and called for revisions of some notions handed down by philosophy. Nevertheless, the formal inauguration of scientific psychology in the 1870's did not signal the substantive influence and direct contribution of philosophy. Henry Misiak notes:

> The language of philosophy and the philosophical notions about man and his mental fictions were still part of psychology, and the various philosophical systems continued to exert a strong influence on psychology and its development. Numerous psychologists, for many years, used philosophical doctrines or certain philosophical notions as their starting points and frames of reference.[31]

Even in the apparent freedom of the clinical setting, they acknowledge not only debt to but genuine need for philosophy.[32]

Concerning the second fact, a review of historical events will reveal that in the interplay between the two forms of knowledge, philosophy cannot always claim temporal priority. In fact, the origins of notable metaphysical systems in the Western world were founded on scientific revolutions. William Levi enumerates the three main ones:

> The first was the revolution of the Ionian philosophers, which, in its search to identify the material properties of all natural substances, was led to seek in rational principles the explanation of the multiformities of change . . . . The second revolution was that of the seventeenth-century philosopher-physicists Galileo,

Newton, and Descartes, which found the rationality of nature to consist in its susceptibility to mathematical treatment . . . .[33]

The third revolution, he goes on to say, was the theory of relativity and the theory of quanta.

The first culminated in the construction of the cosmologies of Aristotle, emphasizing form and matter; of Democritus, establishing atomism; of Plato, based on mathematical relations. The second led to exploitations dominated by the machine-model, the parts of which function harmoniously and regularly, and, hence, are subject to mathematically precise calculation. The third (still following Levi) has philosophical consequences that cannot yet be definitively stated, but has left a profound impression on the philosophizing of twentieth century thinkers.[34]

How deep and to what extent these scientific revolutions affected the philosophies of the time cannot be spelled out here. It is sufficient to state the fact. The claim here is more modest than John Dewey's perception of the influence of Darwin in philosophy (which, he declares, was to show the possibility and direction of the application of scientific method to the problems of mind, morals, and life). What is maintained in this position is only that the findings of science must be taken into account in dealing with the philosophical issues, just as the insights of philosophy must bear upon scientific inquiry.

Such a complementarity is not only convenient but necessary to the reciprocal interest of both. *To the benefit of science*, philosophy can provide it with a systematic theory of nature through which science can justify its perspective. In truth, no science is immune from philosophic backing. This is the case even in the more empirical approach to psychology. For example, the methods and contents of various schools — biophysical (Beuler, Meehl, Sheldon, Kallman, etc.), intrapsychic (Freud, Erikson, Sullivan, Fromm, Hartman, Jung, etc.), behavioral (Pavlov, Skinner, Eysenck, Ferster, Ullman, etc.) and phenomenological (May, Laing, Maslow, Rogers, Buytendijk, etc.) — are ultimately directed by some presupposed philosophy of human nature and some epistemological underpinnings.[35] A.G. Melsen says:

Phenomenologists, existentialists, positivists and Marxists each have not only their own philosophical view about this method but often also pursue the human sciences in their own way. For this reason there exist in the human sciences schools of thought and trends whose differences arise from divergent philosophical views of man and man's cognitive possibilities.[36]

He is saying that the principle of selection indispensably employed by any researcher also has a philosophic root. For (he says in the same text), "one who does not want to drown in a limitless ocean of data must know beforehand what is relevant when he begins to observe or experiment." This claim lends support to the earlier statement made above that the method of science is both inductive and deductive. Van Melsen, again, has the same thought.

> The physicist, chemist or biologist will always place his physical theories and data against a background of certain philosophical convictions. A classical example is provided by mechanism, which accompanied physical science from the seventeenth to the twentieth centuries. In the eyes of many, mechanism, which assumed that material reality is composed of immutable primeval elements and therefore regarded all changes as new arrangements of these elements, was an intrinsic part of physical science itself. As a matter of fact, however, it was a philosophical addition, which could be removed by a careful philosophical analysis. While that analysis cannot offer any aid in solving the proper problems of physical science itself, it cannot contribute to the purification of scientific thinking.[37]

There are other instances. The distinction between mental and organic states presupposes a form of philosophical dualism; theories of learning hinge on the nature of habit and motivation; social and political policies are applications of ideologies antecedently conceived. Scientific psychologists admit these relationships. As Misiak declares,

> Despite emancipation, however, psychology stayed close to philosophy and continued to be influenced by it. The language of philosophy and the philosophical notions about man and his mental functions were still part of psychology, and the various philosophical systems continued to exert a strong influence on psychology and its development. Numerous psychologists, for

many years, used philosophical doctrines or certain philosophical notions as their starting points and frames of reference.[38]

Rollo May is even more categorical.

> . . . every form of psychology or psychiatry rests upon some kind of philosophic presupposition. The only error is not to be aware of these assumptions; the only illusion is to deny them. The presupposition underlying most forms of psychiatric and psychological approaches in the nineteenth and twentieth centuries is the traditional dichotomy between subject and object formulated by Descartes, the father of modern Western thought, some four centuries previously. This dichotomy was assumed by Freud and practically all other scientists and philosophers of the late nineteenth and earlier twentieth centuries, despite the fact that this assumption was so much in the act of modern thought, that they who used it were generally quite unaware they were assuming it. Phenomenology and existentialism consist precisely of an attack on this dichotomy.[39]

To the enrichment of philosophy, science can clarify, confirm, and extend common experience by elucidating the data and, possibly, the conclusions of philosophy. In reflecting upon the facts of man's behavior and experiences in order to see where they lead under the pressure of ultimate and necessary explanation, experimental science is of much use. To borrow Royce's example,[40] Gestalt psychology and Ames' illusion experiments enlarge knowledge of the subjective factors in perception and, consequently, control unwarranted claims in epistemology. Summarily, says Van Melsen,

> . . . the philosophical explication of primary and original experience will of necessity always be influenced by prescientific, primitive-scientific or antiquated scientific data. In other words, authentic primary experience will always be mixed with elements that do not belong to it, but the non-authentic character of these elements will come to light only through the development of physical science. In this indirect way, therefore, the evolution of physical science can contribute to the clarification and purification of philosophical problematics.[41]

But, likewise, in a direct way, discoveries in science can affect specific philosophic claims. Indeed, there were and there can be occasions when the former can invalidate the latter. The view, for example, that life regularly springs from non-living matter by *spontaneous generation* was held for thousands of years, until Louis Pasteur proved it false. The theory that the senses are infallible (understood to mean that there is a one-to-one correspondence between subjective experience and objective conditions) appears haphazard in the face of what experimental psychology and optics have found about perception and what physics has discovered about objective features of the visible spectrum. More instances can be found in the following chapters.

The opinion just cited (on the complementarity of science and philosophy) is, admittedly, not accepted by all. George Klubertanz expresses hesitation. While he concluded that "no propositions of science can be directly and immediately opposed either contrarily or contradictorily to any propositions of the philosophy of nature," he simultaneously defends the community of disciplines.[42] Understandably, he disagrees with G. W. R. Ardley[43] that philosophy can afford to ignore the results of the physical sciences. And to show how scientific theories affect philosophical explanations, Klubertanz cites Aristotle's and Aquinas' assertion that the *virtual presence* of elements in compounds pertains to the order of qualitative accidents. But "our modern knowledge of chemical compounds has led us to transform the causal explanation so that we now think of the virtual presence of elements in the order of substance itself."[44]

This rather lengthy discussion on the distinction and complementarity of science and philosophy is sustained for important reasons, chief among which is to show the justification supporting a position midway between two extreme views, namely, the position that there is nothing in common between philosophy and science such that communication is both unnecessary and impossible, and the conception that philosophy, if not altogether reducible to science, is wholly dependent upon its conditions.

The justification is significant because the two extreme views have already brought about consequences that are unfavorable to the advancement of human knowledge, particularly knowledge about man. The exponents of the absolute autonomy of philosophy have considerably retarded the development of present understanding. A concrete example is the resistance to the theory of evolution on the part of some who were apprehensive about its implications in their philosophical views. The loss to philosophy caused by this posture is incalculable — its very prestige. Says Paul Weiss:

> Fields which philosophers once ploughed have been abandoned in the face of the advance of specialized scientific disciplines. From this a wrong moral has been drawn to the effect that philosophy is anticipatory science, and that it occupies a field only until science is ready to work in its own way . . . .[45]

Experimentalists equally suffer in detaching themselves from philosophy. In promoting an unsound scientism, they have been led to the dead-end alley of mechanistic interpretations. Their reductionism has deprived them of the insights of a personalistic view of man.[46] Many social critics, like Alvin Toffler, lament the evils brought about by twentieth century progress in the forms of scientism and brute technologism — worship of method and impassioned activity to produce new things.[47] They observe that people today are starting to feel negative toward scientists; they are angry at what they regard as the arrogance and dogmatism of some of these men in white coats.

The anger is justified, but more than emotional reaction is needed if change is to be expected. The constructive means to be sought are the alliance of science and philosophy, application of the two disciplines to the problems of men in society, planning for the future wisely. Theodore Puck, writing the introduction to Mortimer Adler's book on man, expresses hope for illumination on "the need to end the artificial separation between science and philosophy in our society — separation which has already been costly to our understanding of the meaning of past accomplishments and to our ability to plan future goals wisely."[48]

Loras College
Dubuque, Iowa, USA

88

NOTES

1. Francis J. Collingwood, *Man's Physical and Spiritual Nature* (New York: Holt, Rinehart and Winston, 1963), pp. 8-9.

2. *View from a Height* (New York: Lancer, 1963), pp. 9-10.

3. Rollo Handy and Paul Kurtz, *A Current Appraisal of the Behavioral Sciences* (Great Barrington, MA: Behavioral Research Council for Scientific Inquiry into the Problems of Man in Society, 1964), p. 9.

4. Ibid. for summaries of results achieved in these fields.

5. Ibid., p. 13.

6. A number of sources are available for this purpose. A basic concept of the scientific method is, for instance, provided in Handy and Kurtz. Refer to the bibliography for other relevant materials.

7. Irving Copi, *Introduction to Logic* (New York: Macmillan, 1972), p. 441.

8. "The Doctrine of St. Thomas and Modern Science," in *Sapientia Aquinatis*, (Rome, 1955), p. 99.

9. Ibid.

10. Ernest Nagel, "The Mission of Philosophy," in *An Outline of Man's Knowledge of the Modern World*, ed. by Lyman Bryson (New York: McGraw-Hill), p. 658.

11. Copi, "Scientists in Action: The Pattern of Scientific Investigation," in *Introduction to Logic*, pp. 444-449.

12. *Logik* (1800), Introduction, part 3.

13. Collingwood, p. 1.

14. Collingwood, pp. 6-7.

15. Collingwood, p. 17.

16. Collingwood, p. 16.

17. James L. Christian, *Philosophy, an Introduction to the Art of Wondering*, 2nd ed. (Corte Madera, CA: Holt, Rinehart and Winston, 1977), p. 100.

18. "What Philosophy Can Be," in *The Key Reporter*, Vol. XXIII, No. 2, January, 1958.

19. *The Sane Society* (New York: Holt, Rinehart, and Winston, 1955), pp. 71-72.

20. *The Difference of Man and the Difference It Makes* (New York: Holt, Rinehart, and Winston, 1967), pp. 36ff. See also his *The Conditions of Philosophy* (New York: Atheneum, 1965), pp. 38ff.

21. Anthony F. Russell, *Philosophy of Man* (Unpublished Notes), 1981.

22. Ibid.

23. Klubertanz.

24. James J. Royce, *Man and Meaning* (New York: McGraw-Hill, 1969).

25. Klubertanz, p. 100.

26. Jacques Maritain, *The Degrees of Knowledge*, trans. from the 4th French ed. of *Distinguer pour unir* (originally pub. 1932) under the supervision of Gerald B. Phelan (New York: Scribner's, 1959), p. 92.

27. Cf. also Pierre Duhem, *La Theorie physique: son objet — sa structure*, second edition (Paris: Marcel Riviere et Cie). The English translation, *The Aim and Structure of Physical Theory*, trans. by Philip Wiener (New Jersey: Princeton Univ. Press, 1964), was used in this work.

28. For a brief discussion of prominent positions on this issue, see F. G. Connolly, *Science vs. Philosophy* (New York: Philosophical Library, 1957).

29. Ibid., p. 11. John Dewey and Ernst Nagel are not rigid reductionists in spite of their espousal of the application of the scientific method in philosophy. Cf. John Dewey, *Experience and Nature* (New York: W. W. Norton and Co., 1929), and Ernest Nagel, "The Mission of Philosophy," in *An Outline of Man's Knowledge of the Modern World*, pp. 643-666.

30. Henry Misiak's *The Philosophical Roots of Scientific Psychology* (New Fordham University Press, 1961) is an excellent treatise illustrating science's indebtedness to philosophy. He concludes (on p. 4) that there are many factors involved in the emancipation of scientific psychology from philosophy, but that these factors can be reduced to "the realization of the incompleteness and inadequacy of solely philosophical treatment of psychological problems, and on the other hand to the progress and findings of physiology which contained elements of psychological significance."

31. Ibid., p. 6.

32. For a confirmation of this view, see Peter Koestenbaum, *The New Image of the Person: The Theory and Practice of Clinical Philosophy* (Westport, CT: Greenwood Press, 1978).

33. *Philosophy and the Modern World* (Bloomington, IN: Indiana University Press, 1966), p. 245.

34. Ibid.

35. Theodore Millon, *Theories of Psychopathology* (Philadelphia: W. B. Saunders, 1968).

36. A. G. Van Melsen, *Evolution and Philosophy* (Pittsburgh: Duquesne University Press, 1965), pp. 34-35.

37. Ibid., p. 31

38. Misiak, p. 6.

39. *Perspectives in Group Psychotherapy* (New York: Science House, Inc., 1972), p. 78.

40. Royce, p. 41.

41. Van Melsen, p. 31.

42. Klubertanz, p. 104.

43. *Aquinas and Kant* (London: Longmans, 1950).

44. Ibid.

45. *Nature and Man* (Carbondale, IL: Southern Illinois University Press, 1947), p. 82.

46. Stephan Evens, *Preserving the Person* (Downer's Grove, IL: InterVarsity Press, 1979), for a vilification of this form of scientism.

47. *Future Shock* (New York: Random House, 1970).

48. Ibid., iv.

THE METAPHYSICAL CHRISTIAN DEMANDS
OF TECHNOLOGY

Richard P. Francis

The purpose of this analysis is to explore the principles of traditional Christian metaphysics as they relate to and function in today's technological world. Metaphysical studies are difficult and, according to Aristotle and St. Thomas, they require a certain maturity and robust intellect.[1] Agreeably, metaphysics in the grand style is presently out of favor because today's thinkers lack intellectual vision, intuitive penetration, and the wider frame of reference, writes Dorothy Emmet.[2] The opportunity to do metaphysics here reinforces the important, central cultural role of metaphysics.

However difficult, everyone ought to pursue metaphysical truths because the rewards are high. Certainly, our eternal happiness consists in attaining the transcendent Truth, God, which can be done metaphysically.[3] This is the God whom we are admonished to know, love and serve in this life. These fundamental admonitions are everlasting, for all times and all peoples. In these enlightened, modern, technological times, as God gives us increasing abilities, so much more responsible and inventive must we be in knowing, loving and serving God and our fellows. Even if our intellectual climate suffers a metaphysical drought, this world cannot be abandoned. Jesus came to this particular world to teach us how to live. We are to use our best abilities, including technology, to carry out his Gospel teachings.

Admittedly, we moderns are very busy, driven in many directions in an increasingly complicated world. Nevertheless, St. Thomas correctly declares that our essential happiness consists in our intellectual perfection, and that our greatest natural happiness consists in contemplating the truths of metaphysics, because these lead to our knowledge of God. St. Thomas writes that the "highest felicity" that we can obtain in this life consists in the contemplation of the first causes. He adds that we are made perfectly happy in the completion of this knowledge after this life. He recalls the Gospel: "This is eternal life, that they may know thee, the only true God."[4]   We are not expected to abandon this world's knowledge, even though a higher wisdom completes and perfects it. Metaphysically we seek God as a self-rewarding task but also as a way to process this world's knowledge.   This includes scientific and technological knowledge.   "By their fruits you shall know them" is a practical teaching.

The poverty of metaphysics, according to Maritain, lies in the incompleteness of human knowledge. The grandeur of metaphysics, he adds, is its awakening in us a desire to know and especially to possess God. Metaphysics itself falls short. But Christians preach a different wisdom, a scandal for the Jews and madness for the Greeks. Thus, beyond human effort, God graces us with the gifts of the Holy Spirit through the mediation of Christ crucified. Metaphysicians, as such, make mistakes, but this divine grace builds upon nature and supplements metaphysics to remove or to reduce error. St. Thomas further reminds us that divine revelation safeguards us against human errors, enriches our knowledge, and adds to the compendium of truths.[5]   Divine assistance is always proffered for our salvation as well as for a better understanding of things.

Technology, as we understand it, must thus somehow fit the plan of salvation. There can be something redeeming about technology. But there persists today an extremely strong tendency worldwide towards secularism with attempts to replace our biblical God with the god-of-the-machine. Of itself, however, technology need not be so pervasively secularizing. Technology can be viewed as God's providence by means of various ways to benefit humankind, to do good, which is essential to the Gospel. Science and technology, after all, originated in and now flourish in Western Christendom. Normally this bodes well.

Maritain, however, has strong doubts about this.[6] He holds that the modern tendency is a progressive dislocation because much of humanity is under the sway of money and mechanics and a materializing world. He complains that by now material techniques should have prepared us for a less materialistic and for a better, more spiritual life. Still, we should not forsake technology, for such has never been the Christian view, declares Maritain.[7] We think that rational, just, charitable and grace-filled ways can be found for technology to succeed in correctly addressing needs. What must be avoided is the inhumane, despotic, dangerous uses of technology.

Clearly, it is the same technology that clothes the naked, feeds the poor, heals the sick, shelters the homeless, builds places of worship, as that which exploits the weak, kills millions of unborn children, conducts aggressive warfare, supports holocaust atrocities, manufactures addicting debilitating drugs, and so on. It is the same technology that holds back devastating nuclear armaments as commits them. Presumably, any nation or people can advance in science and technology and use that knowledge and power for good or for evil. Pointedly enough, Maritain records the present, severe crisis for the West, namely, it has abused divine grace and has lost the gifts of God. It is no longer supported by charity and has corrupted and made useless the order of reason. The world chose to forsake both reason and God in an impossible metaphysical suicide. In the final reckoning, he exclaims, only animality is served.[8] Normally we regard science and technology to be progressively good for us, but obviously just the opposite can and does occur. Abusive technology can devastate a culture and create untold suffering. The enterprise requires a theological-philosophical dimension to keep it safe and beneficial.

Typically, metaphysics seeks after the ultimate causes of things, including that of technology. It cultivates a general wisdom to regulate the other disciplines and our style of life as well.[9] As directive knowledge, metaphysics orders and unifies things. A heterogenous plurality of things, that always naturally exists, will interact and function randomly as well as interfere with each other. Different kinds of things function differently. Some will behave harmoniously, some not. Such various things in the world need some broader metaphysical principles that direct them towards some purpose or end. The major guiding principle for human experience is happiness.

Certainly Christian philosophy teaches us that we are to seek happiness both here and in the hereafter. Christian metaphysics allows for the proper benevolent uses of technology to attain the people's happiness. Happiness is our natural and supernatural goal and it directs, unifies, and guides the different features of human experience. God wants his people to be happy. In fact, all of the diverse things in the world are directed towards God as their goal. Seeking God is our happiness. In truth, heaven is happiness eternal.

Biblical temperament optimistically encourages peace, prosperity, progress, success, well-being and happiness. God's people are not meant to fail. This has its price. We must persist in God's cooperative, covenantal partnership with us. We thus carry our full share of responsibility in pursuing the good life for mankind. And we do this in accordance with the various biblical injunctions of law and love.

Technology can be directed towards human benefit. Indeed, this is correctly the entire role of technology, to benefit mankind. Scripturally, the gospel message can be summed up with this sentence: Jesus went about doing good, making people well and happy. The contrary is unthinkable. Jesus, too, depended on technology, needing the crafts associated with olive and wine pressing, bread making, cloth weaving, sandal making, fishing boats and netting. He needed houses, synagogues and temples, and even the instruments of his passion and death, as well as the hewed tomb for his burial and resurrection. In fact, Jesus and his foster father Joseph were themselves carpenter-craftsmen and used the tools of their trade.

While all of our covenantal activity is directed towards well-being, suffering does persist. Jesus came to heal and make whole, never to cause suffering. Suffering might well be redemptive and somehow meritorious in Christ's mystical body, in the larger scheme of things. But to inflict suffering is not Christian. Instead it is Christian to alleviate suffering of every kind and to use technological means wherever appropriate to make people whole and happy. Certainly, as Maritain said, some people have abandoned reason, have willfully despised charity, abused God's gifts, and greedily surfeit themselves in selfish self-aggrandizement. This is metaphysical suicide, for such sinfulness promotes more sinfulness with overall catastrophic disorder and cultural deterioration. This represents regression to barbarism. Technology fails Christian philosophy when it causes or contributes to evil.

Technology comes from Christianity historically. Christians look to *Genesis* for the idea of this world being created as an artifact and possessing intelligent design. Therein also we find humankind created in God's image and given a share in the dominion of and conservation of creation. From *Exodus* we learn that history is linear, moving purposefully toward an end. Toward this providential, purposeful movement we must contribute by our worldly activities. From the gospel truths of the Incarnation and Resurrection, we learn that matter is not evil but is created for spiritual purposes including regeneration.[10] Overall, our Bible is unique in its account of a progressive salvation history so that the modern idea of progress is unknown outside of Christianity itself.[11] Karl Rahner reaffirms that indeed historically the breakthrough from theory to practice was essentially a product of Christianity,[12] however many Christians opposed this emancipating movement.

Currently, Pierre Teilhard de Chardin explains that after close to two centuries of passionate struggle, neither science nor faith has succeeded in discrediting the adversary. On the contrary, it becomes obvious that neither can develop normally without the other.[13] Scientific progress was expected to eliminate religion. Instead religious beliefs persist even in the most sophisticated technological societies.[14] Because, as Christians, we have invented and nurtured science and technology, we have a continuing obligation to favor their tremendous promise for human betterment. Jesus "came to give us life that we may have it more abundantly" and not more sparingly.

As earlier noted, St. Thomas recalls that metaphysically we are to seek the first causes, meaning also the Cause of all causation. In Christian metaphysics, God is the first cause, the source or origin of everything. God is understood also to be the final cause, the goal, aim, purpose of everything. Immaterial beings, like God, operate higher in the ontological order and more universally in causation than do the lesser causes. If this is correct, then God functions most universally causing the whole universe into existence as the first efficient cause in the act of creation. This highest cause creates *ex nihilo* in a wondrously perplexing fashion, for there is no good logical reason for anything to exist. It appears that this all powerful, universal, first cause, God, simply, freely creates the universe as a gratuity, a gift, out of goodness or love.

Once creation occurs, then God serves as the ordering and unifying principle in terms of his will or providence. As first and final cause, God further sustains or conserves creation over time and place by a kind of concurrence. So significant and inherent is God's sustaining power that, if God were to remove his support for a single instant, the entire universe would immediately disappear.[15] Thus, everything, including technology, depends absolutely upon God's goodness to begin and upon God's sustaining power to continue.

While God exists and functions as the first, principal cause, and as a sustaining cause as well, God also endows his creatures with participant, creative, and sustaining power. Accordingly, creatures act as intermediate or secondary causes.[16] We share God's causal power in our production and management of things. Of course, this causal ability is limited by our human nature. Because such creative sustaining power is freely offered, we can either accept it or reject it according to our ability and willingness. Our gratification rests in that we can do God's work, as intermediate causes, in managing the affairs of this world. Insofar as technology fits into the divine scheme of things and represents God's will, it comfortably enough fits into Christian philosophy. It represents intermediate or shared causation.

As mentioned earlier, God further exists and functions as the final cause. This means that all existence is meant for God. He draws all things to himself. In our own world, all human experience is destined for God, and that also includes technology. Technology is put into the service of creation, redemption, and sanctification. Technology must never be its own self-serving goal, its own God. It is meant to produce the good things in life, always subservient to the higher purposes or causes, especially to the final cause, God. Throughout, God is our partner. Why should our great inventiveness not work for God by improving the human circumstance and serving the divine purpose!

Technological progress, by metaphysical design, can be careful and caring enough to keep within the good stewardship and sacred trust given to us biblically. In *Genesis*, God found everything to be very good, thus encouraging a positive attitude towards this world.[17] In God's sharing dominion with us, we are encouraged to use appropriate means as his good and faithful servants. Unless the world comes to an early and unexpected end, science and technology are here to stay. No one can deny that the world has progressed from ancient to modern times in education, communication, transportation, agriculture, home life, health care, labor conditions, sanitation, religious worship, and in countless ways that make life more comfortable, healthier, safer, happier, and so on. Technologic peoples are not expected to sacrifice their advancement. Their inventions indeed form a cultural, seamless web that cannot realistically be unravelled.[18] Their inventiveness must be used better to know, love and serve God and neighbor and to function in co-creation, co-redemption and co-sanctification.

Arnold Toynbee observes that during mankind's first million years of existence, science and technology have been constantly accelerating in cumulative and enormous progress. And the future advances may well dwarf the past, with promises of more and better to come. We keep increasing our knowledge and control of material nature. Toynbee, however, laments that "In our own time we have seen great nations which had apparently been civilized suddenly lapse into unparalleled wickedness." He complains that as sensational as technology is, it has not changed the essential human condition. "Our behavior to each other is still bad," he writes.[19]

Similarly, Bernard Lonergan respects technology, its human inventiveness and success in mating theoretical science and common sense concerns. But he declares that "we are brought to the profound disillusionment of modern man . . . the focal point of his horror." This consists in our expectation of continuous progress with no decline. Instead, Lonergan deplores our acquisition of "stupendous power without necessarily adding proportionate wisdom and virtue."[20]

Maritain, Toynbee, Lonergan all see the successes and failures of technology with none willing to abandon it. In fact, the overriding, universal, integrating, directing metaphysical principles of genuine Christianity are a necessary concomitant of technology, which must never be neutral. When so-called Christians or others fail to follow the biblical injunctions of law and love, it is not the philosophy that fails but the person who fails individually or collectively. Technological knowledge and activity must constantly be combined with the Christian virtues to produce an acceptable kind of Christian progress. Christianity demands a life of virtue, including the theological virtues of faith, hope, and charity, as well as those of piety, patience, peace, temperance, joyfulness, modesty, humility, peacemaking, long-suffering, wisdom, justice, prudence, among others. These virtues must be applied to our modern scientific-technological culture just as they applied to the pre-scientific age. Christianity is a life of virtue. This represents the character of Christ-in-God as the metaphysical unifying, organizing, directing principle as well as the first, final and sustaining Cause. Intermediate causation is satisfied by our employing the virtues in specific, beneficial, worthy activity including that of science and technology. Seemingly neutral technology, devoid of Christian-humanistic values, will still operate according to certain more secularizing principles and produce a culture inimical to religion. The secular world is simply more dangerous to human life and well-being.

By itself technology can easily become an ideology because of its mystifying power.[21] It can replace the biblical God and become its own kind of god. Herein science professes to be the only true, valid knowledge. Divine revelation is despised and metaphysics derided, all as nonsense or at best immature. We can only note the death-of-God philosophy and its strengthening of popular secularism. In today's secular society, the powerful technocrat rules and can easily rule oppressively and despotically. The believing, religious faithful must never abandon this world to the technocrats whose ambition is likely to be self-serving and repressive of biblical culture. In a secular world, ambitious humans substitute themselves for God. Jean Rostrand warns that "Science has made us gods before we are worthy of being men."[22] A secular, technologic culture also tends to promote the highest production of material goods and goals in a merciless competition that denies the spirit. The frantic pace of life becomes depressing. We know that Christ came not to destroy our world but to save it, and that Christ's Holy Spirit dwells within the faithful. Thus, we must not depersonalize, dehumanize, de-spiritualize and cruelly regiment people to make them only a part of the machine world. Technology tends to do this.[23] Nor need our inventive optimism go so far as to hold that "technology is Christ incognito" as Van Leeuwen teaches.[24]

Modern "post-Christians" and "New Agers" need to know that if historically Christianity has not, and is not working, according to their claims, it may be that it has never been fully tried everywhere. The "failure" is in the ignorance, negligence, ill-will and arrogance, coupled with economic, ecclesiastic, and political pressures of some of the adherents and of others who occasionally violate the principles and norms, and thereby are *not really Christian*. They fail. Christianity does not fail because, in principle, it seeks only the betterment (happiness through salvation) of all peoples everywhere bound together in universal love, justice and peace. Overall, Christianity has worked well in technologically advanced Western Christendom, with the consequence of their enjoying the highest quality of life. Insofar as Eastern Christendom and others also enjoy the working and benefits of Western technology, they too advance in their higher quality of life. This is available to everyone, even to those Africans who are now slaughtering each other in tribal warfare. Anyone anywhere can qualify "to do good" within the predominantly progressive Christian metaphysical standards that guide Western technology. This is an aspect of happiness itself.

In conclusion, this study generally supports modern technology insofar as it can be brought into the plan of salvation. Technology clothes, heals, feeds, houses, transports and teaches us by inventions that usually improve our conditions of life. It tries to make us happy. Scientific technology is a Christian invention, and we are obligated to direct its progress by Christian metaphysical and ethical principles. Technology can fit into the traditional Thomistic metaphysics of causation as intermediate causal operations between the first and final causes (God). Thus, technology serves in the modes of co-creation, co-redemption, and co-sanctification. It also helps us to know, love and serve God and neighbor as good and faithful servants in a sacred trust enacted by the covenantal sharing of dominion over this world. By itself, technology can become despotic and barbarous. A recent Vatican document on higher education succinctly stipulates that ethics has priority over technology.[25] There is no profit in gaining the whole world and losing our soul, which is an attractive temptation in a modern technological world full of material promise. Christians have a passion for a humane social order. We can motivate technology to defend human life, to enhance human dignity, and to secure a just social order. The Church stands in judgment against the modern all-consuming secularistic, materialistic, technologic lifestyle. The Church's distinctive task is to safeguard the human.[26] It encourages science and technology towards that purpose, towards securing a benevolent result. Metaphysics guides ethics which guides technology. All of it can strive to make humankind well and happy in keeping with God's designs in this life with hopes for happiness in the next. And we are all the better for it.

University of Colorado
Colorado Springs, Colorado USA

NOTES

1. St. Thomas Aquinas, *Commentary on the Ethics*, VI, lesson 7, nos. 1210-1211.

2. Dorothy Emmet, *The Nature of Metaphysical Thinking* (New York: Macmillan, 1961), p. 221.

3. Herman Reith, *The Metaphysics of St. Thomas Aquinas* (Milwaukee: The Bruce Publishing Co., 1962), p. 15.

4. St. Thomas, *Exposition of the Liber de Causis*, preface.

5. St. Thomas, *Summa Theologica*, I, q. 1, art. 1.

6. Jacques Maritain, "The Grandeur and Poverty of Metaphysics" in Donald and Gallagher (eds.), *A Maritain Reader* (Garden City, NY: Doubleday and Co., Inc. (Image Books), 1966), p. 56.

7. Ibid., p. 49.

8. Ibid., pp. 50-51.

9. St. Thomas, *Commentary on the Metaphysics*, I, lesson 2, no. 36.

10. Wilhelm E. Fudpucker, "Through Christian Technology to Technical Christianity," in Carl Mitcham and Jim Grote, eds., *Theology and Technology* (Lanham, MD: University Press of America, 1984), p. 57.

11. Ibid., p. 63.

12. Karl Rahner, *Theological Investigations IX, Writings of 1965-67*, Part I., tr. Graham Harrison (New York: Herder & Herder, 1972), p. 214.

13. Pierre Teihard de Chardin, *The Phenomenon of Man, in John Cogley, Religion in a Secular Age* (New York: Frederick A. Praeger Publishers, 1968), p. 69.

14. John Cogley, *Religion in a Secular Age*, pp. 8-9.

15. Etienne Gilson, *The Christian Philosophy of St. Thomas Aquinas* (New York: Random House, 1956), p. 179.

16. Reith, p. 163.

17. Ian G. Barbour, *Science and Secularity* (New York: Harper & Row, 1970), p. 60.

18. Victor C. Ferkiss, *Technological Man: The Myth and the Reality* (New York: George Braziller, 1969), p. viii.

19. Arnold Toynbee, *Preface* to Cogley, *Religion in a Secular Age*, pp. xvii-xviii.

20. Terry J. Tekippe, "Bernard Lonergan: A Context for Technology," in Mitcham and Grote, p. 83.

21. Kai Nielsen, "Technology as Ideology," in *Research in Philosophy and Technology*, Vol. I, Paul Durbin, ed. (Greenwich, CT: Jai Press, 1978), p. 99.

22. Jean Rostrand, in C. S. Wallia, ed., *Toward Century 21: Technology, Society and Values* (New York: Basic Books, 1970), p. 17.

23. Jacques Ellul, *The Technological Society*, tr. J. Wilkinson (New York: Alfred Knopf, 1964).

24. Arend Van Leeuwen, *Christianity in World History*, tr. Hoskins (Charles Scribner's Sons, 1965).

25. Pontifical Document on Catholic Universities (Vatican City, 1985).

26. Barbour, p. 140.

THE HISTORICAL ORIGIN OF THE DIVISION BETWEEN ETHICS AND SCIENCE: THE CONFLICT BETWEEN ARISTOTLE AND CHRISTIANITY

John A. J. Dudley

The value of knowledge is something which nowadays goes unquestioned. No one queries the value of formal education, the improvement of standards of literacy and intellectual cultivation, and as far as possible, maximized opportunity in education. And yet precisely on the level of advanced and systematized knowledge which is called science, a growing problem is seen to arise due to the absence of the application of ethical standards to scientific developments. This problem, which may be called the conflict of ethics and science, is the source of the most serious concern and debate. In the present paper I propose to examine the mentality which I see as the cause of this problem and to show that it can be traced to Aristotle. The Aristotelian mentality will be seen to have penetrated and vanquished philosophy as well as Christianity in its less pure forms. It is hoped, then, by showing the historical origin of this problem, its influence over the centuries and the erroneous reasoning it is based on, that a contribution may be made towards correcting the disorientation of science and technology, which I believe may be held without exaggeration to be one of the most urgent and fundamental problems of our time.

Although it is far from exact that Western philosophy starts with Plato, there would nonetheless be an element of truth in such a statement, since the influence of Plato has so overshadowed his predecessors. Among these predecessors Parmenides, Heraclitus and Democritus in particular, despite the loss of their works, have exercised a substantial influence in later philosophy. Democritus, before Plato, had taken an interest in definitions as well as in both science and ethics.[1] Nonetheless, outside of the schools of materialism, it has been the doctrine of Plato on the connection of science and ethics which has been of decisive influence on Western thought.

As is known, for Plato the word "science" was reserved for knowledge of Being, which for him existed only really in a separate world of Ideas. He placed the various kinds of human knowledge in a hierarchical order, starting with conjecture and belief — both forms of opinion — rising then to reasoning and finally to intellection. For Plato only intellection could truly be called science. The highest object of science was the Idea of the Good, and to achieve this object the ideal man — the philosopher-king — would raise his mind from the lower kinds of knowledge to science and ultimately to the Idea of the Good. The aim of ethics in Plato is equally famous: it is that of becoming as alike to God as possible.[2] The relationship of God and the Idea of the Good cannot be examined here. Although they were held to be identical by Neoplatonists, it would appear that the identification is not historically made by Plato. But for the purposes of this paper it is clear that the Idea of the Good in science and God in ethics are so closely connected as to constitute a unity. Accordingly, the aim of ethics is to become as alike as possible to God, who is the best object of science, and the best object of science bears the ethical qualification of perfect goodness. In Plato it may be said, therefore, that ethics and science are inseparable. This inseparability of ethics and science in Plato prepared the way for Aristotle's ordering of these two disciplines in a manner which would have an immense influence on the future development of Western thought.

For Aristotle, as for Plato, man is a living being composed of body and soul. It is worthwhile noting at this stage that this is clearly also the doctrine of the New Testament. The soul is the principle of life in man. Where Plato had distinguished three parts of the soul, reason, spirit, appetite, corresponding to three aspects of life,[3] Aristotle distinguished four parts. The lowest part for Aristotle is the vegetative faculty, which enables man to grow and to nourish himself, and in general to support that aspect of life which he has in common with plants.[4] The second lowest part is the sensitive faculty, which enables man to perceive through his five senses and in general to support that aspect of life which he has in common with animals.[5] These two lower parts of the soul taken together Aristotle calls the irrational part of the soul.[6] The human soul, however, also possesses a rational part, which plants and animals do not possess.[7] On the model[8] of the irrational part of the soul, however, Aristotle also subdivides the rational part of the soul into two parts, one part, called the *logistikon*, which deals with practical questions of human action, including ethics, and one part, called the *theoretikon*, which deals

with purely theoretical questions of science.[9]   Of these two parts
Aristotle holds that the part which deals with science is superior to the
part which deals with ethics.[10]   It is this doctrine which has had an
immense, one might almost say an inestimable influence on the
development of Western man, particularly in the last 400 years, and more
so today than ever before in the past. Before I proceed to argue against
it, it is worthwhile, however, first to examine the line of reasoning by
which Aristotle arrived at this doctrine.

The origins of Greek philosophy are to be found at the point where
man sought rationally something permanent in the changing world around
him. Thus it is related that the first philosopher, Thales of Miletus, held
that all things are made of water and would sooner or later return to
water.[11] But water was the one thing that was permanent. The history
of Greek philosophy from Thales in the sixth century B.C. to Democritus
at the end of the fifth century, with his theory of atoms, may be said to
a large extent to be the search by man for greater precision in regard to
that which is permanent beyond the changing aspect of the world
observed by man. Plato and Aristotle inherited this tradition, and thus
one of the principles which seemed obvious to them was that that which
is unchanging is superior to that which is changeable. Likewise, Aristotle
held that that which is immaterial is superior to that which is material,
since everything material is changeable to some extent.

When Aristotle came to deal with the problem, which he had
inherited from Plato, of the relative value of the different branches of
human knowledge, he accordingly decided that those branches of knowledge which have unchanging, firmly-established first principles are three
in number: mathematics, physics and metaphysics.[12]   Of these three
branches of knowledge, Aristotle holds that metaphysics is superior to
both physics and mathematics, as its object is immaterial as well as
unchanging, namely the existence of all beings from the lowest up to
God.[13]   Physics is the second-best science, because although its first
principles are unchanging, its object is continually changing, namely the
whole of the universe. The lowest of the three speculative sciences is
mathematics, because although its first principles are unchanging, the
objects of mathematics do not exist in themselves, but exclusively in
other objects.[14] For Aristotle only these three sciences are sciences in
the strict sense, because they alone are purely rational and have
unchanging first principles. These sciences are, then, the domain of the
highest part of the soul, the scientific or theoretical part.[15]

Ethics, however, is not strictly-speaking a science, because it is not a purely rational branch of knowledge. Ethical principles cannot be deduced as if they were mathematical principles.[16] The establishment of ethical principles requires practical wisdom which is the fruit of experience.[17] Human action is the outcome of deliberation: but one does not deliberate about that which does not vary.[18] Man, or the human soul, has an irrational aspect, whereby man is like to the animals, and accordingly ethics has to take into account the irrational aspect of man as well as the rational. Thus Aristotle considered the first principles of ethics to be changeable,[19] as they are based on opinion and experience which cannot be rationally proven. Aristotle classified ethics together with politics, rhetoric and economics, which he called practical branches of thought, which are not strictly-speaking sciences.[20] They are the object of the second-best part of the soul, the lower of the two subdivisions of the rational part of the soul. Accordingly, Aristotle considered ethics to be inferior to science, for it is not a strictly rational branch of knowledge.

Aristotle's subordination of ethics to science did not have important practical consequences for society in his own time for several reasons, one of which is that science was only in its infancy, but the most significant of which is the inseparability of ethics and science which Aristotle took over from Plato. Thus, for Aristotle it was impossible to investigate science without using the ethical criterion of goodness to institute order in the sciences and to understand the relative position of the objects of science in regard to the highest object of science, namely God. Accordingly, for Aristotle science never became separated from the ethical idea of the goodness of the objects of science. However, in his *Ethics* Aristotle held that the best activity for man, the activity which would bring him the highest degree of happiness,[21] is scientific soul (the *theoretikon*), and that moral virtue, resulting from activity of the second-best part of the soul (the *logistikon*), gave only second-rate happiness.[22] For Aristotle this scientific activity is inseparable from the search for goodness, since the highest scientific or speculative activity is the contemplation of God, which in turn should enable man to act better in the sphere of moral virtue.[23] It will be seen, however, that in modern times Aristotle's doctrine of the superiority of science to ethics was retained, while his interest in the contemplation of God was dropped, as it no longer appeared necessary or relevant at a time of specialization in particular sciences.

The influence of Aristotle's doctrine of the superiority of science to ethics has been immense across the centuries. It may even be said that the influence of this doctrine has been greater than that of any other, even greater than his doctrine that the world is the centre of the universe, since the latter doctrine was rejected 400 years ago, whereas throughout the ages and up to the present time, under the influence of Aristotle, the characteristic of man is universally held to be his intelligence rather than his capacity to act morally.

The influence of Aristotle has so penetrated Western thought as to become an unquestioned part of man's way of thinking. Typically, for example, when the protagonists of evolutionary theory sought the origins of the human species, they examined the size and structure of the human brain, whereby the distinctive feature of man was held to be his level of intelligence, not his capacity to act morally. If one goes back to the Middle Ages one finds, following the same line of thought, that angels were interpreted as pure intelligences, on the basis that only pure intelligence could be superior to man, who is a combination of intelligence and intelligence combined with irrationality.[24] Again, St. Thomas Aquinas, under the influence of Aristotle, characterizes Heaven or the beatific vision as the intellectual contemplation of God, rather than, in the first place, as the semi-rational love of God.[25]

However, in the New Testament it is not stated that God is an intellect. But St. John the Evangelist states that God is love.[26] In the New Testament Christ does not say that one should cultivate one's intellect or engage in scientific activity. On the contrary, he says: "Thou shalt love the Lord thy God with thy whole heart, and with thy whole soul and with thy whole strength, and with thy whole mind, and your neighbor as yourself."[27] This sums up the whole of the Law and the Prophets.[28] Thus it would appear that the Franciscan school with St. Bonaventure held the more authentically Christian position by emphasizing that Heaven consists essentially in the perfect love of God rather than the intellectual contemplation of God.[29]

The conflict between Aristotle and Christianity was seen, for example, by St. Thomas a Kempis who writes in a famous passage at the start of his *Imitation of Christ*: "Every man naturally desires knowledge" — this is a quotation of the first sentence of Aristotle's *Metaphysics* — "but," writes St. Thomas a Kempis, "a humble peasant who serves God is far superior to a proud philosopher who watches the stars and forgets he has a soul to save. . . . If I were to know everything in the world and yet lack charity, what use would it be to me in the eyes of God who will judge me according to my actions?"[30]   Here St. Thomas a Kempis is echoing Christ's words: "What doth it profit a man to gain the whole world and to lose his own soul?"[31] and also St. Paul's words: "And if I should have prophecy and should know all mysteries and all *knowledge*, and if I should have all faith, so that I could move mountains, and have not charity, I am nothing."[32]   It is obvious that science gives intellectual truth.   But when Christ said "I am the way, the truth and the life,"[33] he did not mean that he was scientific or intellectual truth, but rather that he was a whole way of life, the one true way of life, the morally good life. Again, when St. John writes: "In the beginning was the Word (*logos*),[34] he does not mean purely intellectual *logos*, since he also writes that "the Word became flesh and dwelt among us."[35]   Finally, Christ chose his apostles from among the ignorant and was born himself in the uneducated classes.   The doctrine of Christianity is thus that love, or the semi-rational combined with the rational, is superior to the purely rational.

A parallel conflict between truth and action may be seen in the virtual universal acceptance, due to the influence of Aristotle, of the notion that man works in order to have leisure,[36] which is justified from the Aristotelian standpoint on the basis that leisure-time is time which one can devote to higher activities, namely activities of the intellect.   Rarely does one hear that the quality of work is of greater value than intellectual thought during leisure-time, and that man rests on the Sabbath day in order to work better during the week.   Here too may be seen an inherited Aristotelian attitude of profound significance due to contemporary economic developments.

It is possible to refute Aristotle's standpoint not merely theologically, but also philosophically.   When Aristotle argues that ethics is inferior to science, he is judging ethics by the criterion of pure rationality. Obviously, if pure rationality were the criterion of what is good, then Aristotle would be right.   But what is good is what is good for man as a whole, not just a part of man.   The purely intellectual corresponds to man's intellect, whereas an action performed out of love corresponds to the whole of man.   It is an error to wish to reduce man to his intellect or to see the human body as an obstacle to the good for man.

Again, to state that science or pure rationality is the good for man is to make an ethical statement.   To claim, indeed, as some have claimed, that scientific progress should not be influenced by ethics, is also an ethical statement.   In fact, ethics extends to every conscious human activity. Science, or the purely rational, on the other hand, is restricted to a very small area of human experience. It is impossible, for example, to reduce ethics to a rational system. This fact, rather than show the superiority of science, as Aristotle claims, shows its limitations. Few indeed are the areas of human knowledge where some aspect of the partly irrational nature of man does not play a significant role.[37] Hence the combination of the rational and the irrational must be superior to the purely rational.

It is true that knowledge of God must precede love of God. However, the precedence of knowledge over love in the temporal order of acquisition in no way implies a qualitative superiority. One cannot read a book without learning the alphabet first. But one cannot, for this reason, argue that learning the alphabet is superior to reading a book.

Again, it might be argued that one can know without loving, whereas one cannot love without knowing, and hence knowing is superior to loving. However, this argument also does not hold, since loving means knowing, and if love is of value, then to know and to love must be superior to merely knowing, as the whole is superior to the part.

The argument that knowledge is free from the passions is also erroneous. Man is never a pure intellect or fully rational. To wish to reduce man to a part of man is an impossible and unwise aim. Rather, for man to control and direct his whole person, intellect and passions, towards his goal in life, is superior to merely doing so with his intellect. In this way, accordingly, Aristotle's doctrine of the superiority of science to ethics can be refuted philosophically as well as theologically.

Finally, it is worthwhile casting a glance at Aristotle's influence on the history of philosophy in regard to this doctrine. The most remarkable growth of the importance of Aristotle's ordering of science and ethics may be traced from the Renaissance, thus, curiously, from the period when many of his physical theories were rejected. With the rise of modern science in the sixteenth and seventeenth centuries, scientists became increasingly more specialized in their individual sciences — mastery of many sciences was no longer possible — and increasingly less interested in seeing science in relation to man and the purpose of his life on earth. Since science, being as purely rational as possible, was held, under the direct or indirect influence of Aristotle, to be superior to ethics, scientists did not see themselves obliged to deal with what they saw as an inferior branch of knowledge.[38] It is well-known that with the rise of modern science, the purely rational or geometrical method of the sciences was held up as the model for philosophical thinking among the early modern philosophers from Descartes to Leibniz. Just as their rational method corresponded only to man's intellect, and not to the whole of man, so too man came to be seen as his intellect or his *cogito*, to use Descartes' term. Following in this tradition, which is of Aristotelian origin, the philosophies of Kant and Hegel thus approach man largely as mind, rather than mind as a mere subservient instrument of man. The culmination of this movement is then reached in positivism, where science is everything and ethics is rejected in favor of sociology.

Finally, if one turns to modern science, one finds that in most cases, due to the attempt at reducing man to the purely rational, they are mere technology and not really sciences. Science, as Aristotle points out, means that a man is more certain of his first principles than of the scientific knowledge deduced from these principles.[39] But how many contemporary professors of psychiatry, masters of the so-called science of psychiatry, write prescriptions and treat their patients for depressions without having any knowledge of the human soul? And how many professors of economics, masters of the "science" of economics, prescribe policies to cure an economic crisis without having any knowledge of the causes of human activity?[40] These pseudo-scientists are like a man operating a machine, who knows that if he pulls a lever or pushes a knob, a particular result will take place, but who has no idea as to how the machine functions or why it works less well at one time than at another. Such is the case with most modern sciences, which accordingly do not deserve the name science at all.

In this paper it has been seen how and why Aristotle subordinated ethics to science. A sketch has been given of the immense influence of this doctrine throughout the centuries. It has been seen that in the Christian view the mere acquisition of knowledge does not contribute to loving God or saving one's soul. A philosophical refutation of Aristotle's viewpoint has also been given. Finally, it has been seen how Aristotle's doctrine of the superiority of the purely rational to the rational combined with the semi-rational has undermined the real claim to science of many contemporary so-called sciences of man, such as psychiatry and economics. It is this doctrine of the superiority of science to ethics, which Thomas Aquinas and other medieval Aristotelians enshrined in Christianity, that is the key to the attitude underlying contemporary scientific developments and the absence of ethical control over them. It is clear, of course, that the solution to the problem of the orientation of technology is not merely a question of believing that ethics is more important than science, but is also a question of putting one's beliefs into practice. In this process, however, it is of the greatest importance to awaken realization of the superiority of ethics to science and of the opposition of the Christian attitude to pure science to that of the philosophical tradition inherited from Aristotle. It is hoped that this paper will have contributed towards that aim.

Catholic University
Nymegen, Netherlands

NOTES

1. John A.J. Dudley, "The Ethics of Democritus and Aristotle," in *Proceedings of the First International Congress on Democritus*, Xanthi (Greece), 1984, pp. 373-4.

2. *Theaet.* 176-a-b; cf. *Resp.* 540 a-b; 383 c, 500 c-d; *Tim.* 90 b-c; *Leg.* 716 c-d.

3. *Phaedrus* 246, 253-6; *Resp. IV*, 431-443.

4. *NE* I, xiii, 15-18, 1102 b 13-31.

5. *NE* I, xiii, 15-18, 1102 b 13-31.

6. *NE* I, xiii, 18, 1102 b 29.

7. *NE* I, vii, 12-13, 1097 b33 - 1098 a 5.

8. *EE* V(=*NE* VI), i, 5, 1139 a 5-6.

9. *EE* V (*NE* VI), i, 5-6, 1139 a 3-15; *Pol.* VII, xiii, 6-9, 1333 a 16 - 1333 b 5.

10. Cf. *EE* V (*NE* VI), xiii, 8, 1145 a 6-7; *EE* V (=*NE* VI), xii, 3, 1143 b 33-34.

11. Arist. *Met.* A(I), 983 b 6 - 984 a 5.

12. *EE* V (=*NE* VI), iii, 2, 1139 b 18-24; *Met.* E (VI), i, 1026 a 6-23.

13. *Met.* E(VI), i, 1026 a 27-32. The dispute on the object of metaphysics for Aristotle cannot be dealt with here.

14. *Met.* (E (VI), i, 1026 a 13-15. Dudley, *Gott und Theoria bei Aristóteles, Die metaphysische Grundlage der Nikomachischen Ethik*, Frankfurt a.M./Bern, 1982, pp. 149-150.

15. *Met.* E(VI), i, 1026 a 18-19 and n. 12 *supra*.

16. Cf. *NE* I, iii, 1-4, 1094 b 11-27.

17. Cf. *NE* I, iii, 5-7, 1094 b 27 - 1095 a 11.

18. *EE* V (=*NE* VI), v, 3-4, 1140 a 31 - 1140 b 7.

19. *EE* V(=*NE* VI), v, 3, 1140 b 1-3

20. *EE* I, viii, 20, 1218 b 13-14; *Rhet.* I, ii, 1356 a 25-28; *EE* V (=*NE* VI), v, 3, 1140 a 31 - 1140 b 2. Of course, there also exist the productive "sciences" which are not really sciences, but are arts or techniques; cf. *EE* V(=*NE* VI), iv, 1-6, 1140 a 1-23.

21. On degrees of happiness in Aristotle cf. Dudley, *"El sentido de la felicidad de la vida perfecta (bios teleios) en la Etica de Aristóteles,"* in *Ethos* (Buenos Aires) 10-11 (1982-3), pp. 39-54.

22. *NE* X, viii, 7-8, 1178 b 21-32; *NE* X, viii, 1, 1178 a 9

23. Dudley, op. cit., esp. pp. 189-192; and Dudley, *"The love of God in Aristotle's Ethics,"* in *Neue Zeitschrift für Systematische Theologie und Religionsphilosophie* 25 (1983), pp. 126-137.

24. St. Thomas Aquinas, *Summa Theologica, Prima Pars*, q.L, aI: "ad perfectionem universi requiritur quod sint aliquae creaturae intellectuales. Intelligere autem non potest esses actus corporis . . ."; a. II: "Substantiae autem angelicae sunt supra intellectum nostrum . . ."; *Summa Contra*

Gentiles I, 3: "Intellectus autem angeli plus excedit intellectum humanum quam intellectus optimi philosophi intellectum rudissimi idiotae: quia haec distantia inter speciei humanae limites continetur, quos angelicus intellectus excedit."

25. Aquinas, *S.C.G.* III, xxxvii, 2160: "ultima felicitas hominis non consistit nisi in contemplatione Dei." St. Thomas, following Aristotle, even subordinates actions according to moral virtue to the end of contemplating God: cf. ib. 2152: "ultima felicitas hominis non consistit . . . in bonis animae quantum ad . . . intellectivam [sc. partem] secundum actum moralium virtutum . . ."; ib. 2158: "Ad perfectionem enim contemplationis . . . requiritur etiam quies a perturbationibus passionum, ad quam pervenitur per virtutes morales et per prudentiam . . ."

26. 1 Jn. 4,8.

27. Lk. 10, 27.

28. Mt. 22, 40.

29. *Itinerarium mentis in Deum* 1,1: "Cum beautitudo nihil aliud sit, quam summi boni fruitio; et summum bonum sit super nos: nullus potest effici beatus, nisi supra semetipsum ascendat, non ascensu corporali, sed cordiali." Cf. also ib. VII, 4; VI, 2.

30. St. Thomas a Kempis, *De Imitatione Christi* I, ii, 1: "Omnis homo naturaliter scire desiderat, sed . . . melior est profecto humilis rusticus, qui Deo servit, quam superbus philosophus, qui se neglecto, cursum caeli considerat. . . . Si scirem omnia quae in mundo sunt, et non essem in caritate, quid me iuvaret coram Deo, qui me iudicaturus est ex facto?"

31. Mt. 16, 26.

32. I Cor. 13, 1-3.

33. Jn. 14, 6.

34. Jn. 1, 1.

35. Jn. 1, 14.

116

36. Arist., *NE* X, vii, 6, 1177 b 4-5.

37. John Henry Cardinal Newman, *An Essay in Aid of a Grammar of Assent* (London: Longman, 1901), VIII, 2, 3, p. 317: ". . . a proof, except in abstract demonstration, has always in it, more or less, an element of the personal . . ."

38. In his *Idea of a University, Defined and Illustrated*, Longman, London, 1923, Newman gives the following reasons which explain the hostility of science to religion and ethics, without, however, explaining the rise of science and the decline of ethics. *Idea* I, 9, 3, p. 322: "Here then is one reason for the prejudice of physical philosophers against Theology: - on the one hand, their deep satisfaction in the laws of nature indisposes them towards the thought of a Moral Governor and makes them skeptical of His interposition . . . "; ibid. I, 9, 4, pp. 222-3: "Another reason of a kindred nature is to be found in the difference of method by which truths are gained in theology and in physical science. Induction is the instrument of Physics, and deduction only is the instrument of Theology . . . . Now this process [deduction] . . . was the very mode of reasoning which, as regards physical knowledge, the school of Bacon has superseded by the inductive method: - no wonder, then, that that school should be irritated and indignant to find that a subject-matter remains still, in which their favorite instrument has no office . . ."; ibid. I, 9, 5, p. 226: ". . . the new and further manifestations of the Almighty, made by Revelation . . . cannot in any sense be gathered from nature, and the silence of nature concerning them may easily seduce the imagination, though it has no force to persuade the reason, to revolt from doctrines which have not been authenticated by facts, but are enforced by authority. In a scientific age, then, there will naturally be a parade of what is called Natural Theology, a widespread profession of the Unitarian creed, an impatience of mystery, and a skepticism about miracles;" ibid. II, 5, 2, 3, p. 397: ". . . thanks to the New Philosophy, sight is able to contest the field with faith. The medieval philosopher had no weapon against Revelation but metaphysics; Physical Science has a better temper, if not a keener edge, for the purpose;" ibid. II, 5, 2, 4, pp. 399-400: "Any one study, of whatever kind, exclusively pursued, deadens in the mind the interest, nay, the perception of any other. . . . And in like manner it is clear that the tendency of science is to make men indifferentists or skeptics, merely by being exclusively pursued."

39. *EE* V (=*NE* VI), iii, 4, 1139 b 33-35.

40. Cf. Newman's splendid attack on economics as ignorant when not subordinated to Christianity, *Idea* I, 4, 10-12, pp. 86-94.

THE CHRISTIAN ETHICS OF TECHNOLOGY

Richard P. Francis

At this late date in today's industrial-technological age, "the most accurate observation to be made about the philosophy of technology is that there really isn't one" complains Professor Langdon Winner.[1] He observes that a society such as the American society with its thorough commitment to making artificial realities would have by now given much thought to that commitment. He is critical of the over one thousand books and articles on the subject of philosophy and technology because they have little well-defined, enduring substance. If there is no philosophy of technology, correspondingly there is no ethics of technology that would be part of that philosophy.

Nevertheless, our culture is based on countless instruments, techniques, and systems geared towards our expectedly relentless progress. That in itself ought to be morally good and valuable. The industrial age taught us to depend on new machines, gadgets and inventions to solve our problems and to grant our pleasures, however specious. Indeed, technology has woven our human society into a seamless web with mutual relationships that cannot be disentangled without profoundly disorienting, grievous results.[2] We fully expect our furnaces, automobiles, telephones, televisions, radios, VCR's and computers to work, our electricity to flow at the flick of a switch, our homes, businesses, schools, churches and places of leisure to be filled with all sorts of equipment. So abundant are they and so dependent are we on our technological inventions that we cannot return to a more primitive, non-technical society. Nor are we expected to. Barring a major global catastrophe, for necessity and comfort, technology is here to stay, even as the world divides itself between the more backward, developing peoples and the more advanced high-tech peoples. The high technology society is portrayed as the better of the two and as a kind of worthy goal for the developing nations. In today's technologically complicated mode of existence, fortunately or not, our simpler, more innocent conditions of existence are forever lost.

Whereas the advanced countries, with their unabashed commitment to technologic industry, rightly enjoy the everyday benefits of such industry, technology is not and cannot be contained solely within their own geographies. Instant mass communication by satellite; international travel by speedy airlines; the cure of malaria, polio, smallpox, tuberculosis, and other killer diseases by medical technology; and similar advances cannot be geographically restricted. The world of technology is everybody's world. Still, just compensation must be made to those creative persons, companies, and countries that are brilliant and resourceful enough to invent our machines, our medicines, our advanced techniques that encourage similar efforts and that make human life safer, healthier, and more bountiful. But, as we live longer in years, are we really happier? Are we better for it?

As in no other century in history, twentieth century people, with all of their beneficial high-tech gadgets, suffer deeply from anxiety, alienation, depression and all sorts of emotional and mental disease.[3] Accordingly, this is the century that invented psychiatry, psychology and social services to help scientifically, technologically advanced people with mental and emotional problems. Could that "dis-ease" be caused by the suppression of moral values? Is there something morally wrong with us, even as we look to technology to effect a cure, to produce drugs that ought to help us, and to industry to ease us with supposedly curative distractions like television? Surely, not all are ill, and many people get along well enough, living healthy, morally worthy lives.

Then again, this is also the most violent century in history, with almost constant wars going on somewhere including two unprecedented global world wars.[4] In warfare, so ingenious are we that every weapon ever invented, from bows and arrows to atomic bombs, was in fact used. And each had progressively more killing power than anything previous. Today, those warriors strengthened with technological advantage, are the most powerful and will be the survivors. While defensive actions against external aggressive forces are ethical as self-defense, what kind of world is it that progressively increases its firepower to kill more people? The morally worthy goal is the people's well-being, and not the reverse. While we need to be vigilant against aggressive forces, ethically our technologic industry ought better to maintain the peace.

Further, this is the age of the holocaust, that well-engineered, legal, efficient Nazi war machine designed for the sole purpose of killing innocent, "undesirable" people. So effective was it that it destroyed millions of people, including six million Jews, with the clear purpose of destroying all of the Jews and any others opposed to the Nazis. While we may be appalled at this atrocity, culturally there is no way to prevent this moral collapse technologically, except by a clear code of ethics that seeks to preserve people's lives.

Similarly, the holocaust against our existing unborn children continues with unprecedented millions of deaths by abortion. Internationally, the medical profession betrays its sacred trust of saving people's lives and becomes "killers for hire," destroying so many of our generation's children. What can we say about technologically advanced people who use the latest means to kill their innocent children? Historically, from ancient to modern times, abortions, known to be criminal barbarity, have been done contrary to ethical norms. But today the reverse happens wherein the ancient brutality of abortion has gained social respectability in many quarters. Technologically, this tragedy cannot be halted except by a clear moral code that forbids killing innocent people.

In this age of increasing violence, no one seems to be safe at home or abroad, as international terrorists shoot travelers in major airports such as in Rome and Vienna, and turn their weapons against state leaders like Egyptian President Sadat, Indian Prime Minister Ghandi, American President Reagan, and even the Vatican emissary of peace, the Holy Father, John Paul II. As the Soviets shoot down a Korean airliner full of civilians over the Sea of Japan, the Middle East becomes the place for terrorists to kidnap and kill innocent people. The streets of many cities suffer from vandalism and hoodlum brutality against innocent people, not safe even in their homes. Should not more technically advanced people be more civilized, living according to established moral codes that cannot justify wanton destruction of lives and property? Technology bereft of ethical civility becomes barbarity. What is wrong is the relaxation or the abandonment of ethical principles. Unfortunately an educated, technologically advanced world is not necessarily a morally good or praiseworthy world.

Arnold Toynbee correctly observed that during mankind's first million years of existence, science and technology have been constantly accelerating in the manner of cumulative and enormous progress. And the future may well dwarf the past with still unimagined promises. Even with our great scientific control of material nature, Toynbee warns that in our own time we have seen great nations, which have apparently been civilized, suddenly lapse into unparalleled wickedness. He laments that as sensational as technology is, it has not changed the essential human condition. "Our behavior to each other is still bad," he writes.[5] Obviously we need clear ethical principles, moral standards that inspire, encourage and sanction people's behavior. And these moral principles need to be as universal as the technological community is universal.

Accurately enough, Daniel J. Boorstein entitles his recent book *The Republic of Technology*, describing a republic that he explains is international or world-wide.[6] He remarks that every year the United States of America becomes less peculiar because the same new forces that have given America its special character now forge the lives and fortunes of people everywhere. Because science is the same equally valid body of knowledge everywhere, technology, as applied science, transcends political boundaries, language, religion and local tradition. Technology, he continues, leads us to conquer or ignore the passions of patriotism and social distrust. He clearly notes that while people around the world may not love each other any more than they did, their ways of life tend to be more and more alike. Our shared technological achievements, like atomic energy, space travel, orbiting satellites and myriad other novelties, have converged the idiosyncratic national cultures, even reducing the differences between big and small nations. Boorstein adds that America aspires to be an international nation. As the most technologically advanced great nation, it serves as a center from which radiate unifying forces of human experience for others in the converging power of technology. But, we ask, should there not also be a convergence of ethics?

Boorstein is well aware that, internationally, persons of common pursuits consider themselves to be freely part of a republic, such as the "republic of letters." The republic of technology, he claims, is democratic because everyone can be its citizen since it is open to all as a community of shared experience. Further, the technologic republic, like technology itself, has built-in obsolescence, as opposed to the usual normal, traditional continuity. Progress is quick and wholesale, while novelty and ingenuity prevail. Everyone can benefit from technology regardless of education or social standing. Everyone everywhere can join the ever changing technological republic.

While theoretically the above is accurate, still most people across this globe have never experienced the life of a republic with its democratic conventions, especially those of freedom and human rights. By far, most people live under dictatorial, autocratic, despotic governmental powers wherein technology, if there is any, is controlled by and is in service to the state. That is not a republic, but a "gulag" or concentration-camp society. Terrorizing force prevails physically, psychologically, economically, religiously and in other ways. The democratic sense of a republic of technology or any other republic is preciously scarce worldwide, being absent in Asia, Africa, Arabia, Eastern Europe and so on. The "republic" belongs mainly to the democratic nations of the West, although a reconstructed post-war Japan and Israel are now members. The notion of a republic of technology under tyranny is clearly nonsense. And until normative civilizing codes of ethics come into play, technology can be and is open to every brutality, viciousness and terror.

At this time, there is unprecedented change in Eastern Europe. The unification of Germany and the overwhelming call for democratic independence in Poland, Czechoslovakia, Hungary, Yugoslavia and the Soviet Union all point towards the dissolution of Communism. In China, though the push for democracy failed, the weakening of Communist authority is inevitable.

By itself, technology, known as the scientific way of doing things, cannot contain or explain what is morally proper for human experience. Often enough, we view technology to be value-neutral, and we usually depend on value-neutral experts or technocrats to help us because of their specialization. But in a civilized moral society, that is insufficient. The experts must follow some kind of ethical code, however implicit or explicit. Technology thus becomes a morally proper means for a morally proper goal.

Sometimes we think that in technology everything is always good, that one size fits all. Contrariwise, evil inherently exists in the design and manufacture of instruments of torture, like the Medieval rack, today's unlawful instruments of harmful pleasure, like designer drugs including cocaine, the instruments of the Nazi death camps including the crematoria, the latest drug that causes abortion, etc. These are all styled to damage or to kill someone, and have no morally good purpose.

Furthermore, in a scientific society, technology may function as an ideology, a kind of mystical expectation and motivation, demanding undue respect or reverence. Kai Nielsen bluntly insists that technology is an ideology. Our ideological mystification about technology obscures this from consciousness. He warns that technology's pernicious function obscures the real nature of our problems. It invests itself with an authoritative monopoly as the only way of knowing and of dealing with things. Its scientific instrumental rationality chooses only the most efficient way for any goal. Humaneness gives way to efficiency, while our citizens remain more and more passive and submissive to the technocrats. Technological ideology, Nielsen adds, is effective and irresistible, with no ethical justification.[7]

Indeed, technology ideologically limits or removes the more humane features, aspirations and needs that are not machine-dependent. As an ideology, technology creates holocausts, destroys millions of lives efficiently, devastates nations and perverts traditional life-respecting values. Obviously the whole scheme can be put to the opposite meritorious purpose of benefiting us in a morally proper fashion. Ideologically we persist in fully believing that science can do only good and no harm.

There seems to be no end to our inventiveness which we firmly believe will solve all of our problems and grant our desires. Even though technology can lead to every kind of excess, we almost unfailingly put our trust into it. Overvalued with its unlimited potential, it is the modern world's salvation and gratification. This can result in dehumanizing ourselves and in humanizing the machinery. We respect our gadgetry more than we do ourselves. The person becomes part of the more important scientific-machine world and loses value if not assimilated into it.[8] He personally fiercely competes with others to gain certain advantages over them by skillfully manipulating the machinery. The power to control is in the machine, without which we are weak. The person or society with the more powerful machinery certainly controls others, for better or for worse. Hence, we may have to submit to the technocrat-experts because of their specialized knowledge, power and control in an otherwise baffling context. To avoid being dehumanized and under the improper control of others, moral principles must prevail.

The attitude of science is objective, uninvolved, and manipulative. The aim is to get results, to get the job done following a pattern of efficiency, measurement and public verification. Science has no inherent moral worth and does not basically add to our moral sociability, freedom, intelligence, responsibility, rights or duties. If science is honest, caring, or sincere, this comes not from science but from ethics. Normative ethics builds moral principles and correct operational standards into the technological process.

While this may at first seem trivial, it bears repetition generation after generation. As elsewhere, so also in the scientific-technological community, the most critical and essential of all ethical standards is "to do good and to avoid evil." Without this real distinction between good and evil, one the opposite of the other, there can be no ethics. Whatever is qualitatively good is ethical, and what is qualitatively bad is immoral. Technology, as a practical science, can and must be ethical. As a means to do something, it must intend a good and proper means towards a good and proper goal.

To "do good and to avoid evil" regarding technology, or any other moral context, is the first driving principle of ethics as it is also, in correspondence, the first principle of the "natural law." Examples of this will follow. For now, to be proper or good, that is, all ethics, including this ethics of technology, flow from the pervasive natural law. The idea of natural law is as old as philosophy and persists to this day. While science as we today know it is "modern," technology or practical science, as the fabrication of things for our proper use, goes back to ancient times, to making tools, weapons, clothing, wagons, shelter, and so on. Anything made for our good, "doing good," was ethical and had to follow the natural law.

The fact that people can and do behave appropriately almost intuitively according to an ethical-rational ingredient implies the pervasive presence of the natural law. This natural law, as an objective fact, serves as the individual and social conscience. As such, it is usually latent and implicit and things go well. But when violations occur, as in crimes against nature, the natural law becomes obvious and operates openly.

The natural law protects and advances our equal, universal, necessary, inalienable human rights including the right to life, health care, family life and sexual responsibility, association and communication, education and learning, work for fair rewards, property ownership, truthfulness, security and privacy, aesthetic and religious experience, justice and freedom throughout, all of these designed for our happiness here and later in Heaven. The sources of these basic rights are nature and nature's God, all reflected in the natural law.

Keeping these rights is consistent with the natural law and our happiness. Violations like murder, abortion, assault, theft, lying, adultery, promiscuity, etc. are crimes against God, against nature and the natural law, and against human nature (against humanity). Natural law tells us what we are and how to behave.

The fact of natural law is the fact of human existence, and thus it precedes written history. It flourishes in the documents of Sumer, Mesopotamia, in Hamurabi's famous law code, with Cicero, with the Greek Stoics, and Aristotle, St. Thomas Aquinas, Grotius, Locke, Blackstone, Maritain, Black, McInerny, and so on. It lives in the American Declaration of Independence, the French Revolution, the bills of rights and constitutions of all democracies, in the unwritten common law, and in the United Nations Charter and Declaration of Human Rights, the Helsinki Accords, etc. In all of them, all of these rights come only from God and the persistent, pervasive natural law.

The workable, classical definition of the natural law comes from Cicero:

> There is in fact a true law, namely right reason, which is in accordance with nature, applies to all men, and is unchangeable and eternal. By its commands this law summons men to the performance of their duties; by its prohibitions, it restrains them from doing wrong. Its commands and prohibitions always influence good men, but are without effect on the bad. To invalidate this law by human legislation is never morally right, nor is it permissible even to restrict its operations, and to annul it wholly is impossible. . . . Neither the Senate nor the people can absolve us from our obligation to obey this law. . . . It will not lay down one rule today and another tomorrow. But there will be one law, eternal and unchanging, binding upon all people, and there will be one common master and ruler of men, namely God, who is the author of this law. . . . The man who will not obey it will abandon his better self, and in denying the true nature of a man will thereby suffer the severest penalties.[9]

Accordingly, there is one permanent, pervasive, universal, irrevocable, all encompassing, God-given law that incorporates and regulates equity or justice throughout the universe. This natural law holds constantly and absolutely for everyone everywhere and cannot be changed or abolished. It contains the rules of conduct inherent in the proper relations between people and is discoverable by reason. It is self-evident and self-validating. It is based upon our innate moral sense. Essentially natural law is a moral law whose prescriptions are reflected in all true and good positive laws. Good positive law is the natural law spelled out, particularized and concretized in many forms, such as criminal, civil, administrative, international, and all laws. This presumes that all good laws, based on the natural law, are just laws. Martin Luther King, Jr. explains that, given the interrelatedness of all communities, injustice anywhere is a threat to justice everywhere.

Regarding how we can break some laws and obey others, King teaches that there are two kinds of laws, just and unjust laws.[10] He agrees, however, with St. Augustine and St. Thomas Aquinas, and with natural law doctrine, that any unjust law is no law at all, and must be disobeyed. In today's technological society, as will be spelled out later, some unjust laws are those that permit and promote racial discrimination, murder by abortion, insider stock market trading to enrich the few and impoverish the many stock holders, invading and stealing privately owned computer information banks, manufacturing and selling cocaine and other "high-producing" drugs, getting drunk, etc.

Similarly, Naim Ateek, in his book *Justice and Only Justice*, stipulates that justice has two dimensions, "the positive and the negative, the inner and the outer, the being and the doing."[11] Each such dimension is a natural aspect of the other. Fairness to self and to others is inherent in all of justice. Accordingly, justice is inherently life-preserving and life-enhancing.

The natural law is justice-laden. It includes everything from "garbage disposal" to "murder prevention" and "international treaties." Other "high tech" examples include, for example, the automobile that was invented to replace the horse and carriage for transportation purposes. Public safety is a virtue based upon our need to survive, or our natural right to life. To protect this right, we design our streets and our cars for safety. From the strictly engineering standpoint a car is an arrangement of various parts and systems intended to work together in the internal combustion medium. Thus, ethically, the car is neither good nor evil. But its ethical quality comes into play in our driving to work, for example, since making a living is a good end and the car a good means. Also, as strips of dirt, concrete or asphalt, our roads are not ethical or unethical. But our correct use of the roads, by careful driving, makes us moral, as our speeding or recklessness makes us immoral. Thus our careful driving to work is "doing good and avoiding evil."

Except for abortions, more people are killed in highway accidents than in any other way. Reckless driving or speeding is unethical. This evil is further compounded by the fact that about one-half of these deaths is caused by drunken drivers. Just like the car, alcohol in itself is neither moral, nor immoral. However, the impairment of the driver by excessive alcohol consumption (or other drugs) is wrong. Both the auto and alcohol are technological devices and can be used ethically or unethically.

We can further look to the workplace to determine if conditions of employment are humane and safe, even in today's technologized factories. Does the greed of the manufacturer to gain unconscionable profits cause excessive stress on the production line, violating the workers' safety and dignity? Are the workers given lesser value than the equipment? This would be unethical. On the other hand, are the workers safety-conscious and doing their fair share of the labor according to established just agreements? Are they absent for faulty reasons, or coming to work with a contagiously debilitating attitude or bad work habits that endanger others and destroy effective production?

Thus "doing good and avoiding evil" here means sharing responsibility between employer and employee, making just agreements regarding wages and production, keeping a positive constructive attitude, observing the safety rules, maintaining the proper production expectation, being honest and sincere, made to feel valued, with the overall workplace being safe and not endangering anyone. Even where hazardous materials are involved, everyone knows that morally the plant cannot be a death trap and that all reasonable precautions must be made and kept. The above principles hold for the more traditional factories as well as for today's high-tech industries.

Another example can be found in the use of television. The television set itself obviously is not moral or immoral. Often enough the viewers will receive accurate, truthful information accompanied by the pictures transmitted. Or we are entertained properly enough by various programs including athletics. The television's transmitting truthful information and correctly entertaining us is morally good. Still the opposite occurs wherein the broadcast industry deliberately falsifies the truth and distorts the facts. The television set becomes the tool for lying and falsified propaganda.

Also by television, the regularizing of pornography, marital infidelity, sexual promiscuity, fornication and homosexuality is immoral. These attack the family which is the basic unit of a stable society. The regularizing of violence encourages like crimes among the more susceptible viewers. Lazy addiction to television viewing at the cost of our other responsibilities is wrong. Regarding television, a high-tech product, ethical norms clarify its proper usage as doing good and avoiding evil, in gaining truthful information and wholesome entertainment.

Additionally, as an inherently value-free instrument, the ubiquitous telephone can be used morally to share information with family, friends and associates, strengthening the bond of friendship, or to conduct legitimate business. To use the phone to harass people, to lie or to slander someone, or for obscene calls, or to deceive anyone about illegitimate criminal business, is wrong.

Computer usage must also be ethical. Computers as machines are inherently neither moral nor immoral. Doing good and avoiding evil means to respect and to use this great machine to collect huge masses of information, various data bases, store and recall information in speedy fashion. Computers help enormously in supermarket inventories, in companies' billings and payrolls, in projecting information for business trends, in idea research and word processing, and many other ways that save us time and help us avoid many errors. Computers fly airplanes and spaceships and guide missiles. The computer is central to the United States' strategic defense initiative which is geared to serve as our umbrella of safety against enemy atomic missiles. Computers help us to hold our nuclear arsenal at bay, or to launch it, even as they help us to monitor whatever is now or will be in space through the North American Air Defense Command in Colorado.

Insofar as human life is valued and to be defended against aggressive power, the computer use in national defense is moral. To launch, by computer, a weapons attack against innocent people is immoral. Computers can further be abused by knowingly falsifying bank accounts or invading the privacy of others by stealing or changing information, by driving the stock market to crash and dangerously weakening the economy, etc.

In the field of medical technology "doing good" exists in sustaining the regular treatments for disease and creating new therapies under new challenges. The impressive new Magnetic Resonance Imaging (MRI) deeply pictures the body's tissues to display differentially our healthy or diseased cells and organs. By itself the "magnet" is neither moral nor immoral, but its use in computerized, skilled, more accurate diagnosis of disease and prognosis and treatment is essentially ethical. With patient use scheduled months ahead of time, everyone expects this busy machine to do a good job. It is difficult to find anything unethical about its use, unless in more experimental features it is used without the patient's informed consent. It might be abused by incorrectly trained technicians or by unnecessary repetition for the same patient (there seem to be no bad effects now) or by excluding financially poorer patients, etc.

The challenge of the worldwide epidemic of the Acquired Immune Deficiency Syndrome (AIDS) takes special creative effort because it is a contagious killer disease, a genetic time bomb that may destroy the whole human race in a relatively short time (some say fifty years). Because this form of virus changes its genetic code, no cure or vaccine is available and may never be. Since this killer virus, which came from Africa, was first predominant among the homosexuals and drug needle abusers in America, one correctly enough might condemn as immoral that kind of lifestyle. The disease was acquired and spread by sexual contact and intravenous blood transfusion, and exchange of body fluids, especially blood. It has now entered the heterosexual population with predictably devastating results. Its incubation period is about fifteen years before the victims die.

Some medical people refuse to treat these patients for fear of getting that killer disease. Since there is no cure, even while the profession encourages its personnel to treat them, ethically the health profession need not do so in self defense. Other contagious diseases are treated, but they are not necessarily killers as this one is. Before people get married, they should seek a test to see if their potential mate is infected and is their future killer. "Doing good" is to seek a vaccine as soon as possible and to treat AIDS patients from a distance to ease their affliction as they die. Some nations are profiling tourists and other visitors to exclude their entry if they are AIDS suspects. This and any measure to save lives is ethical.

Examples can be multiplied, but they all follow the principle of "doing good and avoiding evil" in the modern age. This further translates into the principles of preserving and improving human life. This includes our health maintenance measures, high-tech pharmacology and diagnostic machinery. It forbids murder of innocent people. It encourages a shared responsibility, in justice, for decency and safety at home, in the workplace, and elsewhere. It encourages family values against sexual immorality and debasement of people. It expects honesty and truth not only in family life but also in national and international exchanges. Lying is wrong. All violence and murder are forbidden. Aggression is to be met with a proportional response to neutralize the aggressor and to punish him accordingly. The ownership of property, like food, clothing, housing, work tools, is encouraged because these are all life sustaining. Stealing is wrong. Without following the above moral principles, civilization among honorable people, as we know it, will be lost and barbarism will return. Insofar as we use our technology to preserve and improve human life and experience by means of the above principles, such technology is ethical.

Virtues usually enter our moral experience, including our technological world. Virtues are good qualities in our lives. For example, rationality, or learning, or some derivative value helps to make a person or community morally better. Also, justice conveys a kind of distributive or retributive fairness in our moral relationships. So too with temperance to guard against greed and other excesses, and prudence to guard against indiscretion, and courage to strengthen the right way, and a kind of wisdom to know the principles, etc. All of the virtues add a distinctively good character to our lives, while the opposite is unthinkable.

While shared with other religions, all of these principles and virtues regarding doing good and avoiding evil are still qualitatively Christian. The summary of Jesus' whole life is that "he went about doing good," never evil. This much is thoroughly humanistic. His doing good for us ultimately took Jesus to the greatest act of his being, his passion, death, and resurrection.

Not forced by our sin or by any evil (or by anything else), Jesus freely abandoned his divinity, that is, his divine prerogatives, took on our humanity, and was just like us except for sin. Thus, always doing good, this completely innocent Christ freely redeemed us at Calvary by the horrors of the crucifixion. He did not deserve that. We did, because he died freely to atone for all of our sins, past, present, and future. All time and place collapse in Jesus', God's son's, death. He died once and for all for everyone.

Obviously Christ's redemption is essentially, necessarily, distinctively Christian both humanistically and also spiritually. As the second Adam, he spiritually, fundamentally renewed us, re-created us. Thereby, we are now really empowered to do good and to avoid evil, not only as humans, humanistically, but also and especially as a "saved people," spiritually. We are now empowered to live forever in the spirit of the Christ crucified and resurrected, which is the "holy spirit" of God.

Paradoxically, Jesus saved everyone, the sinless and the sinful, the just and the unjust, all souls for all times and for everywhere. No matter who they are or were, whether Persians, Greeks, Canaanites, Sumerians, Syrians, Romans, Africans, Asians, Europeans, Australians, Americans, everyone everywhere was saved by Christ. By their "baptism of desire," all good people, those who desire to believe and to live like Christ, to do good and avoid evil, are saved. This includes Hindus, Buddhists, Shintoists, Animists, Confucionists, all good people everywhere are "Christian by desire" if they never hear about Christ. Thus by excluding no one, Christianity is the most inclusive of all religions. That is why it is catholic (universal), one, holy, and apostolic. Christianity is like seeds of the Church, sowed everywhere. Some sprout into the Church, others into other confessions, and some remain dormant, but are always there present.

The normal, formal baptism is by water and by word. Besides this form, and the form by desire, the third baptismal form is that by martyrdom whereby people are killed because of their faith.

No matter how we are baptized, that is, made members of the believing community, the reason is our happiness, as saved people, in this life and our perfect happiness in Heaven. Those who do evil, not good, subvert Christ and Christianity and the good in all religions. Their destiny is Hell and eternal suffering.

Because the technological community is becoming international, the above given moral code and virtues ought to be international. They are essentially universal principles.[12] Besides their universal aspect, they are also reciprocal, which means that the same kinds of principles should be enacted everywhere. Moral principles and virtues are never provincial, but belong to all people everywhere in the advanced as well as in the developing groups.

While it was earlier mentioned that people may not love each other any more today and that they are still bad to each other, importantly some common features may be found in Asian and Western thinking which could be reassuring. The code of Confucius prescribes us "to love everyone comprehensively," a universal principle of love. He also taught the reciprocity of the Golden Rule, "do not do to others as you would not have them do to you," a negative variation of the same positive teaching of Jesus. Guaranteed by God, Jesus taught the universal love of God and to love our neighbor as ourselves from Judaism.

Furthermore, the Jewish Ten Commandments from God are universally fundamental to Eastern and Western peoples regarding various immoralities. The lists of virtues from Islam, Confucius, the Greeks, especially Plato and Aristotle, the Jews and the Christians, especially Jesus and Aquinas, are virtually interchangeable if not really the same. Further, the Confucian Chinese, the Greeks, and the Christians all set the common aim of moral life to be "happiness." Thus, we have the same moral basics to serve today's international technological peoples.

As uncivilized terror and brutality still reign in parts of the globe, with these common moral principles and virtues, we can at least hope for a better world and work toward that goal. Scientific technology can be really useful to better the human condition. Ethically that is its only purpose.

University of Colorado
Colorado Springs, Colorado USA

NOTES

1. Langdon Winner, *The Whale and the Reactor* (Chicago: Chicago University Press, 1986), pp. 3-4.

2. Victor C. Furkiss, *Technological Man: The Myth and the Reality* (New York: George Braziller Press, 1969), p. viii.

3. Franklin L. Baumer, *Modern European Thought: Continuity and Change in Ideas, 1600-1950* (New York: Macmillan, 1977), pp. 414-427.

4. Yehuda Bauer, *A History of the Holocaust* (New York: Franklin Watts Co., 1982), p. 53.

5. Arnold Toynbee, *Preface* to John Cogley, *Religion in a Secular Age* (New York: Frederick Praeger Publishers, 1968), pp. xvii-xviii.

6. Daniel J. Boorstein, *The Republic of Technology* (New York: Harper and Row, 1978), pp. xiii-iv.

7. Kai Nielsen, "Technology as Ideology," in Paul Durbin, ed., *Research in Philosophy and Technology* (Greenwich, CT: Jai Press, 1978), p. 132.

8. Jacques Ellul, *The Technological Society*, tr. J. Wilkinson (New York: Alfred Knopf Publishers, 1964).

9. Cicero, in John Cogley, *Natural Law and Modern Society* (Cleveland: World Publishing Co., 1963), p. 15.

10. Martin Luther King, Jr., "Letters from the Birmingham Jail," in James Rachels, ed., *The Right Thing to Do: Basic Readings in Moral Philosophy* (New York: Random House, 1989), pp. 67-73.

11. Naim, S. Ateek, *Justice and Only Justice: A Palestinian Theology of Liberation* (New York: Maryknoll, 1971), pp. 121-122.

12. Carl Wellman, *Morals and Ethics* (Englewood Cliffs, NJ: Prentice Hall, 1988), p. 42.

PART III

HUMANISM AND THE PERSON

THE TRANSCENDING DIGNITY OF THE HUMAN PERSON: KARL RAHNER'S PHILOSOPHY OF PERSON

Robert E. Lauder

In a very provocative essay the late American Catholic theologian John Courtney Murray, S.J., sketched two Christian humanisms which reveal two very different tendencies.[1]   One Fr. Murray called eschatological humanism; the other he called incarnational humanism. Though each, if pushed to an extreme, would be a distortion of Christianity, both humanisms can be orthodox. However, each involves different emphases.   The eschatological emphasizes the cross, the sinfulness of human nature, the absolute gratuity of salvation and the transiency of all things temporal.   If the eschatological were to be summed up in one sentence, that sentence might be "We have not here a lasting city."   Commenting on eschatological humanism Fr. Murray wrote:

> Pushed to an extreme, the conclusion would be that man not only
> may in fact neglect, but even should by right neglect what is
> called the cultural enterprise — the cultivation of science and the
> arts, the pursuit of human values by human energies, the work of
> civilization — in order to give undivided energies to the invisible
> things of the spirit. No Christian of course draws this extreme
> conclusion and makes it a law for humanity, though individuals
> may hear it, in one or other form, as the word of God to them,
> and hearken to it, and be God's witnesses to the oneness of the
> one thing necessary, by the completeness of their contempt of the
> world.[2]

Incarnational humanism stresses the humanity of Jesus, the Resurrection, the doctrine of merit and that all temporal values have been transformed because of the enfleshment of God's Son. We can sum up the thrust of incarnational humanism with Pius X's motto "Restore all things in Christ." Commenting on incarnational humanism Fr. Murray wrote:

Therefore in the perspectives of an incarnational humanism there is a place for all that is natural, human, terrestrial. The heavens and the earth are not destined for an eternal dust-heap, but for a transformation. There will be a new heaven and a new earth; and those who knew them once will recognize them for all their newness.[3]

With its seeming contempt for the world and its emphasis on the next world, eschatological humanism obviously has a sense of man's transcendence. With a proper philosophy of person, incarnational humanism can have an even more extraordinary sense of transcendence. The following is a sketch of a philosophy of the human that leads to the strongest incarnational humanism and also is especially suited to the needs of the Christian today. This philosophy highlights and emphasizes the transcending dignity of the human person as much as and perhaps more than any other philosophy. This philosophy of human nature is that of Karl Rahner, probably the most influential Catholic theologian of the century. Rahner's theology, which of course springs from Divine Revelation and Rahner's Christian faith, is also reliant on Rahner's philosophy of person.

The two key sources of Rahner's philosophy of person are *Spirit in the World*[4] and *Hearers of the Word*.[5] There is an enormously exciting dynamism in human nature according to Rahner's philosophical vision. It is not an exaggeration to say that the word "transcendence" could be used to sum up Rahner's philosophical vision of human existence. For Rahner the human person is a radical desire for Absolute Being and Absolute Good. In other words the human person is a desire for God. To explicate what Rahner means, we have to discuss his view of knowing and of loving.

In the deepest sense of the term, Rahner is a post-Kantian. He has taken the insights of Kant and carried them to their logical conclusion — a conclusion unfortunately not reached by Kant. In his approach to Kant (1724-1804) Rahner was greatly influenced by the pioneer of Transcendental Thomism, Father Joseph Marechal, S.J. (1878-1944). In responding to a question about people who influenced him, Rahner, noting that he was affected by Heidegger, said:

> . . . I have to say that I owe my most basic, decisive, philosoph-
> ical direction, insofar as it comes from someone else, more, in

fact, to the Belgian philosopher and Jesuit, Joseph Marechal. His philosophy already moved beyond the traditional neoscholasticism. I brought that direction from Marechal to my studies with Heidegger and it was not superseded by him.[6]

Immanuel Kant constructed what he called transcendental philosophy, and by transcendental he meant all knowledge which is occupied not so much with objects as with the manner of knowing objects. Kant was interested in the a priori conditions of knowing. These famous lines from the beginning of *The Critique of Pure Reason* suggest Kant's view of knowing:

> Human reason has this particular fate that in one species of its knowledge it is burdened by questions which, as prescribed by the very nature of reason itself, it is not able to ignore, but which, as transcending all its powers, it is also not able to answer.[7]

Kant winds up with a real world, the phenomenal world, and a really real world, the noumenal world. He confines pure reason to the phenomenal world. The human intellect cannot affirm the existence of the noumenal world. Concerning the noumenal order, human reason can have ideas, such as the idea of God, but cannot affirm the existence of realities corresponding to those ideas. So pure reason cannot affirm the existence of God. This is because in whatever pure reason knows, it is tied to the a priori forms of time and space. Situating Kant historically, we can see that to some extent he is trapped by Hume (1711-1776) and the whole movement of modern philosophy toward subjectivism. Though Hume's skepticism awoke Kant from his dogmatic slumber, Kant could not completely escape the subjectivistic current that was sweeping philosophy. Kant established that we could know, that science really worked, that there were causes and effects, but he established all of this within the phenomenal order. Kant's analysis of the human mind tied it to the experiential order, and that order could not be transcended.

A teacher at the Jesuit scholasticate at Louvain for a large part of his life, Marechal applied Kant's critique to the possibility of human knowing but came up with a different conception of human knowing. Like Kant's, Marechal's method is transcendental but, unlike Kant's, Marechal's method views knowing as dynamic rather than static. For both thinkers, knowing occurs essentially in the judgment, but in comparison with Marechal's insights into the nature of judgment, Kant's understanding of judgment seems truncated. One commentator has noted:

> Marechal charges Kant with a fatally incomplete understanding of the judging function. The fault occurs because Kant, operating out of a rationalist bias, conceives knowledge as a mere relating of the data of experience to the conceptual unity of thought. He is preoccupied with the content of the judgment and overlooks the implications of judgment as an activity, as the act of affirmation. But once judgment as an act of affirmation is taken into account, it is seen to involve the objectifying function of relating its content to the absolute order of reality, that is, to the order of that which is in itself.[8]

For Kant any judgment that goes beyond the bounds of sense experience cannot be objective knowledge. In Kant's view, a judgment consists of a synthesizing of sense data through what Kant called the a priori forms of understanding. Marechal criticizes Kant and claims that the German philosopher's error was that he thought of judgment only as a relating of the data of experience to the conceptual unity of thought.[9] Believing that Kant was preoccupied with the content of judgment to the neglect of judgment as a dynamic activity, Marechal was interested in judgment as an act of affirmation and in the implications that could be drawn when judgment was viewed as an activity. Marechal believed that once we focus attention on judgment as a dynamic act, we can see that judgment has an objectifying function. Judgment relates its contents to the absolute order of reality. An act of judgment relates the contents of judgment to reality as it is in itself. For Marechal the relation of knower and known can be explained, not on the level of cause and effect, but only by appeal to goal- oriented action or finality. In every judgment the human mind has a direction. The dynamic drive within every human judgment is a movement towards a goal.

In every affirmation, the human mind moves toward Absolute Being. Present in every judgment, whether it be affirming that something is, or affirming that something is not, there is an implicit awareness of Absolute Being. The horizon against which every judgment takes place is Absolute Being. This horizon works as an antecedent finality. It is present within each judgment and it is the goal toward which each judgment is moving. However each judgment is only a partial fulfillment of the goal. No judgment ever puts a knower in total possession of Absolute Being. But being a partial fulfillment of the goal, each judgment reaches a new stage in the human knower's drive toward its goal. For Marechal this presence of Absolute Being is what accounts for the objectivity of human knowing. In a judgment, the knower discovers either that something really is, or that something really is not. For Marechal an affirmation necessarily objectivates. He wrote:

Is this not precisely the mechanism of the affirmation? Is it not an account of it that affirmation necessarily "objectivates"? Considered as a moment in the intellect's ascent towards the final possession of the absolute "truth," which is the spirit's "good," it implicitly (*exercite*) projects the particular data in the perspective of this ultimate End, and by so doing *objectivates* them before the subject.[10]

According to Marechal, Kant's error was to stop at the form of knowing instead of reflecting on the nature of judgment as an affirmation. Paradoxically Kant's transcendental philosophy is in error not because Kant was critical of human knowing, but because his reflection was insufficiently transcendental. Marechal believed that Kant had shown that the phenomenal objects were absolutely impossible unless they were present in a knowledge that went beyond the phenomenal order. Another way of saying this is to point out that as soon as you recognize a limit, you have gone beyond that limit. To recognize the phenomenal as phenomenal is to go beyond the phenomenal.

St. Thomas wrote:

All knowing beings implicitly know God in everything they know. For as nothing is desirable but through some resemblance with the first goodness, so nothing is knowable but through some resemblance with the first truth.[11]

Marechal uses this text to indicate that St. Thomas alluded to the hidden stage of our knowledge of God. So Marechal concludes that not only is God hinted at by every object of intelligibility, but God's very existence is given to us in an implicit and confused way in the primitive and basic exigency of our intellectual nature. As further evidence, Marechal cites the following passage from St. Thomas:

> To know that God exists in a general and confused way is implanted in us by nature, inasmuch as God is man's beatitude. For man naturally desires happiness, and what is naturally desired by man is naturally known by him.[12]

In his *Spirit in the World*, Rahner follows the lead of Marechalian Transcendental Thomism. The title of Rahner's work reveals his interest. Rahner views man as primarily a questioner, and the question Rahner focuses his attention on in his epistemological masterwork, he articulates early in the book: "How, according to Thomas, human knowing can be spirit in the world, is the question which is the concern of this work."[13] Rahner's answer involves the implicit pre-conscious presence of Absolute Being to every act of knowing and also involves what Thomas called the "conversion of the intellect to the phantasm."[14] Briefly put, what Rahner claims is that in every act of knowing a material reality, the human knower objectivates the reality, and so knows the object as real, but also knows implicitly Absolute Being. The experience of transcendence present in every act of knowing can become more evident to a knower through personal reflection on the nature of knowing. Indeed for Rahner, metaphysics, which asks the most basic questions about Being, and that includes the being of the knower and the being of the act of knowing, is the attempt at thematizing the experience of transcendence present in every act of knowing.[15]

In addition to knowing, we make choices. Every choice is a reaching out for the good. The objects we choose, the decisions we make display an enormous variety, but what is common to all of them is that the good is what draws us. Just as Absolute Being is the horizon against which all our acts of knowledge take place, so Absolute Good is the background against which all our choices take place.[16] Nothing could be chosen without the implicit presence of Absolute Good.

As we choose objects, we choose ourselves. Every choice I make is also a choice of self in the sense that through every choice I make I bring myself about, I make myself the person I am. What you love determines who you are.

In coming to know another person, special demands are placed on me. The other's free decisions are internal and they are available to me only as they appear in the world. If I wish to enter into the personal existence of the other, I must make a free choice to love the other. Love gives the special entrance into the life of the other. It gives me a special knowledge of the other. The maxim "Love is blind" could not be further from the truth if you accept the philosophical vision of Karl Rahner. By loving, I identify with the person of the other and have special access to whom he or she is. This view of love has serious consequences for our knowledge of God.

We do not know God the way we know a material object. In order to know God a "conversion" is required on the part of the knower.[17] If we wish to enter to some extent into relation with Absolute Being, then we must recognize our contingency. As we recognize our contingency we become aware that we are products of a free act of love by Absolute Being. We need not be. We are products of love. For Rahner, freedom and comprehensibility are related by a direct proportion.[18] The following quotation from Rahner is a good summary statement of his view that love is either movement toward or away from Absolute Being:

> . . . the finite has its ground in the free, luminous act of God. Now a free self-present act is love. For love is the luminous will aiming at the person in its irreducible unicity. It is precisely such a will that God sets in action when he creates a finite being. It is his way of loving himself in his free creative power. Thus the contingent is understood in God's love and only in it. The finite contingent being becomes luminous in God's free love to himself and to what he freely creates. Thus love is seen to be the light of knowledge. A knowledge of the finite that is not willing to understand itself in its ultimate essence as reaching its own fulfillment only in love turns into darkness. It must erroneously consider the contingent as necessary, or leave it in its absolute unintelligibility (an unintelligibility which does not exist and which knowledge steadily denies), or it must explain being as a dark urge, in whose depths there shines no light. For the finite may be grasped only when it is understood as produced by the divine freedom. Now this free action of God is luminous for us only when we do not merely take it as a fact. We must also ratify it in our love for it, thus re-experiencing it, as it were, in its origin and its production. Thus love is the light of the knowledge of the finite, and, since we know the infinite only

through the finite, it is also the light of the whole of our knowledge. In final analysis, knowledge is but the luminous radiance of love.[19]

Thus Rahner's philosophy of person in its entirety involves a transcendence toward God. In both knowing and loving, the human person is a transcending movement toward God.

Cathedral College
Dougleston, New York USA

NOTES

1. John Courtney Murray, S.J., *We Hold These Truths* (New York: Sheed and Ward, 1960), pp. 184-196.

2. 2. Ibid., pp. 188-189.

3. Ibid., p. 190.

4. Karl Rahner, *Spirit in the World*, tr. William Dych, S.J. (New York: Herder and Herder, 1968).

5. Karl Rahner, *Hearers of the Word*, tr. Michael Richards (New York: Herder and Herder, 1969).

6. *America*, March 10, 1979, p. 177.

7. *Critique of Pure Reason*, tr. Norman Kemp Smith. Unabridged edition (New York: St. Martin's Press, 1929), p. 7.

8. Francis M. Tyrrell, *Man: Believer and Unbeliever* (New York: Alba House, 1974), p. 171. I am indebted to Father Tyrrell for his clear treatment of Marechal.

9. Ibid.

10. Joseph Donceel, S.J., ed. and tr., *A Marechal Reader (New York: Herder and Herder, 1970), p. 152. Future references will be cited as* Reader

11. Ver., 22, 2, ad 1 in *Reader*, p. 152.

12. *Reader*, p. 152, and St. Thomas Aquinas, *Summa theologica*, I, 2, 1 ad 1.

13. Rahner, *Spirit in the World*, p. LIII.

14. Ibid.

15. Rahner, *Spirit in the World*, p. 34; Tyrrell, pp. 178-180.

16. Tyrrell, pp. 197-198.

17. Rahner, *Hearers of the Word*, pp. 106-107.

18. Ibid., pp. 100-106.

19. Gerald A. McCool, ed., *A Rahner Reader* (New York: A Crossword Book, The Seabury Press, 1975), pp. 39-40. This translation from *Hearers of the Word* is by Joseph A. Donceel and I use it here because it is much clearer than the section from Richards' translation, p. 100.

PERSONAL LOVE AND PERSONALITY PREFERENCE

David Goicoechea

What is the situation of reflection upon the dignity of the person and thus of just peace in our times? Karol Wojtyla is representative of contemporary Christian thinking when he grounds personal dignity in man's double transcendence,[1] in the interplay of vertical and horizontal transcendence. The transcendence of the person involves Wojtyla in the further questions of the irreducibility, the integrity and the interpersonal being of the person. We shall here explore that transcendence in itself and in its relation to irreducibility, integrity and the interpersonal. In our times the exploration of the person has focused upon a series of distinctions: person and thing, person and individual, person and the anonymous one or mass society. We shall attempt to clarify personal being a bit more by working and playing with the distinction, person and personality. But this still remains a vast topic. To limit the meditation further we shall consider personality as the center of preferential love and person as the center of neighborly love. To build a case for the special dignity of the person, we shall try to reveal that personal love as neighborly should not be reduced to personality love as feeling and preference.

Wojtyla in his book, *The Acting Person*, tried to work within the framework of Boethius' traditional definition of person as "an individual substance of a rational nature."[2] However, I will try to show that that Aristotelian direction is not consistent with the emphasis on personal love which is central to the evangelical tradition. Hence, in this paper I shall define person as "a relational agent of loving transcendence." In making this distinction between person and personality I will argue that Boethius' definition fits personality better than person. Thus, I will contrast personality as "an individual substance of a rational nature" with person as "a relational agent of a loving transcendence." This reflection will have four parts based upon the four words of each definition. We shall consider the transcendence of person in contrast to the nature of personality. As we consider the irreducibility of the person we shall

148

contrast the personal agent with the personality substance. In considering the integrity of the person, we shall contrast the relating person with the individual personality. In considering the interpersonal being of the person, we shall contrast the loving person with the rational personality.

In such a way, we can metaphysically thematize the being of person and personality. But there remains the call to ground this distinction in the thinking of our times. This we can do by thinking about the transcendence of the person in the context of Kierkegaard and Nietzsche, the irreducibility of the person in the context of Freud and Scheler, the integrity of the person in the context of Sartre and Marcel and the interpersonal being of the person in the context of Marx and Gutierrez. The point of the contrast will continue to be made that Nietzsche, Freud, Sartre and Marx are dealing with personality preferences while Kierkegaard, Scheler, Marcel and Gutierrez are dealing with personal love. Ideally, the relation between personality and person needs to be clarified.

Once the metaphysical and historical calls are followed, there still sounds the ethical. There remains the question of dignity and a just peace. We shall conclude our meditation on the double transcendence of personal being by relating it to the old Basque proverb that "Every Basque is a King." We shall extend this to say that "Every person has dignity." That dignity will be located in the mysterious touching point of horizontal and vertical transcendence. That realm of stillness is what is not to be reduced to anything less. That shy meeting place which grounds integrity is the sphere of dignity. That spark of each man's dignity, which is his person, is not only his touching point with the Eternal Thou, but with every other thou.

Kierkegaard's book, *The Works of Love*, might be seen as a prolonged reflection upon the existential dialectic of personality's eros-philia and the person's agape.[3] He sees eros-philia as a preferential love that is also a self-love. It says, "I love only you," and, "You are the other half of my soul." Christian love on the other hand is commanded to go beyond such preferential love to a personal love that loves neighbor as self and all neighbors equally. Like Hindu *Bhakti*, Hebrew *Hesed*, and Buddhist *Karuna*, Christian *Agape*, in the mind of Kierkegaard, is a disciplined love. The great commandment with its vertical and horizontal transcendence: "You must love the Lord your God with all your heart, with all your soul, and with all your mind . . . and your neighbor as yourself" is conditioned by the further command: "If any man comes to me without hating his father, mother, wife, children, brothers, sisters, yes and his own life too, he cannot be my disciple." Insofar as I love *my* parent or *my* child or *my* beloved, with the emphasis on the "my," I have a preferential love. In Kierkegaard's context the task of love is to cancel out the primacy of that preference and to allow personal love to become primary.

The existential dialectic of preference and personal love forms the structure of Kierkegaard's authorship. His pseudonyms are each personality centers of a preferential, passionate lifestyle. His task as a writer is to cooperate with the eternal in deceiving persons out of the falsity of their limited personality fixations so that they can grow into fuller personhood. The pseudonyms are literary personifications that call the reader to respond to the challenge of personal integrity. According to Kierkegaard each person has the potentiality to be a relation, related to himself and to God.[4] That vertical dimension of the person by which he is related to the eternal is the coping stone of his integrity. As long as the absolute love of the absolute does not order a person's life, he will be splintered by preferential possibilities wherein he absolutely loves the relative. If he absolutely loves the absolute or the vertical, he will then relatively love the relative or the horizontal. That is, his relative preferences will be integrated by his absolute love. His personalities will be integrated within his person. The entire thrust of Kierkegaard's thinking is to show that a true, existential life demands a continuing relation with vertical transcendence. Without the eternal, each temporal relation will become isolated in the direction of despair. But if one's temporal present is in touch with the eternal, then one's past and future moments can be integrated in an interpenetrational simultaneity.

Nietzsche, like Kierkegaard, was intent upon restoring man's vertically transcendent dimension. He also rebelled against the enlightenment and its prejudice against vertical transcendence. From *The Birth of Tragedy* on, he emphasized the necessity of inspiration and revelation.[5] He began with a double vertical transcendence to Apollo and Dionysus and he retained transcendence to Dionysus. He writes that his *Zarathustra* was an inspired gift that he received.[6] Vertical transcendence governed both the will to power and the love of eternal recurrence. Nietzsche saw the will to power as the ultimate life principle. All living things do not merely strive to preserve themselves in existence, but they seek a higher existence. The notion of higher life and self-overcoming is grounded in the notion of vertical transcendence. So is the love of eternal recurrence. Without the eternal, Nietzsche knew that nihilism would triumph. The "yes" and "amen" saying that overcomes nihilism and its protesting rhetoric is achieved only when the ever transcending eternal is loved. Nietzsche's personification, Zarathustra, moves from nausea in the face of eternal recurrence to love of eternal recurrence through a disciplining and overcoming of preference. He began by preferring the higher man to the lower man and the overman to the higher man. But he comes to see that there can be an overman only when he is strong enough to love the eternal recurrence of the lower man. The realization that there will always be the lower man is what nauseates Zarathustra, but that nausea is overcome in the convalescence that enables him to love the eternal recurrence of the same.

The notion of the same is the telltale difference between Kierkegaard and Nietzsche. Kierkegaard's temporality of personal love which is "Repetition" allows for a future that is truly new. Kierkegaard's redemptive future is grounded in the promise "Behold, I make all things new" (Revelations 21:5).[7] Nietzsche's future which is grounded in the will to power is a future of the same. This shows that Nietzsche's metaphysics is a monism whereas Kierkegaard's is a pluralism. For Nietzsche there are many masks of the will to power. There are many perspectival and preferential personalities, but they are illusory. They do not have any unique being of their own grounded in a unique personhood. The vertically transcendent is immanent for Nietzsche in a different way than it is for Kierkegaard. For Kierkegaard the creature is not identical with the creator. For Nietzsche, just as each moment of time is the same in the eternal, so each individual of nature is really one with the will to power. Thus, Nietzsche does not have a metaphysics of persons, but only of personalities, which are manifestations of the will to power. As he disciplines personality preferences, he arrives at the love of eternal recurrence. This process is one of translating spirit back into nature. It makes vertical and horizontal transcendence one and the same. Kierkegaard, who stresses the personal, does not emphasize nature, but rather a transcending of nature.

Sigmund Freud continued the monistic and therefore transpersonal project of Spinoza, Hegel and Nietzsche. The will to power became for him the "id." In his book on *The Interpretation of Dreams*, Freud brought to attention how the subconscious *id* can produce dream thoughts that are manifest in symbolic pictures that are so extraordinary that the awakened mind could never equal their creative ability.[8] Freud's project might be interpreted as an attempt to prevent the reducibility of man to the *ego*. Even though the scientific method is based upon reduction, the reduction of the greatest number of particulars to the fewest possible number of explanatory principles, and even though Freud was a trained and talented scientist, his life's work showed that man is not primarily an *ego cogitans*. Freud showed that none of our human acts flows simply from our deliberate thinking and willing. He showed how the good intentions of man are just the tip of the iceberg, and thus can "pave the road to hell." It is primarily man's subconscious that moves him to act. Man is not only a thinking and willing being; he is also *super ego* and most of all *id*.

Freud brought to light how man's dreams are condensations of copious associative connections. His contribution to the question of personal dignity is to reveal the vast vaults of the being of man's subconscious depths. Of course, Freud did not develop the concepts of person and dignity. But, when personal dignity is important to a thinker, Freud can help give content to the concept. As he decoded the dream's message, he brought into question the human power of censorship which could be related to the conscience and its vertical transcendence. As he brought into question the revealing-concealing mechanisms of distortion, displacement and transference, he gave evidence for the complex irreducibility of man. As he worked with the relaxation that was necessary for the fruitful associative interpretation of dreams, he explored ways of establishing integrity. As he explored the issues of infantile emotional transference, the libido and the oedipus complex, he could be interpreted as treating love and personal growth. But he did not thematically treat the issues of man's transcendence and the being of the future. His thinking is archeological or past directed and not teleological or future directed. He concerns himself with the sources of action but not the direction of action. Thus, while he overcomes reducing man to the *ego*, Freud ultimately reduces him to the *id*, which implies much the same sort of monism as Nietzsche's will to power.

It was Max Scheler who made a prolonged effort to prevent the irreducibility of the person, and to make sense of human acts in the face of the Nietzschean and Freudian critiques of the *ego*. He showed that the person's being and dignity are greater than the being and worth of his *ego*, his subjectivity, his personality and his selfhood.[9] He argued that the person is not primarily an *ens cogitans* (Descartes) or an *ens volens* (Nietzsche), but first and foremost an *ens amans*. Like Freud and following Pascal, Scheler wanted to reveal man's sub-egological dimensions. He wanted to ground ethics and religion or the realms of justice and peace in a philosophical anthropology which shows that the heart has its reasons which the mind knows not. Scheler phenomenologically clarifies the realm of the heart as being constituted by the conations and feelings of human subjectivity, the preferences of human personality and the love of the person. His chief task was to show that the heart's acts of love, conation, preference and feeling have intentional cognition. He wanted to show how these acts can have a material *a priori* knowledge of value. Scheler with his method of free imaginative variation revealed the essential differences between the acts of preferential and non-preferential love. In this way he clarified why the person should not be reduced to the personality.

For Scheler it is through the acts of preference and placing-after that we know the value hierarchy.[10] In acts of preferring one value over another, we know the grades of physical, vital, intellectual and spiritual values. With *a priori* certitude we can place one value after another. It was upon this knowledge of preference and placing-after that Franz Brentano grounded morality. However, Scheler pointed out that knowledge through preferring and placing-after can become distorted through such phenomena as ressentiment.[11] But, man has a more fundamental knowing and directing power than the preferences of his personality and that is his personal love. The person which is intentionally oriented toward world and being can be the judge of the personality's evaluating of the value hierarchy. There can be split personalities within the person and a disintegrated variety of approaches to the value hierarchy. But, there can also be conversion or a reordering toward the objective value hierarchy because there is the personal love within the person that transcends the preferences of his personality. Integrity of the *ego*, subjectivity and the personalities is possible because of the unifying power of the person.

The person is defined by Scheler as a unity of acts.[12] It is the person which gives unity to the acts of love, conation, preference and feeling. For Scheler, this personal unity is not simply a substantial unity. The person is too much a relational agent to be a thing existing in itself in which relationality accidentally inheres. The person is not a unity of acts by being their sum. The whole in this case is more than the sum of its parts. The person is not the sum and substance of acts, but rather the fundamental moral attitude, the *Grund Gesinnung* giving them direction.

Personhood is that which unifies an individual's many acts by giving them all a certain direction. It is for this reason that the *ordo amoris* is so fundamental to Scheler's thinking. The person's fundamental being is a love which is not to be reduced to the feelings of love and hate, nor to the preferential loves of affection, friendship and eros. This third kind of love, more fundamental than love's feelings and love's preferences, this unique, intimate *ordo amoris* is the ground of personal dignity, justice and peace. This is the crystal form of the person that shapes all the person thinks and does. For Scheler, the loving person is in touch with vertically transcendent love or what Scheler calls the eternal in man.

Sartre's prolonged study of human freedom reveals the non-being that makes relational agency possible. Being-for-itself can be free and transcendent because it is a lack of being that is receptive. It is different from being-in-itself which is a fullness of being associated with necessity. The ultimate human project is to integrate being-for-itself and being-in-itself. If God were possible that is what He would be, the perfect synthesis of being-in-itself-being-for-itself.[13] But, a synthesis of such opposites is, according to Sartre, impossible. Freedom and necessity cannot become one. Man does have a vertically transcendent dimension that touches his every horizontal relation. Man is related to God, but to a God that cannot be. Man is always striving to be what cannot be and, thus, he is a useless passion. For this reason good faith is impossible and love can only be in conflict. Because I am shamed by the look of the other, I try to capture the other's freedom. If I could do this, I would not be objectified by his look. Love is my project of bringing the other being-for-itself into the being-in-itself of his body through my caress and kiss. If this could happen, I know that he would look at me with the eyes of love and I would not need to be anxious. However, the more I succeed the more I work against myself for I do not want to be loved by a robot. Again, in Sartre's terms, the other is either free or necessitated and cannot be both. That is why love fails. That is why the whole human project is absurd.

In his early career Sartre was much like Nietzsche. He saw man as an individual against humanity. However, Sartre did not take the leap of faith into the love of eternal recurrence. He allowed God to remain a dead contradiction and he accepted the consequences: no ethics and no justice, no objective meaning to life and no peace. Eventually, however, Sartre could accept the nauseating nihilism of that position no longer and in response to his conscience he moved toward the thought of Marx.

Sartre moved from defining man in terms of an impossible vertical transcendence to a humanism that dismissed vertical transcendence altogether.

But in the period of his full-fledged existentialism, Sartre's philosophical anthropology was clearly and distinctly consistent though absurdly inadequate. His theory of bad faith shows the implications of his philosophy for the issue of personal love and personality preferences. His complete rejection of even the possibility of vertical transcendence is connected with his complete rejection of any personal love. Sartre does not treat the acting person and his transpreferential love, but only the person as actor and his perspectival projects. The *dramatis personae* of Sartre's world of unlimited freedom are consistently characters of unlimited bad faith. Sartre does not know the world of limited and responsible persons; without God there are no limits. Sartre's actors are not limited by the life script of God and of other persons. They are responsible first and foremost to themselves and thus can start playing a new part any time they wish. They are role players who even in sincerity are telling themselves lies that they believe. Sartre's philosophy clearly shows the dangers of the technological age. As technicians, unlimited by God and other persons, Sartre's personalities can do all. They might feel shame before the other, but they can overcome that with their sadomasochistic projects. Without vertical transcendence and interpersonal being there are no persons, there is no love, there is no integrity. Man cannot make whole his being which is split between the *en soi* and the *pour soi*.

Gabriel Marcel's philosophy of personal love is diametrically opposed to Sartre's philosophy of personality preferences. Marcel's *dramatis personae* face the dangers of a broken world, but with grace and one another they find ways to journey toward the wholeness of integrity. Marcel sees himself as a gardener tending the flowers in the mysterious garden of personal being. It is easy for language to harden into habits of sterility. It is his task to cultivate the freshness of fertility. His notion of the mystery of personal being is indicated by his saying: "I hope in Thee for us."[14] This saying with its "Thee" with a capital "T" contains the element of vertical transcendence. The interpersonal, horizontal structures of the person are indicated by the "for us." Marcel is continuously considerate of the "I-thou" dimensions of the person. By the "I" he does not mean himself or his *ego*, but the universal structures of each subject or of each person. When treating the "I" Marcel pays special attention to the body. When he treats the mind-body problem or what he calls the mystery of incarnation, he clarifies the nuances and difficulties of thinking "I have a body." Then he shows in sensitive detail the shades of meaning in saying "I am my body." His analysis shows that I and my body are related in the mysterious realm between "I am my body" and "I have a body."[15] To keep fresh this personal realm between "being" and "having" is the point of his thinking. By such phenomenological cultivation, Marcel approaches the challenge of personal integrity. He shows how the likes of Descartes and Sartre miss the mystery of the relation of horizontal and vertical transcendence with their hard and fast certitudes which affirm or deny God and the other. My body and I can become whole in a mysterious absence-presence as can I and thou. There is an interplay between the two relations. The integration or disintegration of the I-thou and I-body relations rise or fall together.

But in our times it has been Karl Marx who has brought out the inter-personal structures of personal being most convincingly. From the time of his doctoral dissertation on Epicurus he exhibits an overriding sense of justice. In fact, this is the reason for his atheism. He agreed with Epicurus that the injustice in the world is incompatible with an all good and all powerful God. But, he took a practical approach. He wanted to overcome the unjust place rooted in the religion which is the opium of the people. He analyzed justice and peace in terms of being and having. It is private property born of alienation that is the source of injustice and misery. We can become free persons insofar as we escape being possessed by our possessions. Having, when it is not in the framework of communal being, turns man into an object and a commodity. The solution to man's alienated "having" is communism. In trying to accomplish communal justice, Marx distinguished two possibilities for man. Man could live according to the formula commodity-person-commodity or person-commodity-person.[16] If I use money and commodities in the service of persons I can be a person. If I use persons to make money, then they and I become commodities. What this means is that there is no I; there is only the we. We are all bound together. No man is an island. A person is defined in terms of other persons.

Marx's approach is one of a practical love that works for justice for all or the common good. It is an attempt to overthrow the value hierarchy and the preferences of capitalism. And yet because Marx rejects vertical transcendence, he does not have an objective criterion to guide his love so that he himself falls into a system of preferences rather than neighborly love. He prefers the workers to the capitalists. Even though he sees that masters and slaves are all commodities together and must all become free together, his rational plan for revolution has a necessity to its dialectic, which does not respect the realm of personal mystery. His approach can become very unjust toward capitalists, for the preference of Marx's personality for the oppressed over the oppressors forgets that the oppressors are persons. Marx sees the interpersonal being of the person, but in rejecting the vertical transcendence of the person he opens the door not to a peace without justice, but to a revolutionary strife without justice. Unjust peace is not as evil as unjust war. The end of just peace does not justify the means of an unjust war.

It is here that liberation theology comes on the scene. Gustavo Gutierrez and his brothers and sisters do not want to fall into the trap of moving from the preference for the oppressors over the oppressed to a preference for the oppressed over the oppressors. As Hegel and Marx saw, all, both masters and slaves, are oppressed. The way out is to have a neighborly love based on the common good for all.

Gutierrez begins with two givens: (1) the class struggle is a fact and (2) neutrality in this matter is impossible.[17] The great challenge is to love all on both sides of the class struggle and yet to work for justice for the oppressed against the oppressors. Meeting this challenge leads to a deepening faith and a maturing in love. This challenge can take the person beyond the narcissism of the existentialists. Marcel saw the interpersonal being of the person, but his "I hope in Thee for us" does not have the social dimensions of Marx and the liberation theologians. The perspective of liberation theology and its Marxized notion of the mystical body emphasizes a new aspect of personal dignity in the solidarity of all persons. A poor, illiterate worker is a person of dignity because he is bound together in personhood with all persons. We are all united not only in the spiritual world of vertical transcendence, but also in the material world and its technology. We are the family of man and all brothers and sisters have equal dignity. For the liberation theologians, this dignity is the basis for the value of a just peace. Gabriel Marcel in one of his plays wrote of a woman who was married twice to two brothers. One day she called her second husband by her first husband's name. He was upset and asked her, "Why?" She responded that it is difficult to know where one person leaves off and another begins. So it is with these mysterious persons. They are interpersonal. They are not to be reduced to substantial and individual and rational or irrational personalities. Their very being is a loving interpenetration. Human persons are made in the image and likeness of the trinity of persons, of that God who is love. It is the challenge of human persons as long as they are *homines viatores* to pursue the peace of this love. It is their challenge to pursue just and equal opportunities for all. Every person has the dignity of a relational agent of loving transcendence.

Brock University
St. Catherines, Canada

NOTES

1. Karol Wojtyla, *The Acting Person* (Boston: Dr. Reidel Publishing Company, 1969), p. 119 and following.

2. *The Acting Person*, p. 30.

3. Soren Kierkegaard, *The Works of Love* (New York: Harper and Row, 1962), pp. 58-65.

4. Soren Kierkegaard, *The Sickness Unto Death* (Princeton, NJ: Princeton University Press, 1980), p. 13

5. Friedrich Nietzsche, *The Birth of Tragedy* (New York: Vintage Books, Random House, 1967), p. 13

6. Friedrich Nietzsche, *The Birth of Tragedy* (New York: Vintage, 1969), p. 300

7. Soren Kierkegaard, *The Concept of Anxiety* (Princeton, NJ: Princeton University Press, 1980), p. 17. In this preface to *The Concept of Anxiety*, Kierkegaard picks out the quote as central when he summarizes his book Repetition.

8. Sigmund Freud, *The Interpretation of Dreams* (England: Penguin Books, 1975) see especially chapter VI, "The Dream Work," pp. 381-454

158

9. Max Scheler, *Formalism in Ethics and Non-Formal Ethics of Values* (Evanston: Northwestern University Press, 1973), pp. 32-42 for the conation of the subject, pp. 111-121 for the fundamental moral tenor of the person

10. *Formalism*, pp. 86-100 give Scheler's phenomenology of preferring and placing after.

11. Max Scheler, *Ressentiment* (New York: The Free Press of Glencoe, 1961), pp. 79-82.

12. *Formalism*, pp. 370-386.

13. Jean-Paul Sartre, *Being and Nothingness* (New York: Philosophical Library, 1956), pp. 80-81.

14. Gabriel Marcel, *Homo Viator* (New York: Harper and Brothers, 1962), p. 60.

15. Gabriel Marcel, *The Mystery of Being*, Vol. 1 (Chicago: Gateway, 1950), pp. 113-126.

16. Robert C. Tucker, *The Marx Engels Reader* (New York, London: W. W. Norton and Company, 1978), p. 335.

17. Gustavo Gutierrez, *A Theology of Liberation* (New York: Orbis, 1973), p. 273.

CHRISTIAN MARRIAGE AS A COMMUNITY OF LOVE

John J. Snyder

Central to the renewal of the Christian family in our days is a new understanding of marriage within the Church. Catholic Christians have long understood marriage to be a sacrament, a sacred mystery.[1] However, marriage is not only a sacrament, it is also a natural union. The fathers of the Second Vatican Council have described this natural union as an intimate partnership, a community of love.[2] What is new about this description is not that they have described marriage as a loving union. Over the centuries, many Church fathers have described marriage in this way. What is new is that the fathers of the Second Vatican Council understand the development of an intimate union of love by the couple to be one of its primary purposes.[3]

This new teaching of Vatican II has caused considerable controversy within the Church. Although it is generally accepted that Vatican II has placed a much greater emphasis on the importance of conjugal love in marriage, there is a serious ongoing debate among marriage experts within the Church about whether the development of a community of love is essential to a marriage or not. The traditional position, dating back to St. Augustine, is that the forming of a close and loving partnership between the spouses is *not* essential to a marriage but is simply a perfecting of it. The issue is whether the new teaching of Vatican II is at variance with the longstanding tradition of the Church or is simply an amplification of it.

The main intent of this paper is to support the position that Vatican II has effected a radical change in the Church's understanding of marriage and that an intimate community of love belongs to the essence of marriage. The paper will begin with an examination of the traditional position. Next, Vatican II's new approach to marriage will be presented. Thirdly, a response will be made to some of the arguments given by those who do not think that Vatican II has significantly changed the traditional Church teaching on marriage. Finally, some concluding comments will be given.

The Traditional Understanding of Marriage

Prior to the Second Vatican Council, marriage had been traditionally understood within the Church to be a union of a man and woman for the sake of procreating and raising children.[4] Since the bearing and rearing of children is a long-term process and requires the close cooperation of the parents, a lifelong union and sexual exclusiveness are seen to be essential elements of the union.[5] However, the friendship and companionship of the couple are not deemed to be essential traits of marriage because a couple could mutually agree to have children and functionally cooperate throughout a lifetime in a sexually faithful way to raise their children without ever achieving a close personal or loving relationship. A developed and loving companionship between the couple would provide a better environment for the raising of the children and would also enhance the common life of the couple but it is not an essential requirement for the marriage.[6]

The root of the traditional position rests upon its understanding of sexual intercourse. Drawing greatly upon the teachings of St. Augustine[7] and St. Thomas,[8] it considers the primary purpose of sexual relating to be the having of children. The whole human sexual physiology is clearly directed to that end.

This is not to say that intercourse between a married couple does not have other purposes. It does. The bringing about of a more complete personal union and the relief of sexual desire can also be accomplished through sexual intercourse. However, the unitive aspects and the relief of concupiscence must always be open to the procreative. Sexual intercourse which artificially prohibits procreation, even with the intent to bring the couple closer together or to relieve their sexual desires, is unnatural and immoral. Sexual intercourse must always be open to its primary purpose even when fulfilling other purposes.[9]

Once it is understood that sexual intercourse is nature's instrument for continuing the race, it follows that sexual relations must be reserved to a relationship willing to bear and raise children. Marriage is that relationship and its primary purpose is precisely the procreation and nurturance of the young.

For the traditionalists, a marriage comes into being at the time of the wedding ceremony when the couple mutually contract to give each other the right to have sexual intercourse for the purpose of having children.[10] The agreement between the couple involves mutual rights, not actions.

The couple contract to have the right to sexual intercourse, but it is not necessary that this right ever be exercised, as was the case with Mary and Joseph. There is also no necessity that the couple actually have children. As long as the partners perform acts of intercourse that are open to having children, the basic contract between them is fulfilled.

The Vatican II Critique of the Traditional Position

The new teaching of Vatican II on marriage was derived in large part from some early twentieth century Christian personalist writers, most notably, Dietrich von Hildebrand and Herbert Doms. In essence, these thinkers, basing their positions on the lived experience of contemporary married couples, especially in the Western world, rejected the traditional view that the primary reason for marriage is the procreation and nurture of children.

Von Hildebrand preferred not to talk about the *ends* of marriage. Instead, he wrote about its meanings. The primary meaning of marriage is love.[11] To live in love is why a couple gets married. They do not marry simply to have children or to satisfy their sexual desires, but to create a mutual bond of love. Sexual intercourse between them is not simply for the sake of having children but is fruitful and enriching to the extent that it fosters the couple's mutual love. Children are the natural result of the couple's love-making, not an external goal to which their relationship and intercourse are ordered.[12]

Herbert Doms continued this line of thinking by asserting that the immediate purpose and basic meaning of a marriage is the creation of what he called the couple's "two-in-oneness."[13] Marriage is not just a biological union intended to have children, but is essentially a loving union of two persons of different sex who are drawn together physically and spiritually to form a common life wherein "they can fulfil and help one another."[14] Only through the mutually completing masculine-feminine union can they come to realize all that is human in them. Their human completion cannot be achieved in sexual solitude. The desire for children is normal but is not the usual reason for marrying. In fact, for Doms, the immediate goal of sexual intercourse is not conception but the physical and spiritual union of the couple. In a good relationship, intercourse signifies and brings about the union of love between the pair. Conception is an ulterior goal that is not realized or even desired in every act of intercourse. Although the bearing and raising of children is the natural flowering of any marriage, a marriage realizes its meaning even if no children are ever conceived. Marriage is at heart a union of love, not simply a procreative union.

These Catholic personalists were clearly instrumental in influencing the fathers of the Second Vatican Council in their deliberations on marriage. Despite strong opposition from conservatives who supported the traditional position, the bishops approved a document on marriage that was strikingly in accord with the personalist's basic understanding of marriage. Rather than reaffirm that marriage is primarily for the procreation and nurture of children, the Church fathers clearly emphasized that marriage is a "community of love" and an "intimate partnership of married life and love." While acknowledging that "marriage and conjugal love are by their very nature ordained toward the begetting and educating of children," they were careful to affirm that "marriage . . . is not instituted solely for procreation" and that it "persists as a whole manner and communion of life, and maintains its value and indissolubility, even when offspring are lacking. . . ."[15] To make clear their change in emphasis, they firmly stressed that the formation of an intimate community of life rooted in conjugal love must be considered just as much a primary goal of marriage as is the having and raising of children.[16] Marriage is not just a procreative union.

The intimate community of married life, according to the Vatican II bishops, is brought into being by a "conjugal covenant of irrevocable personal consent."[17] This covenanting is a "human act whereby spouses mutually bestow and accept each other . . . ."[18] It is "a mutual gift of two persons."[19]

Two points need to be made about this novel teaching of the bishops. First, they describe the exchange of marital vows as a covenant rather than as a contract. A covenant is an agreement formed out of love in which the partners freely give of themselves to one another. It is a mutual self-donation. In contrast, a contract, the traditional term used in Church documents on marriage, is an agreement made in justice. The parties have rights and obligations to each other. What is agreed upon in a contract is not a gift, something that is given freely, but something owed in justice.[20] The Church fathers clearly wanted to emphasize the mutual gifting that is marriage rather than the traditional understanding of marriage as an exchange of rights. Secondly, in line with this first notion, the fathers carefully avoided describing marriage as an exchange of rights to have sexual intercourse for the sake of children. Marriage is a covenant in which the partners freely give their whole persons to each other and not just their sexual organs.

Realizing that the term "love" is ambiguous, the Vatican II bishops were careful to clarify what they meant by "conjugal love." For them, it is not to be confused with a highly romantic love, nor is it simply an erotic inclination. Rather, it is a love that actively and willfully seeks the good of the other person.[21] It is a free giving of the self to the other. "Such love pervades the whole of their lives" and "by its generous activity, it grows better and grows greater."[22] Although biblical passages urge this form of conjugal love in several places,[23] it is not just a supernatural love but an "eminently human"[24] love that is being advocated.

The bishops, while still acknowledging that sexual intercourse by its very nature is ordained to the having of children, agreed with the personalists that conjugal love is "uniquely expressed and perfected"[25] through marital intercourse. Marital partners, when they have sexual relations in a truly human way, "signify and promote that mutual self-giving"[26] which enriches their relationship. Sexual intercourse is not simply a procreative act but is a true way for a married couple to express and grow in their mutual love.

Objections to Interpreting Vatican II as a New Approach to Marriage

Not everyone understands the teachings of Vatican II to be a radical break with tradition. Strong opposition has come from some of the judges of the Church's highest marriage courts and from some Church canon lawyers.

A first objection, raised by some judges of the Rota and the Sacred Signatura,[27] is that the document *Gaudium et Spes*, containing the teachings on marriage, is simply a pastoral document that can in no way be considered a definitive doctrinal statement of the Church in marriage matters.

In response to the first objection, although *Gaudium et Spes* was given the title of "Pastoral Constitution," it is not to be viewed as having no doctrinal content. A footnote deliberately appended to the title of the document by the Council fathers makes clear that although the document has pastoral intent, it is grounded in doctrinal principles.[28] To emphasize the doctrinal importance of the document, the bishops voted overwhelmingly to have it called a "constitution" rather than a "declaration" because the former has much greater doctrinal and juridical value within the Church.[29] In addition, a careful reading of the debate surrounding the composing of the section on marriage provides compelling evidence that the vast majority of bishops clearly sought to change the traditional teachings on marriage.[30] Their intent was clearly to effect a doctrinal change. Finally, the revised Code of Canon Law of 1983 changed the canons pertaining to the ends of marriage and to the object of marital consent to be in accord with the basic teachings of the Council document.[31] This is further evidence that *Gaudium et Spes* had significant doctrinal and juridical import.

The second objection, raised in a 1975 decision of the Sacred Signatura,[32] is that the "communion of love" and the "intimate partnership of the whole life" emphasized in *Gaudium et Spes* belong to the essence of marriage only insofar as they are understood to be identified with the partners' perpetual right to conjugal acts. When a couple consent to marry, they agree to give each other a lifelong and exclusive right to sexual acts whose purpose is the generation and education of offspring. The giving of this perpetual and exclusive right to sexual intercourse *implies* an intimate communion of life without which this right cannot be exercised. Thus, the intimate communion of love and life, spoken about in Vatican II, is nothing other than the mutual willingness of the couple to stay together so that they can exercise their perpetual right to sexual relations. No other kind of community of love is necessary and therefore the new position is simply a novel reiteration of the old.

In reply, to identify the lifelong and exclusive right to sexual intercourse for procreative purposes with the "community of love" or the "sharing of the whole life" is to fail to understand that a couple can mutually grant each other the right to have sexual relations but can nevertheless refuse to share any other part of their lives. A classic example is the marriage of convenience, where the partners agree to share a bed and to raise children, but share neither a common life nor an abiding love for each other. An exchange of rights *does not* necessarily imply that the participants love each other.

A third objection, raised by some canon lawyers, is that love is too nebulous to be included in the juridical essence of marriage. A legal definition requires exactness and love cannot be defined with exactitude. Therefore, love cannot belong to the juridical essence of marriage.

Regarding this objection, although it is true that "love" cannot be defined with exactness, the kind of love that is required for a Christian marriage has been described with some care by the Church fathers and has been clearly distinguished from other more volatile forms of love. The fathers wrote about a self-giving love that seeks the good of the other person and distinguished this form of love from romantic passion and erotic inclination. Undoubtedly there will always be a grey area of debate, but this is also true regarding the legal understanding of notions like "just," "honest" and "happiness." The description of love given in *Gaudium et Spes* should be sufficient to resolve most disputes in law. Besides, if the Church fathers understand a community of love to belong to the essence of marriage, it is incumbent upon the Church lawyers to attempt to describe the term for juridical purposes. The tail should not wag the dog.

A final objection, also raised by some canon lawyers, is that love cannot be included in the juridical essence of marriage, otherwise many marriages commonly accepted as valid within the Church, most notably many arranged marriages and marriages of convenience, would no longer be considered marital unions.

In response, the Vatican fathers have clearly understood the creating of a community of love to be one of the essential purposes of a Christian marriage. This means that any marrying couple who do not have the intent to form a community of love or lack the capacity to form such a union are not validly married. This obviously means that some arranged marriages and some marriages of convenience are not Christian marriages. They may be marriages according to the civil law but they are not marriages in the eyes of the Church.

Concluding Remarks

In conclusion, the personalist conception of marriage presented in Vatican II accords well with my experience of marriage and marital sexuality within the contemporary Western world and is indicative of a Church in tune with the "signs of the time." Most couples I know marry because they are "in love." Their love is sometimes shallow and immature, thereby preventing them from attaining a rich and fulfilling marital union, but this does not take away from the fact that they marry out of love. The desire for an ongoing loving union is clearly what

166

motivates most couples to marry. It is the exceptional couple who marry primarily because they want children.

In the strongest marital relationships, the desire is to form an ongoing intimate bond of love. The couple seek to become close friends who share their lives as fully as possible. They deeply care about one another and willingly give of themselves to each other. These marriages are unfortunately in the minority but for those who can achieve them, they offer the fullest possible marital union.

Sexual intercourse in these strong relationships, though clearly a procreative activity, is not primarily done for the purpose of having children. Intercourse is primarily a manifestation of their love and care for each other. It is a way of communicating and strengthening their mutual love in an ongoing repeatable way. When children are desired, they are conceived within this context. It is because the couple love each other that they are willing to allow their sexual relations to be open to having children. In a marital relationship that is truly loving, the personal aspects of sexual intercourse override the physical, even when the desire to procreate is present.

This new ideal of marriage proposed by the Church is not an easy one. Although it is not hard for a couple to have romantic inclinations and sexual inclinations toward one another, it is difficult to sustain an ongoing and exclusive self-giving love throughout the duration of a marriage. Building an intimate and loving relationship takes time, constant effort and continuing perseverance. The ideal that the Church now proposes is difficult but its realization can truly bring about a rich and full life for the persons involved. It is the only ideal that can truly image the eternal love union between Christ and His bride, the Church.

King's College
London, Canada

NOTES

1. Since this paper is being delivered primarily to an audience of philosophers, I have deliberately not developed Vatican II's understanding of marriage as a sacrament.

2. Walter M. Abbott, S.J., ed., *The Documents of Vatican II* (New York: Crossroad, 1989), pp. 249-250.

3. Ibid., p. 254.

4. "The primary end of marriage is the procreation and nurture of children; its secondary end is mutual help and the remedying of concupiscence." *Codex Iuris Canonici* (1917), Can. 1013, 1.

5. "The essential properties of marriage are unity and indissolubility, which acquire a special firmness in Christian marriage by reason of its sacramental character." Ibid., Can. 1013, 2.

6. "This mutual interior formation of husband and wife, this persevering endeavor to bring each other to the state of perfection, may in a true sense be called . . . the primary cause and reason of matrimony, so long as marriage is considered not in its stricter sense as the institution designed for the procreation and education of children, but in the wider sense as a complete and intimate life-partnership and association." Pope Pius XI, *Casti connubii*, N. 24.

7. Augustine held that sexual relations are acceptable within marriage only for the sake of children. Sexual intercourse for the relief of concupiscence, even within marriage, is venially sinful. St. Augustine, *On the Good of Marriage*, Chapter 6, n. 6.

8. Aquinas (1225-1274) agreed with Augustine that sexual intercourse is essentially intended for bearing children. He also rejected sexual relations for the sake of pleasure, even within marriage as a disordered use of the sexual act. St. Thomas Aquinas, *Summa Theologica*, III (Suppl.), q. 41, a. 4c.

9. Pius XI, op. cit, N. 54.

10. "Marital consent is an act of the will by which each party gives and accepts a perpetual and exclusive right over the body for acts which are suitable for the generation of children." *Codex Iuris Canonici* (1917), Can. 1081, 2.

11. Dietrich von Hildebrand, *Marriage: The Mystery of Faithful Love* (New York: Longmans, Green, and Co., 1942), p. 4.

12. von Hildebrand, p. 23.

13. Herbert Doms, *The Meaning of Marriage*, tr. George Sayer, pp. 94-95.

14. Ibid.

15. Abbott, op. cit., p. 255.

16. "Hence while not making the other purposes of matrimony of less account, the true practice of conjugal love, and the whole meaning of the family life which results from it, have this aim: that the couple be ready with stout hearts to cooperate with the love of the Creator and the Savior, who through them will enlarge and enrich His own family." Ibid., p. 254.

17. Ibid., p. 250.

18. Ibid.

19. Ibid., p. 251.

20. Theodore Mackin, S.J., *What is Marriage?* Marriage in the Catholic Church (Mahwah, NJ: Paulist Press, 1989), pp. 268-269. Mackin's book is a superb study on the development of marriage within the Catholic Church.

21. Abbott, p. 252.

22. Ibid., p. 253.

23. See *Gen.* 2:22-24; *Pr.* 5:15-20; 31:10-31; *Tob.* 8:4-8; *Cant.* 1:2-3; 1:16; 4:16; 5:1; 7:8-14; 1 *Cor.* 7:3-6; *Eph.* 5:25-33.

24. Abbott, p. 252.

25. Ibid., p. 253.

26. Ibid.

27. See the decision of Rotal Judge Jose Pinto as reported in *Ephemerides Iuris Canonici*, Vol. 34 (1979, 1-2), pp. 346-353 and the decision of the Sacred Signatura as reported by Mackin, p. 315.

28. Abbott, p. 199.

29. Mackin, pp. 273-274.

30. *Acta Synodolia*, Vol. 3. For a detailed history of how the document was produced see Herbert Vorgrimler, ed., Commentary on the *Documents of Vatican II* (New York: Crossroad Publishing Co., 1990), Vol. 5, pp. 1-76 and 225-245. See also Mackin, pp. 248-282.

31. The relevant canons read: "The marriage covenant, by which a man and a woman establish between themselves a partnership of their whole life, and which of its very nature is ordered to the well-being of the spouses and to the procreation and upbringing of children, has, between the baptized, been raised by Christ the Lord to the dignity of a sacrament." (Canon 1055,1). "Marital consent is an act of will by which a man and a woman give themselves to and accept one another in an irrevocable covenant for the purpose of establishing a marriage." (Canon 1057,2).

32. The argument is reported by Mackin, pp. 317-318.

GUILT AND GRATITUDE: A NEW PARADIGM
FOR DIALOGUE BETWEEN HUMANISMS

John B. Davis

This paper attempts to introduce a paradigm for philosophical anthropology that might provide a broad base for discussion of human nature between Christian and other theistic philosophers on the one hand, and at least some schools of non-theistic humanism on the other. This model is for the moral rather than the ontological structure of humanness, and presents the experiences of guilt and of gratitude as the foundational human condition. These two moral responses, it is suggested here, encompass between them most of the perspectives recent philosophical anthropology has employed in describing the human condition.

Contemporary dialogue between theist and non-theist, or secular humanist, remains badly in need of frames of reference both can share. Christian humanism is often limited to believers, as a conversation with a faith context. Surely this kind of thought is useful, since the believer is always in search of a contemporary articulation of faith. One such effort is Basave's theoretical account of helplessness/hopelessness, of anticipation/actualization as poles of existence, with life viewed vertically: the ascent and descent of the person's life parameters. However, the present paper points to categories that do not necessarily implicate a Someone existing outside this drama of limit and potential, as Basave's model affirms. Is there in guilt and gratitude a capacity for dialogue *between* humanisms, categories acceptable to *both* traditions?

It is true some secular humanists proceed methodologically from the denial of any transcendent Existent, and an effort to clear common ground with these thinkers and their schools will meet this anti-theism in its first stages. Today a variety of secular humanisms are formally atheistic, assuming a confrontational stance with religious belief. Indeed, these postures insist that any transcendent meaning — source or destiny — is precisely what must be overcome before an "authentic" humanism can emerge in our time. Such views are not apt candidates for dialogue.

But there are humanisms — let us title them "consolational" as opposed to "confrontational" — genuinely searching for models of man that could be affirmed by their principles and by those of theistic humanists. Even summary versions of these two broad camps would not be useful here, but it is evident that some views exclude themselves. An anthropology that sees religious belief as illusion or as an escape from the tragedy of human existence, individual or political, would not qualify. Forms of relativism, materialism, versions of deconstructionalism become incoherent without atheism as their foundational principle. Still, trends of humanism stemming from non-Freudian psychoanalysis and hermeneutic methodologies are willing to find common ground with humanisms originating in one of the three major Western religions. In fact, these approaches to human sciences have often looked to the Eastern religions for inspiration. There is much to gain by a search for mutuality in categories.

Acceptability for the basal categories then, is the key to dialogue for the philosophical anthropologist who is also Christian. Here, we take our lead from the tremendous interest in the notion of guilt, even in non-theist ethics, and link it with the fairly novel thematic of gratitude. We have two ideas available for analogical application at varying levels; we find in sum a context for the desired dialogue.

Roger Wescott, a physical and cultural anthropologist, was the first to isolate the unique roles both guilt and gratitude play in a descriptive profile of human nature, although the psychotherapist Melanie Klein had discussed gratitude as foundational in the 1930s.[1] We learn that the human life form is the only one with innate notions of moral boundary, and awareness when this is violated.[2] When the self is the violator, guilt must ensue. Some understanding of what violation of boundary means, not only for actions but also feelings, such as envy, is universally found in human culture with various formats. Gratitude is similarly a universal human experience, an irresistible and spontaneous reaction to any unwarranted benefit. If some theoretical anthropologies insist that guilt is always pathological, no theory could possibly dispense with gratitude in the same way. Wescott's work on this issue is more substantial than the philosopher might first realize. It is difficult to isolate any mode of behavior, individual or social, unique and universal to the human species. Yet in identifying guilt and gratitude as behaviors, let us use this term to satisfy the behavioral scientist. Intimate to the human person, Wescott does not suggest any relationship between them. For him these are not polar opposites nor expressions of some more fundamental structure.

The significance of the doublet is nevertheless the theme of a recent study of the present moral crisis in Western civilization by Joseph Amato.[3]   For this Christian moral philosopher, primitive man's experience of chronic scarcity is the origin of gratefulness for whatever is available. By extrapolation, this becomes gratitude for whatever is, in a sense, for Being. Amato traces the presence of this posture in Western consciousness, or more precisely in Western conscience, down to the eighteenth century.   In the social and political categories of the philosophers of the Enlightenment, gratitude is diminished into various forms of toleration. From that time onwards, acceptance of whatever is the life situation becomes merely bearing with situations which cannot be altered. In our times, this takes the shape of guilt before circumstances beyond our control. The individual experiences a sense of inadequacy in a mass society he neither controls nor to which he can contribute. The primitive human propensity for being grateful in a world of constant limitation has dissolved into a sense of modern society as unbearable. Amato's reflections on this situation constitute what he sees as the malaise of "contemporary conscience" in the West, and it is a largely pessimistic view of our present moral awareness. His anthropology is at best a tragic optimism. His vision resembles E. Mounier's personalism and Ortega y Gasset's critique of industrial society.[4]   It is noteworthy that Amato is able to rely on a veritable chorus of historians and philosophers, political and social commentators who affirm the confusion in the modern person's moral sense.   Guilt over unresolvable responsibility for situations we allow to continue, with even tacit approval, has become the offspring of Enlightenment toleration. Yet it is equally noteworthy that thinkers who have spoken in terms of gratitude rather than guilt in the post-Enlightenment period are few. Amato's chorus is one-sided.   Only G. Simmel, R. W. Emerson and the anthropologist Marcel Mauss see gratitude as equally significant.[5]

As a result, Amato can offer only a dichotomous model of humanity, a paradigm of tension between competing forces in contemporary moral consciousness. Thus for him "guilt and gratitude war within us, as well as the ambiguities . . . and contradictions that have formed around them." In the end, he argues, "if we are to have conscience, we must allow the claims of guilt and gratitude to struggle within us."[6]

174

Here at last we reach our own concern. Granting the centrality of both guilt and gratitude in the structure of human awareness, can this couplet be correlated, or at least brought into contact in some mode that will reveal these two dimensions of the person mutually enhancing each other? Are these moral tonalities to be seen only on a spectrum, and as polar to one another? Or could we more validly perceive them illuminating each other, and the relationship between them as creative rather than destructive, synaptic instead of tensive? This is the point at which the present paper joins the discussions of Wescott and Amato.

The origin of psychic guilt is usually discovered in primitive religion, in the same time frame as Amato finds the origin of gratitude. Guilt finds its way from there into Judaeo-Christian religion, and from there into psychology and with Freud, psychoanalysis.[7] Oddly enough, formal reflection on gratitude belongs to philosophy, not religion. Tacitus and Cicero address the concept as a problem of interpersonal relations, while for Aquinas gratitude is an issue of justice: recognition of a debt of gratefulness due another. Curiously, it is during the Enlightenment period, when the notion is undergoing transformation into toleration according to Amato, that philosophers directly focus on gratitude, giving it an importance in the moral life that a medieval Christian such as Aquinas did not grant it. For Hume, who had little use for religion, ingratitude is "the most horrid and unnatural of crimes" the individual can commit. For Kant, gratitude is a "sacred duty" (a substitute for communal worship?) and his *Lectures on Ethics* classifies ingratitude as one of the vices constituting "the essence of vileness and wickedness."

Today the secular humanist, whatever his views of guilt, will see the capacity to live in gratitude as basic to self-realization. Not to appreciate the benefit of life itself, much more the creative possibilities of living, would be seen as self-debasing. The theist does not tend to so value life as the object of gratitude that primary attention leaves the Giver of life. Here, as elsewhere in a discussion of guilt and gratitude, there is plainly room for accommodation on the side of both humanist traditions, theist and secular. What is undeniable is that every person has moments in life when gratitude arises spontaneously, a feeling due to some intellectual realization that one is the beneficiary of the good, the true, the beautiful. The experience of gratitude must be accounted for by both theistic and secular humanisms in a rational or philosophical anthropology. Sad to note, this task has only now begun, while the literature detailing guilt, either describing it or denying its validity at the individual and communal levels, is immense and growing.

One thinker both humanisms tend to hold in high regard is Martin Buber, who offered his description of man as "the being who is capable of becoming guilty *and* is capable of illuminating his guilt."[8] This effort at definition of the essence of human nature joins a long list of previous attempts to capture this elusive uniqueness, and each has value. But perhaps Buber's has more than many, especially if we interpose gratitude as the "illuminator." What else could uncover guiltiness if not gratefulness? Guilt needs gratitude to name itself, and gratitude discovers its own existence in the very effort to illuminate guilt. We need only return to the ancient myth of the Garden, where desire to know as God knows is the cause of guilt, where the self has become bifurcated in its new knowledge of ingratitude. The powerful first question of the Book of Genesis: "Where are you?" from Yahweh receives its proper response: "We knew we were naked, so we hid." This hiding self is not a *lost* self — a self unaware of its situation — but an illumined self, constituted as such by the memory of benefit; the Lord God would walk with man in the cool of the afternoon.

Even the secularist is willing to see in this text, a primitive articulation of human self-awareness, some profound insight into the human condition as both plight and privilege. Guilt must be the mundane or worldly experience of having fallen from some norm for existence. As experience, it is burdenness; it is self-enclosing and involves the need to hide or escape from the judging self. On the side of the illuminator, there is the experience of openness that gratitude always seems to supply. Gratitude "occurs" or suddenly arises within the self when the norm of life is unexpectedly, and undeservedly, expanded. When the ordinary notion of what is due the self by daily life dissolves, one is affirmed by the gesture of another that springs from no source in obligation, i.e. in justice, and from no reason that can be discerned.

If Buber's description of "grateful guiltiness" or illuminated guilt supplies us with a key to the relationship between the experiences, Heidegger has left us testimony of their mutuality in his writings. The younger Heidegger seems to celebrate gratitude in his image of *dasein* in the world, while after the War an older and perhaps guiltier philosopher attempted to illumine his own condition and that of modern man with darker themes, of which guilt seems the most prominent. Granting that there is difficulty in correlating all phases of his thinking, we still find

176

man "thrown" into a world, responsible for it although not its guardian, a role reserved for Being Itself. Does *dasein*, shining as light in a dark world/forest, experience guilt or gratefulness? Perhaps the different readings of Heidegger are possible because man is experiencing both. Perhaps Heidegger's thought is the articulation of the proper interaction of the two thematics. As a secularist thinker, his work often reverses the categories classical and Christian philosophy suggested for Being and the role of the human in a coherent world. This may well account for the strange sense of familiarity the classical philosopher and the Christian anthropologist discover in the Heidegger texts. It should be remembered also that his close friend Hannah Arendt is the thinker most responsible for current interest in the idea of collective guilt at international levels.

To conclude this introduction to our schema: how can the relationship of guilt and gratitude be visualized? Here Basave's work again provides initiative. It seems best to conceive guilt as a horizontal tangent, the daily experience of obligation and duty never perfectly fulfilled, intersected by the sudden risings of gratitude. We are, each of us, taken by surprise in the passage of routine existence when the completely unexpected, gratuitous gesture is done for us, on our behalf. This gesture can be as simple as momentary help from a stranger, or as complex as those often attributed to a transcendent Source, e.g., those William James describes in his *The Varieties of Religious Experience*. On this account, then, both guilt and gratitude are considered valid constants in human existence, each interpreting the other in a mode we can call, with Buber, "illumination." Our capacity to be grateful actually identifies our condition of guiltiness. We become able to name that capacity Buber merely points towards when he sees human existence as unique in its internal dialectic.

If definition of our two thematics is difficult, then description may suffice: guilt is the sense of being burdened by the self, while gratitude is a sense of being gifted by another self. These descriptions would meet requirements from some secular humanists as fundamental to a valid anthropology. Yet theists could choose to expand these categories in further, faith-based reflection.

Providence College,
Providence, Rhode Island USA

NOTES

1. Roger Wescott, "Of Guilt and Gratitude: Further Reflections on Human Uniqueness," *Dialogist*, 1970.

2. Melanie Klein, "Envy and Gratitude," variously collected.

3. Joseph Amato, *Guilt and Gratitude: A Study of the Origins of Contemporary Conscience* (Westport, CT: Greenwood Press, 1982).

4. José Ortega y Gasset, *The Revolt of the Masses* (New York: Norton, 1957).

5. Marcel Mauss, *Essai sur le don* (New York: Norton, 1967).

6. Amato, pp. 201-2.

7. Roger Smith, *Guilt: Man and Society*, anthology of Nietzsche, Freud, Buber, Mead, Burke and Arendt (Garden City, NY: Doubleday, 1971).

8. Martin Buber, *"Guilt and Guilt Feelings,"* 8. 22in Smith, op. cit.

THE PERSON'S VALUE CONFRONTED WITH DEATH

Kenneth A. Bryson

Our investigation into the religious view of death is guided by two fundamental assumptions. The first of these is that the Christian who follows the teachings of Jesus in this world will survive death and enjoy the vision of God in the next life. This assumption carries with it the beliefs that there is life after death and that the moral habits acquired in this life persist into the next life. The second assumption is that the world of things exists independently of either our sensations of the world or our intellectual awareness of the world. There is a basic givenness about things that commands a prediscursive, spontaneous assent in a theory of direct perception. No attempt is made to prove that things exist, or to investigate the epistemological paradoxes that arise from the attempts to prove the existence of things. There are those who doubt the existence of a world after death while continuing to espouse a belief in the existence of this world. There appears to be some inconsistency about this view. The existence of this world is indemonstrable, and yet it readily commands assent. We would expect those who doubt the existence of a world after death to begin by doubting the existence of this world!

Given the assumptions, then, of life before and after death, and of a continuity between both states, the aim of the paper is to examine the connection that exists between both states. Specifically, the paper examines the nature of our dialogue in being before and after death. For as long as we live, being's revealedness is grasped in a mode that is proper to the human condition as veiled in the garb of contingency. Human death, however, appears to be the condition for a metamorphosis in the nature of our dialogue in being as it emerges to absolute unhiddenness.

There are two radically distinct ways of examining the phenomenon of human death: the one from the point of view of the living, the other from the point of view of the dead. We term these the *existential* and the *ontological* perspectives, respectively. The majority of books or papers on death discuss death from the existential point of view. Heidegger's *Being and Time* contains 33 pages in which he introduces the phenomenon of human death as a possibility rather than an impossibility. The anticipation of our no-longer-being is made to function as an inspiration to make the best of the time allotted us. Sartre's views on death are in sharp contrast to this. He says that the anticipation of our no-longer-being cannot be made to function as a source of inspiration since we do not know the time or the manner of our death. Sartre appears to view death as being an event. Heidegger seems to think that it is a process. Sartre and Heidegger represent two conflicting views in a field of contributors that appears to be growing daily. In our time, the phenomenon of Palliative Care is receiving much attention, as is the general tendency of society as a whole to deny death. The ability of medicine artificially to prolong life indefinitely as well as the ever present threat of nuclear war have also given rise to new ethical questions. But these existential considerations shed no light on the character of death as such.

Can anything be known about death as it is to the dead? Do MacQuarrie's appeals to analogies, Tillich's discussions of the "impenetrable darkness of the no longer being" and Marcel's "relationships in mystery" provide an insight into the state of death? The difficulty is that there is no data on death as such. Death is not the kind of activity that we live to talk about. It is not an experience. While it is possible for me to imagine my own funeral, I do not expect to live through it. It seems inevitable that the discussion of death will take the form of death as it appears to the living. The Ontologists are asking the following kinds of questions: What is death like to the dead? What would the dead tell us about themselves if they could speak? Is death an experience? What do the dead do? Are the dead in some kind of state? The obvious difficulty with raising such questions is that we who are not yet dead are forced to use imagery or analogy to investigate what death is like to the dead. Is there a more direct route? Do the experiences of attending the dying shed light on this problem? It seems not. The clear thing about death is that we are never more or less dead. Attending to the needs of the dying may well remind and prepare us for our own deaths, but this is not a substitute for it. The expression "you look half dead" really means that you look to be well on with dying and not half living and half dead as such. It appears that dying and death are mutually exclusive concepts. If death is thought to be the absence of all life, the total absence of all activity, does the Ontologist examine what it is that we have when we no longer have anything, or what it is that we do when we no longer do anything? There is a certain madness about this line of inquiry.

The difficulty appears to arise from the point of view of conceptualizability and language. The statement death is the absence of life has nothing to do with the nature of death as such. Death as absence is a statement of privation with respect to the living not the dead. It says something about what death is like to the living; it says nothing about what death is like to the dead. Rather than investigate what one has when one no longer has anything, let us recognize that death is inconceptualizable. But this is not to say that we can have no insight into the nature of death. Given the truth value of the assumption that the Christian who follows the teachings of Jesus in this life will see God in the next life, there must be a connection, or continuity between both states of death. Saint Thomas Aquinas thinks that it is habit that persists from one state to the other. Those individuals that pursue the will of God in this life will, out of habit, seek to see God in the next life. The inconceptualizability of death is the gateway to the ontological issue and the metaphysical connection that exists between the two states of death. It leads us to the observation that the phenomenon of human death is to be *explained* rather than *understood*. The distinction between explaining and understanding something is critical. In the latter, the intellect comprehends the phenomenon directly in its essence, whereas in the former, the phenomenon is discussed in its relatedness to an antecedent sufficient condition. Explanation according to Leibniz and others after him consists in discovering the sufficient reason of a consequent from within the folds of an antecedent. The antecedent sufficient reason of consciousness is to be found within the folds of being's revealedness. Specifically, we concern ourselves with the nature of our dialogue in being. The issue of what death is like to the dead is not examined from the conceptual point of view but from the side of the objective correlate of consciousness. The ultimate root of the possibility of knowledge is not consciousness knowing being but being's revealedness of self to consciousness. We are immersed in the mystery of dialogue in being. The connection between being's disclosure of self and the subject's openness towards being forms a unit. What did Descartes find when he turned into the *Cogito*? He saw what he put there and not what was there. Having called all things into doubt there could be nothing left to safeguard the possibility of knowledge. Being and consciousness form an inseparable unit. The self does not exist abstracted from the objective correlate of consciousness. Death is not something that happens to consciousness abstracted from being but to consciousness in its relational existence to being. The revealedness of being is the objective correlate of consciousness. It is consciousness from the objective point of view. The revealedness of being contains within its folds the sufficient reason of the possibility of consciousness. The explanation of human death is traceable to an activity within the folds of being itself. The attempt to understand something of death from the point of view of consciousness led to the absurdity of the ontological quest, but the attempt to explain death from the point of view of the objective correlate of consciousness holds greater promise of success. In particular, it seems possible to argue that the sufficient reason of death can be traced to being's reclaim of revealedness. Death is at the place of a hardening in being in which the ultimate ground of the conceptual union is withheld. Death is at the place in being, bordered by nothingness, where revealedness suddenly becomes concealedness. It is a mysterious cessation in being in which the gratuitous (indemonstrable) disclosure of being is withheld. Whereas dying is the gradual estrangement of consciousness from being, death is being's refusal "to be" for consciousness. It is a metaphysical hardening of things in which the translucence of being acquires opacity and impenetrability. Death is a reclaim of being by being. It arises at the place of silence in being. Death is not the absence of life but the removal of ground in which the possibility of absence (or presence) arises.

Does this explanation of death enable us to establish a connection between the "before death" and "after death" state of the Saint? It is necessary, first of all, to turn our attention to the silence of being. What becomes of being's revealedness? It seems possible to suggest that being's revealedness will on occasion of human death emerge to absolute unhiddenness.

It may seem strange to argue to "the other side of revealedness" without understanding death, but the explanation of death suggests that the infolding of being's revealedness will result in a mirror image of revealedness rather than its annihilation. For those who might ask how this is possible, it is no more difficult to imagine a mirror image of revealedness than it is to assent to the givenness of being in this world. The existence of things is indemonstrable, yet it commands spontaneous assent. Two brief considerations are adduced for those who doubt the existence of this state. The first is that continuity is always presumed in logic. It does not seem possible to suppose that Divine Wisdom, having seen fit to create, would then proceed to annihilate all things. Matter as eternal is just as it has to be to satisfy the ways of human understanding. The second consideration has to do with the concept of annihilation as absolute privation. The explanation of death suggests that death arises on the occasion of the removal of grounds of the possibility of privation, not on the occasion of privation as such. To conceive of death as being absolute privation is to confound dying and death and to lapse into the ontological absurdity of inquiring into what remains when nothing remains.

The connection between the state before death and the state after death can now be made clearer. For as long as we live, we are affected by the contingent nature of worldly things. We are contingent beings and pursue truth on the installment plan. The human intellect sees that a course of action is good and the will gives the command to pursue it. But the human act is rooted in corporeity. Our vision of the Eternal is blurred by the garb of the temporal, and we sometimes mistakenly pursue a course of action that does not perfect us. But for as long as we live, the possibility of making amends exists. We correct ourselves and continue to perfect ourselves as we actualize our human potential for good. Our dialogue in being comes to an abrupt end at death. For the first time in our existence we can no longer repent.

How are we to make sense of the eternal, obstinate condition of the dead? It seems necessary to suppose that something radical happens to us in human death. But it does not happen without reference to the temporal scheme of things. On the contrary, the temporal life of the individual is what paves the way for eternal destiny. In order to explain the immutable plight of the dead it seems necessary to recognize that something profound happens at death. For as long as we live, our dialogue in being is veiled in the garb of contingency. We do good here and now in accordance with the perspicacity of the intellect and the determination of the will to pursue it. The human condition is such that we see the will of God obliquely. The revealedness of being and the acuteness of the human intellect *is* (they form a unit) clouded by the spatio-temporal character of the dialogue. But the nature of the dialogue must change at death. How else can we explain the obstinacy of the dead. It seems to us that the phenomenon of human death is the occasion for a metamorphosis in the character of our dialogue in being. If the dead are obstinate, it is because they lack no data. Human death, then, is an occasion for data input, an occasion in which being's spatio-temporal revealedness will emerge to absolute unhiddenness. It is the occasion for the individual's final insight and irrevocable decision to side with either God or the Fallen Angels.

The recalcitrant revealedness of being will, on occasion of human death, emerge to absolute unhiddenness. Such must be the knowledge of the Angels. Aquinas says that it is absolute. The Angel intuitively sees the end directly. How else can we explain the obstinacy of the damned? If the Demons do not repent, it is because they cannot. We must seek for the cause of this obstinacy in the condition of their nature or state.[1] The Demon lacks no data. The natural gifts of knowledge were not diminished in them. All of the data is eternally present to them.

There is a strict parallel between the plight of the Demons and the plight of the living who are damned. They are likewise obstinate in sin. For as long as we live, we are affected by passion and errors in judgment. We perfect ourselves inasmuch as we succeed in actualizing the unit we are. But for as long as our decisions are so affected, the obstinacy of the damned is unintelligible. We cannot suppose that the final decision to side irrevocably with either God or the Demons takes place on this side of death. We develop habits of that sort while we live, but our finite nature is such that we cannot aspire to it absolutely. And yet, how imagine God forcing us to make the decision before all the data that is required for the decision is made available? The soul's departure from the body is the fundamental psychological thing that happens to us. To suppose that our final decision is executed before this separation takes place is to impose a burden upon man that God did not see fit to impose upon His angels. Human death, then, must be an occasion for data input and for a final decision. This decision can only be made in the full intuitive disclosure of being's revealedness, in the after death state rather than in the before death state. This new view does not undermine the significance of the before death act. On the contrary, it recognizes that the moral habit that is acquired in the before death state will continue into the after death state. It recognizes, too, that the individual's dialogue in being is likewise continued in the after death state. But the fact that the possibility of repentance does not exist in the after death state also implies that the nature of dialogue is transformed. The objective correlate of the dialogue - being - will not be veiled in the garb of spatio temporality, but will emerge to absolute unhiddenness. The subjective correlate of the dialogue, consciousness, will not perceive truth piecemeal, but will emerge to full intuitive insight. Such is the knowledge of the Angels.

Is there a time lapse of greater or less duration in the after death state to allow for the final decision? It seems not. The individual's final decision does not take place in time. It occurs neither before death nor after death as such but in death. The dead are neither in time nor are they out of time. This is the plight of the living. It is a possibility that is removed on occasion of death. It is the occasion for a reversal from time into duration without extension. Everything is eternally present to the dead. There is no time after time, but there is eternity above time.

The condition or nature of the Saint persists from the before death to the after death state. But with this difference: Death is the final occasion for the Saint to submit his will to the will of God.

To summarize, we have suggested the following sequence from before death to after death: (1) the intellect's dialogue in being is veiled in the garb of spatio temporality; (2) human death is not the estrangement of consciousness from being, but being's refusal to be for consciousness; (3) being's refusal to be is not the annihilation of revealedness, but the occasion for a mirror image of revealedness; (4) being emerges to absolute unhiddenness; (5) the intellect's grasp of being emerges to full intuitive insight; (6) a final decision is taken; (7) the decision takes place in duration; (8) habit persists, condition or nature hardens; (9) the dead are obstinate as are the Angels and the Demons.

In conclusion, it seems that the sorts of things we encounter in the next world will be very much like the sorts of things we encounter in this world, but with this difference. The individual's dialogue in being will emerge from relative unhiddenness to absolute unhiddenness. We will see being as it is in itself, from itself, for itself. We will see being fully, at once, intuitively and not the bits and bites we grasp in the temporal horizon. The presence of God will become explicitly manifest in His effects. Those who habitually seek God in this life will enjoy the full vision of God in the hereafter. The life of moral habits in the concrete immediacy of the present is what pours the mould for this vision (or lack of vision) and tempers the soul's obstinacy in death.

University College of Cape Breton
Sydney, Nova Scotia, Canada

NOTE

1. St. Thomas Acquinas, *Summa Theologica*, 1, 64, 2.

THE CONCEPT OF SUBSTANCE AND LIFE PRESUPPOSED BY CHRISTIANITY

John A. J. Dudley

Christianity, as represented in the New Testament, presupposes the existence of two ultimate realities, a material reality and an immaterial reality. The theory that the universe can only be explained in terms of two ultimate realities will be referred to as dualism. Thus it will be argued that Christianity can only make use of a philosophical theory which is dualist.

Looking at the history of philosophy it is remarkable to discover that the only dualist Greek philosophers of note were Plato and Aristotle. Furthermore, since the time of Plato and Aristotle there have been few dualist philosophers of any consequence who have not based themselves on the two greatest Greek philosophers. From the point of view of the Christian philosopher, the dualism of Plato and Aristotle must therefore be of the most fundamental concern.

If, however, Christianity is compatible only with a dualist philosophy, and if the most noteworthy dualist philosophies are those of Plato and Aristotle, it still remains to be ascertained whether these dualist philosophies are compatible with Christianity or whether they require adaptation. A task of this magnitude cannot, of course, be undertaken in the space of a single paper. The present paper will, therefore, be restricted to a single point of fundamental importance. It will be argued that the metaphysics of Plato and Aristotle are unrealistic and that Aristotle's hylomorphic theory has remained unrealistic in the forms it has taken on in Thomism and other adaptations thereof. Given that Christianity requires a realistic philosophy as its basis, an attempt will be made to adapt the hylomorphic theory in such a way as to render it realistic and hence acceptable to Christianity.

The paper is divided into four brief sections. In Part I, will argue that the New Testament presupposes the existence of two ultimate realities: the material and the immaterial. Part II, traces the emergence of dualism with a view to seeing why Aristotle formulated the hylomorphic theory as he did and what is wrong with his formulation.

Part III, shows that Aristotle's theory of substance should be restricted exclusively to living beings. Finally, in Part IV, shows that for Aristotle himself the term substance is applicable properly only to that which possesses life.

Part I: The New Testament Presupposes the Existence of Two Ultimate Realities: The Material and the Immaterial

This section will be very brief, as it is maintained that the entire mainstream of Christian thinking over two thousand years understands an irreducible difference in reality between this world and the other world and between the material realities of this world and three immaterial realities, namely God, angels and the human soul.

In the New Testament, it is very clear that mention is made of a number of realities which cannot be explained in material terms. It is stated, for example, that in heaven "neither moth nor rust consumes.[1] In heaven human beings are like angels and there is neither marrying nor giving in marriage."[2] Again, it is stated: "Do not fear those who kill the body but cannot kill the soul."[3] Soul is a reality distinct from body and necessarily immaterial, as being imperceptible by the senses.

It is unnecessary to insist on the obvious and well-established fact that the New Testament thus presupposes the existence of both material and immaterial reality. It follows, then, clearly that only a dualist philosophy, i.e., only a philosophy which accepts the existence of both material and immaterial realities can serve as a philosophical basis for Christian thought. This fact is taken as the basis for the argument of this paper and understood as so basic as not to require further argument.

Part II: The Emergence of Dualism

This section traces the emergence of dualism with a view to seeing why Aristotle formulated the hylomorphic theory as he did and what is wrong with his formulation. For this purpose it is necessary to go back to the Pre-Socratics.

In the words of Aristotle, that which most of the Pre-Socratics investigated was the material cause.[4] By this statement Aristotle meant that matter in his theory of substance is the same kind of thing as Thales' water, Anaximenes' air, Empedocles' four elements and Democritus' atoms. However, although Aristotle equated the primary materials of most Pre-Socratics with his own theory of matter or the material cause, one does not have to look far to notice an important distinction between the theories of most Pre-Socratics and Aristotle's matter. The primary materials of most Pre-Socratics, such as water, air, homeomeria, and atoms, are claimed to be realities, whereas Aristotle's matter is an abstraction and by definition could never exist on its own. It is to be noted, accordingly, that the most important investigations of the Pre-Socratics are recognized by Aristotle as having led to his own theory of matter, which is one of the two constituents of his dualism.

To trace the origins of the second constituent of dualism, namely the reality of the immaterial, it is necessary to account first for the development of Plato's metaphysical theory. Without entering into detail, it may be said that there are some recognized influences on this theory. The first is Heraclitus' pessimistic observation that everything changes permanently on earth. Second, in Parmenides' theory of Being, change is impossible, because that which is is and cannot not be. Third, the Pythagoreans held to the eternity of the soul, which they took over from Orphism. Fourth, Anaxagoras admired the human intellect, which led him to set up intellect as the source of order in the universe. Finally, Anaxagoras struggled to express the notion of the immaterial.

As well as these influences, the causes which led directly to the establishment of Plato's world of Ideas may be said to be first his pessimism, his feeling that Heraclitus was right, that all things change and nothing remains the same, and second his insistence that science must be possible. If all things are changing and cannot form the basis of science, and if science must be possible, then there must be another world, which is also a real world, which is unchanging, which can be and is the basis of science. This other world which is real can only be immaterial, because it is precisely other than the material or changing world. Therefore, one might conclude that Plato is a dualist because he maintains that all of reality, namely this world and the world of Ideas, cannot be explained in terms of a single ultimate principle, but only in terms of two ultimate principles: the material, which is the basis of this world, and the immaterial, which is the basis of the other world. However, one cannot declare Plato to be a dualist without qualification, because precisely for Plato this world of permanent "becoming" lacks reality. There is an anomaly here, because, on the one hand, Plato maintains the unreality of this world, while, on the other hand, he treats this world in practice, i.e., when explaining it or speaking about it, very much as real. It may be said accordingly that Plato is rather a semi-dualist than a dualist in the full sense.

It was stated at the outset that dualism may be said to be the tenet that there are immaterial as well as material beings. For Plato man is a combination of these two ultimate principles. His soul is one of the Forms and is eternal both before birth and after death, while his body is a perishable being composed of earthly matter. Not all of the soul is eternal, however, but only the intellect or reason, the highest or most important of the three parts of the soul. The part of man which is chosen out as being immaterial and eternal is thus man's intellect, which is held to be part of the soul. The other two non-eternal parts of the soul are spirit or will and appetite.

The dualism initiated by Plato is accordingly a dualism of a very particular type. It consists of entirely rejecting the attempts by the Pre-Socratics to explain change in this world and claims that the other world is the real world, and it picks out the human intellect as being the one captive part of the other world which can be seen at work in this world.

If one turns, then, to Aristotle it is clear in the first place that he is apparently a dualist because he believed that two ultimate principles are necessary to explain the universe, namely form and matter. Aristotle's matter, like Plato's matter, has been seen to be the successor to the ultimate principles proposed by most Pre-Socratics. Like Plato's matter, however, and unlike the first principles of most Pre-Socratics, Aristotle's matter is not real, as it never exists on its own. It is a mere abstraction, which in combination with form is used to explain the universe. Just as Aristotle's matter is the successor to Plato's matter, so too Aristotle's forms are the successors to Plato's Forms. Aristotle saw that science was possible without duplicating this world. Hence he abolished Plato's second world of Ideas. However, when he combined each of Plato's Ideas with matter to make a composite which he called a substance, he declined to attribute any real status to form in the combination of form and matter. Thus, where Plato had maintained that a Form or Idea is real and immaterial, for Aristotle such form is neither real nor immaterial, with only two exceptions, namely the Unmoved Mover and, with certain qualifications, the soul.

Aristotle's theory of substance may in a sense be called the ultimate in chicanery, since he claims that the universe is real and made up of substances, but that every substance is composed of two unreal components, namely matter and form. If this were all Aristotle had to say, one would have to regard his system as brilliantly absurd, since there could be nothing more absurd than to claim that by combining two unreal components one could obtain a reality.

Thus, it has been seen that both Plato and Aristotle are dualists, but that their dualistic theories must be qualified in the case of Plato as only partly, and in the case of Aristotle as entirely unrealistic. Before making proposals to render these theories realistic, it is important to note first that both Plato and Aristotle are part of a tradition which goes back to two exceptional Pre-Socratics, namely Pythagoras and Parmenides, who may be held not to have investigated the material, but rather the formal cause, and hence to belong to a separate school of thought to that of the other Pre-Socratics. Thus the Pythagoreans held that all things are made of numbers. In histories of philosophy, attention is devoted to explaining how this is so. It is also pointed out that Pythagoras emphasized the formal cause, where the Milesians sought the material cause. However, the most astonishing aspect of the philosophy of Pythagoras is generally ignored: namely, that he was the first philosopher to state that the ultimate constituent of things, number, is an abstraction and is something which in the strict sense does not exist.

It is frequently held that Parmenides was the founder of metaphysics, since he was the first philosopher of being. If one accepts Aristotle's definition of metaphysics or first philosophy as the study of being-*qua* being, then this claim is doubtless true. However, looked at from a different point of view, Parmenides was doing something very similar to Pythagoras by holding that everything is "being." He was trying to describe everything in terms of something which for us is an abstraction and as such does not exist. It is a truism to say that everything that is, is. But things are not made of being, since being is an abstraction and does not exist.[5]

The line of thought followed by Pythagoras and Parmenides is doubtless made clearest by Plato who holds that the world around us is not the real world and that the real world, namely the world of Ideas, is imperceptible. Thus, this school of thought diverts attention from the world surrounding man to another world, a world of Ideas.

It is of the greatest importance to realize that Aristotle's metaphysics, which is usually taken as the basis for what is called realist philosophy in the traditional sense, is in fact no more realist than the philosophies of

Pythagoras, Parmenides and Plato. Thus, it has been seen that Aristotle's form and matter no more exist than Plato's Ideas. The adaptations of Aristotle's hylomorphic theory by Thomas Aquinas and other medieval thinkers also in no way contribute towards making the theory more realist, but rather simply add to the number of abstractions or unreal components in the theory. It is not the purpose of the present paper simply to reject Aristotle's metaphysics because it is not realist. Rather it is aimed first to reformulate the hylomorphic theory in realist terms, and secondly, by means of an examination of what Aristotle has to say about substances, to show that the proposed reformulation is in fact something which Aristotle himself supported implicitly.

Part III: A Reformulation of Aristotle's Theory of Substance

The account which has been given up to now has been historical. I come now to the fundamental reasoning of this article, which is speculative. Christianity requires as its basis a dualist philosophy, that is to say, a philosophy which believes in the reality of both material and immaterial beings. The only Greek philosophers of note to come close to believing in the existence of two ultimate first principles of all reality, namely a material and an immaterial first principle, were Plato and Aristotle. However, for Plato the material principle was not genuinely real, and for Aristotle — apart from the case of the Unmoved Mover and, with reservations, the soul — both the material and immaterial principles were abstractions and were real only in combination. The question then arises as to how to correct the lack of reality in these two fundamentally dualist philosophies. It may be asked: to what reality do Plato's and Aristotle's matter correspond? Here the answer is clear. They correspond to the first principles of the Pre-Socratics, and of these the most refined and sophisticated, as well as the latest in chronological order, was, of course, the atomic system of Democritus. The contemporary successors to the atoms of Democritus are then the ultimate principles of modern physics, which until recent times were in fact still held to be atoms, and have now been refined to even more elementary particles. It is of the greatest importance to emphasize that the ultimate particles of modern physics are realities, i.e., they really exist, and to this extent differ fundamentally from Aristotle's matter, which is an abstraction.

One may then raise the question as to what reality Plato's and Aristotle's forms correspond. Plato's Forms were of course full realities. However, they are open to the overwhelming objection that they involve an unnecessary duplication of the world. For this reason and for many others, Aristotle rejected Plato's theory of Forms. It has been seen, however, that Aristotle's forms are unreal, since they are abstractions and are regarded by him as realities only when combined with another abstraction, namely matter. There are, however, two exceptions. First, the Unmoved Mover is held by Aristotle to be a pure form and to be immaterial and a full reality. It can also be established historically that during most of his career Aristotle continued to hold with Plato that the soul is a full reality and a pure form.[6] Only at the end of his career, in the *De Anima*, did Aristotle reduce the soul to the status of an abstraction, as is the case of all other forms compounded with matter.

The indications are, then, that the material realities underlying Plato's and Aristotle's matter are the ultimate particles of modern physics, and the immaterial realities underlying Plato's and Aristotle's forms are God and the soul. But of the immaterial realities, God is unchanging and in no way compounded with physical particles. It remains, then, that only the soul is compounded with physical particles, namely the body. Hence the only occasion when two full realities are compounded is in the case of soul and body which make up a living being. If this theory is correct, then only living beings can be called substances, since a substance is a reality composed of two ultimate real principles, an immaterial principle and a material principle. All other Aristotelian or Thomistic substances, such as artifacts, must be held to be substances only by analogy. An artifact is something purely material, but has a form imposed upon it by man, not, however, a real or permanent form, but merely an idea in the human mind.

Part IV: For Aristotle Himself the Term Substance Applies Properly Only to Living Beings

The final section of this paper shows that the above speculation in regard to substance is one which Aristotle himself supported in his philosophy of nature.

It is to be observed that in a number of passages Aristotle states that substance pertains in the first place to living beings. Thus in *Metaphysics* Z, in his discussion of modes of generation, Aristotle writes:

> Processes of generation of natural things are those, the generation of which is from nature. That from which it occurs is what we call matter; that by which it occurs is some being which exists by nature; that which it becomes is a man or a plant or something else of this kind, which we most of all call substances.[7]

Thus for Aristotle a substance is in the first place a natural substance, and then in particular a living natural substance, such as a man, a plant or an animal. In the following chapter of the *Metaphysics* Aristotle again states that living beings are most of all substances.[8] In accordance with this view, he also gives animals as an example of his doctrine that for every substance that is generated there must be another substance which preexists it in actuality.

Again, in his account of nature in *Physics* II, i, Aristotle divides up the moving universe into that which is by nature and that which is due to other causes.[9] As examples of natural substances, he then gives animals and their parts, plants and simple bodies, such as earth, fire, air and water.[10] All natural beings are said to differ from non-natural beings by having within themselves a principle of movement and rest.[11] For Aristotle, therefore, the essential division of the moving universe is that between substances which have within themselves a principle of movement and rest, i.e., an internal purpose, and substances upon which movement or purpose is conferred from without.

The source of purpose conferred on substances from without is man. Thus the essential division of the moving universe is that between natural objects and artifacts. Whatever is not an artifact is a natural object. Aristotle classified living substances (namely animals and plants) and inanimate natural substances (e.g., the four elements) together. Both groups are natural beings, as both are said to have within themselves a principle of movement and rest.

It is significant, however, that the classification of animate and inanimate natural objects together caused difficulties for Aristotle. The difficulty arises from the notion that inanimate objects have a principle of movement within themselves. In what follows, an attempt will be made to show that Aristotle was aware of this difficulty and that in practice he associated nature primarily with living beings and then transferred the characteristics of living beings to inanimate beings in order to unify his view of the universe.

The first meaning of "nature" given by Aristotle in his list of the meanings of the term in the *Metaphysics* is the genesis of growing things.[12] Aristotle thus shows in this carefully drawn-up list that he is most conscious of the connection between nature and living beings. Again, at the start of the *De Anima*, where Aristotle deals with the importance of the study of the soul, he writes "It also appears that the knowledge of [sc. the soul] contributes greatly to the entirety of truth, especially to nature, since it is as it were the principle of living beings."[13]

Here too an association is made between nature and living beings. In *Metaphysics* Z, vii, in his discussion of modes of generation, Aristotle also gives living beings as an example of things generated naturally.[14] Such examples of living beings as exemplifications of nature occur very frequently, especially the example of man begetting man.

Again, in *Physics* VIII, iv, Aristotle clearly implies that his definition of a natural being is applicable primarily to living beings, and furthermore he implies that it does not fit in well with inanimate beings. In his argument that whatever is in movement is moved by something else, he writes that that which is moved by itself is moved by nature, and gives as an example any animal.[15] Again, he writes that of things which move naturally the clearest examples are those that are moved by themselves, i.e. animals,[16] thereby implying that it is not so evident that non-living beings move by themselves. Aristotle's greatest difficulty in the chapter in question is the explanation of how things can move naturally and yet be moved by something else.[17] In his argument, he writes of inanimate beings that: "It is impossible to say that they are moved by themselves; for this is an attribute of living beings and proper to those beings possessing soul."[18] Thus Aristotle clearly states that only living beings move themselves, a statement which apparently conflicts openly with his inclusion of inanimate beings as natural and yet possessing an internal principle of movement within themselves. He also adds the further argument which tells against the inclusion of inanimate objects as natural, namely that, in his view, that which moves itself is capable of standing still and of moving in the opposite direction to its natural place.[19] A physical object by definition has an internal principle of movement and rest. Hence fire, if it were moved by itself, ought to be able to both stand still and to move downwards. Thus in this passage Aristotle effectively refutes his own inclusion of inanimate objects in his definition of a natural object.

Thus it would appear that for Aristotle the concept of nature is in the first place applicable to the living world. The concept appears to have been applied by him to the heavenly bodies by extension on the basis that these are also living beings. If one may speculate as to why Aristotle considered inanimate beings to be natural, two answers seem possible. First, his division of the world was essentially that between the products of art or human free will and the products of nature. Whatever was not produced by art was accordingly classified by Aristotle as natural. Second, Aristotle was possessed with the idea of final causality and the unity of the universe. By means of the notion of natural place, he thought he could harmonize inanimate beings with animate, since inanimate beings could then also be said to have a natural movement. The natural movement of both inanimate and animate natural objects could then be said to be an imitation of circular movement and, in this way, all movement could be harmonized under the final causality of the Unmoved Mover.

It has been seen, accordingly, that there is a tension in the works of Aristotle between the desire to regard all beings as substances and the recognition that only living beings properly fulfil the definition of the natural being or a substance. A further explanation of this tension is possibly an element missing in Aristotle's understanding of substance and likewise missing in his account of time in *Physics* IV, xi-xiv. This element is that in the sublunar area, a substance, to be a substance, must be in a process of constant change and at the same time retain its identity. Thus man is in a process of constant change, and yet is aware throughout his life of being the same person. All living beings possess this sameness in the midst of change. Artifacts and inanimate beings, however, have no principle of permanency in the midst of constant change. Thus it is known that every particle of the human body is different every seven years and yet the person is the same. But one could not say of a table or a stone, when every particle had been changed, that it was the same table or the same stone. Accordingly artifacts and inanimate beings are substances only by analogy, to the extent that their permanence, relative to the duration of human life, makes them significant to man. It is precisely this intuition which is implicit in Aristotle's account of substance and nature in spite of the tension which it causes with his desire to unify the universe by regarding inanimate beings as substances on a par with animate beings. It has been seen, accordingly, that the speculation in regard to the real meaning of substance, which was set out in the last section of this paper, is one which is confirmed by Aristotle himself through a strong tendency within his philosophy of nature.

Conclusion

In this paper it has been maintained that Platonism and Aristotelianism must inevitably be of the greatest interest to the Christian philosopher, since these are the only Greek philosophies, and are among the few major philosophies of any era, which hold that the universe can only be explained by means of two ultimate principles, namely the material and the immaterial. The difficulty with both Platonist and Aristotelian metaphysics, however, was seen to be that neither is fully realist, since Plato's matter is unreal and Aristotle's form and matter are unreal except for the Unmoved Mover and, with certain reservations, the soul. Nonetheless, one could render Platonic and Aristotelian matter realistic by replacing it with the ultimate particles of modern physics. Of Plato's Ideas and of Aristotle's forms, the two full realities agreed on by both philosophers are, on the one hand, the supreme Being (the Idea of the Good or the Unmoved Mover) and, on the other hand, the soul. If, then, the term substance is to be reserved for a reality, and if a substance is a composition of two ultimate principles, namely a formal and a material principle, then only living beings are substances, since they alone are composites of two realities, namely soul and body. Finally, it is precisely this intuition which is latent in Aristotle's philosophy of nature.

The advantage of regarding substance as applicable only to living beings is not merely that of rendering Platonism and Aristotelianism realistic. It is to be considered above all to be of major importance in emphasizing that life is something fundamentally different from that which is inanimate. Because of Aristotelianism based on the *De Anima*, as found in Thomism, for example, living beings have been considered to be substances composed of form and matter like all other substances on earth. It is of the greatest importance to regard soul in a living being as a reality and hence as something fundamentally different from all other so-called forms in other Aristotelian substances. It is only by regarding the soul as an immaterial reality that the value of life, especially human life, can be maintained in an era when life is threatened. And again, in an era of naturalism and materialism, it is only by regarding the soul as an immaterial reality that it is possible to maintain the supernatural destiny of man in an immaterial world after death.

Catholic University
Nijmegen, Netherlands

NOTES

1. Mt. 6, 20.

2. Mt. 22, 30.

3. Mt. 10, 28.

4. Aristotle, *Metaphysics* A(I), 983 b 6-8; 984 a 16-18; 988 b 22-23.

5. It might perhaps be thought that Anaximander was doing something similar when he went behind the phenomena and posited his "Unlimited" as the source of all things. However, it seems likely that Anaximander's "Unlimited," although not perceptible to the senses, was nonetheless conceived as a body, a neutral body from which the extremes of fire, water etc. were sifted out. Thus to posit that Anaximander was doing the same as Pythagoras and Parmenides would appear to be an anachronism.

6. John A.J. Dudley, *Gott und Theoria bei Aristotles, Die metaphysische Grundlage der Nikomachischen Ethik* (Frankfurt a.M./Bern: 1982), pp. 57-9.

7. *Metaphysics* Z(VII), vii, 1032 a 15-19.

8. *Metaphysics* Z(VII), viii, 1034 a 4.

9. *Physics* II, i, 192 b 8-9.

10. *Physics* II, i, 192 b 9-11.

11. *Physics* II, i, 192 b 13-14.

12. *Metaphysics* (V), iv, 1014 b 16-17.

13. *De Anima* I, i, 402 a 4-7.

14. *Metaphysics* Z(VII), vii, 1032 a 23.

15. *Physics* VIII, iv, 254 b 14-17.

16. *Physics* VIII, iv, 254 b 27-8.

17. *Physics* VIII, iv, 254 b 33-255 a 5.

18. *Physics* VIII, iv, 255 a 5-7.

19. *Physics* VIII, iv, 255 a 7-10.

PART IV

METAPHYSICS OF THE PERSON

ON RECOGNIZING THE MYSTERY OF THE SOUL

Thomas A. Michaud

The Irony and Challenge of the Copernican Revolution

A frequently proffered claim is that the Copernican revolution, including its Galilean developments, overthrew the Medieval Christian anthropocentric orientation. With the Copernican/Galilean discoveries, humankind lost its literal cosmic centrality, and, it is said, also lost its privileged status as the axiological center of the natural universe. However, the historical irony which this claim fails to recognize is that *the* principal thematic orientation for all of the philosophical and scientific movements which emerged in the post-revolutionary Modern era was nothing but anthropocentric. Both Rationalism and Empiricism explicitly designated their philosophical and scientific starting points as the study of human being such that "man" was indeed hailed as the measure, the focal point of reference, for all things. Descartes' Rationalism, for instance, posited that the only certain basis for knowledge and for reconstructing all of the sciences was the human *cogito*. Hume, although certainly not enamored of most of the desiderata of Rationalism, clearly propagated Rationalism's anthropocentricity with such mandates as, "As the science of man is the only foundation for the other sciences, so the only solid foundation one can give to this science itself must be laid on experience and observation."[1]

No, the Copernican revolution did not expel the Medieval anthropocentric orientation; it reappraised and leavened the significance of that orientation. Nevertheless, it was with the Modern's reappraisal of anthropocentricity that there was indeed a challenge issued to the Medieval Christian views.

As the last phrase of the above-cited directive from Hume implies, modern anthropocentricity evolved a predominate emphasis on the empiricistic approach. Investigations of human being found their paradigms in the cause/effect, empirically verifiable sorts of mechanistic principles that Galileo and Newton unreservedly ascribed to the universe

204

at large. The challenge to Medieval Christian anthropocentricity was, of course, a metaphysical one. The Empiricists, and their kindred successors the Positivists, refused to accept the existence of the human soul with the properties of intellect and will. They denigrated such a conviction as emerging from naive religious sentiment, without any verifiable bases, and, thus, a pernicious superstition which should be exorcised. To be sure, currents of a secular type of humanism flowed through such Modern attitudes, but to the dismay of those who still maintained certain Medieval Christian convictions, Modern humanism was bereft of any metaphysical bases. Without affirming the spirituality and consequent metaphysical value and dignity of the person, Modern humanism, the believers fearfully charged, was founded upon sand and subject to dissipate into views which would ultimately erode if not flatly deny the profound, sacred value that should be accorded to persons. And, unfortunately, 20th century developments have shown that such fears were not at all gratuitous.

The reductionist materialism of Hobbes, the psychological behaviorism of Hume, the physiological mechanisms of Harvey and Galileo have indeed developed into views which patently devalue the human person in that they consider persons as nothing more than organic machines functioning within a clockwork universe, perhaps the most complex machines in that universe, but machines nonetheless. Skinnerean psychological behaviorism, Wilsonean sociobiology, social Darwinism and certain forms of dialectical materialism all demean the value-status of persons by proclaiming that all human behaviors are reducible to and fully explainable as the mechanistic cause/effect operations of physiological processes. Any value attributed to persons excludes any profound, sacred significance and is merely of the order of the kind of value one might place on a highly sophisticated, multi-faceted and virtually irreplaceable computer.

For the contemporary Christian philosopher, the challenge posed initially by the Copernican revolution clearly persists. How in the face of proliferating physiological reductionisms can the Christian philosopher aver that the human person, as a union of body and soul, is, thereby, in possession of a fundamental spiritual worth? How can the Christian philosopher in the context of a culture which admits only empirically verifiable explanations *reasonably* maintain a belief in the human person as a union of body and soul, as a metaphysically free being, as a being whose dignity is ultimately rooted in its spirituality?

These questions are truly some of the most critical issues confronting the contemporary Christian philosopher. How they are dealt with will significantly determine the vital longevity of the Christian perspective in the contemporary world.

The Mystery, Not Problem, of the Soul

A possible, reasonable way in which the Christian philosopher can confront contemporary objections to accepting the person as a union of body and soul has been offered with Gabriel Marcel's well-known distinction between problem and mystery - a distinction which can be aptly characterized as a variation on the Kantian phenomenon/noumenon distinction. Like Kant, who insisted that certain metaphysical issues, viz., the existence of God, the actuality of human freedom and the reality of the immortal soul, were of noumenal status and not explicable by reason, Marcel maintained that such issues are not solvable by reason as problems, but should be acknowledged as mysteries.[2]

In elaborating his problem/mystery distinction, Marcel introduced a corresponding distinction between primary and secondary reflection. Primary reflection is characterized as intellectualizing thinking which seeks objective and universally valid solutions to all philosophical issues. It pursues verifiable knowledge to resolve issues, i.e., knowledge which can be proven to be definitely certain through logical/theoretical "scientific" demonstrations. Secondary reflection, in contrast, does not aim for such verifiable knowledge, but is our contact with mystery. It arises when primary reflection hits a dead end, when the problem-thinking of primary reflection cannot locate an objective, universally valid answer for an issue. Secondary reflection then recognizes that the issue should not be considered as something *before us* as a problem, but as something *within us* as a mystery, a mystery in which we participate, and through secondary reflection's non-intellectualizing, intuitive "knowing," of the mystery, our lives are made more meaningful. Such "knowing" Marcel emphasizes, is not an empty, vague feeling, but is and should be aided by conceptual processes of explication. This explication does not yield verifiable knowledge but does engender a knowledge which serves to illuminate our lives, make our existences more intelligible and understandable.

The first important lesson the Christian philosopher can glean from Marcel's problem/mystery descriptions appears in his very specific articulation of the way in which an issue originally broached as a problem reveals itself as a mystery. Marcel states that a "mystery is a problem which encroaches upon its own data, invading them, as it were, and transcending itself as a simple problem."[3] What Marcel means here is that an issue should be recognized as a mystery when the problem-thinking approach begins to fold back on itself in that the very principles, the data, the approach employed to frame and solve the problem preclude the possibility of reaching an objective solution.

For Marcel, like Kant, one of the fundamental mysteries of the human being is the existence of the soul which in union with the body forms the person. By acknowledging Marcel's identification of the person as the mysterious union of body and soul, the contemporary Christian philosopher can receive reasonable support for believing in a spiritual soul and, thereby, for confidently asserting that the human person is endowed with a sacred dignity. The exact way in which such support would be forthcoming would be, with Marcel, to show why the issue of the existence of the soul, the human person as a union of body and soul, is one which defies problem-thinking attempts at denial or confirmation insofar as such attempts self-defeatingly fold back on themselves. Moreover, again with Marcel, the Christian philosopher can further support a belief in the person as a union of body and soul by conceptually articulating the ways in which human behavior can and should be understood in light of this mystery.

As indicated earlier, physiological reductionism presents a very serious challenge to the contemporary Christian philosopher. Rejecting the existence of a soul, or what in this context should be more appropriately termed as a non-physical intentional mind or consciousness, the reductionists assert that any human behavior can be fully explained by the cause/effect functions of its component parts. That is, for every behavior there is a specific identifiable physiological cause which makes that behavior occur. The problem, as the reductionists see it, is simply to identify the cause, and thereby, the behavior is explained and understood. But are such identifications really possible for *all* types of human behaviors? In fact, the reductionists are not capable of logically maintaining their cause-identifications and their claims fold back on themselves.

Consider the common behavior of raising one's arm which can be performed for a variety of intentional purposes such as waving, signalling a vote or indicating a desire to ask a question. According to the reductionist, there would have to be a different physiological component in each one of these apparently identical actions, and these different components would be the functional causes of the different intentional purposes of the actions. But, to press the reductionist, one need only ask what causes those different components to function in the first place. To maintain his position consistently, the reductionist would have to respond that yet another component causes the previously identified component to function. Still, again to press the reductionist, one need only ask what causes those newly cited components to function.

Without pressing further, it should be clear that the reductionist cannot successfully identify some first, primary physiological cause for such an intentional behavior. The reductionist, with his principle that for every effect there is an identifiable cause, fetters himself by extending *ad absurdam* his chain of causes. And, with such a result the reductionist certainly cannot be accepted as offering a final objective demonstration of his claim.

But, on the other hand, is it possible to demonstrate and/or explain objectively the Christian view that the human person is a union of body and soul? The most common approach which aims to do so follows a Cartesian line of dualistic causal interactionism. Cartesians categorize all existents as either physical or spiritual substances.[4] The human person, however, is said to be a being composed of body, a physical substance, and soul, a spiritual substance. Now, what arises as the crucial problem for the Cartesian is to explain somehow logically his claim that in the human person there is causal interaction between body and soul.

The reason why this problem presents itself is because of the Cartesian's conception of causal action. Employing a mechanistic understanding of causality, the Cartesian asserts that just as one moving billiard ball strikes another ball causing that ball to move, or just as very strenuous exercise causes fatigued muscles in the human body, so too does the soul cause events to happen in the body and *vice versa*. But as Descartes himself at least implicitly recognized, there is a difficulty in maintaining that a spiritual substance can cause events to happen in a physical substance and *vice versa*. The difficulty is simply this: How can a spiritual substance causally impact a physical one when logic would dictate that a spiritual substance would pass right through a physical one and *vice versa*, just as a poltergeist is said to pass right through physical objects, e.g., doors, walls, human bodies, or have physical objects pass right through it? In other words, is it reasonable to maintain that the causal interaction between body and soul is just like the mechanistic causal interaction between physical substances?

As indicated, Descartes was at least tacitly aware of this problem, but his resolution makes his position fold back on itself. In order to explain the causal interaction between body and soul, Descartes conjured up entities which he designated as animal spirits. These entities apparently had the remarkable capacity of metapmorphosing, when appropriate, from physical to spiritual substances or *vice versa* and thereby mediated the causal interaction between body and soul. More specifically stated, the animal spirits when in a spiritual state could be causally affected by events in the soul and then could metamorphose into physical substances in order to transmit the message they causally received from the soul to the body. Or, in a physical state these entities could receive causal input from the body and then by metamorphozing into spiritual substances, they could cause the soul to receive the input that the body originally impressed upon them.

However, given Descartes', or any Cartesian's, basic principle that all existents are physical substances, spiritual substances or composites, it is logically inconsistent to invoke entities which *in themselves* are capable of being physical *and* spiritual substances. Such entities just could not be admitted in a Cartesian universe without contradicting the basic categorization of existents with which the Cartesian begins.

Still, regardless of the problem of conjuring up such entities as animal spirits, a Cartesian position ineluctably hits a dead end. Any claim that there is causal interaction between body and soul when the concept of causality, insofar as it is understood in the Modern era, implies a mechanistic sort of operation cannot be logically explained. The problem of showing how a spiritual substance can in a mechanical way causally interact with a physical substance is insurmountable. Hence, Cartesian dualisms have not and will not solve the issue of the human person as a union of body and soul.

Since neither reductionism nor a Cartesian type of dualism yields a final, objective resolution of the issue, acknowledging the issue as a mystery, as Marcel recommends, becomes the only sensible recourse for the Christian philosopher. Recognizing that the issue is not amenable to any sort of problem-thinking solution and accepting that intuition and belief are the only reasonable ways to affirm that the human person is a union of body and soul becomes *the* alternative. However, in following Marcel, the Christian philosopher can articulate his belief through conceptual processes of explication. Secondary reflection's intuitive apprehension of the mystery can be intellectually unpacked (an effort of primary reflection) by formulating certain principles with which human behavior can be understood and made intelligible as the behavior of a being which is a union of body and soul.

Articulating the Mystery of the Soul

The most fundamental principle for understanding human behavior as the behavior of a spiritual and physical being is that human behavior is the behavior of an embodied consciousness.[5] What this principle implies is that in order to understand a behavior, it should be investigated in terms of two aspects, its physiological aspect and its mental (consciousness) aspect. However, to attempt to reduce one aspect to the other, or to explain "objectively" how the mental causally interacts with the physical would be to adopt a problem-thinking approach which, as was shown above, would eventually fold back on itself. A human behavior should be examined as a complex, an integrated whole of mental and physical aspects, while admitting that the precise way of integration is an inexplicable mystery.

This holistic approach can be further illumined by specifying two propositional guidelines. First of all, it should be recognized that physiological processes are necessary conditions for, but insufficient explanations of human behavior. As *embodied* consciousnesses, human persons are incapable of performing mental acts if they lack the appropriate physiological bases. For instance, one cannot calculate trigonometric functions or write a philosophical essay if one's brain is anesthetized. Or, one cannot simply will to run a marathon successfully if one's heart and muscles are not in fine tone. However, to ignore the mental and to explain behaviors exclusively on the basis of the physical would be insufficient as was evidenced by the dead end which reductionists encounter.

Secondly, it should be acknowledged that mental processes are characteristic aspects in, but insufficient explanations of human behavior. Any attempt to explain human behavior exclusively on the basis of acts of consciousness would also be grossly inadequate. As embodied consciousnesses, our physical and mental aspects are "intervolved" in our behaviors. Our mental acts involve certain specifically related physical processes such as neuro-chemical patterns, regional functionings of the

210

brain and even genetic codings. To refuse to admit such involved physical processes when explaining human behavior would be to "detotalize" the human person, to render an account which does not encompass the totality of the human being.

Summary and Conclusion

With the recognition that the issue of the person as a union of body and soul is a mystery, the Christian philosopher can reasonably assert his belief in the profound sacred value and dignity of the person. Such reasonability, as has been detailed in this paper, is ultimately derived from the fact that neither reductionism nor Cartesian dualism can offer an objective, universally valid demonstration of their claims. These problem-thinking approaches prove to be impotent when broaching the issue as to whether the person is an entity with spiritual and physical aspects. And, because they do prove to be so ineffectual, it is then reasonable to affirm that the spirituality or non-spirituality of the person is a mystery which cannot be unraveled. Moreover, because the issue does disclose itself as a mystery, it is again reasonable for the Christian philosopher to express confidently a belief that there is a spiritual dimension to the person. This confidence can be further bolstered by showing how, as was done in the previous section of this paper, one can fruitfully investigate human behavior while respecting the belief that there is a spiritual, mental or consciousness aspect to the human person.

With accepting mystery and eschewing self-defeating problem-oriented approaches, the Christian philosopher can clear reasonable room to insert his belief in human spirituality and consequent metaphysical value into the contemporary world. A recommendation of the acceptance of mystery may perhaps disturb some, but until it is acknowledged, it is unlikely that the Christian philosopher will uncover any other way to proclaim reasonably his belief in the person's spirituality and sacred dignity.

Wheeling Jesuit College
Wheeling, West Virginia, USA

NOTES

1. David Hume, *A Treatise of Human Nature* (Oxford: Oxford University Press, 1968), p. xx.

2. This discussion of Marcel's problem vs. mystery distinction is based on Gabriel Marcel, "On the Ontological Mystery," in *The Philosophy of Existentialism* (Secaucus, NJ: The Citadel Press, 1973) and *The Mystery of Being*, vol. 1: *Reflection and Mystery* (South Bend, IN: Gateway Editions, 1980).

3. Marcel, op. cit., p. 19.

4. This presentation of the Cartesian line of thought is primarily based on Rene Descartes, *Discourse on Method*, Part V and *The Passions of the Soul*.

5. This term "embodied consciousness" has widespread use in phenomenological philosophy. Maurice Merleau-Ponty, Stephan Strasser, William Luijpen among many others have employed it.

A PHENOMENOLOGICAL AND CLASSICAL METAPHYSICS OF THE PERSON: COMPLETION AND CRITIQUE OF ARISTOTLE'S METAPHYSICS

Josef Seifert

The nature and greatness of man is intimately connected with his ability to engage in metaphysical inquiry. We could speak of a constitutive metaphysical character of human nature which is expressed in Max Scheler's assertion that man possesses *Welt* (world), the animal only *Umwelt* (surroundings). Man is related to the world as such precisely by being open not only to certain limited categories of being but to being-qua-being, as Aristotle says who, in fact, defines metaphysics as the science of being-qua-being.[1]

In reflecting on this definition given in his *Metaphysics*, we encounter at least four different possible interpretations of being-qua-being as object of metaphysics.

First, being-qua-being can refer to the most universal principles and features of being which constitute a bond of unity among all things. Subjects of metaphysics as general ontology are particularly the first principles of being, that of contradiction, of identity, of excluded middle and of sufficient reason. Medieval philosophy later added the immensely interesting discourse on the transcendental properties and pure perfections of being which are not limited to single categories of being.

We can understand by being-qua-being, secondly, the distinct categories and fundamental divisions which are characteristics for being as such. There is a third way of interpreting being-qua-being as that which possesses the character of being in the most proper and paradigmatic sense: the model-case of being. Finally, there is a fourth way of interpreting being-qua-being to which we shall return at the end of this paper.

Metaphysics, inasmuch as it investigates being most properly speaking, was identified by Aristotle as "ousiology," as the science of substance. Without any doubt Aristotle has made an extremely important contribution having shown that there are some things, such as color, which can only be *in* something and have accordingly a heteronomous

214

mode of "being," whereas there are other more foundational entities, which exist in themselves, in the sense that they are not attributes and properties of another thing. A being which simply possesses *esse* (existence), not only *in-esse* (existence in), Aristotle and Aquinas respectively call *ousia* and substance. Yet while discovering philosophically substance and the true ontic superiority of substance over accidents, Aristotle failed by not going sufficiently beyond this point. As we shall briefly indicate in the following, the question about being in the most proper sense necessarily involves us in an investigation into being as person. Metaphysics should be defined more deeply than "science concerning substance" as "science concerning person."

But how and why should this be necessary? Is a person not also a substance? If we readily grant this, one could say that Aristotle's definition of metaphysics as the science concerning substance already includes metaphysics as science of the person but is broader than "personology." Yet one forgets in such an objection that, while the features of substance are common to persons and to non-persons, an investigation into the most proper meaning of being must not stop at this more general level. On the contrary, it must proceed to ask the question whether all substances possess the general features of substance in the same degree of perfection and whether, furthermore, there are not, among the features peculiar to some substances, only such properties which lift these above and beyond all other entities. Specifically, we shall ask whether the essential marks of personhood endow the person with being in a more exemplary sense and with a greater dignity than any non-personal being.

Metaphysics as Personology

Now we shall not investigate, in this paper, the extremely intriguing question as to whether each of the seven characteristics which Aristotle ascribes to substance is embodied on the level of personal being in a fundamentally superior mode and sense. We have done so elsewhere.[2] Rather we shall try to test our claim that metaphysics ought to be better characterized as personology than as ousiology by investigating the criteria which Aristotle presupposes for making the judgment that substance excels over other categories of being and embodies the *ratio essendi* in the most proper sense.

Autonomy and Self-Possession of Being Through
Consciousness + Cognition

Aristotle explicitly mentions that substances are "being" most properly speaking for the reason that they exist autonomously and possess an autarchy of being. Now, the autonomous character, the self-standing, accrues to the substance-qua-substance simply from the fact that it does not inhere in another thing but constitutes a certain end-point in reality. For this reason the substance possesses its own being more properly than accidents which inhere in substance. But one brief philosophical glance at the nature of personal consciousness, at human cognition and self-knowledge, reveals that the person possesses his own being in an incomparably superior sense to the one which is exemplified in the substance-qua-substance. For in knowledge the spirit possesses the beings of the world rationally, through consciousness and cognition. Compared with this form of possessing being, non-rational substances do not "possess" any being at all. Least of all can they possess their own being in the most proper sense, while they not even know it, nay, in many cases have no inkling of it. The person, by consciously living his own being and by being reflectively conscious of himself, possesses his own being in a unique mode.

Moreover, *knowing oneself*, as Augustine has shown in his version of the *cogito*, surpasses unreflected consciousness of self and involves *cogitatio*, intentional cognition and even the self-possession of knowing oneself with indubitable and infallible certainty. Through the cognition of himself the person more truly "is" and possesses his being in a mode to which the mere self-possession of the substance-qua-substance must be compared as a non-possession of being. In and through consciousness and cognition, "being" becomes present to itself, discloses itself, is spiritually and really possessed in a unique way, compared to which any mere ontic substantial self-possession of being-as-such is like non-possession and alienation of being. For this reason, a definitively non-conscious mode of existing would amount to the person being deprived of existence, to annihilation. So profoundly is the self-possession in consciousness linked to ontic possession of one's own being.

"Being" in things and plants is external to itself, has not returned to itself, does not possess itself. Here lie important insights of German idealism which can be perfectly liberated from the subjectivist connotations and implications they have in Hegel or Schelling.

Do we deny the importance of the objective substantial nature of the person by emphasizing consciousness? Not in the least! The subject who is conscious of himself experiences and knows himself also as substance. The self-standing of the substance is fulfilled, not cancelled on the level of the person. Only the person is an "I" and therefore subject and substance in a far more precise and proper sense than "things." This becomes even clearer when we consider freedom.

Autonomous Self-Possession of Being and Freedom

An entirely new mode of personal self-possession occurs in and through freedom. A substance which is determined by its own nature and by causes extrinsic to itself, such as the stone or the tree, does not truly possess its own being. Only in and through freedom, in virtue of which acts proceed from the spontaneity of the self and are truly dependent on the free self and determined by it, does the person possess himself. Only in and through freedom, the person shapes his own being, determines, governs and possesses it. In our time, in the work *The Acting Person*,[3] Karol Wojtyla, as philosopher, has elucidated these great insights of Stoic and medieval philosophers (particularly Augustine, Anselm, Bonaventure, and Duns Scotus) who have achieved the philosophic discovery of personhood and freedom.

When we consider the heteronomy of any being which is not free but determined by forces outside of itself, it becomes quite evident that in freedom we find a unique mode of possession of one's own being. This self-possession of the person is something immensely great, not only because it makes history and culture possible but also because it allows the person to become morally good and freely to bring acts into existence which would not exist without the free subject who possesses his own being in a most marvelous sense. But the same freedom which allows the person to possess himself and to bring about moral goodness also makes it possible for the person to lose himself, to throw himself away and to auto-destruct himself through moral evil. Only in virtue of his freedom, man is able to bring about a metaphysical disharmony which expresses itself in the phenomenon of guilt. While animals do not possess themselves, they cannot lose themselves like a free agent.

Axiological Dimension of Personal Self-Possession

The unique self-possession of the person through knowledge of the world and of himself and through freedom involves also an important axiological dimension of self-possession. In general, it is not most profoundly being-qua-real and the mere act of existence which make a thing possess its own being. Only the dimension of value and goodness gives the being its *raison d'etre* and thus makes it good that a being exists. The value and dignity of being account for an axiological self-possession, however, which is equally overlooked in Aristotelian *Metaphysics* and calls for a further dimension of *metaphysics* as *agathology* or as science of the metaphysical role of the self for the self-possession of being.

A being possesses its own being, in the axiological sense of the term, to the extent to which it not just "is" but might, axiologically speaking, just as well "not be." Or consider even the case of a person for whom it would be better that he were never born because he is forever afflicted with pain and moral evil. Only the good, and most of all the good person, possesses his own being in the axiological sense, because the good alone sits, as it were, on the throne of the justification of his own being. The good alone and most of all the person, in virtue of his dignity, combine being as reality of his being with the *justification* of being. Therefore Nietzsche observes rightly that the most terrible nihilism is not the cancellation of all being but real things deprived of goodness, value, and purpose.

In this light, it becomes apparent that the person-qua-person, being capable of knowing and freely partaking in the good and realizing it, possesses an inalienable dignity which makes the violation of the person, the free acting against the person, morally evil and throws light on the agathological dimension of ontic self-possession of being.

Completion of Aristotelian Metaphysics Through an Agathology of Accidents and of Freedom

Another completion and critique of Aristotelian metaphysics is called for at this point. Aristotle explicitly excludes an ontology of accidents from metaphysics. However, the person does not possess his dignity primarily in virtue of his substantial being as such but through the right use of his freedom. This deeper value, which involves another dimension of the self-possession of personal being, is achieved not primarily on the level of the substance of the person as such. We must consider here an insight of Thomas Aquinas, which Thomism normally gives very little weight to but which cancels the Aristotelian restriction of metaphysics of being in the proper sense to ousiology: namely the insight that while the being of a thing derives primarily from its character as substance, its goodness derives primarily from the *actus superadditos*, from the accidental order. For we do not call a man primarily good because he exists or is a man, but in virtue of his good acts and habits.[4]

In the person, however, these accidental reasons for the goodness of the person do not depend, as in aesthetic objects, on forces and powers outside the entity itself which bears value. Rather, in the person the deepest actualization of the value and axiological self-possession of being and of the *raison d'etre* for being is tied up with personal freedom, without the cooperation of which that most profound actualization of self, which occurs only in the goodness of the person, is impossible. Hence we must distinguish that axiological self-possession of being which is inseparable from the character of a person endowed with inalienable dignity, and that deeper axiological self-possession which is tied up with the right use of personal freedom.

To see that the axiological dimension of self-possession of being is achieved through accidents and in the person through freedom demonstrates another weakness in Aristotelian metaphysics. Aristotle, as is well-known, explicitly rejects the idea that the study of accidents as such belongs to the subject matter of metaphysics. In fact, he says that metaphysics must be defined as ousiology also in the sense that there cannot be a metaphysical science of accidents. If we recognize, however, that the deepest level of axiological self-possession of being is inseparable from freedom and from those ontic accidents which are, however, in no way accidental or non-essential for the actualization of the being of the person but have the utmost importance for it, we then recognize that a study of the good and of "accidents" belongs definitely to metaphysics. Thus metaphysics may still be defined as *ousiology* but not to the exclusion of *symbebekotology* and of *agathology*.

Personalistic Completion of Aristotelian Metaphysics as Aitology

There is still another consideration in the light of which we may see that metaphysics as a science of being, in the most proper sense, can only be fulfilled through a metaphysics of the person. I refer to another definition which Aristotle gives of metaphysics when he calls it aitology (the science about ultimate reasons).

Everybody is acquainted with Aristotle's distinction of four different kinds of causality. He says that the question about the ultimate reasons, conditions and causes of things, the question about the principles which explain being, can refer to four and only to four different kinds of cause: the material cause or that out of which something is or becomes; the formal cause as the form and essence of a thing which Aristotle deems to be the supreme cause; the efficient cause or that through which something is or comes about; and the final cause as that for the sake of which something is or becomes.

Now it could be shown that each one of these causes requires, in the last analysis, an ontology and metaphysics of the person, in order to find an ultimate explanation. Let us consider just efficient causality and final causality, in order to demonstrate this point. As Kant has shown in the third antinomy of pure reason, efficient causality without reference to freedom is ultimately entirely inexplicable. For if a cause "A" exists and unfolds its causal power only in virtue of a dependence on cause "B," and "B" only in virtue of "C," and so on, the explanation of the chain of causality will eternally be incomplete. For only if there is some absolute beginning of efficient causality, only if there is a cause which is not, as Augustine puts it in the fifth book of *The City of God*, only efficient to the extent to which it is effected, but more than that, i.e., in an original grounding way, will there be an answer to the question as to why there are efficient causes at all and as to which is the ultimate cause of things. Yet such a cause, which is not determined extrinsically but which proceeds spontaneously from the agent, is only realized on the level of personal being and in freedom. For this reason, efficient causality remains entirely inexplicable without reference to freedom as its absolute beginning.

We must also not be misled by Kant's view that efficient causality, simultaneously with requiring it, contradicts freedom, in which contradiction Kant sees the third antinomy of pure reason. A careful investigation may bring out the fact that only if we absolutize "efficient causality in accordance with laws of nature," as Kant does, and take it into the definition of causality that one event must follow upon another one, according to a general law, only then does the universal principle of causality appear to negate freedom. If we recognize, on the contrary, that efficient causality by its essence only involves that one being come about *through* the power of another, then it emerges that "efficient causality in accordance to general laws of nature" is only one type of causality, such as when an event "A" determines an event "B," the movement of a billiard ball "A" determines that of a billiard ball "B," in accordance with some general laws of nature pertaining to motion and inertia in material objects. But the mere fact as such that "one" event "B" is causally dependent on another event "A," through the power of which it comes about, does not "universally" involve such a dependence on laws of nature. On the contrary, we may see that a classical case of efficient causality is found wherever the agent truly causes the event; and this is only achieved fully by causality through freedom.

Not only would efficient causality remain entirely without explanation, if we were not to take into account personhood and freedom as important metaphysical notions of a metaphysics as aitiology. Rather, causality through freedom is also the archetypical instantiation of causality. The nature of efficient causality, that which is meant by saying that one thing is *through* another, emerges in an entirely new and more perfect way only on the level of the free personal act. Only here it is fully *through* the free agent that something is, only here the pure character of the relationship of "A" being *through* the power, activity and agency of "B" is realized. For this reason, only here do we find an agent or subject in the full sense of this term, rather than an anonymous cause. Only here do we find an *aitios* (a personal cause) rather than a mere *aition* (an impersonal cause).

Final causality remains entirely inexplicable without reference to the person. For final causes do not possess any causal power in and of themselves, in sharp contradistinction to efficient causes. Rather, the purposes and end which presuppose in most cases the value and meaning of a thing, the final cause, "for the sake of which" that thing is, unfolds its crucially significant causal activity only in and through the mediation of persons, through the cognition of persons, who understand values and turn them into ends and goals, and through the freedom of persons, who alone can order means and direct them to the realization and actualization of ends.

Seen in this light, the modern dispute as to whether we might eliminate final causality altogether from the explanation of value (impossible as such an attempt proves in biology, as recently Reinhard Low and Robert Spaemann have proven)[5] has its root precisely in an impersonalistic metaphysics. In Aristotle, who denies that the absolute first mover be efficient cause of the world and claims that he is only a final cause, final causality does not become intelligible. For how should the end-qua-end determine anything at all? It can do so only if a personal efficient cause *understands* the end and *acts for the sake* of it. For this reason, finality and meaning in nature give witness to a personal ground of the world. Thus finality must be rejected by an atheist metaphysics and even by Aristotelian metaphysics. Although it recognizes the influence of intelligence, it does not provide a sufficiently deep metaphysical understanding of final causality, which could render the latter's efficacy intelligible, because it lacks a grasp of efficient causality in terms of freedom. The dependence of final causality on personal agents may be one of the reasons why in modern science a war is being fought against the existence of final causality, although each organ and each function of organs which the biologist or doctor explores, prove the presence and crucial role of final causality in nature. Inasmuch as final causality appears not in nature but in the human world, and ends determine the actions of architects, doctors, authors of books, actors, craftsmen, in fact of any human agent, the evident link of final causality to the person becomes even more apparent.

The personalistic structure of final causality or the necessary link of final causality to the person emerges ever so clearly through another consideration. We call the directly and freely intended object of human actions the *end*, the *finis operis*, and we speak also of the subjective purpose of actions, the *finis operantis*. The essential end of human action embodies quite another sense of end than the purpose to which, objectively, means are directed without involving a conscious directedness. This new meaning of end reveals, however, that the ultimate character of an end and of a purpose is essentially related to the person. The purely ethical and anthropological sense of the end or purpose of an action is unthinkable outside of the sphere of consciousness and freedom. Only the freely intended object of the moral act as such, and the reason of it as intended, can be called the *finis operis*. All other finality outside of personal action presupposes, in order to become intelligible with respect to the finalistic order of means and ends, a person's intelligence and action. Thus a penetration into the *actus humanus*, or into the relationship of all finality to the *actus personalis* and its essential end, would reveal even more clearly the need to complete the Aristotelian metaphysics of the *aitiai* through a metaphysics of the person.

Still another reason can be named why only a metaphysics of the person can complete metaphysical aitiology. If we consider things carefully, we find on the level of the person other and new types of causes which have no analogue outside of the sphere of personal being. Think of the dependence of the act of knowledge on the object known. The object of knowledge is not just the efficient cause which produces knowledge in the person. This emerges from the fact that it "produces" cognition essentially necessarily through the medium of consciousness. It brings about the act of cognition by revealing itself to consciousness and by engendering knowledge in and through the essentially conscious contact between subject and object. Any interpretation of cognition as a mere instance of efficient causality would destroy knowledge because it would precisely omit consideration of the intentional and cognitive relation itself. It could never explain why the mere result or causal effect of something would be similar to the cause, let alone know the cause. Without explaining this any further, we now turn to a final reason why metaphysics, and precisely classical and Aristotelian metaphysics, calls for a completion through a metaphysics of the person.

Metaphysics of the Person as Completion of Metaphysics of Pure Perfections

One criterion, which Aristotle fails to mention, could be developed, taking our starting point in the medieval metaphysics of pure perfections. Anselm made the tremendous metaphysical discovery that there is a radical distinction between two kinds of properties and perfections. Some perfections are such that we may say it is absolutely better to possess them, or to be them, than not to be, or not to possess them. Thus being itself, unity, value or goodness (bonum), beauty, and others are such pure transcendental perfections.

Anselm contrasts these in the fifteenth chapter of the *Monologion* with those perfections which were later called mixed perfections and which are perfect only *secundum quid* and in some cases only. Thus to be gold is possibly to be the most perfect form of a metal but by no means a pure perfection. For it limits that which possesses it to a relatively inferior form of being. For this reason, to be human or to be a spiritual substance, which clearly excludes being gold, is more perfect than the highest splendor which is possible within matter but which necessarily presupposes materiality and its limitations.

Without investigating the difference between pure and mixed perfections any further, we might introduce as an important criterion of perfection whether a being possesses pure perfections which not all other beings likewise possess. Now if it can be shown that the specifically personal properties, in particular consciousness, knowledge and freedom, are pure perfections, then it can be shown that the person is being in a far more perfect sense than any other substance and that metaphysics must necessarily be also metaphysics of the person. If it becomes clear, moreover, that countless other personal qualities such as wisdom, justice, faithfulness, happiness, love and others can be realized only in persons and are simultaneously pure perfections, then it becomes evident that a whole host of pure perfections, which to possess is absolutely better than not to possess, are necessarily tied to personal being. Yet if this is so, it is entirely clear that any metaphysics which is not also and in a primordial way metaphysics of the person, is gravely deficient.

Metaphysics as Personalistic Theology

Aristotle defines metaphysics also as theology, as the exploration of absolute divine being. If there are truly many pure perfections which to possess is absolutely better than not to possess and which are simultaneously necessarily personal, then it also becomes clear that there is a further reason why metaphysics and metaphysics of the person are inseparably tied to each other. For as could be shown, all pure perfections admit of absolute infinity and in fact are only truly themselves when they are free of the limitations which we encounter in their worldly embodiments. If this is true, it is also clear that the absolute and divine being which is the supreme object of metaphysics can only be understood when grasped as a personal being. For if personal perfections are absolutely better than any mode of their non-possession, including any form of attributes which are incompatible with them, then it is also clear that God, as the supreme and absolute being, must be a personal being. That this metaphysical insight ties in with so many other central issues of metaphysics and renders an ontology of the person indispensable for metaphysics can no longer be shown in this essay. It could be brought to evidence, however, that the very contingency of the existence of the world and many other facts would remain entirely without metaphysical explanation if the absolute, divine being were not free and freely creating. For an absolute being which is and acts by necessity could, as Parmenides has already recognized, never bring about contingent, becoming, temporal being. Thus the *raison d'etre* of being, the question "why is there something rather than nothing?" which constitutes another central entrance door to metaphysics, could never be answered without reference to a personal being who provides the ultimate explanation to the question "why?" Thus we may have received a glimpse of the fact that Aristotelian metaphysics must both be criticized and perfected by means of a metaphysics of the person.

International Academy of Philosophy
Furstentum, Liechtenstein

NOTES

1. Adolf Reinach, *Was ist Phänomenologie?* (München: Kösel, 1951); Dietrich von Hildebrand, *What is Philosophy?* (Milwaukee: The Bruce Publishing Company, 1960); Josef Seifert, *Erkenntnis objektiver Wahrheit: Die Transzendenz des Menschen in der Erkenntnis*, 2nd ed. (Salzburg: Universitätsverlag A. Pustet, 1976); Seifert, *Back to Things in Themselves: A Phenomenological Foundation for Classical Realism* (London/ Boston: Routledge and Kegan Paul Press, 1987); Seifert, *Verso una Fondazione fenomenologica di una Metafisica classica e personalistica* (Mailand: Centro di Richerche di Metafisica, Vita e Pensiero, 1987).

2. Joseph Seifert, *Leib und Seele. Ein Beitrag zur philosophischen Anthropologie* (Salzburg: Universitätsverlag Anton Pustet, 1973); see also of the same author, *Das Leib-Seele-Problem in der gegenwärtigen philosophischen Diskussion. Eine kritische Analyse*, 2nd ed. (Darmstyadt: Wissenschaftliche Buchgesellschaft, 1987).

3. Karol Wojtyla, *The Acting Person* (Dordrecht/Boston: Reidel, 1979).

4. Thomas Aquinas, QDV q. 21 a. 5) where he speaks of contingent beings and goods saying:

> . . . aliquid dicitur esse ens absolute propter suum esse substantiale, sed proper esse accidentale non dicitur esse absolute . . . De bono autem est e converso. Nam secundum substantialem bonitatem dicitur aliquid bonum secundum quid; secundum vero accidentalem dicitur aliquid bonum simpliciter. Unde hominem iniustum non dicimus bonum simpliciter, sed secundum quid, in quantum est homo; hominem vero iustum dicimus simpliciter bonum . . . non perficitur nisi mediantibus accidentibus superadditis essentiae. . . .

5. Reinhard Löw, *Philosophie des Lebendigen* (Frankfurt a.M.: Suhrkamp, 1980); R. Spaemann/R. Löw, *Die Frage wozu. Geschichte und Wiederentdeckung des teleologischen Denkens* (München: Piper Verlag, 1981).

HUMAN DIGNITY AND SELF-CONSCIOUSNESS ACCORDING TO MICHELE FEDERICO SCIACCA

Francisco L. Peccorini

> What a piece of work is man! How noble in reason! How
> infinite in faculties! in form and moving, how express and
> admirable! in action how like an angel! in apprehension, how
> like a god! the beauty of the world! the paragon of animals!
> (*Hamlet, Prince of Denmark*, Act II, Scene II)

Shakespeare, in order to describe the paroxysm of Hamlet's depression by showing that not even man's beauty can lift his spirit, ponders human greatness in the above quotation. He presents us with a select list of human actions that find no equal in other creatures (not including angels, of course, who surpass men in perfection) and somehow bring us closer to God. And rightly so for there is nothing that makes man more similar to God and in a true sense to his son as the human spirit, which constantly reflects its face on our self-consciousness; and because if there is anything that our spirit can be proud of, it certainly is the infinite reach of its actions, which determines its dignity and its rank among spiritual beings. However, Shakespeare did not give us the reason why man can attain a nobility so worthy of respect. Fortunately, Aristotle had put us already on the track to such an excruciating question.

It is a well known fact that Aristotle, in his *De Anima*, falls prey all of a sudden to a seizure of childish babbling, for lack of adequate terms, to describe the nature and the depth of the human soul. Furthermore, in addition to this difficulty, we his readers have suffered the consequences of a defective translation of the most significant passage, which turns the soul into a mere field for the action of two independent faculties of which one shows all the traits of an immortal entity, whereas the other appears to be no more than a transitory and temporal power. Moreover, even if we eliminate such a problem by means of a new translation that I am about to propose, the depth of the mystery remains and still keeps the great Stagirite puzzled.

228

Let us first accept the principle that whatever is said by Aristotle about both the possible and the agent intellects is to be referred to the soul, which is the only agent that works through those powers, which, in turn, are but ways of acting belonging to the human subject. In order to establish this principle better, let us propose a new translation such that in it, the case in which the articles preceding those names are found be taken into consideration. In particular, let us note that they are not in nominative — indeed, if they were, then each one of those faculties would be principles of different actions — but in dative (which is the ablative of the Greek language), thereby pointing to faculties which are but instruments of one and the same subject. This yields the following picture:

> Since just as in the whole of nature there is something that is the matter of all and every genus (that which is all of them in potency) and something else that is the cause and the effective principle, whereby nature produces everything, and which behaves towards the former as the act does in regard to the material, so also and by necessity the same distinctions hold true within the soul. For there is first that mind whereby [the soul] becomes all things, and there is also that mind whereby [the same soul] makes [actually intelligible] all [the potential intelligibles], and this is a positive state, such as light.[1]

In the foregoing text the following ideas stand out: just as in the external world nature is a principle of determination of matter, in like manner the soul does not operate through the agent intellect as an efficient cause but rather as a determining principle. But by the same token the soul, in its capacity as the possible intellect, must offer a corresponding aspect of indetermination that may be able to lend itself to the determining action that the very same soul is called upon to exercise on itself in its capacity as the agent intellect. On the other hand, the soul cannot be a "thing," i.e., it cannot be tied up to one particular nature, precisely because it is the possible intellect. "It is necessary," says Aristotle, "for the mind not to be mixed with anything, since it is capable of thinking of everything; as Anaxagoras puts it, such is the condition for the soul to be in control, that is for her to be able to recognize things since the least thing that would show up in her makeup would be an obstacle and an impediment."[2]

But, if such is the case, the following question arises: is the soul, which is neither this, nor that, nor anything else, pure nothingness? It is here that Aristotle brings in a middle term which is both unique and indescribable, but most of all full of unheard of consequences which must be analyzed most carefully. "It ensues from this," says the Stagirite, "that [the soul, in its capacity as possible intellect] cannot have another nature but to do what it is doing." In the remnant of the quotation Aristotle does not only affirm the soul's spirituality while denying that it is a thing, he does also confirm the conclusion that we had reached at the end of our own translation, namely, that it is the soul that works through the agent and the possible intellects. It reads:

The part of the soul that is called mind (and by mind I mean that by means of which the soul thinks and judges) is not anything that actually exists before it thinks. Hence it would be pure nonsense to suppose that the soul and the body make up a mixture, because if they did we would not have to say that the soul is of a determinate kind — hot or cold — or, that at least it enjoys an organ as the sensible faculty does, which is false.[3]

The preceding unique *status* of the soul prompts a "riddle" which is most fascinating and, certainly, for a hypercritical objective mind, most intriguing: what can that be which is such that things cannot become actually intelligible unless they identify themselves with it, and yet itself is neither this, nor that, nor anything else? The least that one can say is that being endowed with one of the most outstanding powers of *Initial Being*, namely, the power of being the source of intelligibility for anything that "is," it might as well stand as the surrogate of Being, if need be. Furthermore, such a reality does not only share with Initial Being the power of founding intelligibility: just as Initial Being, it cannot either reach its own total actuality unless it identifies itself with the divine actuality and behaves as God's mind, which contemplates the Objective Being in its inexhaustible actuality; "human mind," the Stagirite tells us, "cannot be fulfilled with this or that particular thing; only a totality which is the supreme good and is different from anything else, can really satiate it." And he adds: "and such is also the way in which the subsisting thought that thinks itself behaves eternally."[4] No wonder that in his opinion the mind deserves the adjective "divine" while it is thinking. After all, as Aristotle tells us textually, ". . . the intellect is the natural container of the actually intelligible substance, without the actual possession of which it will never be able to reach its own actuality."[5] The soul, then, in her capacity as the possible intellect, is Being itself knowing itself, but only as *Initial Being*, which means that such a knowledge takes place in time.

St. Thomas points out that same characteristic when he tells us that "if the agent intellect presented to us Being in its total objective actuality instead of giving us only *Initial Being*, the soul would know all things at once and thus she would not operate as a possible intellect."[6] It follows, therefore, that Aristotle does indeed affirm without any hesitation that the human soul is an entity with a natural capacity such that in it *Virtual Being* can be present to itself as *Virtual Being* and that, consequently, in it all things can appear actually intelligible in time in the same way in which words can progressively appear in a *tabula rasa*. This, of course, is a mystery that entails a dignity almost infinite in man.

If I have dwelt on the exposé of Aristotle's sentence, it was because the latter, in its capacity as a precedent of Sciacca's position, is likely to enable us to accept the latter without disturbing misgivings. Besides, let us not forget that Sciacca himself went through agonizing pains until he finally adopted such a thesis. The following question that he formulated to Father Bozetti, in his capacity as the top authority in Rosmini's philosophy, surmises the crisis that he endured. The question itself points in the direction of the ontological knot that Aristotle showed in the junction between the soul as the seat of Being's existential subjectivity and Being as object. "In sum," he writes, "the light of Reason winds up being both at once, object and light of Reason. Yet, whereas in its capacity as object, such a light is not one thing with Reason. As a constituent of its essence it is indeed inseparable from it. Query: how can light be at once the object and the form of Reason?"[7]

Bozetti's answer — namely, that such a light is immanent insofar as it is a function of Reason, but transcendent as Reason's essential object — was not satisfactory on the grounds that in it the "subjectivity" of light did not come out in the right light. It is all the more so if we take into consideration the emphasis placed by Bozetti on Being insofar as it constitutes the other millions of human beings in exactly the same way and at the same time that it constitutes me. Fortunately, Sciacca managed to eliminate such an "Avicennian" bent by focusing his attention on the Idea insofar as it is both at once, *manifesting*, through its constitutive work on the soul, and *manifested*, in the same intuition of Being that constitutes the subject.[8] In a memorable article that he wrote in 1955 in the *Revue de Metaphysique et de Morale*, Sciacca sheds further light. Taking off from the same difficulty that he had objected to in Bozetti, and that Rosmini had already acknowledged explicitly — namely: "How can the same reality be both at once the form of the act of knowledge and the form of the knowing faculty?" Sciacca introduces a pertinent distinction: "Insofar as it is *manifesting*," he says, "[the Idea] is called *form of the soul* on the grounds that without it the soul would not be a soul and, by the same token, the cognitive faculty would not be such. On the other hand, insofar as it is *manifested*, it is called the *form of knowledge* because, as such, it constitutes the object of knowledge and, by the same token, of whatever is objective and formal in any act of understanding."[9]

But from this to the Aristotelian position there was only one step, and apparently Sciacca took it. Indeed, the Professor from Genoa could not justify the combination "manifesting-manifested" without resorting to the consciousness of the self. On the other hand, such a consciousness, in his view, could be only the consciousness that Being enjoys of himself insofar as *here and now* it is being perceived by Peter's and John's minds. As individual thoughts, therefore, Peter and John are but appropriations of Initial Being insofar as the latter is the subsistent subject. Sciacca tells us "Such is the reason why self-consciousness is the primordial and originary determination of . . . the pure intuition . . . of the subsistent existential Being."[10] It should be noted that as much as this may seem scandalous and unbelievable, the common sense alternative is not Sciaccan at all.

Indeed, if the subject of self-consciousness were only the soul *as an individual entity*, the following text would be absolutely meaningless: ". . . self-consciousness discovers and reveals the Being of all things within the order of Being, which constitutes self-consciousness as an objective interiority because it is present to it in its infinite extension."[11] If, on the contrary, such a subject is Being knowing itself, everything falls into place. By definition, indeed, self-consciousness must bear directly and exclusively on the subject; on the other hand, though, such an act consists in a direct intuition of Being as Idea. It follows, therefore, that according to Sciacca the subject of self-consciousness and the Idea are one and the same reality. In other words, objective interiority, i.e., the Idea, inasmuch as it is actually being intuited, cannot correspond to any other agent but Initial Being. It is, therefore, a case of Being knowing itself; and it is quite normal that self-consciousness should be able to discover and reveal the Being of all things within the order of Being.

Furthermore, the following paragraph, in which it is said in an Aristotelian vein that when the understanding knows an object, it becomes that object in the sense that the latter begins to enjoy the actual intelligibility of the subject, makes full sense. Indeed, if self-consciousness is Being itself in its actual intelligibility, nothing stands in its way towards being the subject to which Sciacca is referring when he writes: "Self-consciousness turns into the known thing, i.e., it gives itself to it in order to take hold of the object, and it takes hold of the object by giving itself to it in order to be able to know it as it is in itself in the light of Ideal Being, i.e., in the light of objectivity by means of which it is itself constituted as self-consciousness."[12]

But Sciacca seems to go farther than Aristotle in connection with the question on which the whole Aristotelian theory rests — which he answers explicitly in contrast with Aristotle, who answered it only implicitly — namely, "Why is the soul's gift of actual intelligibility to the object, by means of which the latter can be known, so effective a gift?" In the following quotation Sciacca explains very clearly that it is Being itself that gives itself and undergoes a process of transformation in the soul as in a stage, the very same Being which is conscious of existing through its own self-consciousness, which is the feeling of existing pure and simple, i.e., the existing of Being itself. This clearly confirms the Aristotelian theory insofar as it extends to the fundamental act of knowledge, which is the very intuition of Being, the general rule stating that to know is to become the object: "But before the objective interiority transforms itself into the known thing," he says, "it converts itself into the Being where it is rooted, i.e., into the subject of which it is the interiority and which is interior to it as the feeling of its own existing and thus it becomes consciousness of itself, a synthesis between the objective interiority (the intuition of Being as Idea) and the subjectivity"[13] — and, we might add, a subject actualized with the actuality of Initial Being.

Sciacca is most careful to assert unequivocally that the "I" that knows is Being in its totality. This prompts him to state, in almost Marcellian terms, that self-consciousness includes also the consciousness of the world, or the consciousness of my being in the world. Indeed, he says, the fundamental total feeling is "a primary experience, which is immediate and complex — although it is not yet an objective or reflective experience — it is a vital experience of the whole man and of the universe in its totality."[14]

Under the circumstances, then, we must say that to be a human being amounts to owning a nature (or a degree of participation in Being), such that whoever is endowed with it is automatically "equipped" to share in the self-consciousness of Being if only Being's presence is granted to it, or to put it otherwise, that it is automatically equipped to lend itself to Being's takeover so that Being may know itself, although finitely and in time only. But this prerogative, which constitutes human dignity, is exclusively a human prerogative, as can be seen from the examination of the three following hypotheses in which the objective presence of Being encounters different responses. In the first place, if Being presented itself objectively to a rock, the rock, which lacks a "possible intellect," i.e., a capacity of becoming everything, would not even realize such a gift. If Being did the same thing in regard to a dog — dogs do also lack a possible intellect although they have what we might call a "possible sense," if we were willing to extrapolate the semantic power of words a little bit — the dog would not grasp *intellectually* the presence of Being as Being, but it would realize it *sensibly* — and in fact does so since it feels the attraction of certain beings and runs away from others, thereby carrying out its vital animal activity.

Finally, human beings, who even before the constitutive intuition of Being, do already possess a nature that we might call a possible intellect *in actu primo remoto*, will automatically start to enjoy the self-consciousness that belongs to Being in its existential respect as soon as Being is presented objectively to them. If such a condition takes place, which is the case as soon as objective interiority is granted when man is constituted, man's possible intellect passes automatically from the state in which he was *in actu primo remoto* to his permanent state of *tabula rasa*, in which he is already *in actu primo proximo* in regard to all possible acts of knowledge.

Being, therefore, is not only in us as an "*actus essendi*"; it does really "inhabit" in us as an infinite subject who knows and loves himself in our soul in a finite and temporal way. According to Sciacca, by "existing" through the soul, Being constitutes man into a *triadic* being, which naturally reveals the Divine Trinity by means of a very imperfect analogy with the Father (Being knowing infinitely), and the Son (Being actually being known infinitely), and the Holy Spirit (Being actually being loved by the Father and the Son), which is faintly visible in it. Our natural makeup does, therefore, surmise a forthcoming dwelling of the Divine Trinity based on grace, which, in turn, is called upon to transform itself into the eternal union by means of the *lumen gloriae*. Consequently, the very fact that we enjoy such a direction enhances our dignity to inconceivable heights; and it is this destination of our nature to be united with God that Sciacca calls the *trinitary* character of men. Of course, it goes without saying that if our soul, in its capacity as possible intellect or subject, were not Being knowing himself in a finite and temporal way, such an analogy would not exist and therefore man would not enjoy a *trinitary* Being.

In fact, though, our nature is already of itself a natural revelation of our vocation to a mystical and supernatural union, the possibility of which looms already in the existential presence of Being which grace is only called upon to intensify. "Insofar as he is a triadic being" — says Sciacca — "man constitutes the proper object of ontology or speculative anthropology; but if we take into consideration the revealed datum of the Trinity, it is possible to discover at any time in its triadicity a very imperfect connection . . . of an analogical participation in the Trinity, and as a result its triadicity winds up being trinitary. Consequently, when God later on unites himself in a formal manner to the creature, not indeed anymore through the divine operation of creation, but by means of Grace, human action is suddenly lifted up to the supernatural order and the divine Trinity unites itself to the intelligent being through its three Persons."[15] In other words, the magic bridge had been there all along from the outset in the very *nature* of the soul, all set to cooperate with the Grace.

St. Thomas Aquinas did not overlook it in the thirteenth century. He reasoned as follows: since man includes a divine element in his very natural constitution, it is no wonder that a power consisting in sharing in the divine knowledge should arise out of the essence of the soul. His premise is in the *Summa*: "Since the essence of the soul is immaterial"; in other words, since the soul is a being, the creation of which depends, not only on an act of the divine will, but also on the gift of the actual intelligibility of Being, which in turn calls for a certain cooperation between the divine mind and the human mind; a being, therefore, whose immaterial essence must be "created by the supreme mind," we can add with Aquinas: "nothing prevents the power which it derives from the supreme intellect, and whereby it abstracts from matter, from proceeding from the essence of the soul, in the same way as its other powers."[16]

Indeed, man is so unique that we can only say "ECCE HOMO," and remain silent.

In summary, this paper establishes first that in the *De Anima* Aristotle identifies the possible and the agent intellects as two different aspects of the activity of the same individual soul, and that in this sense the former is but the soul insofar as, upon intuiting Being as an object, it becomes Being in the latter's capacity as a subject, thereby allowing it to know itself in the soul. This, in turn, gives the soul the power of knowing everything (*tamquam tabula rasa*). Then the paper goes on to analyze what Sciacca says about self-consciousness and he finds that everything he says could be reduced to the Aristotelian position. It shows, in the first place, that the "I" would not be able to feel himself "existing" *in the world* with an infinite cognitive horizon if he were not Being knowing itself; after that, the paper explains how such a character, which Sciacca calls *triadic*, makes it possible and forecasts the intimate union that grace operates between the soul and the Trinity, a fact that allows the Being of man to show also the title of *Trinitarian*.[17]

California State University
Long Beach, California, USA
El Salvador, CA

NOTES

1. Aristotle, *De Anima*, III, 5, 430a10-15.

2. Op. Cit., 4, 429a17-27.

3. Ibid.

4. Aristotle, *Metaphysics*, 1075a6-27.

5. Op. Cit., 1072a22-23.

6. *Aristotle's De Anima with the Commentary of St. Thomas Aquinas* (New Haven: Yale University Press, 1965, paragraph 739).

7. Michele Federico Sciacca, *Interpretazioni rosminiane* (Milano: Marzorati Editore, 1963), p. 97.

8. Op. Cit., pp. 110-111.

9. Sciacca, "Le problème de l'origine des idées et de l'objectivité de la connaissance selon A. Rosmini," in *Revue de Métaphysique et de Morale*, 1955, #3, p. 304. See F. L. Peccorini, "Sciacca and Kant On 'Interiority': Variations On the Same Theme?" in *Studi Sciacchiani* 1 (1985), #1, pp. 26-27.

10. Sciacca, *Interiorita Oggettiva* (Milano: Marzorati Editore, 1967), p. 98.

11. Op. Cit., pp. 97-98.

12. Op. Cit., pp. 99-100.

13. Op. Cit., p. 100.

14. Ibid.

15. Ibid.

16. Sciacca, *Ontologia Triadica e Trinitaria* (Milano: Marzorati Editore, 1972), p. 101.

17. St. Thomas Aquinas, *Summa Theologiae*, I, 79, 4, *ad 5m.* See Peccorini, F. L., *From Gentile's "Actualism" To Sciacca's "Idea"* (Genoa: Studio Editoriale de Cultura, 1981. Currently being distributed by *The University Publications of America*, Frederick, Maryland), pp. 82-83.

This paper, which is the English translation of the paper that the author presented to the II International Congress of Christian Philosophy at Monterrey, Mexico, was first obtained by *Studi Sciacchiani*, of Genoa, from Prof. Dr. Agustin Basave Fernandez del Valle, the President of the Congress, and scheduled for publication in the first issue of 1987. It is being published here with permission granted by *Studi Sciacchiani*.

THE ONTOLOGICAL STRUCTURE OF MANKIND:
A CONTRIBUTION OF ONTOLOGY TO WORLD PEACE

Heinrich Beck

Fundamental ontological insights, which have been gained in the history of thinking, have to prove and are able to prove their unfading value by turning out to be principles of discovery even for the empirical research in the different branches of science. If empirical phenomena are investigated ontologically, ontology itself as well as the different branches of empirical research may advance immanently. Ontology may advance by discovering new dimensions of its traditional propositions; and the different branches of empirical research may advance by receiving new pregnant aspects for the order and the sense-finding synopsis of facts that are already discovered, and it may also advance by finding new facts.

Ontology is taken into consideration not in its special branches, but only in its fundamental and everlasting propositions, that is in its doctrine of the three transcendental determinations of being, which are "unum" (one), "verum" (true) and "bonum" (good), and ontology is also taken into consideration in its doctrine on the metaphysical analogy and the mutual participation of all things being. In the following the ontological connections that are meant here will not be presupposed as a dogma; we shall do it the other way around. We shall begin with the *phenomena* and then show that the ontological connections (structures) are the conditions for their possibility, and that they are the principles for understanding them.

It is quite natural that a preliminary programmatic draft may be easily misunderstood; but the intention of the following explanations is to stimulate further empirical research and its philosophical penetration.

Up to now the order of people seemed in the first place to be a political problem. But more and more the realization forces its way that this is not only a political problem; for behind the political problem there is the ethical problem. We cannot found a social order politically if we do not have ethical foundations in the common sense. But in the same way as ethics is the foundation of politics, ontology is the foundation of ethics. For the ethical norm is founded on the sense of being. The measure for the ethical behavior of people to each other is founded in the *sense of their existence* through which they are related to each other. Ontology, as the science of existence as such, as the science of the sense of being, is therefore the basic science for ethics and politics. And so, to the same degree as the political problem of the order of people tapers off today, to the question of to be or not to be for mankind, it is absolutely urgent to contemplate the sense of being and the conditions of existence for people.

If we contemplate the structure of people from this ontological point of view, we will find therein the ontological aspects of unity, truth and the good — the transcendental determinations of being into which the character of being is divided. Tradition expressed this interpretation of being with the words: "Omne ens est unum, verum et bonum" (All being is one, true and good), a proposition whose meaning must be struggled for again and again.

In the following, these transcendental moments of sense are to be demonstrated in the existence of mankind. They reveal themselves in typical cultural phenomena or even in a cultural anthropological structure of mankind. In this structure of mankind, we find prefigured an order of people according to the sense of existence, and in this structure of mankind we also find the dimension of what peace can mean and must mean.

The Unity of Mankind

The sense of unity reveals itself more distinctly than ever in the present period of world history. Today it reveals itself as the first condition for the possibility of existence. In the same degree as mankind is in disagreement, as people isolate themselves and fight each other, their existence is diminished and the continuation of their existence is endangered. Absolute quarrelsomeness and the rejection of their unity would finally bring about the extinction of their existence. A mankind without any degree of unity would not have existence at all. For being means first of all unity, "omne ens est unum" (all being is one).

But if a plurality — in this case a plurality of people — must necessarily form a unity in order to be able to exist, it follows logically that this plurality can only exist in an order. For order means plurality that is intrinsic unity. Order means neither an unsegmented unity nor a disjointed plurality and variety. Order means neither unity without any plurality nor plurality without any unity, but a unity dividing into a plurality or a plurality united under a uniform point of view, in short, a plural-unity. Every part of a plurality has its solid position in it from the unity-giving point of view or law.

Under which connecting, unity-creating point of view are the different people ordered? First of all it is the basic way of existence that offers itself; it is the universality of humanity. For within this humanity — in the meaning of the totality of attributes which distinguish Man from other beings — all races, people and cultures come together and have their solid position in it. They differ, however, in the way they embody it; Eastern people for instance show another kind of humanity than Western people. This means, however, that the order of people interprets itself in the sense of the "analogia entis," which means: neither absolutely univocal unity and identity nor an absolutely equivocal plurality of different entities, but intrinsic similarity which is deeply rooted in being; and this similarity is in the middle. Within the bounds of human existence people are neither absolutely equal nor absolutely different; they are only similar, they are analogous.

It is now of the highest importance that both aspects of "analogia entis," the analogy of being, the aspect of community and unity as well as the aspect of variety and plurality, are taken into consideration equally. Only if this is done, the order which enables the existence and the continuation of the people can fully be realized. The rationalistic metaphysics of entities after the end of the Middle Ages overemphasized the unity of the common human nature and neglected the plurality and variety of their concrete characters which were regarded as insignificant and accidental. So the genuine character of the analogy of being of people was not really looked upon, and the concrete variety of human existence remained not understood in its necessity and was not investigated ontologically.

Against such an infertile rigidity of the general notion of human nature, the empirical-phenomenological method soon arose as the advocate of the neglected concrete abundance of reality. And this abundance was described from the viewpoints of ethnopsychology, ethnology, ethnography and sociology. But in the course of time the common basis of human nature was pushed into the background, and finally we believed that human nature was nothing but the sum of ethnic characters. The former notion of human nature which had overemphasized its homogeneity was replaced by the one-sided view on the diversity of human ways of existence (or of life); monism was replaced by pluralism, the rationalistic-idealistic notion of the unity of mankind was put aside by a mere empiricist-positivist view on the plurality and variety, even heterogeneity, of the people. But now as the unity of people and civilizations could not be really understood from its roots in human nature, it became negative, for this unity could hardly be made visible by the philosophical trick of composing mere disparities and antithetical empirical phenomena in a dialectic way. But antithesis and heterogeneity, if made the foundation of politics, will destroy the unity, and that also means the existence of mankind. Therefore two things are very important today. On the one hand we must see the metaphysical unity behind the empirical disparities of people, and on the other hand we must display the concrete plurality of the ways of life on the general basis of human nature. So we can succeed in applying deep and far-reaching possibilities of the "analogy of being" in a full ontological understanding of the ethnical structure of mankind.

If we really comprehend the whole of mankind as an analogous unity of a plurality of people, it will become clear that the people intrinsically incline to mutual completion and partnership. If the same human nature is realized in the different people in a different way, it follows clearly that a single people for itself can realize the possibilities of humanity never completely, but only in a limited manner. However, it may liberate itself in a high degree from the limitations and the narrowness by establishing close participating contacts to other people which have exactly those qualities which this people itself does not have. Such a participation enriches that people's own way of life, and so the whole people will gain a richer and deeper existence. The more the different people gain and show sincere concern for each other, approach each other and complete one another, the more the inner unity and at the same time the ability of existence will grow for the whole of mankind in all its parts. The more they refuse partnership and abandon mutual completion, the more the inner unity and vivacity of mankind and of all people will decrease.

Consequently the order of people does not mean something rigid; on the contrary it means inclination to animation of its analogous unity by mutual participation. This is the task of history and peace.

The Structural Moments of the True and the Good in Mankind

The role a certain people has to play in these mutual relations is defined by the aspect of order which characterizes that people, for instance the aspect of unity or the aspect of plurality. An order as a "plural-unity" is only possible if both aspects are taken into account in the proper proportion. Therefore it is quite all right that one part of mankind is more inclined to differentiating and analyzing the unity into the plurality, and that another part is more inclined to integrate the plurality of parts into the unity of the whole. In the first inclination there is, if we have a deeper look into it, a relation to the significance of truth; in the second, an inclination to the significance of the good. For, by unfolding in its parts, a unity *reveals* its intrinsic substance, but by binding together the parts, it comes to completion as they also complete the whole in the being.

So an ontological view on the order of people unfolds before us in the light of the axioms "omne ens est unum," "omne ens est verum" and "omne ens est bonum." It turns out that the so-called West of mankind inclines to the "verum," the East to the "bonum"; for the West has always shown a more differentiating and analyzing basic attitude. The East, however, shows a more integrating and synthesizing basic attitude towards being. That means that the East and the West both have the ability for analysis as well as for synthesis, yet not in the same, but in a similar, analogous way, that is, in an exactly reverse accentuation. This can be shown by a comparative reflection on the several departments of culture, from the political and social to the religious department. The West or the so-called Occident is above all Europe and the New World of America as far as it emerged from the European civilization; the East or the Orient means above all Asia and Africa as far as it is similar or related to Asia. Here the notions East and West are meant in the sense of cultural anthropology, and geographically they can be demarcated exactly.

In the West individual character, the individual rights and the freedom of the various people and parts of people against the whole have been accentuated since time immemorial. We may think of the development of a plurality of city-states and national states, sometimes exaggerating to nationalism and even chauvinism, and we may further think of the symptomatic Wars of Liberation and other struggles for emancipation. The East on the other hand has always shown a tendency towards integrating mankind into continental or global empires, from Attila and Genghis Khan over the China of later ages, India and Czarist Russia to Communism which is expanding from the East over the whole world. In a stricter social and economic sphere, the West has soon developed a combative sense of individual rights and freedom against the higher entity of the people that was exaggerated to Liberalism, whereas in the East the person, the individual, demanded fewer rights of free development, and the safety in tradition was stressed as we see in the dominating position of Confucianism.

In contrast, the development of sciences is a typically Western phenomenon. For science is directed towards analysis and dissection of entities which are originally experienced in a more intuitive way. The scientific attitude of analysis and dissection increased even to the extreme by dividing science into the many sciences which split off from the whole of life and proclaimed their autonomy. Similar to scientific research also the other departments of culture such as art, economy and politics did not want to find their fundamental sense in the whole but in themselves and declared comprehensive ethical norms to be invalid; think of the slogan "l'art pour l'art" for instance. In contrast with that, the way to understanding in the East shows less analytic and more synthetic or even meditating traits. Western art, for instance, has a less decomposing character, which may also make things visible, but Eastern art shows us the way to the middle, to the centre, leads us to self-communication in calmness. In the dimension of religion, finally, the West-East polarity culminates: Whereas the West emphasizes towards God the attitude of free *partnership* which is even exaggerated to religious individualism, the East, on the contrary, has always accentuated the connection of the individual to the unity of the whole and its divine cause, with the immanent danger of going astray into the pantheistic exaggeration of fusion with the Universe.

In conclusion we may even say that the accentuated gravitation to analysis and truth has become manifest in our days in the distortion to Western individualism, liberalism and pluralism. In the same way, the accentuated gravitation to synthesis and to the good becomes manifest in a corresponding distortion by Eastern communism which tries to monistically uniformize the individual character, the individual value and the individual rights of the departments of life and culture to an all-embracing monotonous and homogeneous unity of aims. The deeper such a gravitation is rooted, the more it may be exaggerated into the negative if it falls out of the order.

Therefore, we can recognize how in the entire order of mankind, East and West are intrinsically inclined to mutual completion and could not even exist without each other. Without a sympathetic partnership with the synthesizing powers of the East, the analyzing powers of the West would disintegrate and corrode the unity and the substance of human life; without the sympathetic partnership with the analyzing and dissecting powers of the West, the synthesizing powers of the East would level out the life of mankind into the Nirvana of an empty and monotonous uniformity. Hence the ontological context proves that it is the consequence for ethics and politics that none of the partners may self-sufficiently retire into himself, but should, fully aware of his lack of completion, open himself from the bottom of his heart and apply to the other because of his own imperfection, for only in this way, order, and consequently the existence and continuation of the whole of mankind, are possible. Here we see revealed the perspective of a *peace* not paralyzing us in a balance of terror, but liberating us in a mutual acknowledgment of partners and a creative interrelationship!

Hence, in the present hour of the greatest threat to the existence of mankind, there appears the transcendental import of "being." Being, as a well-ordered unity, can be realized only in the adequate (rhythmical) complementary relationship of revealing analysis and completing synthesis, and this is its beauty.

In summary, the propositions of the classic ontology on the analogous unity of being, and the true and the good, have been proposed to make them profitable for the problem of a peaceful order of people; for politics has its foundation in ethics, and ethics finally in ontology. In doing so it has been shown that the classical ontological propositions, if confronted with concrete modern problems, will reveal and define themselves in a perhaps unexpected way, whereas ontology can stimulate and contribute to discovering and interpreting new empirical facts and thus can also animate the interdisciplinary discussion. On this basis it becomes clear that a peaceful political order of people can be found neither in a monotonous unity nor in a radical contrast and a balance of terror but only in a creative completion of partners. In this process the so-called West has the anthropological task of emphasizing the differences in the unity or the "truth," whereas the East has the task to lay stress on the unity above all differences, that is on the "good."

University of Bamberg
Germany

THE SIX THOUSAND SHOES: DO CLOTHES MAKE THE PERSON?

Mary L. O'Hara

Dialectical Considerations

In a Marxist analysis of work and consumption Lucien Seve has remarked that an adequate theory of human personality has not yet been developed.[1] He offers a theory of the relation between persons and work at various stages of life. But psychologists and anthropologists as well as philosophers must contribute to a theory of the human person today; and such a theory must take account of the essentially bodily reality of the human being.

During the Patristic and Medieval periods, discussion of this topic centered upon the notions of substance and rationality, as Greek-speaking and Latin-speaking theologians debated appropriate translations of these and similar terms into their respective languages.[2] In modern times disaffection from the old metaphysics led to a neglect of the question of the nature of the person.

Recently philosophers have taken it up again, often reflecting in their discussions a Cartesian division of mind from body. Thus they typically ask about the effect of brain transplants (that is, the bodily) or loss of memory (the mental) upon personal identity.[3]

An Indian anthropologist, Veena Das, criticizes what might be called a quasi-Cartesian distinction made by Victor Turner and others between "bodily experiences and phenomena" supposedly "given" in nature, and, on the other hand, "ethical principles and values" lacking this givenness.[4] She finds this distinction unfortunate, as it assumes that the

body is something given in nature and its experience is universally shared; that the experiences of the body are concrete rather than abstract; and that the body in consequence can be described and made the subject of conative and affective aspects of experience alone. It is these experiences that are given priority over the body as a culturally cognizable object. It is for this reason that many authors have shown such hesitation in describing the role of the body in Christian thought. . . .[5]

She favors seeing the body as a "system of meanings," as a symbol "culturally created," rather than merely a "biological substance." Similarly, clothing itself (and nudity) functions as a symbol. The person who "goes around naked or dresses himself with . . . bark, leaves or skins of wild animals, fasting, living on fruits and leaves, . . . is, in cultural terms, an asocial being."[6] In contrast to this Hindu *sannyasin*, the Buddhist monk is to wear clothes that are patched and thus look "like a ploughed field."

Without going into the distinctions of kinds of bodies to be found in Indian systems of thought, Das here makes clear that clothing and the body are to be regarded not simply as brute facts with no import for culture, but as radically involved in human culture. In this she echoes statements of Aristotle and Saint Thomas Aquinas about the dynamic, willed character of human dress and about the reflection of the human spirit to be found in ways of dressing as well as in the body itself.

The failure to treat the body adequately in Christian thought is to some extent being remedied today, but much remains to be accomplished before the human spirit can be seen to be as it were completely incarnate in the body.[7] A long history, going back to the very beginnings of Christian thought, of dependence upon Stoic and Platonic philosophy, accounts in large measure for this failure.[8] It is time, however, to move beyond the constricting effects of these ancient doctrines and strike out on a new path.

A generation ago the French philosopher Jacques Maritain put forth a theory of the nature of the human person in which the body figured prominently. He began by introducing a distinction between "individual" and "person." In *The Person and the Common Good* Maritain discussed, in the face of the totalitarian governments of his day, the relationship between human beings and political societies.

. . . though the person as such is a totality, the material individual, or the person as a material individual, is a part. Whereas the person, as person or totality, requires that the common good of the temporal society flow back over it, and even transcends the temporal society by its ordination to the transcendent whole, yet the person still remains, as an individual or part, inferior and subordinated to the whole and must, as an organ of the whole, serve the common work.[9]

Maritain's distinction between the partial, material individual and the whole, somehow transcendent person smacks of Cartesianism, even though it was not his intention to be Cartesian, and he is careful to note that his distinction between person and individual is a distinction without separation. Such a distinction, nevertheless, can become the basis for the sorts of attack upon human persons that are common today.

Maritain himself had no personal experience, as those of the present generation have, of totalitarian governments lasting for generations. On the basis of his distinction it can be argued that the lives of individual human beings can be sacrificed for the good of the whole state in time of war, for example; but if a protracted conflict, such as that against Communist aggression in various parts of the world today, requires the subordination of the bodily welfare of human beings for their entire lifetime to an alleged political necessity, this supposed distinction between a material individual and a spiritual person may become useless or even dangerous. It is, after all, the person as a bodily being that is under attack today, through torture, murder, abortion, and starvation; a useful theory of the human person must be such as to offer a defense for the person against oppression by a totalitarian government. While Maritain's theory does not make spirit, soul, or mind identical with person, his person/individual distinction approaches a Cartesian view of "I" as "thinker."

Derek Parfit in a recent book rejects a Cartesian-ego view of the person, but he introduces a distinction between "human being" and "person" that has a Cartesian flavor. He says:

If we know that a human being is in a coma that is incurable . . we shall believe that the person has ceased to exist. Since there is still a living human body, the human being still exists.[10]

Parfit prefers a reductionist approach which does away with the "self" considered as something over and above the body, coming to a "no-self" theory he likens to Buddhist theories:

> I claim that, when we ask what persons are, . . . the fundamental question is a choice between two views. On one view, we are separately existing entities, distinct from our brain and bodies . . . . The other view is the Reductionist View. And I claim that, of these, the second view is true . . . . *Buddha would have agreed.*[11] A person is like a nation. . . . But persons are not separately existing entities.[12]

> Thus, . . . in a superficial sense--the birds are *as much* my relatives as my own children.[13]

> We can now deny that a fertilized ovum is a person or a human being. This is like the plausible denial that an acorn is an oak tree.[14]

Whereas Maritain fails to give sufficient importance to the bodily reality of the human person, Parfit can be said to "de-hypostatize" the person in according to persons no greater substance than that of nations. This redefining of the word 'person' by Parfit does nothing to help solve the very real questions involving persons and human rights today.

Aristotelian Contributions

It has been pointed out above that Stoic and Platonic philosophical doctrines have dominated the mainstream of Christian thought for two millenia. In an impatient dismissal of ancient doctrines, it has been usual to assume that if Platonism no longer serves our needs, neither can the thought of Aristotle. In the case of the question of human personality, however, it was Aristotle who supplied the very terms in which "person" was first defined. Thus, although Aristotle says nothing in his extant works about the person as such, he lists in his *Categories* ten sorts of predicates, substance and nine "accidents," and it was substance that Boethius used in the definition of "person" that became normative: a person is an individual substance of a rational nature.[15]

Some theologians have claimed recently that the categories elaborated by Aristotle "correspond to the being of nature, but not to the being of the person. . . ."[16] In fact, however, each of the ten categories sheds light upon the body, but all, even time and situation of limbs, upon the soul through the medium of the body. An example will serve to show this.

In what follows, the category of "*habitus*" or clothing will be examined for the light it can cast upon the nature of human personality. It should be remarked first of all that the word "habit" is ambiguous: it can refer to a quality, like the habit of smoking, as well as to clothing, like a riding habit. It is the latter sense that is under discussion here. To mark it off from the other sense, it will be referred to as "habitus."

Aristotle lists all ten categories in only one of his books, that entitled *Categories*. In other works he lists those of the ten that are of interest to the particular work, depending upon its intention: *Metaphysics* deals with being, *Physics* with movement, and *Topics* with argument. Here the category of habitus will be treated according to Aristotle's *Metaphysics* and *Categories* and St. Thomas' commentary on the *Metaphysics*.

Habitus

As Aristotle makes clear in his *Categories* and elsewhere, the word "to have" is not a univocal term. One can be said to have qualities or quantities, a fever, or a certain form; Atlas "holds" the earth; a tyrant "has" his city; a container "has" the contained. What "holds" things together as a continuum is another example of the use of this term. One "has" property, the parts of one's body, even, though in a probably unjustifiable sense, one's wife or husband.[17]

In the book of definitions in the *Metaphysics*, Aristotle says that "having is a kind of act (*energeia*) of the one having and the thing had . . . as between one who has a garment and the garment which is had."[18] One treats what one has according to one's nature or desire, which is why "fever is said to hold a man, or a tyrant, a city." And when we are clothed, we "have on" or "wear" our clothes.

Of all these meanings, however, it is particularly the last one that he uses to instantiate habitus in his list in the *Categories*: ". . . of possessing, 'is shod' and 'is armed'; . . ."[19] This is the third sense in the list of non-univocal senses in the last chapter of the *Categories*: ". . . something he wears, such as a coat or a tunic, or something he wears on a part of his body, such as a ring on the hand . . . ."[20]

The list of Aristotle's sense of the category of habitus is: is shod; is armed; wears a coat or tunic; wears a ring. Each of these predicates

250

speaks not only about the nature of the one thus described, but also about the individual himself or herself. Each will be examined in turn.

1. To be shod is important in a country like Greece, with its wide variations of temperature and mountainous terrain. Even the nude statue of Praxiteles' Hermes is sandal-shod. Footgear, like other clothing, can identify a group of people: jogging shoes differ from tennis shoes and mountaineers' boots. Ideally, a shoe takes on the form of an individual foot. Animals can be shod, as horses are, but only by human beings, for human purposes.

2. To be armed is something chosen by a human being. Other animals and even plants can be said to be armed, but in a somewhat different sense, since human armaments are artificial means of defense not naturally given.

While it can be said to belong to human nature to make and use implements such as arms, each individual human person will choose the particular tools he or she prefers, including perhaps a left-handed monkeywrench. Thus when the proverb says that "It is a poor workman who blames his own tools," it is on the supposition that a good workman would have provided himself with the tools appropriate for his work. It is as a bodily being, with a definite potentiality for development, that a person needs possessions. A worker needs to know where his tools are, to have them at hand, in order to work efficiently. Gerard Manley Hopkins' "gear, tackle and trim," everything human beings need to live and work, is what Aristotle understands as belonging to *habitus*. Keys, pens, paper, even one's personal papers for international travel — these objects make easy, or in some cases even possible, human creative work.

3. To wear clothes is at once proper to human nature as contrasted with animal natures and also characteristic of each human being. Clothing symbolizes the person in many ways, as the expression, "Clothes make the man," indicates. A "power suit" is worn by successful businessmen and women. The infant's powerlessness is symbolically indicated by its nakedness.[21]

One's individual taste in dress enables a person to be picked out, identified as this individual. Clothing tells something about the individuality of persons, and even about one's dispositions and temperament. It is said proverbially that "The habit does not make the monk": more is required than merely a change of clothing to make one a spiritual person. The whole question of the relation of clothing to holiness (like that of the relation between person and symbol)[22] invites further reflection. Sahi has observed that the Indian holy man's nakedness symbolizes both his detachment and also an erotic quality.

4. Finally, a person can wear jewelry, and this may be the most personal of the types of habitus. Even a member of an equatorial tribe otherwise naked will wear bracelets, necklaces, and finger, nose, or ear rings. Whether or not some of these are (as I was told in India) related to acupressure in some way, they can in any case indicate a great deal about the status as well as the individual taste of their possessor. The pope's signet ring is broken when he dies. Animals can be furnished with harness and decoration, but these are put on them by human beings, often precisely to indicate that they are someone's possession. Cows in India and ancient Greek sacrificial animals often had gilt horns.

Thomas' Observations

Regarding accidents in general, St. Thomas Aquinas remarks that the existence of accidents is in-existence in the appropriate substance. Even a simple accident, lacking any composition in itself, nevertheless "does form a composite with something else, namely the subject in which it inheres."[23] For this reason, a complete treatment of habitus would have to include reference to the person as its subject. For the sake of simplicity, however, the accident alone is treated here.

Regarding habitus, Thomas explains that "tyrants are said to have cities"[24] because "civic business is carried out according to the will [voluntatem] and impulse of the tyrants." Here Thomas introduces the notion of will with no advertence to the fact that it is not a term that figured in Aristotle's discussion of the same questions.[25]

Thomas explains that the person wearing clothing is somehow impressing himself upon it, since it is made to fit this one individual. Thus, wearing clothes is, in the last analysis, a question of my choice, of my imposing my *will* upon the cloth, as well as of making my bodily impression upon it, because "clothing is fitted to the one who wears it and so it takes on something of the wearer's natural way of being."[26] Because human beings, for Thomas as for Aristotle, are naturally social animals, Thomas will apply a social standard to judging modest dress in the *Summa Theologiae*.[27] To have a thing is to treat it "according to one's own nature in the case of natural things, or according to one's impulse in the case of voluntary matters."[28] "In this sense, . . . those who are clothed are said to possess or have clothing. . . . And to have possession of a thing is also reduced to this sense of to have, because anything a man possesses he uses as he wills."[29]

A complete treatment of the "in-existence" of the accident of habitus according to Thomas would certainly involve reference to subsistence, substance, and personality. Here, some less often noticed aspects of Thomas' views will be treated, and in particular the notions of will in relation to habitus and of habitus as having a cultural bearing.

The accident of habitus as it is treated by Thomas reveals some essential features of the nature of the human being, but just as one can imprint one's fingerprints on leather gloves, one can also express one's personal style in the way one wears one's clothes. A person is thus, in the way he or she dresses, reflecting very precisely and accurately his or her personal way of being, and this not merely as an individual but as a socially integrated being. Relations of possessing have this social character, something important for the question of the way in which human beings hold property and assume social obligations with regard to it. This topic is of overriding importance in nearly all aspects of human life today, especially those involving the competing economic systems of East and West and of communist and capitalist societies.

In distinguishing natural from voluntary (we should probably say "cultural" today) matters, Thomas points to but does not enter the field of interest of the cultural anthropologist of today. Scientists working in this area supply metaphysicians data for reflection.

Finally, Thomas' use of the term "will" invites reflection upon the question of the nature of human agency. Lacking a clear concept of will, the ancients tended to see human acts as emanating almost by necessity from the rational faculty in human beings, making virtue simply the result of knowledge and thus making no place for either good or bad will as distinct modes of responding to and using knowledge of the right course of action. Because the person today is frequently identified in terms of responsible action, the notion of will is an important ingredient of the notion of human personality.

Having considered Aristotle's and Thomas' views of habitus, let us turn now to some conclusions suggested by the findings so far.

Concluding Reflections

From what has been said it can now be seen that the category of habitus tells much about the person as well as about his or her nature. Habitus has been called the most human category precisely because clothing, decoration, and tools do not have much relation to subhuman, angelic, or divine beings, but solely to human beings as such. It can also be called the most personal of the nine accidental categories, at least as these refer to human persons.

From the first moment of conception, the human being as a soul-body composite is a person, but every human person is eminently potential. It is in order to realize one's potentialities as far as possible that one needs possessions. An infant depends upon other persons to provide for its needs; so does a person too old to work. It is as a bodily being, with a definite potentiality for development, that a person needs possessions. To deprive him or her of them is to stunt that person's growth.

The history of workers' relations to their tools remains incomplete, if only because the effects of the information revolution upon society are as yet incompletely understood. What seems clear already, however, is that the work force can be divided into those who produce goods and services that are immediately marketable and those who create primarily for the sake of the joy the creative process gives them. Economic laws concern principally the first group. They are said to be employed or not and to have or lack the means to buy what they need. With changes in the world economic situation, such persons can change in a very short time from workers earning their own living and contributing in this way to society to an impoverished proletariat.

In technologically advanced societies today, computers and robots are replacing workers in such a way that women and men who had prepared themselves for lifetime employment in a particular field may find that, after having lost a job, they are unlikely ever to be hired in the same field again. It is therefore evidently important that every person be educated to realize the creative side of his or her personality so as to be able, when possible or necessary, to engage in the kind of making and doing that is less obviously immediately marketable than is ordinary gainful work.[30]

Possession has meaning only relative to others. A person alone on the planet would possess all and none of it. Possession shows the person as a related being in the very act of owning or claiming for himself or herself what each needs to live. Perhaps the most important question relating to the meaning of habitus today concerns the fact that possessions and access to possessions can mean the difference between life and death for a human person. Thus the whole area of human rights in all circumstances is bound up with this category.

Animals exhibit a form of behavior called "territoriality" manifest in their marking a certain piece of ground which they undertake to defend against aggressors. Such behavior is in some sense related to human ownership, but unlike human beings, animals do not aspire to set up empires.

Society as a whole, and each state, needs to find ways to assure for every human being adequate access to what each needs to live. Capitalist and communist states compete in this endeavor, the one emphasizing freedom, the other control and planning. Condemning persons to a life of slavery in the name of a classless society, or to a life at a lower than subsistence level in the name of defense against communist aggression, as alternatives, these are equally unacceptable. As has been remarked before, a new order must be found combining the better features of both systems for the good of human beings. Only in such a society can human persons enjoy the peaceful possession of what they need to live. A consideration of the category of clothing makes plain some of the requirements for a society enhancing the lives of persons.

The views of the nature of human personality alluded to in the first part of this paper — those of Seve, Parfit, and Maritain — have been seen to suffer from a too narrow and at times too Cartesian emphasis upon a *part* of human personality, whether this be the person as worker, as spirit, or as mere aggregate. A new theory is needed to justify human rights under attack today. And while some theologians find Aristotle's categories of little help in dealing with questions about the person, an attempt has been made above to show how one of these categories, at first sight the relatively unpromising one of habitus, can in fact say something about the human person, especially as a bodily being.

Recently the attention of nearly the whole world was focused on the extraordinary sight of rack upon rack of shoes — 3,000 pairs, it was said — in the presidential palace of the Philippines. Mrs. Marcos felt no embarrassment about going into the slums dressed like a princess. That was what people expected of her, she said. The Philippine dictatorship was justified on the grounds of its necessity for opposing communism.

But human beings, for optimum health, need clothing; what one person possesses of superfluous wealth can be said rightfully to belong to a person in extreme need.

A philosophy of the human person adequate to meet the challenges to human dignity today must explicitly recognize the bodily character of human persons. A Cartesian approach to human personality fails to do this. An approach like that of Parfit, doing away with the person as a subsistent being, attacks the person rather than defends him or her. Thus while it is not true in an ontological sense that "clothes make the man" or the habit the nun, yet shoes, clothing, and other possessions can affect the development of the person.

College of St. Mary
Omaha, Nebraska, USA

NOTES

1. Lucien Sève, *Marxisme et théorie de la personnalité* (Paris: Editions Sociales, 1975). See also M. L. O'Hara, "Marxist Theories of Human Personality," in *The Human Person*, Proceedings of the American Catholic Philosophical Association, LIII (1979), pp. 115-23.

2. M. L. O'Hara, "The Human Person, Mask or Presence?" in the *Bulletin* of the National Guild of Catholic Psychiatrists, 23 (1977), pp. 123-32, and "The Person and the Body: Roman Rhetors and Greek Naturalists," *Apeiron*, XI, 1 (1977) pp. 43-48.

3. Derek Parfit, *Reasons and Persons* (New York: Oxford University Press, 1984).

4. Veena Das, "Paradigms of Body Symbolism: An Analysis of Selected Themes in Hindu Culture," in Richard Burghart and Audren Cantlie, eds., *Indian Religion* (New York: St. Martin, 1985), pp. 180-81.

5. Ibid., p. 181.

6. Ibid., p. 193. On clothing and nudity, see also Jyoti Sahi, *The Child and the Serpent: Reflections on Popular Indian Symbols* (New York: Viking Penguin, 1990), pp. 118, 202. On women as clothed, see N. Shanta, *La voie jaina* (Paris: Auromere, Inc., 1985), pp. 493-95.

7. Karl Rahner, "Death as an Event Concerning Man as a Whole," in his *On the Theology of Death* (New York: Crossroad, 1961).

8. On the influence of stoic thought upon Christian teachings, see James A. Brundage, "'Allas! That evere love was synne': Sex and Medieval Canon Law," *The Catholic Historical Review*, LXXII, 1 (January, 1986), pp. 1-13, and, on stoic and neoplatonic influence upon Christian spirituality, Mary L. O'Hara, "Truth in Spirit and Letter: Gregory the Great, Thomas Aquinas, and Maimonides on the Book of Job," in E. Rozanne Elder, ed., *From Cloister to Classroom: The Spirituality of Western Christendom* (Kalamazoo, MI: Cistercian Publications, 1986).

9. Jacques Maritain, *The Person and the Common Good* (Notre Dame: University of Notre Dame Press, 1966), p. 60. Maritain cites *Summa Theologiae*, 2-2, 64, 2, and 1-2, 96, 4; 2-2, 61, 1; 22-, 65, 1; 1-2, 21, 4, and 3.

10. Parfit, p. 323.

11. Ibid., p. 273.

12. Ibid., p. 275.

13. Ibid., p. 316.

14. Ibid., p. 322.

15. Boethius, *Contra Eutychen*, II-III.

16. Michel Schmaus, *Katholische Dogmatik* (Munich, 1956), III, II, p. 51.

17. Aristotle, *Categories*, XV, 15b18-34; see also *Topics*, I, ix, 103b22-36, and *Physics*, III, 1 200b28-201a3.

18. Aristotle, *Metaphysics* V, 20, 1022a8-25.

19. *Cat.*, 2a3.

20. *Cat.*, 15b21-24.

21. Sahi, p. 201, note 2.

22. Sahi, pp. 53-54. Sahi also remarks that "the feminine . . . is clothed in space (digambara)." *Digambara* refers to nakedness. Is this a statement about the powerlessness of women in Indian society?

23. Saint Thomas Aquinas, *Commentary on the Metaphysics of Aristotle*, V, 5, Lec. 7, No. 865.

24. Ibid., V, 23, Lec. 7, No. 1080.

25. Albrecht Dihle, *The Theory of Will in Classical Antiquity* (Berkeley, CA: University of California Press, 1982), pp. 177-79 et passim.

26. Thomas Aquinas, *Commentary on Metaphysics*, V, 23, Lec. 20, 1080.

27. *Summa Theologiae*, 2-2, 169, c.

28. *Commentary on Metaphysics*, V, 23, Lec. 20, 1080.

29. Ibid.

30. The question of the maintaining of a standing army precisely to absorb the portion of the labor force not otherwise employed, as well as that of violent images and their effect on personal growth, or that of the acting out of violent behavior by children using toy guns, etc., needs to be considered, also.

THE BEING OF PERSONHOOD IN MARY AND HER ROLE BEFORE "THE TECHNOLOGICAL MAN"

Elena Lugo

Introduction

In this presentation I wish to show the sense in which it is possible to apply the Christian concept of Mary, as the Immaculate and Permanent Companion of Christ the Redeemer, in a critical reflection on the negative impact a positivistic, naturalistic and utilitarian technology might have on the integrity of the human person. I attempt to derive metaphysical significance from a specifically theological category in order to apply it as criterium in the interpretation of a secular theme. This is a daring enterprise.

What constitutes the being of person can be expressed in various ways. I choose to do so in three relational phrases which I consider basic. First, *one is a person in relation to one's self.* That is to say, a person strives to gain self-consciousness, self-acceptance, self-knowledge in order to attain a certain degree of self-identity, autonomy and self-reference in one's activities. In this fashion the person recognizes his/her proper dignity, inherent truth and goodness as well as discovers his/her finitude and contingency. Second, *one is a person in relation to the other than self, and/or to other persons.* A person longs to exert a formative, creative, humanizing influence on natural as well as on artificial environments without rejecting the being of the other as such. Moreover, a person longs for encounter and for communion in reciprocal complementarity with other persons conceived as a "personal you" and not merely as a "functional other." And likewise the person seeks to comprehend events by articulating a history in view of lived temporality, individually and collectively, and in attunement with a universally shared humanity. Third, *one is a person in a recognized dependency toward an*

Absolute. The Absolute, be it God or an Ideal worthy of unconditional surrender, presents itself as transcending the subjective, individual, finite and contingent condition of the person. The Absolute provides a foundation to the values that inspire the person, represents an ultimate explanation to the existential questions, and presents itself as the final purpose or end of human endeavors.

To summarize, the ideal of each person is to realize self in its proper identity in terms of a complementary encounter with others, of a creative relationship with the physical and cultural environment and in dependence on an Absolute correctly conceived. In becoming a person one must develop intimate, radical, permanent bonds with ideals, persons, places (things and events) and with the Absolute.

I believe that a technology founded on positivistic, natural-mechanistic, and utilitarian presuppositions interferes with the search for personhood as outlined above. We must now describe the "technological man" as a cultural category or rather as the human agent within technology understood as a cultural phenomenon. In so doing we shall discover that the "technological man" suffers under a vital anguish which in turn might be indicative of a triple depersonalization in each of the dimensions of person as already presented. At the end of my exposition I will introduce the concept of the *Immaculata* as a contrast to the "technological man" and I trust as a counterbalance to the process of depersonalization in the technological culture as here conceived.

Technological Man

In relation to himself, the "technological man" is less concerned with who he is in his intimacy and more with what he can do exteriorly or what he can accomplish with his power. He makes use of technology to control, manipulate and use the available resources or those he strives to make available. He tries to place at his disposal new resources in order to enhance his self-determination and self awareness for attaining self-sufficiency and full satisfaction in his search for pleasure, honor, and power. His own humanity appears as an object for innovation, modification, experimentation, control and technical projections in his attempt to surpass the inherent limitation and/or spatio-temporal conditions of human contingency (illustrated in genetic engineering, conditioning of behavior, social control). There is a longing for a secular-anthropocentric redemption.

In relation to the other/to other persons, the "technological man" overestimates the power of practical reason as oriented toward productivity, efficiency, utility, control and manipulation of natural resources and artifacts. Practical reason thus oriented emphasizes the instrumental value of object, the informational data, the measurable as calculable, while underestimating the intrinsic value of whatever he encounters and disregarding the ultimate criteria for appraising reality in terms of the final causes, and for the objectivity of values in themselves. Nature is viewed as neutral in its truth and goodness, and hence at the indiscriminate disposal of man's productive power.

Human conduct and the most intimate aspects of being a person become the objects for techniques which collectivize individuals, easily disregard or openly violate privacy, and often manipulate man's distinctive rational and volitive capacities (e.g. artificial reproduction, extension of the span of life, the maintenance of the dying by indiscriminate use of extraordinary clinical means, conditioning in behavioral therapies, some forms of group dynamics, mass social policy). As far as the guidance of moral conduct is concerned, the technological man appears unconcerned with objective norms expressive of duties, rights, and of natural law inherent in human nature. He is inclined to follow an ethics which fosters the probabilistic calculus of cost/benefit, risk/achievement without inquiring into the justification of this calculus or the utilitarian presuppositions this entails.

In relation to the Absolute, the "technological man" at present experiences a remarkable anxiety. He is already keenly aware that a secularized redemption or an attempt to transcend the limits inherent in the human condition is utopian or at least unattainable given the spontaneous resistance of man to manipulation.

"Technological man," as a cultural category, suffers anxiety before the possibilities of the misuse of technology, of despair before the suspicion that technology might not after all improve the human condition, and of panic before the anticipation of a cosmic holocaust. "Technological man" begins to experience the emptiness of his power and the unavoidable presence of his contingency. He acknowledges the inescapable responsibility for the proper use of technology in behalf of present and future generations, but his pluralistic, secular, liberal and pragmatic system of values does not provide him with a clear and solid point of reference. He seems, in short, lacking of the necessary wisdom to establish a secure foundation for his practical-technical knowledge and his secularized vision of nature, and to orient his fascination with instrumental goods.

Mary, Immaculate and Permanent Companion of Jesus Christ the Redeemer

The image of Mary, as the Immaculate and Co-redeemer, entails an ontological value with anthropological practical implications. The *Immaculate* reflects the order and harmony of the being of person as originally created by God, the incarnate ideal of the Christian as another Christ. The greatness of human nature and the dignity as well as nobility of personhood are fully evident in her. She is the microcosmos, the living and integral unity, the archetype for the person who longs to elevate and perfect his being to plenitude in contact with God. In her mission as co-redemptrix she is the way for and dynamic force within a Catholic Humanism which has singular relevance in questions of personal identity, communion with nature, and binding with God which so much concern man today before the challenges of technology.

Mary in Relation to Herself

Upon acknowledging her own proper identity, in knowing herself as "the full of grace" and thus the possessor of an ordered heart, Mary surrenders herself completely (*Fiat-Annunciation*), and in the freedom of her self-possession she affirms her own self (*Magnificat*) as well as becomes all servitude (*Visitation*) and renunciation under the most personally demanding of circumstances (Calvary).

One must understand by "heart" not merely feeling and emotions but rather what the German word *Gemüt* entails. This word designates the very essence of interiority, the unifying center of the intellectual, the volitive as well as the affective. An ordered heart represents the harmony of the human faculties in their singular orientation toward the full realization of being a person. Self-assurance in Mary serves as a foundation to her freedom and is also the antidote to the contemporary emancipation from and manipulative power over nature. In her silence and spiritual solicitude she cultivates self-identity without the need of restless productive activity as a means for self-estimation.

Mary in Relation to the Other and to Other Persons

The *Immaculata* entails a diaphanous and clear mind, a balanced and sure judgment, a correct and decisive will and, as well as all of these, is integrated in the finest of emotional sensibility. That is, in her we have a knowing capable of integrating all experiences into an organic totality which encompasses the theoretical and the practical, the ideal and the concretely real, the conceptual as well as life itself, the effective and the affective. From the integrative form of knowledge (natural wisdom + supernatural wisdom under the influence of the Holy Spirit) one may conceivably derive those cognitive functions which complement the knowing of "technological man," such as: appreciation of the intrinsic truth and goodness proper to each mode of being, discernment between the essential and the accidental, capacity to distinguish between ends and means, between depth and superficiality, and to coordinate the whole and the parts. And in general the Immaculata entails a certain openness, receptivity, appreciation of the other as well as willingness to realize in concrete life what is acknowledged as true and good.

The natural/supernatural wisdom of the Immaculate One, as imitated by the Christian, leads him/her to a unity and harmony of modes of knowledge, in themselves at first disarticulated in clarity and rectitude, before the ambiguity and ambivalence that positivistic technological knowledge often presents. Technological activity can become personal, be almost divinized, while subordinating its utility to the full development of the person according to spiritual values.

The practical-technical know-how of the means and processes of productivity will then be complemented, perhaps subordinated, to the theoretical-ontological wisdom which in itself entails an intuition of being and of the end of human activity. This wisdom admits the value of meditation, of the creative silence before the contemplation of a mystery, of the symbolic expression as ways to contact the Divine. The utilitarian manipulation of artifacts, and even of living beings, would be coordinated with the urgent need for the conservation and preservation of nature. Historical events will reveal the dispositions of Divine Providence.

Mary in Relation to the Absolute

The Immaculate is inexhaustible receptivity for the Divine. It is partly a passive receptivity for she recognizes her radical dependency on God the Father, but it is also active in her total self-surrender to the difficult and complex mission as co-redemptrix of all creation, of the technological order included. Thus it is that she becomes for us modern human beings an antidote to the very arbitrariness, irrationality, uncertainty and general anxiety that weighs upon the "technological man" in his presumed self-sufficiency, power and domination over his being and over nature in general.

Only in reference to the primary, creative and providential Cause, all intelligent and all powerful, can the intrinsic truth and ontological goodness of nature and of man himself be restored. Only thus can reverence, a sense for the mysterious, become the guiding spirit of the conservation and preservation of nature while maintaining a prudent utilization of natural resources. Openness, receptivity, and appreciation of the incommensurable value of each human life in relationship to God sustain a true bond of self in one's intimacy with a personal "you" and of all in loving communion with God the Father in one Church conceived as a Family.

Mary Immaculate integrates the temporal into the eternal, the finite into the infinite, that is into an organic whole which preserves the value of the temporal and finite. This whole is reflected in her being as a person who thinks, wills, and loves in harmony of being. In her the smallness of her temporal and finite self reveals the instrumental character of every human being and hence the secondary causality each being is able to exercise in dependence, disposibility and trust toward the Primary Cause. A link with the Supreme Wisdom, Power, and Goodness of God transfigures the ambition of secularized redemption, due to be destructive of the person, into a participation of Divine Providence in the world.

Technological activity can then become theocentric. It will represent a collaboration with the creative and providential activity of God in the world. The cosmos appears then as God's own invitation to man to unfold himself as inquirer, inventor, and maker of the world in accordance with ontological truth and goodness. But this unfolding, thrown off by original sin, has demanded the redemption of Jesus with and in Mary so that technology can in truth be the self-projection of man in authentic freedom.

Conclusion

In Mary Immaculate one can see how sanctifying grace leads to inner freedom, to the surrender of one's self (heart/*Gemüt*) as organic unity of the human faculties, to the full realization of God's providence in the world. Bonded to God the person discovers his/her true dignity and unique value of being in his/her intimacy and hence the authentic justification for self-affirmation and autonomy as a child of God. This person-child of God can then be responsible, in wisdom and prudence, for technology's spiritual value of nature and power before nature. The Incarnation is the decisive event for the orientation of technological culture. The Immaculate Virgin and Mother in relation to the Incarnation has served us as a model emphasizing the necessity of a lay spirituality rooted in the proper valuation of created being. As a summary, I should like to mention now the main qualities this lay spirituality must embody: first, a meditative or contemplative outlook enabling one to grow in faith, hope and love and in the discernment of the metaphysical value of the cosmos, of its mystery and symbolic meaning beyond utility and efficiency; second, the striving to secure the following virtues: *reverence* toward the truth and good proper to each created being, *courage* to unfold its inherent potential, *responsibility*, before the entire cosmos and toward future generations, in renunciation to secure inner freedom and resist the trend of consumerism, in *patience* and *confidence* regarding the future of technology. Technological culture, as guided by prudence and wisdom, cannot only contribute to the God-willed unfolding of the cosmos and of man but will also be viewed as a manifestation of Divine Providence.

University of Puerto Rico
Mayaguez, Puerto Rico

PART V

THEOLOGICAL DIMENSIONS
OF HUMANISM

GOD OF REASON AND GOD OF REVELATION

Terry J. Tekippe

Pascal is famous for his dictum that the God of the philosophers has little to do with the God of Abraham, Isaac and Jacob.[1] What does the austere, abstract prime mover of philosophical deduction have to do with the concrete, passionate God of the Hebrews? The question is rhetorical; they have nothing in common. The thesis of this paper will be the opposite: that the God of revelation and the God of reason are highly compatible, that the knowledge of God enjoyed by the Christian is a continuation of that elaborated by the philosopher.

This is not, of course, to deny differences in the two accounts, or to say that the content of the philosopher's knowledge is the same as that of the theologian. That would result in a rationalism, an emptying out of faith. But it is to reject any radical incoherence between the two conceptions.

A simple example may help. Suppose a blind man is introduced to a woman. Suppose he is allowed to touch her face. Obviously he does not know her as another person with full vision does. But, equally obviously, it is not a different women that he knows; and what he senses with his fingers is not incompatible with what someone else can see. Such is the relation between reason and faith in knowing God. And lest a philosopher resent being compared to the blind man, I appeal for warrant to Aristotle, who says that in knowing divine things we are like owls staring at the sun.

The argument will be threefold: from metaphysics, from epistemology and anthropology, and from history.

1) The claim here is simple: If the God of the philosophers is different from the God of Christians, and if the Christian God is the true God, then the philosophers' God must be a false God. This may be taken in either the religious sense of an idol, or the philosophical sense of an untruth.

The conclusion appears necessary. Unless one succumbs to the medieval temptation to a "double truth", or unless one holds the simultaneous existence of two Gods, then on the suppositions above, it is clear that any God different from the true God is not God at all, but simply an unverified idea.

E converso, if the God of the philosophers is known truly, then he must be identical with the God of revelation. Consequently the knowledge of the philosopher and the Christian must be complementary, not contradictory.

Of course, some would deny this. The atheist holds that neither the God of the philosophers nor the God of the Christian exists. But this position may be left out of the discussion, as the atheist is not likely to be concerned with the question whether the God of the philosophers is other than the God of Christians. There are Christians, however, who deny the God of the philosophers; Karl Barth, in his rejection of natural theology, would be an example.[2] This question will recur at the end of the paper; suffice it to opine here that Barth maligns reason, which is also God's creation.

How does the philosophical account differ from the revelational? As abstract differs from concrete. Another simple analogy can be used, taken from Aristotle. A man at a distance can be recognized as human, without any personal recognition. As he comes closer, he is revealed as Callias. First nature, then person is distinguished. So with God. The philosopher recognizes the divine nature, as from a distance; the Christian knows Emmanuel, God-with-us: Jesus, who reveals the Father, and promises to send the Spirit.

2) The philosophical and theological accounts are coherent because they both stand in the one human drive to transcendence. ". . . for thou hast made us for thee and our heart is unquiet until it finds its rest in thee," said Augustine in the *Confessions*.[3] But this is just as true for our philosophical as for our theological knowledge of God.

Plato is continually illustrating this process of "going beyond." One begins to learn beauty by falling in love with an individual beautiful body, Socrates says in the *Phaedrus*.[4] But gradually one is in pursuit of the very Idea of Beauty. Similar is the Idea of the Good in the *Republic*.[5] "Seen and hardly seen" is the way Socrates phrases it. It too is arrived at by a philosophical ascesis, a painful birth from the womb of the cave of images into the light of the Forms. Similar is the Idea of

Love, the final secrets of which are revealed to Socrates only by the wise woman Diotima, as recounted in the *Symposium*.

Whoever has been initiated so far in the mysteries of Love and has viewed all these aspects of the beautiful in due succession, is at last drawing near the final revelation. And now, Socrates, there bursts upon him that wondrous vision which is the very soul of the beauty he has toiled so long for. It is an everlasting loveliness which neither comes nor goes, which neither flowers nor fades, for such beauty is the same on every hand, the same then as now, here as there, this way as that way, the same to every worshiper as it is to every other. . . . It will be neither words, nor knowledge, nor a something that exists in something else, such as a living creature, or the earth, or the heavens, or anything that is — but subsisting of itself and by itself in an eternal oneness, while every lovely thing partakes of it in such sort that, however much the parts wax and wane, it will be neither more nor less, but still the same inviolable whole.[6]

The very structure of Aristotle's *Metaphysics* reveals the same sense of direction. It climaxes in Book XII where Aristotle treats the highest object of metaphysical speculation, divine reality. As thought is the highest vocation of humankind, so what should God be but Self-thinking Thought?

But the same thrust toward transcendence appears in the Scriptures. Already in Genesis later myths are used to purify earlier ones. In the course of the Old Testament development, a spiritualization of God occurs, reaching a notable high point in Second Isaiah. "As high as the heavens are above the earth, so high are my ways and my thoughts above your thoughts" says the Lord (Is. 55:9).

In the New Testament John affirms: "God is spirit" (Jn. 4:24). Arguably the Evangelist does not have the full philosophical equipment to make the precise affirmation of later Christian metaphysics. But he is clearly launched on a trajectory which heads in that direction. Similarly James: "Every worthwhile gift, every genuine benefit comes from above, descending from the Father of the heavenly luminaries, who cannot change and who is never shadowed over" (1:16).

3) Let history here be considered an Hegelian experiment. History itself reveals the possibilities of thought. Does the God of revelation

embrace the God of Greek philosophy? Indeed a synthesis occurs. It begins already in the Book of Wisdom, clearly influenced by Greek culture. "For from the greatness and beauty of created things their original author, by analogy, is seen" (Wis. 13:5). Paul not only echoes that in Romans 1, he also speaks to the philosophers at Athens, offering to make known to them the "Unknown God" whose monument he had seen (Acts 17:23). The situation here is clearly that envisioned above of an unfolding knowledge. The God the Athenians knew could not have been totally unknown, or they could not have dedicated a monument to him. He was only relatively unknown. But Paul offered to make him more fully known, to tell his name.

The Church Fathers were of two minds about Greek philosophy. Some rejected it as simply pagan, opposed to Christianity. But the majority, and the triumphant position, was that the treasures of Greek philosophy were booty belonging to the victors, like the tribute the Israelites exacted from the Egyptians. The synthesis they essayed reached its high point in the Scholasticism of Anselm, Peter Lombard, Thomas Aquinas and Bonaventure. Here was elaborated the idea of the Infinite, the grandest idea of human conception, that greater than which, in Anselm's phraseology, nothing could be conceived.

Ab esse ad posse valet illatio. If a synthesis between the God of Christians and the God of the philosophers took place, it is obviously possible. The God of the philosophers is not inimical to the God of Christians.

An adversary might object with a similar historical argument. Since the Middle Ages this synthesis has broken down. Kant held that we could have only a regulative idea, but no true knowledge of God. Karl Barth insists that a Christian does not need, indeed must spurn, a natural knowledge of God. But if it happened, it's possible; this argument cuts both ways. If history reveals a medieval synthesis, it also exhibits a manifest dissolution. If the dissolution took place, it is obviously possible; and it furthermore suggests that the union was merely an artificial one in the first place.

At the risk of being blunt, and perhaps unecumenical, I will speak with that *parrhesia* highly prized in the New Testament. The synthesis of faith and reason broke down due either to a defective Christianity or a defective philosophy.

A strand of Christian thought downplays or denies the philosophical approach to God. Luther stated that reason was a whore, and vehemently attacked Aristotle.[7] Karl Barth follows in that tradition in rejecting natural theology. Jansenism was an attempt to compromise between Catholicism and Lutheranism, so Pascal may be tinged with the same tendency.

But this is not the main tradition of Christianity, which is voiced much more by Shakespeare: "What a piece of work is man! how noble in reason! how infinite in faculty! in form and moving how express and admirable! in action how like an angel! in apprehension how like a god!" (*Hamlet* Act ii, 2). Reason is God's creation. One does not honor the Creator by vilifying his creation. The bulk of the Catholic tradition is clear on this point, so much so that Vatican Council I solemnly defines that God can be known by natural human reason (DS 3004).

But philosophy which rejects a knowledge of God is equally defective. This is particularly clear in Kant. He intends a survey of the scope of the human knowing power. He ends by rejecting most of metaphysics. In this realm the mind flaps its wings vainly for lack of air. Reason is obviously corrupt: it produces only antinomies by thinking of such subjects.[8]

But Kant's project is inherently incoherent. No scientist would use a defective instrument as a standard by which to test itself. Yet Kant is using the defective instrument of reason to measure the deficiencies of reason. The project must be stillborn. Ironically, as Whitehead points out, it was the medieval thinkers, who most firmly subordinated reason to faith, who also accorded to reason the greatest ambit of operation!

My topic has been the compatibility and continuity of the metaphysical God of reason and the Christian God of revelation. A metaphysical analysis eschews two Gods or a double truth to leave only two alternatives: either the God of philosopher and theologian must be fundamentally identical, or one or the other must be fundamentally false. Within the human knower can be discerned an infinite wonder (Aristotle), an intelligence so unlimited it is *quodammodo omnia* (Thomas), a seeking against an infinite horizon (Rahner), an unlimited drive to know (Lonergan). Object of that single thrust is both the God of the philosopher and the God of the theologian. History reveals in Patristic and medieval thought a wonderful synthesis of revelation and reason. When that synthesis dissolves, it reveals not so much the weakness of that intellectual achievement, as the decline of philosophy, or Christianity, or both.

274

The conclusion may be succinctly stated: the incompatibility of the God of the philosophers with the God of Abraham, Isaac and Jacob has been greatly exaggerated.

Notre Dame Seminary
New Orleans, Louisiana, USA

NOTES

1. *Pascal's Pensees.* Tr. M. Turnell. (New York: Harper & Brothers, 1962), 381-82.

2. Karl Barth, *Church Dogmatics*, v. 2. (Edinburgh: T & T Clark, 1957), pp. 75-128.

3. Augustine, *Confessions*, X:6. tr. Vernon Bourke. *Fathers of the Church*, v. 21 (Washington, DC: Catholic University Press, 1953), pp. 270-71.

4. *Phaedrus*, 249e. Hamilton, E. and Cairns, H., *The Collected Dialogues of Plato* (Princeton, NJ: Princeton University Press, 1961), p. 496.

5. *Republic* 514-17. *Collected Dialogues*, pp. 747-50.

6. *Symposium*, ibid., pp. 210-211.

7. Martin Luther, *Luther's Works*, v. 39 (Philadelphia: Fortress Press, 1970), p. 209; and v. 44 (Philadelphia: Fortress Press, 1966), pp. 200-201.

8. Immanuel Kant, *Critique of Pure Reason*, tr. Norman Kemp Smith (New York: St. Martin's Press, 1929), p. 500 (A 591) and p. 569 (A 702).

INTIMATIONS OF GOD

Dominic A. Iorio

Belief in God, and even a certain "knowledge" of God, has been the possession of mankind for as far back in his history as we are able to reach. Nor has this belief, or "knowledge," been devoid of some attempt at rational justification. Those earliest attempts to probe the incipient meaning of God may appear to us today as feeble and unconvincing expressions of rational insight, but they are nevertheless genuine attempts to formulate in rational terms the implications of a fundamental experience of God-reality, of a felt presence of God, however feebly understood.

In our own day, we find new gropings for a rational rephrasing of the very meaning of God. Philosophers and theologians alike have as a major preoccupation the possibility, the validity, the meaningfulness of "God-talk." How are we to speak of God? What new categories of thought and expression are required to speak once more of the God we are convinced by faith to be and to be present to us?

The search for God can have meaning for the contemporary man only to the extent to which he returns to the primordial encounter with God-bearing experiences to which his forebears attended. Further, only if such a return is successfully undertaken can the classical proofs of God's existence be rephrased as a natural reflective concomitant and expression of these primordial experiences.

Because we no longer share the primordial roots out of which these proofs were developed and to which they were tied, contemporary man does not find these proofs persuasive, but only intellectually challenging at most. They have been reduced to logical puzzles, insolubilia, transcendental illusions, tricks of the mind, or irrelevancies. At best, they are seen as interesting, but not by themselves necessary or sufficient complements to a knowledge and faith which, for the believer, are grounded in other experiences and other reflections both deeper, more meaningful, and more compelling.

The total rationalization of the primordial experience that these proofs bespeak has left us with the abstraction without the concrete experience that gave birth to these proofs and nourished their meaning. The rationalization has led to an abstract "God" incapable of commanding worshipful assent and love.

Let us look at the primordial experience to find where we have lost our way, how to get back to it, and how we might rephrase a rational, not rationalistic, demonstration of God's existence.

Intimation is the first response of man to God. Intimation means the intellectual, moral, aesthetic, sensuous contact with any object or state of affairs capable of eliciting a human response that moves the person beyond the object or state of affairs in such a manner as to suggest more in or about the object or state of affairs than its purely factual experiential status, quality, character, or relationship with other similar factual objects or states of affairs. Intimation is distinct from symbol, since in the experience of symbol there is a consciousness of the meaning beyond the object's facticity, e.g., two crossed sticks become a cross. In intimation the object bespeaks more but does not do so with precision. The object does not become something else (e.g., a cross) while remaining its factual self (e.g., crossed pieces of wood). Rather, in intimation the "factual" remains purely and simply, but suggests vaguely beyond itself a "more" that challenges definition. In the end, the consciousness remains intimately conjoined to the factual experience as it is confronted. An example may help here. When I view the heavens on a clear, unimpeded night, I see celestial specks of light against a black sky. That is, simply put, the experiential fact. I apprehend sensuously only the mere facticity of the celestial phenomenon. But assuming a relatively unbiased and unreflective apprehension initially, I cannot refrain from a sort of "further glance," a "second concomitant look" at the celestial phenomenon, the beginning of wonder, but not yet wonder.

That concomitant second look may express itself simply as a gasp, as a primitive unreflective awe, a feeble first attempt to gauge or encompass, a primordial merging of the attention with the attended. These are all movements beyond the factual. They constitute a response to the seen. It is in the nature of that response that we first encounter the stirrings of intimation. Before a fact can symbolize, it must first intimate, suggest, dissociate the attention from the object of attention to some "other," not yet defined. At this stage to which I refer the intimacy of consciousness is still on the side of the factual experience. It is still rooted in the here and now, in the "this" lying before consciousness.

Intimation here precedes definition. It has no clear object. It is only an attentive, unreflective movement beyond and toward an I-know-not-what. It is in the multiplication of precisely these kinds of experiences that an aura of wonder, of surprise, of expectation, of anticipation begins to form. In one case it may involve awe, in another fear, in still another exhilaration. An object may touch us by its beauty, its strength, its power, its swiftness, its immensity or by some other character that suggests a "more."

Within this "aura" reflection is born. The question arises, why is it so and not otherwise? What does it mean? What is it to me? For most of such experiences, reflection barely arises only to be relinquished for other more pressing matters affecting one's existence and welfare. But there are those relatively few, superimposing, imperious experiences of this type which not only transfix the attention, but engender consistent, sustained reflection which demands resolution, satisfaction, completion. It is here that intimation emerges at its strongest and becomes one with the experience of the fact, a "face" the fact presents only to the reflective mind. The fact is seen as faceted, like a well-cut diamond. It now begins to appear as multidimensional in its meaning. It is what it is, but it is also what it is not. The fact becomes a sign, pointing beyond itself to another dimension of meaning, to another object, to an explicator of its being.

The intellectual movement to "explain" is not, however, a direct or simple one. Initially "primitive" in the sense of a hesitant, tentative intellectual effort to "grasp" the meaning of the factual situation and to relate it to other meanings already more firmly grasped. By such multiple, repeated incipient intellectual movements a "world" of meaning is constructed, lying close to the experiences that gave rise to these insights. This "meaning world" not only organizes the common factual world but, more significantly, structures a world of meta-factual meanings to which become attached the values that give intellectual and moral support and foundation to the individual and community. In all its complexity it becomes the *lebenswelt* of Husserl, the breeding ground of insight into God and man. Here is found the meaning (and the implications of that meaning) of good and evil, right and wrong, order and chaos, the reasonable and the irrational, and the honorable and the despicable. Here too is fixed the meaning of person, of family, of community, as well as of discourse and gibberish. All the meanings that are serviceable to man and all the values that attach to those meanings are rooted in those intimations of the "more" of the purely factual world.

It is out of these meanings and values that the notion of God is first proposed to reason as a possibility, albeit a poorly understood possibility. That notion of God is gradually, continuously, and collectively generated out of the complex of life-experiences that constitute the understood world. And that notion makes sense only in the context of the life-experiences that gave rise to it. To take the notion of God developed out of one complex of life-experience and to suggest it to those living out another complex of such experiences is to render it an almost meaningless abstraction. It does not fit because it was not born out of nor is tied to the experiences that would render it meaningful or relevant.

Given this intimational experience, the first human response to God is inevitably a response to God as immanent, not as transcendent. He is at first transcendent only in the sense that God rises above, beyond the factual, but so closely attuned to it, so intimately involved with it that the first natural state of human consciousness *vis-a-vis* God is a sense of the Divine Presence in and of things. This inevitably must lead to a first expression of God-reality as immanence and, thence, to monism as an almost natural first conclusion drawn from such experience.

The purpose of rational proofs for God's existence is not to establish that existence so much as it is to establish the ineffable, absolute transcendence of God. Whether we speak of a First Mover, First Cause, Perfect Being, Supreme Good, or Last End, we speak always and only of a transcendent being, unapproachable by human intelligence which ultimately remains silent in the presence of such a being. The adored being, however, is not the transcendent but the immanent, the one who resides close to life, close to the person, close to experience, close to prayer and worship. Here alone have we the beginning of religion and of religious consciousness.

One can certainly proceed from here, as Feuerbach does, and speak of a dissociation of consciousness that occurs which leads to the objectification of human consciousness and to its infinitization. But Feuerbach moves too far too quickly and thereby loses the truth. The intimational experience is never lost, even when it moves self-consciously beyond the factual to its transformation into sign or symbol. It is rational reflection that pushes the factual beyond itself, forcing it to assert more of itself than it is initially willing to provide. What rational reflection finds, however, is not a mirror of itself in the object, but rather a stepping stone to another reality that is neither the object in experience nor the experiencer. The mind in reflection is driven outward, not inward, away from the attended and the attender and toward the implied, the suggested, the intimated. Both knower and object become self-effacing signs, the one intending, the other referring beyond itself. The first act of reflection, therefore, is one that seeks to remain close to the factual object. How immense is this thing, after all? it may ask. How far does this extend? it may ask. Or it may initially ejaculate "How magnificent it all is!" Or, "How terrible this wrath!" The focus has shifted ever so slightly, from the object to its immensity, its extension, its magnificence, its wrath. But not to a clear and distinct idea of any of these, only to the concrete experience of them here and now.

The play of reason upon the factual-as-intimation inexorably leads, sometimes painfully and fitfully, to the attempt to come to rational grips with the meaning of the factual as intimater. The intellect focuses increasingly and insistently on the meaning of the intimation, on what might be suggested by the existential fact. But the movement of the mind is by a logic that keeps the intellect always close to the fact. It is, after all, the fact that needs to be explicated. It is the fact that suggests beyond itself. And the fact suggests beyond itself a something that is close to the fact, intimately conjoined with it, almost another "face" of the fact. This is not simply the connection of the fact with other facts, although these connections certainly enter the consciousness of the thinker and may themselves intimate a presence beyond their connectedness. Rather, the suggested "face" of the fact, while standing in a certain intimate, logical connection with the fact itself, begins to reveal itself as "meta-fact," an extension of the factual world, a dimension of it that reveals itself through the experienced fact. This "meta-fact" is no less real, no less existential, than the fact by which it is intimated. It presents itself as a revelation, as a noumenon that shines *through* the fact, *in* the fact, *beyond* the fact, and *with* the fact. Its reality is one with the fact's reality.

The "meta-fact" always presents itself as a "more." So the "meta-fact" is the "more" of the fact, not the "other" of facticity. It is this sense of the "moreness" of facts, rather than their "otherness," that constitutes the ground out of which the first conception of divinity is formed, the Divine as immanent in nature. Only when the rational reflection is developed in its purity, that is, within the limits of logical necessity, does the Divine begin to emerge as a rational "other," above, beyond, and totally other than the world of experienced fact. These pure rational reflections constitute the beginning and the end of the classical proofs of God's existence. At first primitively stated, the logical necessity that gave birth to them finds its fulfillment in the highly refined demonstrations we have come to know in Anselm, Aquinas, Descartes, or Leibniz.

A peculiar history, however, surrounds these classical demonstrations. Theirs is a continuous history of rational development and refinement. At first we find them stated in as close a factual context as possible. Aristotle's First Mover, for example, is not a transcendent being, but simply an explanatory principle of the world's motion. The interest is in explaining motion, not in describing God. Even in St. Anselm, the ontological proof is not so much a demonstration of God's existence-as-other as it is an attempt to describe rationally what the believer "knows" in his heart through faith. The attempt here is to define a faith in a God already known, not to establish the existence of an unknown God who is absent from human consciousness. That is why an Anselm or a Scotus will cast their proofs in the form of prayers to a God already known and ever present in consciousness, waiting to enlighten the understanding by becoming intimately present to it. Both Aristotle and Anselm remain close to the primordial experience to which we earlier referred.

When Aquinas, however, becomes intent on developing a rational theology in the manner of an Aristotelian science, the phrasing of rational demonstrations of God's existence assumes a decidedly different and new aspect. Their interest, though not St. Thomas', is to establish the existence of an object no longer in evidence. The conclusion of the argument is not *a priori* known in any manner, but needs to be established by means of a rigorous logic that is inventive. Philosophers have, since St. Thomas' day, been attempting to establish the existence of an object called "God" by means of a logic of invention. In the process, the believer, the worshipper, has been left out. Disengaged from the kind of experience that can alone give muscle to such arguments, the demonstrations have been reduced to little more than logical exercises for young philosophy students who find that they can agree with the premises and conclusions of such arguments and still deny that God exists. Just as the student is reduced to silence by the power of such arguments, so also the believer is reduced to religious silence by these same arguments.

What are these everyday experiences that intimate God? They are myriad, and because of their number and diversity, it would be clearly impossible for us to make much headway in describing even some of them. But some direction can be given.

The person who worships provides us with the best clues. The worshipper sees an intimation of God in the flight of a bird, lazily circling above, taking advantage of the warmer, uprising air currents to sustain its glide. The perfect attunement to nature intimates a truth about the world and about us. To be at one with nature, its laws, its opportunities, its freedom, suggests a harmony, a balance, a firmness, a unity that extends beyond the merely factual (the bird in flight). That bird's flight intimates perfect conformity to "what is." It is right, it is good, it is as it should be. Rectitude, goodness, oughtness, harmony, and unity are all intimated by that single flight. The believer, of course, "sees" God in that flight. But the primordial experience that supports and confirms that faith in God for the believer is an intimation that only begins to go beyond the fact, that begins to offer another "face" of the fact.

It would carry us well beyond the limits of this paper to explore in detail what some of these intimational experiences reveal to us about the rational meaning of God. Suffice it to say, that among these we must include the renewed understanding of God as person, as hope, as promise, as immanent in the world, as suffering, as caring, as having a stake in the world He created, as love, as partner, etc. All of these dimensions of God-meaning have yet to be explored with the rational precision formerly accorded to the categories of the classical proofs. These are categories whose meanings are only now, despite their years of association with the believing consciousness, being deepened, made more precise, and translated into God-talk. The task ahead for the theologian and the philosopher of religion is formidable, but invitingly challenging.

Rider College
Lawrenceville, New Jersey, USA

ANALOGY OF THE TRINITY: A KEY TO STRUCTURAL PROBLEMS OF THE CONTEMPORARY WORLD[1]

Heinrich Beck

Christian Belief in Trinity as a Key

The statement of the inner personal structure of God — God is one in three persons — depicts the central mystery of Christian faith;[2] all further statements of faith covering creation, salvation, and perfection of the world can only be understood in this context.[3] But its meaning stretches beyond. When all finite being is a creation of God and this necessarily means a similarity and participation of its creator, then all being is an image of the Trinity: *analogia entis ultimatim est analogia trinitatis*. Resulting from its divine basis, all being in itself has a trinitarian structure. Thus "analogia trinitatis" is the deepest basis of understanding of the ontological structure of nature and culture; it is the last "hermeneutic key" of all structural problems.

There could be, however, this objection: The divine Trinity is the darkest and therefore the most severe mystery of faith to us. A problem, however, cannot be enlightened by an even more obscure principle. Consequently this "Trinity" principle is not qualified to master the problems of our world.

One has to inquire about the principal relation between Christian faith and human understanding, especially scientific rationality. Very likely Christian faith exceeds human understanding. If it, however, should be reasonable and involving responsibility, it must necessarily be expressed in our rational wording and has to penetrate into it. We have to know what we believe. In other words, the substance of belief penetrates into our limited human reason and simultaneously exceeds it by a "more than" sense. And this is the relation of correspondence and analogy.

Out of this, however, there results that from the very beginning, philosophical and scientific rationality must not be barred from faith; it must, on the contrary, be ready to be questioned by it. We have to try to answer such questions by using the free space of strictly rational

284

methods. To say it in a modified term of Kant: Faith goes into reason not as a constitutive, but as a regulative principle. Thus it can even more arouse reason within its own possibilities, proving hereby that it is rational and reasonable without being "swallowed" by reason. Neither shall theology be deduced out of philosophy, nor shall philosophy be falsified into theology. "Christian philosophy" is rather a strictly rational philosophy, in its philosophical character still increased by the inspiring force and vigor of faith. Only on the basis of such a philosophy can a theology be erected which is able to continue philosophical onsets. This in particular applies to the problem of the Trinity.

In what then can now be perceived the essential content of the Christian Trinity-belief, by which the philosophical-rational penetration of the world can be fundamentally stimulated, and which thus can give concretely and actually evidence of its credibility? The only personal, infinite and eternal God begets and speaks Himself perfectly in the Logos, who consequently as He-Himself is personal, infinite, and eternal. Both persons have their lively unity and community in the Holy Spirit, who therefore as the third person is perfectly equal to them according to his essence. It is well known that Augustine relates in a psychological analogy the bringing forth of the second person out of the first person in a special way to cognition and truth, the bringing forth of the third out of the first and second, however, to love and joy.[4] In this perspective it is told by Thomas Aquinas: "Like in God so is in us a circulation [circulatio] in the works of the knowing mind [intellectus] and the loving will [voluntas]; for the will returns into that, from which the intellect has its origin".[5]

Corresponding to these statements coming out of the tradition of Christian and Occidental philosophy and theology are statements of the Asian cultural sphere. In the old-Egyptian myths and conceptions of Gods, the triad played an important part. And according to the Upanishads of early India the name of God is Sat-Chit-Ananda, that is, being-logos-delight or also unit-thinking-joy.[6] When reality in its divine ground is a trinitarian movement of life, we must not be surprised when we find outlines of it also in the reality-experience of non-Christian religions. This is not simply a question of relativity, but rather that a confirmation of truth of Christian belief becomes clearly visible.

From the point of faith we are about to conceive the whole reality as a movement, impressed by the divine trinitarian ground: Being goes infinitely out of itself and returns to itself. The first means opening and truth, the last fulfillment and accomplishment. In a corresponding continuation of the doctrine of analogy of Thomas Aquinas here in the finite world, we can only find a remote and faint participation in the infinite God, which above all gives way to the liberty of creator and creation. In the explaining of Hegel's dialectical idealism, however, and its inversion to the dialectical materialism of Marx, the infinite ideal, material being and the finite being are molded respectively into one necessary dynamic identity. Also in the empiricism and positivism of the Western world, a modification of the original trinitarian conception of reality is displayed, insofar as here the reality is coming forth by experience and should be processed into a governed unity by the rationality of society.

The trinitarian conception of reality, suggested by Christian faith and in various forms modified by history and the present time, can indeed give us a key for enlightening the structural problems of today's world, which include the discussion with various ideological positions. Above all, we now have to outline the structure of trinitarian movement in nature and culture, in order to gain the existential-spiritual dimension of mastering the problems.

The Trinitarian Rhythm of Nature

The results of modern physics suggest the hypothesis that cosmic masses swing out of themselves and extend by themselves in space as if exploding, filling at the same time the newly opened space by forming new masses. Further to the general theory of relativity of Einstein, the physicist de Sitter concluded that the largeness of the radius of the universe cannot be constant. Facing this background, the red-shifting in the spectral light of the spiral nebulas, as stated by Hubble, could be understood, analogous to the Doppler effect in acoustics, as an expression of a flight motion of the stars, in the course of which the flight velocity increases corresponding to the distance. According to the general theory of relativity, a certain radius of the universe always corresponds to a certain total mass of the masses of the universe, so that an increase of the radius of the universe must run together with the new forming of mass. Now the physicist Unsold, and others in fact, came to the opinion, when discovering relatively young fixed stars, that the total mass of the universe did not exist as it is from the beginning, but grows continuously by repeated births of stars, the so-called supernova-phenomena.[7] In

286

philosophical interpretation of the empirical results and corresponding physical theories, the material being is represented as a pulsating rhythm, because (1) it proceeds out of itself and forms new potential space, in order to (2) accentuate itself at the same time into that space in a more deepening way. With the first, we can combine the nature-philosophical term "extensive quality," and with the last, the term "intensive quality."

To this motion-structure of the *macrocosm*, there responds in the *microcosm* the so-called "double nature" of material energy, which can be represented in the figures of wave and corpuscles. According to the conditions it swings between both habits, from a wavy-ecstatic radiation into space to a corpuscular condensation into static presence at one place. In such an energetic oscillation of the microcosm, investigated above all by the physicists Einstein, Planck, Heisenberg, Shrodinger and de Broglie, the described dynamics of expansion and contraction of the macrocosm are representing themselves.[8]

Only on the basis of this *physical* rhythm, a further actuating and concretion of mass in *chemical* processes is possible. In its chemical evolution, mass was formed to increasingly more different and complex molecular structures. Thus, as its potentiality was developed and disposed satisfactorily, a new and more intensive reality could be born, *life* itself.

The rhythmical contrary of the swinging-out-of-itself and the swinging-into-itself can also be perceived in the evolution of life following the great steps of plant, animal, and man. In the *plant*, life is totally turned outwards. According to the principle of maximum corporal outside independence — as of light, temperature, and conditions of air and soil — the plant is vertically built into the room of light. The evolutionary stage of the *animal* turns the life back to earth. According to the principle of minimum corporal outside and inside independence, in general it is horizontally built, which signifies a greater independence of environment and the ability of free local motion. That is, at least for higher animals, the expression of an "inwardness of sensual conscience," as Adolf Portmann says.[9]

At the stage of *man*, life turns basically from the horizontal to the vertical line, in which by the erected shape of the body is figured the transcendency of mind into the realm of truth and freedom. Thus man is, as Hans Andre says, the transcending repetition and synthesis of the structural principle of the plant and the animal.[10] Whereas the plant possesses the sexual organ as generic pole above and the root as individual pole below, the animal carries both poles in front and behind at the same ontic level. Man, however, has the individual pole as "head" ordered over the generic pole. The cosmic principle of the plant is overturned when reaching man while passing through the animal stage. So finally the evolution of life describes, in the whole comparable to the masses, the figure of a whirl or spiral movement.

The dynamic rhythm of the *phylogenesis*, almost a biological macrocosm, is mediated by a corresponding rhythm of the *ontogenesis*, which is almost the biological microcosm. The individual, as such, rises in the genus by sexuality, which is analogously structured. For the sexes are in their character and way of motion designed to reach mutual completion: The male principle is specially directed from the inside to outside, the female from the outside to inside. That is, in corporal structure and function the first one is more eccentric, the last one more concentric; and as a (remote) psychological equivalent, the first one is objective (abstract and distanced), the last one subjective (receptive and valuing). This contrary psycho-physical opposite, however, is only a relative one.[11]

So the life of the genus separates itself into both opposite sexes and embodies, upon their meeting, new individual possibilities. The child is the confluence, the transcending synthesis and continuation of the parents' life; and therefore it is similar to both of them. The inseminated cell, out of which it develops, differentiates by homologous division of the cell and parts out of its originally indeterminate unity into a plurality of opposite organs, by which its hidden character appears (the event of opening and truth). The parts, however, do not decay into an incoherent plurality. They complete themselves mutually to the unity and wholeness of the organism, by the means of which it grows into its own fullness and becomes accomplished (the event of integration and subsistence).[12]

This rhythm of "out-in" or "asunder-together" (structure of motion and embodiment) is also realized in other temporal forms of life, in the rhythm of the day, of the year, and of the ages. Every morning, life has a new beginning; it will grow silent in the evening. Analogously we can say: With the blossom of spring it breaks open, in order to return into itself with the fruit of autumn and to reappear with strength and vigor next year. In another analogy the time of development in childhood and youth can be described as the morning or spring of life, and the time of a last maturation and introversion in seniority, the evening or autumn of life.

The last aspects, however, are already going across the ontic dimension of mere nature as we come now to cultural phenomena.[13]

The Trinitarian Rhythm of Culture

The basis of all culture is the individual person, whose existence can be understood according to the above-mentioned trinitarian analogy of Augustine. By self-knowledge man goes intellectually out of himself and is placed in front of himself. In an "inward word," he speaks to himself, expresses himself, stands face to face with himself and looks upon himself. In this way, self-valuation and self-affirmation become possible, whereby man, in reasonable self-love, accepts himself, goes together with himself and into himself. But self-knowledge gives him also a critical distance to himself, so that he can work out his moral character and unite himself in creative liberty. Thus, man continually states new possibilities of his own existence, in order to actuate himself into them. His actuality is the process of self-actuating, which has the structure of the spiral rhythm of swinging out of himself and into himself. But this more or less explicit dialogue of the individual person with himself is very imperfect because it does not lead to self-satisfaction and needs, in its concrete form, the mediation of society. Such agrees with modern social philosophy. Already the language by which the individual man meets himself, criticizes himself, and cultivates himself, originates from the surrounding culture, which is emphasized, for example, by W. v. Humboldt, Herder, Dilthey and Wittgenstein.[14] The smallest cell of this cultural event is the concrete *interpersonal meeting* and relation. Man goes out of himself to his fellowmen; in every sentence, he speaks out, he exposes himself to them. By reaction and answer of his fellowmen he experiences and finds himself. Enriched and changed, he returns from every meeting to himself and so he actuates himself in continuously newly produced possibilities and forms, which is specially investigated in the phenomenological, respectively hermeneutic social philosophy and philosophy of language, existential philosophy and philosophy of meeting.[15]

By such "micro-events" is mediated the "macro-occurrence" of universal history. By the common work of culture, by labor and technique, mankind expresses itself by means of creative formation in the material nature, in which it consequently reflects itself, observes and meets itself. Thereby it can and must continually order, strengthen, and actuate itself. And that is the motivation of the progress of history.[16]

At first, mankind had to spread from its original place to all over the earth, in order to condense in different places and to culturally fulfill and actuate its territory. By this streaming into their own possibilities, the separated parts of mankind got and get a permanently increasing importance for each other. They went out of their dispersion into a community of destiny. Once the different fields of life and culture were dissociated in their qualitative structure, here and there cultural synthesis came into existence, such as in Europe in the Middle Ages. But the once gained "qualitative unity" of a culture had, as in modern times, to break again and, so to speak, to open itself by means of the achievements of the quantifying sciences and techniques. Now new quantitative far-reaching effects to all parts of mankind and the cosmos could begin. Mankind is brought now to the universal and total decision, either to accept itself mutually in its parts and to complete itself towards a communicative world-culture, or to perish entirely in a worldwide catastrophe.[17] Viewing that fact, the rhythmical actuating process of divergence and convergence, embracing nature and culture, today comes into crisis, in which the "to be" or "not to be" of the future of the world will be decided.[18]

This critical tension is accentuated in the political and cultural contrast of West and East, which in its destructive danger and constructive task can be understood again by the "hermeneutic key" of trinitarian structure. Europe and the New World, as far as it has developed culturally out of Europe, incline to analysis, dismembering, and separation of all fields of life, also to a strong accentuation of individual differences reaching to individualism and radical pluralism. Asia, Africa, and the New World, as far as it is related to it, incline to a stronger accentuation of the unity in all plurality, of the connection with all fields of reality and of nations and men ending in the relativity of all differences in a radical monism of being and consciousness. This accentuatedly different expression in culture and anthropology of West and East can be remotely compared with the above-mentioned contrariety of male and female. Thus the polar contrasts in mankind are summoned to a partnership and solidarity in mutually creative completion, that is, to a living order of freedom, which overcomes in its distorted picture, the paralyzed balance of terror.[19]

The Existential and Spiritual Dimension

These philosophical perspectives, shown in the discourse with sciences of nature and culture, can move us to an existential break-up in faith, which offers the deepest basis for mastering the problems of our world. Nature and history swing as an analogous participation in the trinitarian rhythm of God as out of Him and into Him. In that, God becomes more and more powerful. Thus, He Himself can be the vigorous source of solution, as far as the being opens itself by faithful confidence in His actuating actuality. Then the mastering of problems does not happen out of a man, selfishly closed in himself (in all events it would exceed his finite abilities) but out of the freely working and penetrating trinitarian actuality itself, at whose disposal he wants to be. Not the man, who in his finite essence is overstressed and overtaxed, is able to take the task, but only that one, who loses himself in God, that is, who lets God approach and actuate him.

If mankind starts leaving its self-constructed systems of solving problems, its attempts of securing and its precautions of anxiety by transgression of devotion and confidence, it would be in accordance with the outlined history of nature and culture. For every higher and more compromising new forming in nature and culture requires the dissolution (and in critical cases of induration the often painful breaking-up) of old forms. Such a deprivation (or steresis) of all fixed and, as it seems, of holding and security-giving structures, means for the being the precondition for receiving new things. The hope that this also in the future will succeed motivates the stepping forth of historical inevitability, either to perish in anxiety and isolation, or, by the decision for risk, to incur the provocation of history and to be at its disposal.

In history, this offer of sense was long ago symbolically prepared before the destiny of nature; for always during the phylogenetical or ontogenetical realization, the old form was broken up by the pressure of a more comprising and higher form, in fact a new actuality took place. That is, the actuality is always fundamentally approaching and offering itself, so that being only has to open itself and to receive it.

By this knowledge, the fundamental actuality does not retain itself but goes out of itself and approaches the event of Christ in its trinitarian depth and is disclosed. For in Christ the infinite divine actuality itself goes out of itself and becomes a man, has left the godhead and taken the form of men[20] in order to finitely invite and redeem mankind by the completion of the Holy Spirit.[21] By that it becomes apparent that God in Himself is this motion, an infinitely going-out-of-Himself and making Himself of no reputation in order to return infinitely to Himself and to complete Himself. While He totally speaks Himself in the "word" (or begets Himself in the "Son"), He as well is originally and infinitely in Himself (= "Father") as therefore infinitely out of Himself and in front of Himself (= "Son"). This infinite space, in which God communicates Himself, is infinitely filled by the "effusion" or "spiration" of the Holy Spirit, who "penetrates the depths of the godhead."[22]

As the trinitarian cyclical motion of God means, that infinite being goes totally out of itself and totally into itself, this motion is ever and always absolutely and perfectly before all things and over them, whatever may go out of it and return to it. Anything else can only be a free and symbolical continuation of the original process. Thus the event of incarnation in time, in which God leaves his godhead and accepts the fellowship of men, can only be an image of his eternal trinitarian going out of Himself, to which basically nothing new is added. Incarnation is the "super-fluous" and free continuation of the eternal and infinite going out, in the mission of the Spirit, the continuation of the eternal and infinite spiration. All that can be seen in the infinite humanity of Jesus: He understands, forgives, suffers, risks and loves infinitely. But to be infinitely human, that is, to be as man infinitely actual, can only be an infinitely actual existent, God Himself. As finite being, a mere man is also only finitely human; to be human can be declared by us only with finite truth and relative authorization. In nothing else but in the infinite humanity of Jesus, the infinite being steps out of itself and opens the access to itself.[23]

This trinitarian going out of the divine substance itself can be observed until the extreme desertion of every community at the cross; God leaves here not only his godhead but also his being human. As man He is totally devastated; He has no longer a "human form,"[24] and in His cry of despair, "My God, my God, why hast thou forsaken me?"[25] He makes our desertion of God His own.

Yet by means of this extreme loneliness and frankness of God, the Holy Spirit becomes free and brings with Him salvation as the most intimate completion possible. The crucified "spirates" out His "life" and He "commends His spirit,"[26] which is received on the day of Pentecost and founds a new community, the "church." In the church the going out of God Himself is realized by another step: God loses His outer human form, assumes the forms and sensual qualities of food and drink, in order that all men can anywhere and always "live by and out of Him." This sign of "ec-in-sistence" is to the incarnate so essential and characteristic that the disciples of Emmaus recognized Him by breaking bread.[27] Such an offering and going out as food for all builds up His community as His new body in the Holy Spirit; it is, so to speak, the continuation of incarnation through space and time, as the last and actual "ec-in-sistential" sense of nature and history.[28]

The entrance into this spiritual dimension of "ec-in-sistence" as a participating cooperation and further mediating actuation of trinitarian motion through nature and history happens in "baptism" as a "rebirth out of water and [fire] spirit":[29] The man has to be newly "born," i.e., he has to leave his protecting, but afterwards suffocating, room of his merely natural and finitely ensured existence. That happens by break-up and dissolution of his old structure: The "water" dissolves, so to speak, the physical basis, while the "Spirit of love" dissolves the personal center of the human being. This "baptism" as immersion into the dissolving elements (water and fire) penetrates and alters the whole man, as far as he abandons himself to them and actually lets them loosen and liberate himself. Thus, "baptism" is the beginning of a new spiritual and organic structure that originates from the nourishment and "wedding" in continual eucharist. This, however, means that God and men expose one another, that they mutually penetrate themselves, that they have mutual confidence in themselves. Such an existentially rooted execution of the eucharist is according to its meaning the pulsating center of dedication and actuality in historical progress.

But in this "salvation-history" the going out is deepened, as it seems, by alienation and perversion of its sense. When, for example, the official Christian Church takes some precautions and attempts to establish itself in dogmatic, moral and juridical fields (likewise when certain groups start anti-actions), so then can be perceived a mistrusting anxiety, which does not seriously rely on God. Should the destiny of Jesus be repeated on behalf of His church? The crisis of nature and culture, the whole structural problem of the modern world, requires an existential and spiritual engagement, in which man extensively breaks up himself, transcends himself to his ground and approaches it in the courageous and trusting risk of active self-possession.

Conclusion

God, the ground of all actuality, goes out of Himself by the word and completes Himself in the Holy Spirit. This mystery of faith can be a light and an invitation to discover empirical facts of our world and to understand them in new connections. According to scientific hypotheses following up the general theory of relativity, the cosmic mass opens in spatial extension ontic possibilities, which it completes in a new forming of masses in the supernova-stars. In a similar way, life describes in its phylogenetical and ontogenetical evolution, a rotating spiral in which it continuously produces new possibilities and actuates itself into them. According to the trinitarian psychology of Augustine, the spiritual ontogenesis of an individual person is also analogously structured. And in the discourse with the sciences of culture, the essence of human communication, human work in culture, technique, and history, until the present structure of mankind, can further be understood in this light. It prepared finally the knowledge for the existential transcending of itself and for the completion of faith. In this way, the loosening ground of the structural problems of today's world is unlocked.

Thus "Analogia Trinitatis" proves to be a "hermeneutic key" for a better rational understanding of the empirical world out of the faith and, of the faith, out of the experience of world. So the abstract and, as it seems, remote principle of faith and of Christian metaphysics must and can be fruitfully mediated with the concrete and near results and problems of the empirical sciences of nature and of culture and with the human existence. Analogy means dynamic difference in the unity and the unity in the difference; it determines the relation as well of the world and of God as also of fields in the world to one another. The conception of analogy is in itself an analogous conception, which always newly breaks up from itself and transcends itself into a deeper actuality. It distinguishes and unites, and therefore it differentiates and integrates science into an "ec-in-sistential" motion.

(Tr. by Erwin Schadel)

University of Bamberg-Salzburg
Germany

NOTES

1. According to a lecture at the World Congress of Christian Philosophy, 21-28 October 1979, in Embalse (Cordóba, Argentina), plenary session 1: Christian Metaphysics. The manuscript, simultaneously published in Spanish (in: Actes of the Congress, Cordoba 1980), in Portuguese (Rio de Janeiro 1980), and in German (in: Salzb. *Jahrbuch für Philos.* XXV, 1980), was, compared with the Congress-lecture, enlarged by chapters 4 and 5 and the footnotes. A first historical and comprehensive systematical foundation of this sketch was tried in my work: *Der Akt-Charakter des Seins. Eine spekulative Weiterführung der Seinslehre Thomas v. Aquins aus einer Anregung durch das dialektische Prinzip Hegels,* München 1965 [the same under the title: *El ser como acto,* Pamplona 1968]. Here can only be presented the draft of a research-project that includes the critical and constructive dialogue between philosophy, theology, and the single sciences of nature and culture. It is intended to invite all interested scholars to communicate their critical analyses.

2. See Denzinger-Schönmetzer, *Enchir.* symbol. 75 (the formerly to Athanase ascribe symbolon "Quicumque"), 125 f (Nicaenum I), 150 (Constantinopolitanum I), 525-531 (11th Council of Toledo), 88 ff; also: Michael Schmaus, *Katholische Dogmatik,* Bd. 1, Munchen 1960, p. 194-678.

3. Compare the relation of "immanent" and "economical" Trinity, for example, by Leo Scheffczyk, *Der Eine und Dreifaltige Gott,* Mainz 1968; Karl Rahner, *Bemurkungen zum dogmatischen Traktat "De Trinitate,"* in: Schriften zur Theologie, Einsiedeln 1960, pp. 103-133; *the same,* Der dreifaltige Gott als transazendenter Urgrund der Heilsgeschichte, in: *Mysterium salutis.* Grundrib heilsgeschichtlicher Dogmatik. Arsg. v. Joh. Feiner und Magnus Löhrer. Bd. II, Einsiedeln 1967, pp. 317-401.

4. Compare the main qualities of the soul "esse-nosse-velle" (*Confessiones* XII, 11, 12) and the corresponding ternaries "memoria-intelligentia-voluntas" and "mens-notitia-amor" (*De Trinitate* X-XV); also: M. Schmaus, *Die psychologische Trinitätslehr des heiligen Augustinus,* Münster 1927 [Photomech. Repr. with an addendum and supplements of literature, Münster 1967].

5. *Pot.* q. 9 a. 9; the full text:
Intelligere nostrum est secundum motum a rebus in animam;
velle vero secundum motum ab anima ad res . . . . Est ergo tam
in nobis quam in Deo circulatio quaedam in operibus intellectus
et voluntatis; nam voluntas redit in id a quo fuit principium
intelligendi. Sed in nobis concluditur circulus ad id quod est
extra, dum bonum exterius movet intellectum nostrum, et
intellectus movet voluntatem, et voluntas tendit per appetitum et
amorem in exterius bonum; sed in Deo iste circulus clauditur in
seipso. Nam Deus . . . omnia intelligit intelligendo seipsum: et
ex hoc . . . procedit in amorem omnium et sui ipsius."
Compare also *S. theol.* I q. 27-43; further: P. Vanier, *Theologie trinitaire
chez S. Thomas d'Aquin*, Paris 1953. - Systematic sketches of a trinitarian
ontology, that are related to the sketches of Augustine and Thomas
Aquinas, by Gustav Siewerth, *Der Thomismus als Identitätssystem*,
Frankfurt/M. [2]1961; Hans André, *Annäherung Gleichnis des dreieinigen
Gottes*, Salzburg 1952; Walter Simonis, *Zeit und Existenz. Grundzuge
der Metaphysik und Ethik*, Kevelaer 1972. (Eichstätter Studien. N.F. Bd.
7.) [Rec.: H. Beck in: *Theolog. Rev.* 70 (1974) 493 f.]; Hans-Eduard
Hengstenberg, *Seinsüberschreitung und Kreativität*, Salzburg-Munchen
1979 (Salzburger Studien zur Philosophie 12.); Heinz Wipfler,
*Grundfragen der Trinitätsspekulation. Die Analogiefrage in der
Trinitätstheologie*, Regensburg 1977. [Rec.: Willy Bongard, in: SJPh
XXV (1980).]

6. Compare also the three great Gods Brahma, Vishnu, Shiva, that are
sometimes collected to a triunity (trimurti). To Brahma is ascribed the
"creation," to Vishnu the "conservation" and to Shiva the "destruction,"
but also the "sanctification" of the world. To that: Helmut Glasenapp,
Die nicht-christlichen Religionen (Frankfurt: 1957), p. 164.

7. See Albert Einstein (1879-1955): *Die Grundlage der allgemeinen
Relativitätstheorie.* Leipaig 1916; *Über die spezielle und allgemeine
Relativitätstheorie* 21. ed., Braunschweig 1969; *Grundzuge der
Relativitätstheorie.* 5. ed., Braunschweig 1969; Willem de Sitter (1872-
1934): *Kosmos.* A course of six lectures on the development of our
insight into the structure of the universe, Cambridge 1932; the
astronomical aspect of the theory of relativity, Berkeley 1933.
(Following up the general theory of relativity in 1917 he propounded the

first cosmological model of an expanding universe, which is called the *De-Sitter-World*); by Edwin Powell Hubble (1889-1953): *Redshifts of the spectra of nebulae*, Oxford 1934; *The realm of the nebulae*, London 1936 (dt. Braunschweig 1938); *The observational approach to cosmology*, Oxford 1937 (As far as the observed red-shifting can be declared by the Doppler-effect, the Hubble-effect confirms the relativistic cosmology, developed by Willem de Sitter); by Albrecht Otto Johannes Unsöld: *Physik und Sternatmosphären*. 2. ed., Berlin 1955; *Der neue Kosmos*. 2. ed., Berlin 1974; popular: Sterne und Mensche, Berlin 1972. Compare Otto Heckmann's presentation of different theories on the phenomena of red-shifting of the spectral lines and their interpretation as present expansion of the world: *Einstein und das Weltsystem*, in: Von Erde und Weltall, Stuttgart 1958 (Kröner Tb. Bd. 236), p. 149-160. Critically to this interpretation of red-shifting Freundlich's merely empirical formula, according to which the red-shifting can be calculated by the temperature of the radiating field, ibid. 165-167. Further: Joseph Meurers, *Allgemeine Astronomie*, Frieburg 1970, 121; Wolfgang Büchel, *Philosophische Probleme der Physik*, Frieburg-Basel-Wien 1965; Zur Geburt neuer Sterne: Hans Kienle, *Die Vorstellungen von der Entwicklung der Welt*, in: Von Erde und Weltall, Stuttgart 1958, p. 18; Hans Vogel, *Vom Atom zum Universum. Einführung in die Kosmologie*, Nürnberg 1953, see spec. p. 231, 253 s., where P. Jordan and C. F. v. Weizsäcker are cited as representatives of an interpretation of the super-novae in the sense of a new forming of stars. A special problem seems to be their compatibility with the sentence of the conservation (resp. "constant total quantity") of energy, as also the energetic identity and invariability of the world, expressed by Heisenberg's world-formula "0 = 0": Every increase of "positive" energy is compensated by exactly the same increase of "negative" energy. For solving this problem you have to pay attention to the sense of physical theories and conceptual constructions: There are only functional conceptions, which are used to as simple and elegant as possible calculating of empirical phenomena and which therefore cannot directly by interpreted as "ontological" statements. So, for example, an ontological content cannot be coordinated to the mathematical functional conception "$\sqrt{-1}$." In this context is a special question, whether the (increasing) "positive" energy has another relation to reality as the (proportionally increasing) "negative" one. Concerning the fundamental methodological difference of scientific functional conceptions and ontological intentions compare: Hans André, *Urbild und*

Ursache in der Biologie, München 1931; dispositions to an interpretation of various components of the modern physical "Weltanschauung" in direction to a trinitarian conception of reality by: Bernhard Philbert, *Der Dreieine,* Stein/Rh. 1976.

8. Max Planck (1858-1947): *Vorlesungen uber Thermodynamik,* Berlin [11]1964; *Physikalische Abhandlungen und Vorträge.* 3 Bde., Braunschweig 1958; *Die Quantenhypothese,* München-Battenberg 1969; Werner Karl Heisenberg: *Die physikalischen Prinzipien der Quantentheorie,* Leipzig 1930. Machdr. Mannheim 9. ed., Stuttgart 1959; *Die Physik der Atomkerne,* Braunschweig 1943; *Das Naturbild der heutigen Physik,* Hamburg 1955; *Physik und Philosophie,* Frankfurt 1959; *Einführung in die einheitliche Feldtheorie der Elementarteilchen,* Stuttgart 1967; *Der Teil und das Ganze,* München 1969; Schritte uber Grenzen, München 1971. In the thesis of Louis de Broglie: "Recherches sur la théorie des Quanjta" (Paris 1924) are developed the fundamental ideas of the wave-corpuscle-dualism. By his introduction of the conception of material waves (=Broglie-waves) he was able to explain Bohr's condition of quanta and the occurrence of stable electron-courses in the atoms. Simultaneously he initiated the discovery of wave-mechanics by Erwin Schrödinger (1887-1961). Compare further: *Einführung in die Wellenmechanik,* Leipzig 1929; *Licht und Materie,* Hamburg, Baden-Baden 1949; Following up the ideas of L. de Broglie about material waves and wave-corpuscle-dualism E. Schrödinger developed in 1926 the wave-mechanics as a kind of non-relativistic quantum theory; compare his Collected Papers on wave mechanics, New York 1978 (= *Abhandlungen zur Wellenmechanik,* 1927); *Die Wellenmechanik,* Stuttgart 1963; further: *Briefe zur Wellenmechanik.* Briefwechsel Erwin Schrödingers mit Max Planck, Albert Einstein und Hendrik Antoon Lorentz. Hrsg. v. K. Przibram, Wien 1963. Schrödinger turned the quantum theory, created by Planck, Einstein and Bohr, to a non-relativistic one.

9. Compare A. Portmann, *Biologie und Geist,* Frankfurt 1973, pp. 15-17, 135 (162), 239 f., 284.

10. Hans André: *Die dreieinige Selbstüberschreitung als Urprozeß alles Lebendigen,* Braunsberg 1935; the same, *Sinnreich des Lebens,* Salzburg 1952; *Licht und Sein. Betrachtungen über den ontologischen Offenbarungssinn des Lichtes und den Schöpfungssinn der Evolution,*

298

Regensburg 1963. [Rec. H. Beck, in: Salzb. *Jahrb. fur Philos.* VIII (1964) 272-274.] Concerning the rhythmical occurrences in nature see: Hans André, *Ausbergungs-und Schutzhullenereignungen in der Schöpfung*, in: *Innerlichkeit und Erziehung*. Gedenkschrift G. Siewerth. Hrsg. v. F. Pöggeler, Frieburg 1964, pp. 193-205. On the dynamical view of reality by André see: Heinrich Beck, *Natur-Geschichte-Mysterium. Die Materie als Vermittlungsgrund der Seinsereignung* im Denken von Hans André, in: Salzb. *Jahrb. für Philos.* XII/ZIII (1968/69) 95-129.

11. Compare to that: Philipp Lersch, *Vom Wesen der Geschlechter*, München 1968; Frederik J. J. Buytendijk, *Die Frau-Natur, Erscheinung, Dasein*, Köln 1953; Heinrich Beck, Arnulf Rieber, *Anthropologie und Ethik der Sexualität. Zur ideologischen Auseinandersetzung um körperliche Liebe*, Salzburg-München 1981.

12. To that also: Adolf Hass, *Das Lebendige: Spiegel seiner selbst. Versuch einer naturphilosophischen Lebensdefinition*, in: Scholastik 36 (1961) 161-192; the same, *Der Präsenzakt, ein unbekannter fundamentaler Lebensakt*, in: Scholastik 38 (1963) 32-53.

13. Concerning the cyclical (resp. spiral) motion of cosmos and the evolution of nature in their relation to divinity see: Heinrich Beck, *Die rhythmische Struktur der Wirklichkeit*, in Philosophia naturalis 9 (1965) 485-504; the same, *Der Akt-Charakter des Seins*. Eine spekulative Weiterführung der Seinslehre Thomas V. Aquins aus einer Anregung durch das dialektische Prinzip Hegels, München 1965. Here in particular pp. 321-334 about the progressive rhythm of material, organical and intellectual life; subsequently pp. 334-343: outline of an analogous (and free) structure of history and culture.

14. Compare, for example, Wilhelm von Humboldt's speech of the "Weltansicht" of the language of single nations in: *Schriften zur Sprachphilosophie* (= Werke in funf Banden, III), 5 ed. Darmstadt 1979 [pp. 230-367 about the relation of language and nations]; Johann Gottfried Herder, *Sprachphilosophische Schriften*. Hrsg. v. Erich Heintel, Hamburg 1964, specially: Vernunft und Sprache. *Eine Metakritik zur Kritik der reinen Vernunft* (1799); Wilhelm Dilthey, *Der Aufbau der geschichtlichen Welt in den Geisteswissen-schaften*, Stuttgard-Göttingen 1973, pp. 146-152; Ludwig Wittgenstein, *Philosophische Untersuchungen*

(1958), in: Wittgenstein, Schriften I, Frankfurt 1960, 1962. [There is no private language. We use interpersonally obligatory rules of speaking. There are as many plays of speaking as there are forms of life. Compare Wittgenstein's influence on Oxford Orginary Language Philosophy.]

15. For perspectives of individual development and education, that result from a spirally rotating structure of human communication, see H. Beck, *Philosophische Grundlegung zu Begriff und Sinn von "Erzeihungsmitteln,"* in: the same (ed.), *Philosophie der Erziehung*, Freiburg-Basel-Wien 1979, pp. 196-203. When man speaks out himself, he founds a relation to fellowmen. Compare the widespread tendency of contemporary philosophy to begin from "we," and not from an isolated "I," for example in the *Phenomenological Explication of Social Experience* by Edmund Husserl, Die Krisis der europäischen Wissenschaften und die transzendentale Phänomenologie. Eine Einleitung in die phanomenologische Philosophie. Hrsg. v. Walter Biemel (= Husserliana, VI), 2 ed., Den Haag 1962; Alfred Schütz, *Der sinnhafte Aufbau der sozialen Welt.* Eine Einleitung in die verstehende Soziologie, Wien 1932. Repr. Frankfurt 1974; Bernhard Waldenfels, *Das Zwischenreich des Dialogs.* Sozialphilosophische Untersuchungen in Anschluß an Edmund Husserl, Den Haag 1971; the same, *Der geistesgeschichtliche Hintergrund: Vom Ich zum Wir,* in: Claus Heitmann u. Heribert Mühlen (ed.), *Erfahrung und Theologie des Heiligen Geistes,* Freiburg-München 1974, pp. 162-175. About the meeting of "I" and "you" ("Philosophie der Begegnung" in a strictly speaking) see: Ferdinand Ebner, *Wort und Liebe,* Regensburg 1935; Martin Buber, *Das dialogische Prinzip,* 3. ed., Heidelberg 1973; *Urdistanz und Beziehung. Beiträge zu einer philosophischen Anthropologie,* 4. ed. Heidelberg 1978; to that: Josef Boeckenhoff, *Die Begegnungs-philosophie. Ihre Geschichte ihre Aspekte,* Freiburg-München 1970.

16. Concerning self-objectivating and acquisition of one's own essence by labor and techniques see: H. Beck, *Kulturphilosophie der Technik. Perspektiven zu Technik* - Menschheit - Zukunft, Trier 1979 (spec. pp. 32-38: The "ontological place" of techniques, and pp. 48-72: The positive sense of techniques in world-history). Because of their Feuerbachian-dialogical coning became important for the "Begegnungsphilosophie" the Economical-philosophical or Parisian Manuscripts of the young Marx of 1844, in: *MEW Erg. 1,* Berlin 1968,

300

spec. pp. 536-546 and 568-588. In the last-mentioned place Hegel is valued, because he sees the essence of man in labor (which for Marx, however, is illusiorily idealistic and perverse because of the theological and "heilsgeschichtlichen" foundation).

17. In comparison with a romantic conception of the Middle Ages is here — at least partially — accepted, what Hans Blumenberg calls the "Legitimität der Neuzeit" (Frankfurt 1966, enl. single ed. of the parts 1 and 2 under the title: *Säkularisierung und Selbstbehauptung*, Frankfurt 1974, and of the part 3 under the title: *Der Prozeß der theoretischen Neugierde*, Frankfurt 1973). In a more positive manner then by Heidegger person (subject) and techniques are appreciated here as legitimate occurrences of Western modern culture. Compare to that also: Denis de Rougement: *L'aventure occidental de l'homme*, Paris 1957, who calls person and machine two excellent actualities of Occidental culture.

18. The positive or negative end of history, i.e., the question whether mankind will master its provocation in our view philosophically is left open. In contrast to that, certain deterministic and teleological philosophers of history believed, impressed by the biblical expectation of salvation, that history in spite of all accidental absurdities is fundamentally meaningful because of the future and certainly coming positive end. According to Karl Löwith (*Weltgeschichte und Heilsgeschehen. Die theologischen Voraussetzungen der Geschichtsphilosophie*, Stuttgard-Berlin-Köln-Mainz 1953, 5. ed. 1967) mean the modern theological conceptions of history, nominally by Burckhardt (27-37), Marx (38-54), Hegel (55-61) Proudhon (63-68), Comte (68-87), Condorcet and Turgot (87-98), Voltaire (99-108), Vico (109-128), Bossuet (129-135) secularizations of the theology of history, especially of Joachim de Fiore (136-147), Augustine (148-158), and Orosius (160-167), that directly can be referred to the biblical explanation of history. The question is, however, whether the sense of history is founded only by its factually god exit, or it primarily means, by its essential relation to such one, the encouraging invitation to liberty, simultaneously, however, the possibility of failure. Such a "sense as essential relation" is philosophically accessible to an onto-dynamical analysis of structure, but "sense as factually good exit in future" is a thing of believing. A "philosophy of history," based in argumentation in the last "sense," would be in fact nothing other than a disguised theology.

19. For further characteristics of the difference between West and East see, for example: Denis de Rougement, *L'aventure occidental de l'homme*, Paris 1957; Jean Gebser, *Asien Lächelt anders*. Ein Beitrag zum Verständnis östlicher Wesensart, Berlin-Frankfurt-Wien 1968; the same, *Ursprung und Gegenwart*. Bde. 1.2., Stuttgart 1953; Walter Schubart, *Europa und die Seele des Ostens*, Luzern 1943; Ursula v. Mangoldt, *Buddha lächelt, Maria weint*, Munchen-Planegg 1958; Heinrich Beck, *Kulturphilosophie der Technik. Perspektiven zu Technik-Menschheit-Zukunt*, Trier 1979, pp. 118-122; the same, Aufriß eines Forschungsvorhabens zur Grundlegung einer "Ethik der Politik" als Beitrag zur Friedensforschung, in: *Internationale Dialog-Zeitschrift* 3 (1970) 345-347, und in: *Zukunfts- und Friedensforschung - Information* 6 (1970) 65-67; the same, *Bietrag der Ontologie zu einer sinnvollen und friedlichen Ordnung der Völker*. Zur kulturanthropologischen Struktur der Menschheit. Referat 4. Internat. Kongreß für Christliche Philosophie Curitiba/Brasil 1978, in: *Acts of the Congress 1979, and in: Zeitschr. fur Ganzheitsforschung* 23 (1979) 85-91. Concerning the dimension of the West-East contrast in the philosophy of religion see: the same, *Anthropologischer Zugang zum Glauben. Eine rationale Meditation*, Salzburg-Munchen 1979.

20. St. Paul even says: "Who, being in the form of God thought it not robbery to be equal with God, but made himself of no reputation and took upon him the *form of a servant*" (*Phil.* 2, 6 s).

21. This is the "comforter" (*St. John* 14, 16.26) and the "essence of the good" (see synoptically *St. John* 6, 63.68; 14, 16; 15, 26; 16, 7; *Rom.* 14, 17; *Gal*, 5, 22; *Eph.* 4, 3; 2 *Tim.* 1, 7; *Acts* 2, 38; 10, 45).

22. Compare 1 *Cor.* 2,10.

23. Concerning further anthropological and epistemological reflections see: H. Beck, *Anthropologischer Zugang zum Glauben. Eine rationale Meditation*, Salzburg-Munchen 1979.

24. Compare *Is.* 52, 14.

25. *St. Matt.* 27, 46; *St. Mark* 15, 34.

26. St. Luke 23, 46. See also Felix Porsch, *Pneuma und Wort. Ein exegetischer Beitrag zur Pneumatologie des Johannesevangeliums*, Frankfurt/M. 1974, for example 339 s. Here also is to refer to the trinitarian conception of Passion by Origen, *Entretien avec Héraclide*, 7. Publ. par J. Scherer, Paris 1960 (Sources chrét. 67), pp. 70-73.

27. *St. Luke* 24, 30 s.

28. *Concerning the historical and ontological foundation of that formula see:* H. Beck, *Ek-in-sistenz. Sum Seinsvoll-zug des Menschen, in: De homine. Studia Hodiernae Anthropologiae. Acta VII. congressus Thomistici Internationalis*, Vol. II, Rom 1972; and the same, Statische Wesensontologie oder modernes dynamisches Weltbild? Die Aufgabe einer ek-in-sitentiellen Synthese, in: Salzb. *Jahrb. für Philos.* XVI XVI (1971/72) 21-25; concerning anthropological aspects: the same, Existenz in Freiheit-Geborgenheit in Ungeborgenheit. Die christliche Existenzphilosophie des Peter Wust, in: *Wissenschaft und Weltbild.* Zeitschr. für Grundfragen der Forschung 23 (1970) 304-313; the same Materie-Geist-Gemeinschaft. *Philosophische Vorüberlegungen zu einer Theologie des Geistes unter der Provokation der Sinfrage*, in: *Lebendiges Zeugnis* (1973, H. 1-2), 39-49.

29. *St. John* 3,5.

CHRISTIANITY AND METAPHYSICS IN A HUMANISTIC CULTURE

Mary-Rose Barral

Metaphysics is often thought of as the third degree of abstraction, the highest type of philosophizing, the investigation of being itself as it is in its very nature. Metaphysics, for some, seems to imply a type of reflection totally separate from or above our everyday contact with reality, the reality of this planet and of the human beings who make it a world by reason of their conscious lives. These allegations are true in a sense, for that kind of metaphysics which is concerned only with "thinking about thinking," forgetting concrete experience.

If philosophizing is "reflecting on experience," then a true metaphysics must be concerned with the world in all its mysterious and complex reality vis-a-vis human beings, in their immediate relation to the Creator. Seen in this light, metaphysics must take into account not only the physical configuration of the planet and its inhabitants but also the complex of all that which human beings have created, that is, the cultures which express the human concerns of the ages past as well as present.

Cultures reveal human wisdom in the context of nature and of historical events, the understanding of the purpose of human life, and the aspirations of the human soul in any given time and place. Doing metaphysics is then a learning to view the world and human beings in a new light, not just a method for abstracting from reality a series of theoretical hypotheses or a chain of logically related concepts.

Metaphysics is then a study of being, and of beings, in daily human relations, work, joys and sorrows, triumphs and trials. Seen in this light, metaphysics is found to have its roots deep in the fabric of life, and metaphysicians attempt to discover and illuminate the common elements of the beings of our experience, whose essential and existential source is Being itself.

It may be objected that this is not metaphysics but rather a description or evaluation of life. It is a beginning of analysis. However, the ascent to metaphysics is inevitable. Just as in the understanding of religion and in a philosophy dealing with God, it is easy to ascend, from the recognition and study of Being, as revealed by the beings of our experience, to the Being who transcends all nature and creation, so too, from the lower reaches of metaphysical reflection, we learn to recognize both the simple and complex natures of our experience as real manifestations of Being in nature: physical, sentient, human, spiritual.

Is it necessary for metaphysics to arrive at the highest universal concepts, embracing the widest possible range of beings, in order to claim true knowledge? It seems not. Granted, universal concepts are useful tools for the communication of ideas, but the heart of metaphysics cannot be found in abstraction, just as the heart of religion is not found in theoretical notions of what the "nature" of God might be.

Wherein, then, does one find a valid and relevant science of being, a metaphysics which really touches the lives of human beings and becomes the foundation of a spiritual light to guide both thought and action?

There is a notion of a Christian metaphysics, open to the true believer, one which does not refuse an Absolute, which rests on a valid body of eternal truths as found in Revelation. This notion seems to point out that there are really two sets of truths, one sacred and the other profane. True, one can begin philosophizing either from a purely human point of view, or from a religious premise. Does the search for truth differ depending on the point of departure? It seems clear that the metaphysician, in trying to ascertain the nature of beings and of Being, has to arrive at the truth, and will eventually recognize the contingent nature of the beings of our experience, the only beings to which we have access. From this discovery, the step to an Absolute of some kind seems inevitable. The difference between the two is that the Christian begins with a certitude, the non-Christian with a basic question about reality. It is at least debatable whether there is such a thing as a purely profane approach to Being. It seems more sensible to see any approach to being as a step in the direction of Truth, which is, in every sense of the word, "sacred."

The investigation of the world, with all its mystery and with its load of ambiguities, must then take into consideration not a neutral nature or a "natural" human being, but a transformed world and a human being already enriched beyond the natural condition, because of the cultural influences which have a bearing on every creature coming to life. Cultures, however, also work in reverse by depriving the individual of the richness accumulated by the wisdom and ingenuity of ages past and of present accomplishments. A true metaphysical investigation must take all this into account in order to have a true picture of the human person in the world today. But then, what happens to the notion of a universal definition, applicable to all genre of beings, to all human beings in particular, one which adequately describes human nature and every single concrete existent? Must we renounce metaphysics, as understood traditionally, for some relatively contingent kind of description? Or, must one absolutize the accidents of time, place, relation, etc. to make them part of a universal concept of nature in general and of human nature in particular? And if we arrive at the highest level of metaphysical reflection, must we relativize also the notion of God to present Him as perceived by the understanding of the various cultures?

These questions are very relevant to our discussion: there are no easy answers. Many works have been written to sustain the theory of a relativized world, of a relativized human person, even of a contingent God. We cannot digress into a discussion of these ideas, but generally, they deal with the points already mentioned of the real transformation of the world and the human person by cultures. What then, can a metaphysics in a Christian context preserve as basic truth in this context? It seems that it is precisely in a Christian context that the notion of a person in the world cannot be taken as pure nature, abstract and disincarnate. It is precisely the Christian faith which has given us an incarnate God to dramatize the human condition and to show that the human being is not a disincarnate soul, but a being-in-the-world whose nature, essentially identical in every individual, is nevertheless molded by the culture within which life evolves. It is then necessary, in order to understand the human being, to understand culture and differentiate among the different cultures which form the "Lebenswelt" of each people, of each region, of each epoch. Christianity is not a theory, but a way of life, based on solid truths, but flowering in many ways at different times and places. Metaphysics, to take notice of these differences, must study human nature and derive the principles of being from the concrete manifestations of the beings of experience as they appear in the world. It is not a question of *thinking* what being must be, but of *experiencing* this being. It is entirely possible to come to a generalization sufficient to affirm the unicity of being among the multiplicity of manifestations, taking account of cultural diversities; for only in their concrete reality do we discover their essence. A purely theoretical reflection does not reveal the reality in question, but only the "thought about" the reality. It is this way of doing metaphysics that discredits the science of being which metaphysics purports to be.

It is not an easy task to penetrate the intimate reality of beings immersed in an all encompassing reality called "culture." It is a much easier task to view being stripped of all existential, cultural endowments, neatly classified as if its actualization were accomplished in a vacuum, ahistorical and unrelated to any other being capable of transforming it in any way. The being of which metaphysics strives to attain radical knowledge can only come to our scrutiny, not in its naked nature, but clothed in cultural garments which make it difficult to penetrate its inner reality. But then, its inner reality is not separate from its phenomenological revelation to us.

In order to discover the true reality or nature of being, it is then necessary *to accept the fact of cultural transformations* outside of which we do not find being. The metaphysician has the doubly difficult task of discovering the reality of being and of assessing value: Being is, by definition, convertible with *good* and *beautiful*. Therefore, the metaphysician must see to what extent being and good are one in the cultural structure which presents itself to human inquiry, for instance, the good in persons, the beautiful in the environment. In particular, it becomes a serious problem for the Christian metaphysician, who is seeking the "trace" of God in creation and the "image" of God in the human person, to see to what extent a particular culture may approach the good.

The human person actually decides on the goodness or the lack of goodness of a philosophy of life. So culture is the human touch upon "raw" nature. This, however, has happened at various levels from the beginning of time, so, at this moment, we do not know what "raw" nature might be. However, we do recognize certain humanistic traits now shaping human society.

Humanism can have many faces: the original Renaissance attempt to reinstate man in the sublime position of a being superior to nature and not bound by fate or cosmic order, the Sartrean affirmation of absolute liberty to create the human nature in oneself, the Marxist declaration of human dignity against the alienation born of oppression, the pragmatist's self-assurance of the person as "measure of all things", the contemporary glorification of human reason as all powerful and sufficient to carry the human being to the highest reaches of knowledge and the religious-oriented personalism affirming the capability of the person to touch the divine. All kinds of humanism have in common a profound respect for the dignity of the person, confidence in human capabilities, and the importance of humanizing the individual through the liberal arts.

In practice, the vision of the humanist is not always carried out. One kind of humanism fairly prevalent today strongly denies the possibility of admitting a God while retaining the exalted idea of the dignity of the person. It affirms the infinite perfectibility of the human being, and promotes an atheistic philosophy. In what was called Humanist Manifesto II, the proponents of this philosophy affirmed that reason and intelligence are the most effective human instruments for which there is no substitute, and human striving is, and ought to be, for the good life here and now. There is nothing further to be desired or looked for. It is an explicit denial of transcendence diametrically opposed to the spirit of Christianity.

However, humanism *per se* is not necessarily atheistic. Erasmus, the Father of Humanism, was a Christian. Christian or religious humanism finds it not only compatible but necessary to affirm the dignity of the human being in the light of a Transcendent God. The existence of God is the reason for the existence and the dignity of the human self; the exalted rationality of the human being is the human participation in infinite wisdom. Even Existentialism, a humanism, can be theistic; one needs only mention Soren Kierkegaard and Gabriel Marcel. The transcendental dimension of humanism, which was never entirely abandoned after Erasmus, is recaptured by those who follow the existentialist movement in the Christian Church, evident among others, the Lublin School of Thomism.

This Christian humanism is based on a philosophical anthropology and a Thomistic metaphysics of the person, revealed in human action. This school encompasses methods, phenomenology, and insights from contemporary thought, from Existentialism, in its investigation of the metaphysical structure of the human being as person, and in the description of the experience of the self, while retaining the traditional foundations of Christian morality of St. Thomas Aquinas, reinterpreted in the light of contemporary cultures.

The human person, according to this Christian humanism, is a value not in *having* but in *being*; the fundamental relation among human beings is love, which is seen as the measure of human dignity. Love is directed to God in a way that allows the person to achieve the maximum of development in every sense. "God, Who is the goal of all creatures, does not tear them away from themselves and from their own immanent perfection. On the contrary He places and grounds them in it even more securely."[1]

This type of humanism is most needed and extremely valid today because it maintains a proper balance between a theocentric and an anthropocentric view of the human person. If considered from an exclusively theocentric point of view, then it is easy to lose sight of the person and related problems, but if human reality is viewed from the sole position and principles of anthropology, there is risk of denying the divine.[2] The Christian understanding of the human condition as life within the all-encompassing care of a loving God, whose children are free to shape their lives according to their inner light, cannot but disclose the wisdom of a life totally human, yet anchored on God.

The human venture on this planet is fraught with risks and beset with dangers; yet it is a challenge to the human person who experiences the fascination of reaching for a goal almost beyond reach. The achievements of science cannot be the answer to all questions, nor be the assurance of happiness. Knowledge, however, increases the person's joy in the contemplation of creation and deepens the dignity which is the human prerogative. Metaphysics discloses the treasures of the beings of this world and permits a glimpse, at least, of the Being who is the Source and Matrix of all that is. But the real contact with beings and with Being can only come in the concrete and daily exchanges between person and person in the world, that natural beauty and grandeur which has been and is the human dwelling, transformed and enriched by the human mind and action. Yet, is it not by reason alone that the humanist strives to improve life, but also, and especially, by refining the spiritual element in the interior life and by deepening love in the interchange with others, whose presence is integral to humanistic development, to life itself?

Gannon University
Erie, Pennsylvania, USA

NOTES

1. Andrew N. Woznicki, *A Christian Humanism: Karol Wojtyla Existential Personalism* (New Britain, CT: Mariel Publications, 1980), pp. 2-3.

2. Ibid., passim.

THE HISTORICAL MODEL: HUMAN AND DIVINE DIMENSIONS

Evanghelos A. Moutsopoulos, Ph.D.

Definitions

History is likely to be defined as the succession of events which forms the itinerary of mankind within a temporal framework, and which directly involves the participation of human consciousness. Indeed, geological events, for instance, which have occurred during millions of years and which have shaped the actual appearance of the earth differ from historical events in that they are completely independent from the presence of man on earth, unless they have influenced the course of civilizations, e.g., the earthquakes, around 1400 B.C., that destroyed the Minoan civilization, or the earthquake that destroyed the city of Lisbon in 1755, and produced in Europe an important philosophical movement dealing with the ontological and moral meaning of evil.

Apart from such cases, historical events are to be considered as implying a direct or indirect participation of human consciousness, and consequently of human intentionality understood not in a scholastic and Husserlian sense as a passive aptitude of consciousness to be its own experiences, but in a rather Bergsonian sense, as an active aptitude of consciousness to conceive of and to reach aims, goals, projects and "designs" beyond its own experiences.[1] In this respect, history may be understood as the succession of events which manifests the dialectics of continuity and discontinuity[2] at the level of human becoming.[3]

Analytics of History

There are two basic conceptions to which the various models of the historical process as a functionality may be reduced: a balanced one which has been illustrated by Plato[4] and the Stoics,[5] according to which history moves like a pendulum or like a cyclic recurrence or reversal; and an unbalanced one which has been illustrated both by the Greeks (e.g.,

312

Hesiod)[6] and by Christian thinkers (e.g., by Augustine, influenced by Hebraic thought),[7] according to which history moves in a descending or ascending flow, or in both directions. Both these conceptions, however, be they balanced or unbalanced, imply that historic continuity is disturbed by historic discontinuity, in that both periodical and non-periodical historic motion are interrupted at certain important "points" which determine an essential shift of this motion, since they are common extremes at which a given phase of the historical process ends, and from which a new phase is supposed to start.

Such "points" are particularly salient, prominent and substantial, since they display both a double meaning and a double power of stopping a given movement and producing a new one. Even the compounding and combining models of the historical process, the spiroidal one conceived of by Gianbattista Vico[8] and the helicoidal one conceived of by Hegel,[9] obey this general rule. The same occurs with the positivistic model of Arnold Toynbee,[10] according to which civilizations emerge successively or simultaneously, to grow and decline following ascending and descending curves.

This is also the case of the model of the historical process, as the author of this text has elaborated since 1966,[11] according to which the essence of the historical process is fundamentally "fugical" or "phygoidal," since the structure it alludes to reminds us of the structure of a musical fugue where the various constituting elements merge into each other while keeping their individuality, in a contrapuntal way, to form autonomous movements strictly related to each other, with dramatic effects. More recent, also musically inspired, models which refer to "serial" musical processes, and which are finally reducible to the classical model of recurrence, are themselves in no way capable of escaping the obligation to refer to the existence of such extreme "points."[12]

It becomes obvious that the diversity of the conceptions and models mentioned does not impede them from referring in common to the notion of an extreme point (or zone) which indicates both the final outcome of a phase of the historical process and the initial impulse which generates a new phase of it. In this respect, the extreme understood here acquires a significant ontological value which is worthy of being analyzed.

The Notion of Kairicity

The threefold system of fundamental temporal categories - "past," "present," "future" - helps to define and concretize the scheme that contains "becoming." However, besides this distinction, another distinction is also possible. Whereas the system of temporal categories is strictly static and refers to objectively considered data, since it implies that propositions formulated according to it are entirely independent from any kind of commitment of consciousness to the process of becoming,[13] the system of "kairic" categories implies such a commitment. Its meaning will be clarified through some examples.

The following propositions - "it rained yesterday," "it is raining today," "it will (probably) rain tomorrow" - imply no immediate consequence for the consciousness itself which remains that of an indifferent observer.[14] Consider, however, the following propositions - "it has not rained yet," "it will (probably) not rain any more (this autumn)." In these propositions the commitment of consciousness to the facts described is obvious and direct. Suppose these statements belong to a ploughman. They immediately acquire a very precise meaning. They respectively express, on one side, the ploughman's concern, anxiety and hope, and, on the other side, his frustration, for his own existential activities are tied to the "weather" facts as stated by him. They express his deep interest in determining an advantageous moment to be located between two distinct periods.[15] In this sense, more than statements, they are, to some extent, axiological propositions, for they indicate the intention of a consciousness[16] to recognize the advantageous moment in question as a "kairos," i.e., both as a minimal and as an optimal moment.[17]

Divisibility and Discontinuity of Becoming

"Not...yet" and "...any more" represent the two elements of a twofold or dual categorical system which one may call "kairic," and which is generally disguised and screened by the former static system of temporal categories. The "kairos" is defined and determined by the minimal difference between the period covered by the application of the category of "not yet" and the period covered by the category of "not any more" (or: "never more"). This implies a uniqueness of the "kairos," because of its objective impossibility to be repeated within the limits of the process it engenders. It actualizes the future and the past as well, depending on the process' orientation, and reduces that to the present.[18] It further contains the intentionality of consciousness, understood as an orientation towards an aim to be reached.

Combined with the "kairic" categories, these notions allow us to understand the "vectoral" attitude of consciousness when introduced and integrated into reality. Such an attitude entails, on behalf of the consciousness, the possibility of restructuring reality itself by dynamically imposing on it a discontinuity which makes possible a radical distinction between its two subsequent, yet irreducible, portions.[19] The "kairic" moment definitely inserts into and imposes upon the process of becoming a restructuring and catalytic distinction between what precedes and follows. Division, in this sense, does not disrupt continuity of becoming. "Kairification," on the contrary, implies a fundamental discontinuity according to which there is no way to reconcile "before" and "after." The whole life of consciousness is thus reducible to a chain of "kairifications," its main activity consisting in conceiving intentionally the aim of its immediate or remote, subsequent action.[20] Thus, history, as the process leading to the promotion of mankind, is in fact a chain of "kairic discretions" due to the initiative of the historical hero's consciousness.[21]

Kairicity in Providential History

Since history is the field *par excellence* of human exertion, it is manifest that it concentrates on the major part of man's intentional activity. History of mankind is mainly a succession of "kairifying" actions. From this level, the notion of intentionality may be easily raised, by means of an "economical" transfer (in the theological acception of the term), up to the level of divine action.[22] At this level, God is considered mainly as an *acting person* who plans, decides and executes his acts by actualizing, through "kairification," the moments at which his activity will prove more efficient. In the perspective of divine absoluteness, this "economical" conception of a "kairic" moment seems, of course, to be meaningless. In fact, it emerges out of a process of projection of the human intentionality to that of the Divine.[23]

Thus the history of the deeds of the Divine since the creation of time, in the sense attributed to it by Augustine,[24] is a series of actions, of what one might improperly call "timings," but which is, in fact, a series of "kairifications," according to the nature of the Divine's own intentionality, the most prominent of which, in a Christian perspective, for instance, are creation and redemption, completed by the prevision of the last judgment. An infinity of major or minor acts scheduled and executed according to the same model of divine activity, and which are interpolated between these basic actions, then incorporated and integrated into their fundamental system, constitute its comprehensive form, namely divine providence.[25]

Considered under this viewpoint, divine providence proves to be a continuity of discontinuous acts, which is elaborated upon the basic model of "kairification," i.e., of actualization of remote instants within the range of divine intentionality. In this way, time turns out to be a typical illusion, and its creation, in fact, only a static form of the dynamic reality of the Divine's activity. Such an activity actualizes eternity itself through a series of successive disruptions. These disruptions entail the existence of gaps which the activity of the Divine fills up simultaneously, and finally surpasses by means of a series of "stridings" and "overlappings."

Providential history thus acquires the meaning of a highly dynamic field in which divine intentionality is exerted under a creative form which is inconceivable through the static system of temporal categories, but which is fully realizable through the dynamic system of "kairic" categories. Such a system acquires the importance of an instrument which helps to understand divine activity as a creative historical process comparable to usual human creativity,[26] a comparison which would be otherwise unacceptable, namely under the shape of traditional insights based on mere temporality.[27] Moreover, God's activity itself thus acquires a meaning which, even if not fully understandable, is necessarily the very reason of providential history.

Hermeneutics of History

In order to shape any functional model according to which history, as a process, may be interpreted and be given a meaning, one is constrained to take into consideration the notion of *kairicity*, which, in its turn, involves that of *intentionality* of the human consciousness (even projected to a divine level). This is necessary both in a microhistoric and a macrohistoric vision. Outside of kairicity history remains meaningless, since it implies no conscious historical activity and, therefore, no historical perspective at all. To be relevant, any historical hermeneutics has to take into consideration the intention (or system of intentions) of

316

the historical agent or agents as far as such an intention is the driving power of historical activity. In the same order of ideas, historiography has to proceed through the investigation of the motives that justify a historical action with reference to the precise, direct or remote, purpose of human consciousness, and its organized undertakings as well.[28]

In terms of kairicity and intentionality, the proposition "Julius Caesar crossed the Rubicon" remains meaningless inasmuch as one fails to consider the real aim of such an event, which was to suppress the power of the Roman senate, by choosing the "kairic" moment for acting in this sense. This is only one example among others referring to a series of actions aimed at the realization of a precise goal. Likewise, any hermeneutics of divine actions, seen from a historical viewpoint, should ponder their "economically" presumed aim, as far as their meaning for universal history is concerned.

Conclusion

It becomes obvious that the historical process, in both its human and divine dimensions (the latter, though with human criteria), acquires its full meaning through a high profile, when reduced to a "kairic" scheme of discretional choice applied to historical events. Viewed under such an angle, history becomes a locus of actions aiming at the conscious evolution of mankind on its way towards its own accomplishment.

University of Athens
Athens, Greece

NOTES

1. H. Bergson, L'évolution creatrice, ch. IV, in *Oeuvres*, Paris, P.U.F., 1959 (Edition du centenaire), p. 761; cf. E. Moutsopoulos, *La critique du platonisme chez Bergson*, Athens, Grigoris, 1980 (ch. L'idée et le temps), p. 43; Idem, Historiologie philosophique et philosophie d l'histoire, *Diotima*, 6, 1979, pp. 151-153.

2. Continuity and Discontinuity in History, Ibid., 7 1980, pp. 200-202.

3. Idem, Une catégorisation de l'historique est-elle possible? Ibid., pp. 206-208.

4. P.-M. Schuhl, Sur le mythe du "Politique," *Revue de Métaphysique et de Morale*, 39, 1932, pp. 47-53.

5. V. Goldschmidt, *Le système stoicien et l'idée de temps*, Paris, Vrin, 1953, pp. 45 sq.

6. Evanghelos Moutsopoulos, Structure et valeurs de l'historicité humaine dan quelques aspects de la poésie épique, didactique et tragique grecque, *Diotima*, 7, 1980, pp. 142-146; Idem, Geschichtliche Modelle und Kulturelle Modelle, *Dialektik des Geschichtsprozesses*, Berlin, Dietz, 1980, pp. 313-314.

7. J. Guitton, *Le temps et l'éternité chez Plotin et Saint Augustin*, Paris, P.U.F., 1953, pp. 57 sq.

8. Moutsopoulos, Historical Crises, *University of Athens, Official Speeches*, 22, 1977-1978, pp. 57-72.

9. Moutsopoulos, Kairos and History, *Proceedings of the Academy of Athens*, 59, 1984, pp. 532-553.

10. Man and History, *University of Athens, Official Speeches*, 15, 1970-1971, pp. 201-215.

11. Kairos and History, *loc. cit.*, p. 546.

12. History of Philosophy as a Historical and Metahistorical Science, *Parnassos*, 1966, pp. 367-387; Historical Crises, *loc. cit.*, p. 68; Kairos and History, *loc. cit.*, p. 547.

13. Kairos and History, Ibid.; Possibilité et limites d'une histoire "serielle," *Diotima*, 7, 1980, pp. 204-205.

14. L'idée de développement, *Revue Philosophique*, 1978, pp. 79-84.

15. L'histoire comme tradition: acceptation et dépassement, *Actes du XVIIe Congrès des Sociétés de Philosophie de Langue Française*, Abidjan, 1977, pp. 141-143; Histoire et mythes historiques, *Atti del Congresso Internazionale "Teoria e Prassi"* (Genova-Barcellona, 1976), t.1, Napoli, Ediz. Dojmenicane Italiane, 1980, pp. 281-290; Historical Time in the Philosophy of J.N. Theodoracopoulos, *Desmos*, Athens, 1975, pp. 369-379.

16. La fonction du *kairos* selon Aristote, *Revue Philosophique*, 1985/2, pp. 223-226; Kairos et activité kairique chez Plotin, *Estudios Clasicos*, 26, 1984, fasc. 87-88, pp. 443-447; *Kairophuès*: sur la conception finaliste de l'intentionnalité chez Proclus, *Mélanges Edouard Delebecque*, Paris, Laffitte (Publications de l'Université de Provence), 1983, pp. 313-320.

17. Will and Intentionality, *Philosophical Concerns*, t. 1, *Consciousness and Creation*, (Athens: Hermes, 1971), pp. 149-253.

18. Maturation et corruption. Quelques réflexions sur la notion de "kairos," *Revue des Travaux de l'Académie des Sciences Morales et Politiques, et Comptes Rendus de ses Séances*, 131, 1978/1, pp. 1-20.

19. "Irréversibilité" du present chez Husserl?" *Diotima*, 11, 1983, pp. 193-194.

20. Quelques comentaires sur la notion d'homme kairique, ibid., 12, 1984, pp. 178-182.

21. In the sense William Dray conceives of such an activity. Cf. *The Itinerary of Consciousness*, t. 3, *Values*, Athens, 1977, p. 291. Cf. Idem, La notion de "kairicité" historique chez Nicéphone Gregoras, *Actes du XIVe Congrès Internat. des Etudes Byzantines* (1971), t. 2, Bucarest, 1974, pp. 217-222, et *Byzantina*, 4, 1972, pp. 207-213, The Meaning of Error According to Nicephorus Gregoras, *Memory of A. Yannaras*, Athens, Papazissis, 1981, pp. 126-132; L'idée d'intentionnalité en histoire, *Pela Filosofia. Homenagem a Tarcisio Padilha*, Rio de Janeiro, Pallas, 1984, pp. 581-585.

22. Prospective et historicité de la présence divine, *Il senso della filosofia cristiana oggi, Atti del XXXII Congresso del Centro di studi Filosofici*, (Gallarate, 1977), Brescia, Morcelliana, 1978, pp. 103-104.

23. On the Reduction of Temporal Categories to the Interventional Activity of the Divine, *Diotima*, 7, 1979, pp. 202-204.

24. Augustin, *Confessions*, 13.

25. E. Moutsopoulos, Une archéologie chrétienne de l'être est-elle possible? *Diotima*, 8, 1908, pp. 184-186.

26. Moutsopoulos, Alternative Processes in Artistic Creation, *Proceedings of the 8th International Wittgenstein Symposium* (Kirchberg am Wechsel, 1984), Part I, (Wien, Hölder-Pichler-Tempsky, 1984), pp. 107-113; Artistic Approaches of the Absolute, *Scientific Yearbook of the Faculty of Philosophy, University of Athens*, 28, 1985, pp. 378-393.

27. Moutsopoulos, The Ultimate: Insight and Reality, *God: The Contemporary Discussion* (New York: Paragon, [under publication]).

28. Moutsopoulos, Historiologie philosophique et philosophie de l'histoire, loc. cit.; History and Science, *Stasinos* 6, 1978. pp. 119-140.

PART VI

HUMANISTIC SOCIAL PHILOSOPHY

MARXIST ESCHATOLOGY AND CHRISTIAN ESCHATOLOGY: MARX AND THE STORY OF MAN'S DELIVERANCE

Robert C. O'Brien

How can one explain the persistent allure of Marxism[1] in light of the disillusioning experiences of its institutional embodiments in state and party, of the demonstrable inadequacy of its economics, of the predictive failures of its scientific history, and of the dogmatic sterility of its philosophy? A rhetorical *tu quoque* addressed to the Christian in the light of its historical institutional faults would bring a similar mode of response that would penetrate the phenomenal embodiments, institutional forms and practice, to the noumenal heart of the matter which is, put in a literal sense, religious — a *re-ligio*, binding men together in a mutual commitment for an ultimate concern, the meaning of man's story on earth and his destiny. One explanation, then, for the paradoxical phenomenon that in inverse proportion as Marxism is discredited in its failure to fulfill economic, political, and social expectations, many men, under no duress, are attracted to it as a total story of man's life, of its meaning and fulfillment[2] to the extent that Marxism stands alone in the Western world as the secular competitor of the Judaic-Christian saving history (or, for some, a secular complement).[3]

We witness, then, an encounter, if not conflict, of faiths, "each fundamentally inspired with an equal faith in man."[4] It is a competitive eschatology, a prospective view from the present situation in history to a final fulfillment when the full scope of salvation is finally revealed, and thus the truth that constitutes this world is disclosed in all its fullness. The light of a future hidden in the present renders the meaning of the present intelligible.[5]

Each of these eschatologies proposes the meaning of the story of man, of his-story. A story is a primary way of disclosing a truth. Marx discerns the meaning of his story within the linear, natural world-historical axis, totally within this-worldly experience, for therein alone lies the truth: "the truth of history, therefore, since the world beyond truth has disappeared, is to establish the truth of this world."[6] His story is that of the deliverance of man from the misery of intolerable oppression into a state of harmonious well-being in a perfected community of unrestricted self-fulfilling creative activity.

The need to elucidate a meaning for life in the world, to discern its truth, becomes acute when it arises out of crisis situations threatening meaninglessness, of limiting situations of suffering and death, of evil and injustice whose apparent senselessness raises the questions: why? what is the meaning of our role in such a story, in this history? If the end of Marx's story is a culmination of man's history in a state of peaceful earthly harmony and complete self-fulfillment, its beginning is with discord and dividedness under the cruel rule of necessary labor and of hostile powers, in "a world torn apart."[7] It parallels the Genesis account, but with an economic depiction, thus it is a "story of salvation in the language of economics,"[8] a story of the fallenness of man from a primal state of immediacy with nature, his "inorganic body," and of simplicity in communal life into a condition of arduous labor intruding between man and nature and into a divisive condition in his social life, intruding into his relations with others. Hence Marx begins with the experience of suffering and oppression, of the misery of man now exiled in the conflicted, alienating environment that constitutes modern industrial society, in short, with divided man.

The pre-fallen era of harmony and simplicity in providing for subsistence and producing tools for working with nature gave way to the complexity of tasks required of familial life in the larger social context and ultimately to the "division of labor" that typifies modern industrial production. By virtue of the ineluctable dynamics of growing industrial capacity, by historical necessity, man finds himself in a divisive situation. He is alienated from the objects he produces which he does not directly enjoy, from the very producing activity itself by "forced labor" restricting him to one mode of labor, and by a class-divided society of producers against the owners of the means of production. The more the worker produces, the less he consumes as he works to live rather than lives to work; the more value he creates, the less he is valued. So enslaved is he to the world of commodities that he himself in his labor is a commodity, alienated from his own worth and sundered in alienating social relations: this is the misery of man in a commodity world he produces. "Capital is man lost to himself."

The radical nature of this alienated condition is manifested in Marx's insistence that the essential character of man is his productive creativity in dialectical relation to nature. As "objectively active," man expresses his own self in the objects that bear the stamp of his essence, and as an activity essentially social, it bears the social dimension of his essence in his co-laboration, co-operation with others. Until the ideal condition is realized when "in community with others . . . each individual has the means of cultivating his gifts in all directions, [for] only in community, therefore, is personal freedom possible,"[9] he dwells in the misery of alienated unfreedom. The evil that is alienation is the loss of his essential self, of his existence divided from his essence, of an essential dismemberment in which he falls into thralldom to objects and powers hostile to him: he is not his own master, he is not free. Exiled from the essential context of his selfhood in a socially inimical environment of class conflicted society whose rule is greed and avarice, his worth is evaluated simply by what he has, not by what he is.

First: Marx's anti-theism has its roots in this prophetic protest against evil, calling his age to account for unjust and intolerable evil. Granted other facets of his anti-theism, especially his position on the incompatibility of the givenness of the God-creature relationship with real human creative freedom, his Godlessness is also grounded in his moral stance against a biblical God who will not immediately eradicate evil, but who permits it to stand, who judges it to be evil but not intolerable, who shows forbearance towards it insofar as it serves the vindication of His justice. "This is the purest and most passionate form of atheism when man rejects God in the name of his more God-like morality . . . Marx's atheism rises toward, if it does not reach, this height of purity and passion."[10]

Second: the fallenness of man is the consequence of his doing, of his labor under pre-ideal conditions, but, Marx holds, it is by historical necessity. The fall is not by man's choice, it is not his fault or falling; rather, it has befallen him out of the ineluctable historical development of the division of labor which has dismembered his life, personal and social. Man is not intrinsically at fault, it is not his originating sin nor guilt out of the misuse of his freedom. It is the historical case that his life does not express his essence, that his historical situation does not actualize his freedom, that he dwells in the toils of necessity. Given this presupposition of faultlessness, intrinsic goodness and innocence, Marx and Marxist culture critics of our day plunge into a sort of "demonology" to seek out the demonic source of evil outside of man in his historical situations, social structures and powers which, when eradicated or "revolutionarily transformed," would purportedly deliver him from evil and restore him to pristine conditions of unhindered freedom.

Third: recalling Feuerbach's theory of the projection of man's perfected, ideal essence into an illusory objective deity whose apparent autonomy would dissolve upon enlightened disillusionment, Marx further grounds this projected division of man from himself in the socio-economic conditions of a divided world of inhuman relations, of which religion is a symptom as well as a protest.[11] Marx holds that, like this Godhead, and like the oppressive power of the political state, so too the alienating forces and structures of industrial Capitalism are in fact man's *own* doings, the products of his own powers. All that appears in these illusory forms of alienated otherness are the dismembered products of the only creative power there is, his own. Out of confrontation with his misery, enlightened to its cause by Marx's theoretical recognition of the necessary dynamics of history, and encouraged to practical revolutionary activity then, since God is seen to be man's own creature, man alone can master history so as to re-appropriate these powers, to re-member himself in undivided wholeness in membership with others in a condition beyond labor, in unrestricted multidimensional creativity, finally having transcended the age of the dominance of economics. "He can think and act and shape his reality like a man who has been disillusioned and has come to reason, so that he will revolve round himself and therefore round his true sun."[12] Man can save himself from the evils that had befallen him. Marxian self-sufficiency and encapsulated naturalism permit no gratuity of an extrinsic source of saving power. It is a "do it yourself" salvation.

This is already the middle of Marx's story. His secular replication of the biblical drama of man's saving history has often been recounted in its many parallels.[13] The triadic dialectical unfolding of Paradise lost, man's fall from primal innocence into the fallen state of toil and misery, dispossessed in a sinful world surrounded by hostile forces; then, the exile of a chosen people destined for a promised land, the locus of judgment on the world as well as the locus of the messianic message and saving action; finally, the climactic apocalyptic struggle culminating in the triumphant denouement of the restoration of the redeemed, delivered and transformed humanity to the Kingdom of Heaven, thus ending its earthly travel and travail, Paradise Regained — or "True Socialism."

Attention must focus on the proletariat, "the poor who shall inherit the earth," the chosen, or now historically determined instrument of revolutionary deliverance as well as its beneficiary, which is already operative within Capitalist society. One can discern here also the secular symbol of the Suffering Servant of Deutero-Isaiah. This proletariat is the locus of the saving promise and action, the one universal class, representative of all human impoverishment whose self-wrought liberation delivers all who are dehumanized by greed and misery, both capitalist and proletariat. Since for Marx human life is evaluated essentially by its productive creativity, the poverty of the proletariat, however moral and personal its consequent suffering, is nevertheless socio-economic in nature, its origin lies in productive diminishment, its loss is one of materiality and power. On the other hand, biblical poverty exceeds the limits of socio-economic status, of materiality and power, to include rich and poor, the powerful and the powerless, all who are in need of the saving power of the Lord in a "comprehensive community-in-poverty before God."[14] Before Him all are exigent, although this spiritual status is most materially manifest in the weak, the outcast, the ill and the poor. All yearn for Him who will "deliver the weak from him who is strong, the weak and needy from him who despoils him" (Ps. 35:10) and seek deliverance from power. Absent here is the self-righteous vindictiveness of the proletarian revolutionary overthrow and its redistribution of power for itself, a power not yet relinquished.

Fourth: as the immanence of a revolution spontaneously springing from the economic dynamics of history receded farther, as it failed to materialize in the passage of opportune occasions, Marx increasingly placed it in the voluntary agency of the enlightened proletariat now politically agitated to action. If history does not make man, but man history, then if history will not make a revolution, then man must — he is his own saving instrument by his own unaided action for his own social improvement. The biblical vision, on the other hand, is not that of a self-emancipating revolutionary transformation into a new, improved social order, nor is it an "e-vent" out of man's autonomous history. It is a transfiguration, an "ad-vent," a gift of precisely what man cannot give to himself,[15] for what man has lost, he cannot give to himself. And it is a new sort of life, not simply a better one. Marx, however, finds unacceptable any freedom granted to man by any power other than man.[16] Hence the proletariat is the recipient of its own giving, its motivation is the recall of conditions for the fulfillment of its own needs, the completion of its own immanent possibilities; it is not a response to the call of Another Who alone can give what has been lost.[17]

Finally: the proletariat is the repository of hope, of a promised future luring man in hope. The end, and moral, of Marx's story is hope — hope for man in a future delivered from the despairing misery of oppression into communal unity of freely self-directed multidimensional creativity, an earthly eschaton worthy to be sought; and one in which those here and now struggling to actualize it (if one is to remain faithful to Marx's naturalistic immanence in which death is not overcome) will not even participate, hence requiring a courageous, selfless devotion which Christians, who have at least the rewarding promise of personal participation in "the new heavens and the new earth," might well emulate. The Marxian eschaton promises a better world for its "new man" who is not yet existent, a "land of milk and honey" — but only that. The Judeo-Christian eschaton is one of radical discontinuity from the immanent possibilities of perfected human progress, one exceeding the confines of encapsulated naturalism and the finality of death. "The supernatural end of man which is to consist in a union with God himself can never be found in this world, be man never so happy in classless societies "[18]

The allure of Marx, then, is the lure of a promising future to hope for. The future, it is said, is the horizon of hope.[19] Because man exists historically he "ex-sists" in a hope which is constituent of his ontological structure — it is that about man which is-not-yet, his "may-be-ness," and thus is that by which he is "sent forth" in a "pro-mise" — it constitutes his "mission." But the Marxian horizon recedes interminably farther, unveiling itself as a utopian imaginary projection of an exclusively linear history yet historically unrealizable in time while the conditions for the universally representative revolutionary eruption Marx relied upon is indefinitely postponed. Even then, there is no verifiable guarantee that the hope for a harmonious City of Man in which man's transcendent exigencies will simply dissipate is realizable, nor that the conflict between man and nature, and between man and man, between the factual and the ideal existence of man, can be resolved within the framework of immanent human historical processes. Marx's ideal eschaton refers to "a situation as unhistorical as the term 'Kingdom of God'. . . it is incapable of realization in history . . . a utopia . . . never to be discovered on earth."[20] It is a promise that cannot be kept, if for no other reason than that it separates the openness of the future from a giving, fulfilling reality: "Marxism . . . has not given a guarantee for the existence of a genuine future, for genuine openness."[21]

The Christian eschatology is not utopian. Man's existence is eschatological because man's worldly history is eschatological. The Christian
eschatological expectation — of which man can speak only by pointing
ahead out of the signs of the present because it is not-yet, because it is
a future anticipated but not yet disclosed, because ". . . it has not yet
appeared what we shall be" (1 John 2:3) — is a hope founded on the
promising God of Israel before Whom man travels. "Through promise
man is bound to the future. It is only in the horizon of God's promises
that we know God in relation to his historical activity."[22] It is a promise
kept, validated by the inbreaking ad-vent of God into man's own history,
a future already made present here and now in the presence of the Risen
Christ whose own fulfilled promise is the foundation of the confidence
in God's historical loyalty to His promise.

Because the eschatological fulfillment is that of the City of God, of
which God is the architect, and not a City of Man, of which Man is the
architect, Marx's challenge, which must be taken seriously, is that it
deflects man's struggle with this-worldly evil into a complacent tolerance
out of other-worldly distraction and reward. His challenge is that
Christian eschatology does not take this world seriously enough to devote
itself to its transformation; and hence, that Christians tolerate its evils and
merely sanctify the *status quo*. But the Christian "pro-mise" is precisely
a "pro-mission," a "mission to go forth" in and through this worldly
history to an end that is not merely extrinsically rewarded, but rather a
future in the making now, in whose construction all men, theist and non-
theist, co-operate, co-create in solidarity with corporate mankind. The
Christian eschatology, as operative presently, requires as one of the concrete forms of Christian hope a constant critical concern for and protest
against secular social structural evils and a responsibility, every bit as
militant as the Marxist's, for their ongoing transformation.[23] This is the
Christian "praxis" and, I take it, the essence of "Liberation Theology" in
its predilection for the poor.[24]

Marx rightly indicated that man does not now dwell in the immediacy
of nature as originally given, but in a second phase of man-created nature,
and, within the Christian eschatological perspective, this second stage
represents man's "renewal of the face of the earth" in co-action with
God's creative agency, a worldly transformation as a fulfillment of God's
creation commitment to man. Yet this requires a gift of transfiguration,
a third stage as it were, even for the secular to fulfill itself if it is ever to
become the material of "the new heavens and the new earth," for "an

330

outside force is needed if the secular is to have an interior life that is free."[25] The essential discontinuity of the Christian eschatological fulfillment that is not simply the result of immanent human progress, but gifted also, cannot exclude the co-operative co-action of the non-theist, who is also under the dynamism of grace,[26] in working toward a future that does not depend on man alone. The transcending hope for eschatological fulfillment must permeate all processes and structures of secular life and must appropriate as its own, too, that historical experience through which Marx arrived at his eschatology, for only then would Marxism really "establish the truth of this world." Marx's eschatology, however, falls short of fulfilling its promise because of its reliance on the total self-sufficiency of man and in its ultimate insufficiency for man.

Fordham University
New York City, New York, USA

NOTES

1. Reference is made solely to the thought of Marx and not to the subsequent devolution of his philosophy by others.

2. Two recent statements of erstwhile converts to Marxism bear witness to this: Czeslaw Milosz, *Native Realm* (New York: Doubleday, 1980), p. 143, explains his attraction to Marxism as "the key that would explain everything," so that "when the Kingdom of God received the name of Communism one had at least the consolation that an earthly iron necessity led up to it . . . one brought the Great Day that much closer." Sidney Hook, American pragmatic secular humanist, writes of his attraction to Marxism in *Marxism and Beyond* (Totowa, NJ: Rowman & Littlefield, 1983, p. 88): "Communism functioned more and more as a religion in the lives of its intellectual adherents, as they believed that theirs was a kind of historical and cosmic support for their generous ideals."

3. Nicolai Berdyaev long ago recognized Marxism as a spiritual doctrine. Cf. especially *The Origins of Russian Communism* (1937) and *The Realm of Spirit and the Realm of Caesar* (1949). In 1959, Henri de Lubac wrote: "Of all the modern doctrines it is the one which most clearly

poses the problem of the total man and tries to find a total solution . . . it has not shirked final questions and for that reason it is legitimate to compare it with Christianity . . . we are forced to confront the one with the other." *Cross Currents* I, 1, Sept. 1959, p. 76. More recently, Alasdair MacIntyre, in *Marxism and Christianity* (University of Notre Dame Press, 1968, p. 115), wrote that Marxism was "the only systematic doctrine in the modern world that has been able to translate to any important degree the hopes that men once expressed, and could not but express in religious terms, into the secular project of understanding societies and expressions of human possibility and history as a means of liberating the present from the burdens of the past and so constructing the future." One Marxist expression of this is by Jaroslav Krejci ("The New Mold of Scientific Atheism" in *Concurrence* n. 1, Winter 1969, pp. 94, 96), to the effect that Marxism is a "detheologized belief in man . . . a revolutionary faith. . . . It is a faith, a continual evaluation and cultivation of the ideology of belief. . . . [It] does not reject belief as a motive force in history."

4. P. Teilhard de Chardin, *The Future of Man* (New York: Harper & Row, 1964), chapter 18, "The Heart of the Problem"; chapter 21, "Faith in Man."

5. K. Rahner and H. Vorgrimmer, *Theological Dictionary* (New York: Herder & Herder, 1961), pp. 149-50.

6. "Contribution to the Critique of Hegel's Philosophy of Right" in *Marx & Engel's Reader* (New York: Norton & Co., 1978, 2nd ed., ed. Robert Tucker), p. 54.

7. "Notes of the philosophy of Epicurus," ibid., p. 11.

8. Karl Lowith, historian of philosophy cited in J. Bentley, *Between Marx and Christ* (London: Verso Editions, 1982), p. 80.

9. "German Ideology," Tucker, p. 197.

10. John Courtney Murray, *The Problem of God* (New Haven: Yale University Press, 1964, p. 108).

332

11. "On the Jewish Question," Tucker, pp. 26-52; "Contributions to the Critique of Hegel's Philosophy of Right," Tucker, pp. 53-54.

12. Ibid.

13. Cf. Mircea Eliade, *The Sacred and the Profane*; K. Lowith, *Meaning in History*; C. Dawson, *The Dynamics of History*; M. D'Arcy, *Communism and Christianity*; W. Herberg, "The Christian Mythology of Socialism," *Antioch Review*, March 1943, pp. 125-32.

14. K. Blaser, "Christianity, Marxism and the Poor," *Theology Digest* 29/3 Fall 1981, pp. 218-19. Cf. also Jose Miranda, *Marx and the Bible* (Maryknoll, NY: Orbis Books, 1974), and *Marx Against the Marxists* (Maryknoll, NY: Orbis Books, 1980).

15. ". . . man's historicity needs a salvation beyond the scope of his own human dynamics." Louis Roberts, *The Achievement of Karl Rahner* (New York: Herder & Herder, 1967), p. 85.

16. J. Metz, "Emancipation by Universal Suffering," *Theology Digest* 21/3 Autumn 1973, p. 243.

17. Richard Lischer, *Marx and Teilhard* (Maryknoll, NY: Orbis Books, 1979), p. 159.

18. Martin J. D'Arcy, *The Meaning and Matter of History* (New York: Farrar, Straus & Cudahy, 1959), p. 105.

19. K. Rahner, "Towards a Theology of Hope," *Concurrence*, n. 1, Winter, 1969, pp. 23-33. Reference here must be made to the theologies of hope, especially to the work of Ernst Bloch and Jurgen Moltmann.

20. A. van den Beld, "Karl Marx and the End of Religion," in *Theology Digest* 25/1, Spring 1977, pp. 67, 69.

21. Ernst Bloch, "Man as Personality," *Cross Currents* 18/3, Summer 1968, p. 280.

22. G. Collins, "Hope Seeking Understanding," *Theology Digest* 16/2, Summer 1968, p. 157.

23. Rahner, ibid.

24. Cf. Miranda, *Marx and the Bible.*

25. W. Lynch, "Towards a Theology of the Secular," *Thought,* v. 41, 1966, p. 350.

26. Rahner, ibid., p. 76.

THE CRISIS IN CONTEMPORARY DEMOCRACY

George J. Lavere

The present crisis, which threatens the continuation of Western democracy in its traditional form, has been occasioned by a radical shift in the structuring of political authority and in the relationship of the state to the body politic and to the individual citizen. In its original form, in the theory of John Locke for instance, individuals who had grown weary of the uncertainty of the "state of nature," however free it might have been, contracted among themselves, established a consensus and founded a society. Only then did they structure a governmental mechanism to accomplish the purposes of their communal undertaking, thus insuring that the state would be subservient to the political community and its purpose and general welfare as articulated in the terms of the original contract.[1] What is noteworthy here is the fact that the direct line of authority reaches from society to state and from state to society. Laws are made for the people and it is the people, taken collectively as the body politic, who confront the state.

Over time but especially since the end of World War II, these relationships have changed. Increasingly, groups and even individuals within the body politic have commenced to negotiate directly with the government, asserting a variety of claims in the name of freedom and equality as applicable to their particular group and without advertence to the terms of community consensus and majority rule. The immediate result has been to fragment the body politic into semiautonomous interest groups or constituencies, each seeking its own advantage in dealing with the government which, for its part, is no longer accountable to a unified political community. Instead, the role of the government in most democracies has become that of mediator of conflicting claims to rights and guarantor of rights, however conflicting. With the breakdown of political and moral consensus, the state has become both less and more than it should be if it is to continue as a constructive agency in human affairs. In its role as mediator, it is reduced to the level of the competing parties and is, in fact, their hostage, since it must render a decision that pleases both parties, or the conflict, however disruptive, will continue.

As guarantor of rights and provider of the means to achieve and sustain them, the state moves beyond all limits and approaches the absolute, since it must respond to a potentially infinite series of claims and demands. It is becoming increasingly clear that this condition cannot continue much longer; either the state will succumb altogether and anarchy will prevail, or the state will absorb the remnants of the body politic into an authoritarian regime. A third possibility remains — restoration of political consensus and with it the body politic and the democratic state.

However unlikely it might seem at the moment, the third possibility offers the only genuinely human solution to what appears to be a terminal crisis for Western democracy. So pronounced is this malaise that it has prompted Professor Edward Shils to question whether any government is capable of responding to the demands made upon it by its members. These include:

> A higher standard of health, longevity, consumption, physical comfort, convenience, justice, emotional gratification, and individual fulfillment . . . . There is an incessant search for the "problems" which are constituted by conditions below a certain standard and which therefore stand in need of remedy. It is widely believed by theorists and publicists that all is remediable if the will to remedy is there and that human beings have a right to these remedies.[2]

While some of these claims are unquestionably valid, others are not. Health, longevity, justice and a reasonable degree of physical comfort and convenience are properly public concerns. Levels of consumption, emotional gratification, and "personal fulfillment" are highly subjective and therefore not of direct public concern, if only for the fact that no government can effectively provide for the complete satisfaction and total happiness of each one of its citizens. Moreover, this is especially the case in an age of esoteric individualism when value judgments have been reduced to personal taste and whim. Nevertheless, and without regard to their plausibility, both types of claims are being advanced by individuals and groups who typically espouse a single cause, for instance, free speech or women's rights, and pursue it relentlessly with little concern for public consensus or democratic process. Furthermore:

> This situation is aggravated by the "emancipationist" ethos of many of the intellectual leaders of modern societies; for them self-restraint, self-discipline, inhibition, respect for conventions are thought to be remnants of an out-of-date outlook which should be dispensed with as soon as possible.[3]

Thus, the aggressive and singleminded pursuit of individual and group rights by various constituencies, the disdain for convention and morality on the part of certain fringe groups, the libertarian and reform projects of some influential social and political leaders, and a fairly numerous but disorganized segment of the body politic who, for a variety of reasons, whether economic, political, social or ethical, remain outside the mainstream of organized society have effectively nullified any consensual agreement about the meaning of the political community. The notion of communal unity based upon common and accepted purposes has given way to individualistic and opportunistic interpretations and applications of freedom, equality and justice. Since the original consensus has been effectively discarded and since a new consensus has not emerged and, in fact, cannot emerge under the present circumstances, these fundamental concepts — freedom, equality and justice — have come to mean whatever interested parties want them to mean to the extent that they are able to sustain their views in the political market-place. Torn between the irresistible ideological appeal of freedom and equality, on the one hand, and its traditional role as guardian and inter-preter of the common good, on the other, the state has elected to expand freedom and equality at the expense of the common good. The result has been confusion and conflict since one person's freedom is often achieved at the expense of another person's freedom. The lack of a common and accepted standard — a consensus — has reduced the political community to competing, even warring, factions each self-centered and jealous of its prerogatives.[4]

Lacking a common standard for the adjudication of competing claims, all must be considered equal in merit and, since each claim is advanced by a pristine individual equal in every way to every other individual, no claim may be justly dismissed either by popular opinion or majoritarian vote. In recognizing the individual rather than the body politic as the prime political entity with which it must deal, modern democracy has moved outside the Western tradition. In a spirit of naive optimism, it has set about dismantling its carefully crafted institutions of governance and justice, its accumulated wisdom and, above all, its moral vision and commitment, in the interest of a new concept of humanity — the totally democratic man.

Such a man, a completely free and equal individual following his own inclinations, would be either the pre-social man of Hobbes, Locke and Rousseau, the victim of his freedom and equality, living in fear of his life, or mass-man compressed in perfect equality with his fellow-citizens into an authoritarian regime. These are not satisfactory alternatives. However, twenty-five centuries of political experience have verified the Aristotelian dictum: ". . . that man is by nature a political animal."[5] The issue is not whether there should be political arrangements for the governance of men; rather it is a question of what form these arrangements should take. Viewed in this perspective, the relative merits of *consensus* and *common good* as organizing principles of political association assume a position of primary importance at this critical juncture of Western democracy.

Consensus and Common Good

In general appearance and function, the notions of consensus and common good are strikingly similar. Both provide a basis for political organization and a ground for authority, law and justice. There is, moreover, a considerable overlap in what they formulate — the good things for which a society is founded. Whether we take the statement of John Rawls[6] or that of Jacques Maritain[7] in this regard, similar concerns for basic freedoms, economic opportunity, justice and the family are stressed, among other things, as fundamental social values. On the surface, at least, as presently formulated, either statement could serve as the point of departure for a political system. The question remains, however, would they serve equally well?

The issue turns upon the manner in which social and political values are generated. Do they come about by postulation and contractual agreement or are they formulations of actual qualities found in human nature? If liberty and equality, for instance, however reasonable and desirable in themselves, are not universal qualities which actually inhere in real flesh-and-blood human beings, then it is unrealistic and eventually tragic to declare this to be the case and to formalize these assumptions into principles by mutual agreement. What is created by agreement can be undone by agreement with equal validity. The ideological history of the 20th century provides ample testimony of the consequences of shifting assumptions concerning man and society. Consensus alone is not enough; it must be underwritten by real human qualities perceptible in ordinary experience and sustained by metaphysical explanation and moral justification, since not every human quality is admirable and worthy of being incorporated into a political principle. With the introduction of these considerations — a realist anthropology and ethics — into the political dialogue of the present, an essential but long missing link with the past could be reestablished and, with it, much needed perspective on the contemporary situation.

The link in question is the notion of "the common good," an integral part of the political wisdom of the West reaching back to Plato and beyond, but simply ignored during the crucial period of the formation of the Western democracies in the sixteenth and seventeenth centuries. For a variety of reasons — the repudiation of the old order and a sense of new beginnings, a scientific conception of man in place of a metaphysical and theological conception, a preoccupation with liberty and equality, and, finally, a legalistic desire for precise origins and conduct of government which could only be satisfied by consensual agreement to values and principles — the theorists of the new democracies settled upon consensus, with its fundamental provisions for consent of the governed, to principles established by contract. Recent dissent from the presuppositions of founding contracts and serious challenges to majority rule as the means of determining policy suggest the need to return to substantive rather than contractual principles, that is, to the common good as the basis for social and political organization. For it seems to be the verdict of history that unless the state is built upon the proper moral foundation, it cannot endure.[8]

The common good is the communal good of a society of persons:

The common good of the city is neither the mere collection of private goods, nor the proper good of a whole which, like the species with respect to its individuals or the hive with respect to its bees, relates the parts to itself alone and sacrifices them to itself. It is the good *human* life of the multitude, of a multitude of persons; it is their communion in good living. It is therefore common to both *the whole and the parts* into which it flows back and which, in turn, must benefit from it. Unless it would vitiate itself, it implies and requires recognition of the fundamental rights of persons and those of the domestic society in which the persons are more primitively engaged than in the political society. It includes within itself as principal value, the highest access, compatible with the good of the whole, of the persons to their life of person and liberty of expansion, as well as to the communications of generosity consequent upon such expansion.[9]

Moreover, according to Jacques Maritain, the common good is a moral good, "an end, good in itself," and not merely by agreement or practicality, since it is "the good of a people and a city, rather than of a mob of gangsters and murderers."[10] Although it includes all of the material and cultural conditions requisite to the good life of mankind, the primary emphasis of the common good is upon those values and relationships which pertain especially to human persons as transcending matter, namely, truth, liberty and love. For it is as person that man is capable of social relationships and most in need of them, for the privileged communication of truth, the affective union which is love and the prerogative of liberty are fully realized only in relation to other persons in a communal setting. Thus the community is both natural and necessary to man, as Aristotle taught,[11] if man is to reach his full stature as a human being. But the community itself must be a fully human community attuned to the highest good — the common good — what is good for man *qua* man as evinced in the fact of a common human nature accessible to intellectual understanding.

Thus the common good represents what is best in man and what is best for man, that is, the human person, "what is most perfect in all nature, a subsistent individual of a rational nature," according to the description of Aquinas.[12] While only individual things exist, and man is no exception to this, it is not quantitative or circumstantial uniqueness which specifies man; rather it is the fact of rational nature, intellect and will, as powers of the human soul, which impart meaning to man and the possibility of community. What enhances the person as such is the measure of the common good which, in turn, serves as the primordial principle of political unity. All claims, laws, public and private actions alike affecting the body politic in a well-ordered society would be compared to the same universal standard. Groups and constituencies could claim no special prerogatives in the name of freedom and equality precisely because persons operative within such a society would already be afforded a maximum of freedom consistent with the requirements of the common good and the same equality afforded all persons. With the primacy of person situated within the context of the common good established, the unity of the political process would be restored and the present crisis alleviated.

Christian Renewal of the Political Order

In a world which is becoming increasingly secular, materialistic and technological, it would be highly impractical to propose specifically Christian solutions to social and political problems of contemporary concern, since, in all likelihood, they would be ignored or rejected simply because they were Christian. Despite this disability, the Christian political philosopher can make a meaningful, even crucial, contribution to current political dialogue by drawing upon the riches of Christian tradition which has historically provided Western culture with its ideals of humanity and the spiritual dynamism to accomplish them.[13] These ideals are not moribund; ironically, distortions of them animate the various movements which threaten Western democracy today. The essential dignity of man, the individual rights of life, freedom and equality, as well as justice and happiness, are, after all, Christian in their inspiration. They are part of the Gospel message which, over time, has become so identified with Western culture that its Christian origins have been forgotten or ignored, to the point that many believe that purely secular values, or what they believe to be secular values, are capable of sustaining both private and public life.

Close inspection of these values reveals that what is truly viable in them is Christian in its inspiration, however exaggerated or diluted it might be. Where, for instance, could we find secular justification for individual freedom and equality? Surely there is nothing conclusive in science, history, philosophy or even in personal experience to validate these claims. They remain empty and futile until they are vivified by Christian love — the love one bears toward the neighbor for the love of God — the love of one person for another, dimly reflective of the supreme prototype of love found among the Persons in the Trinity.[14]

342

Centuries of Christian reflection have produced insights and analogues of the Divine order of things making them available not only to the believer but also to the rational knower. Concepts such as "person," "common good," "justice" and "love" evoke both natural and supernatural meanings, the natural leading to the supernatural for those who are willing and able to follow, while the supernatural illumines the natural meaning without in any way distorting it or making it less accessible to the non-believer. Moreover, these concepts represent both Divine and human wisdom and, properly understood, could resolve the present crisis in Western democracy. Christian philosophers could hardly do better than to re-introduce them into contemporary discussions of political and moral values. In fact, it would seem to be their duty to do so.

Canisius College
Buffalo, New York, USA

NOTES

1. John Locke, *Second Treatise of Government*, Chapter VIII, 95-97.

2. Edward Shils, "On the Governability of Modern Societies," *Notes Et Documents d l'Institut International "Jacques Maritain,"* nouvelle serie 7 (1984) p. 40.

3. Ibid., p. 48.

4. "It has been said that there are three nations in the United States: a black nation; a Woodstock nation; and a Wallace nation. The first one is self explanatory. The second takes its name from the great political and musical convention held at Woodstock, New York, in 1969 . . . . It includes the hippies and the radicals. The third nation is composed of 'lower middle-class whites' whose symbol is the 'hard hat' worn by construction workers." Jean-Francois Revel, *Without Marx or Jesus: The New American Revolution Has Begun*, tr. Jean Francois Bernard, (Garden City, NY: Doubleday, 1971), pp. 150-51.

5. Aristotle, *Politics*, Bk. I, ch. 2, 1253a 1-3.

6. "Thus the legal protection of freedom of thought and liberty of conscience, competitive markets, private property in the means of production, and the monogamous family are examples of major social institutions. Taken together as one scheme, the major institutions define men's rights and duties and influence their life-prospects, what they can expect to be and how well they can hope to do." John Rawls, *A Theory of Justice (Cambridge, MA: Harvard University Press, 1971), p. 7.*

7. "Man's right to existence, to personal freedom, and to the pursuit of moral life, belongs, strictly speaking, to natural law. The right to the private ownership of material goods pertains to natural law, insofar as mankind is naturally entitled to possess for its own common use the material goods of nature; it pertains to the law of nations, or *jus gentium*, in so far as reason necessarily concludes that for the sake of the common good those material goods must be privately owned." Jacques Maritain, *Man and the State* (Chicago: The University of Chicago Press, 1951), p. 100.

8. In the fifth century A.D., Saint Augustine of Hippo recognized the difference between *consensus* and *common good. In his analysis of Cicero's claim that the Roman Republic had been a just state (City of God, XIX, 21), Augustine remarked that since justice based upon virtue was lacking, Rome was not a true commonwealth (City of Godne common good* was lacking and therefore the Romans were not a "people" in the proper sense, they were in a secondary sense by *consensus*: "a multitude of reasonable beings voluntarily associated in the pursuit of common interests." These interests, however, could be anything, moral or immoral. It was agreement not virtue that made such an association valid, if not a genuine society. *(City of God*, XIX, 24). Saint Augustine, *City of God* (New York: Fathers of the Church, Inc., 1950, 1952, 1954).

9. Jacques Maritain, *The Person and the Common Good* (Notre Dame, IN: University of Notre Dame Press, 1966), pp. 50-51.

10. Ibid., p. 53.

11. Aristotle, *Politics*, Bk. I, ch. 2, 1253a 1-35.

12. Maritain, p. 32.

13. "It is only in Western Europe that the whole pattern of the culture is to be found in a continuous succession and alternation of free spiritual movements; so that every century of Western history shows a change in the balance of cultural elements and the appearance of some new spiritual force which creates new ideas and institutions and produces a further movement of social change." Christopher Dawson, *Religion and the Rise of Western Culture* (Garden City, NY: Doubleday Image Books, 1950, 1958), p. 21.

14. "To say, then, that society is a whole composed of persons is to say that society is a whole composed of wholes. Taken in its full sense, this expression leads us directly to the society of the Divine Persons (for the idea of society is also an analogical idea). In the Divine Trinity, there is a whole, the Divine Essence, which is the common good of the three subsisting Relations. With respect to this whole, the Three who compose the trinitarian society are by no means parts, since they are perfectly identical to it. They are three wholes who are the Whole." Maritain, pp. 56-57.

HUMANISM IN AFRICA: A PHILOSOPHY OF LIFE

Robert Rweyemamu

Introduction

In an interview given twelve years ago, Leopold Senghor, talking about *Negritude*, stressed his belief that it was a Negro-African answer and contribution to the twentieth century humanism. He went on to elaborate what he thought "negritude" really was.

As is well-known, after the years we may call African Renaissance, which were characterized by the Rediscovery of African History and Identity in the 1920s,[1] Senghor and some of his friends and colleagues, including Aime Cesaire, embarked on the cultural offensive by proposing the concept of "negritude." It was not in order to fight against White cultural supremacy or domination as such, an opinion which Arnold Toynbee later advanced.[2] Rather was it intended by them as a search for Africa's future role in a developing universal humanism.[3] And, when Africa was on the point of gaining political independence with her new States taking part in the world's human family, the prospects which count for much were those of having her way free to speak to the world in her own language as well as giving something for other Nations to acknowledge and receive: not gold nor ivory nor slaves, this time, but her soul, her personality and her civilization, namely the product of her thought and way of life.

African Civilization and Culture

Objectively, Senghor explained,[4] negritude was to be understood as a civilization which is the result of the cultural values of the Negro-African world. Here the emphasis is not so much on the values as on the source and origin from which they stem and grow, the cultural context itself. It is an affirmation underlying the principle of the idea which determined the birth of the "Société Africaine de Culture" in 1947, notably, that there exists a cultural unity of the Negro-African world.[5]

The original connotation of the "Negro-African" serves to bring out the doctrine that this civilization or culture is not limited to the geographical element, but it extends itself to embrace what Frobenius somewhere calls "das Afrikanische" wherever it has a strong social representation as is the case in the Americas, in Oceania and even in Asia. At the Panafrican Festival held in Algeria in 1969, the reaction from North Africa proposed that "African" be used to replace "Negro-African" for the obvious reason that the distinction between "black and white" was to be avoided.

Without going into the theory that establishes relationship between civilization and culture in terms of cause (culture) and effect (civilization), to which Senghor himself subscribes,[6] it is clear that culture, in any case, is understood to comprise not only a way of life but also, and primarily, a way of thinking. Thus we underline the fact that any civilization is an expression of a philosophy. On the other hand, being culture-connected with human society, culture in Africa is a predicament related to African societies.

Diversity and Unity

Whereas G. P. Murdock brings the number of African societies to 850 on the basis of the large ethnic groups, and J. H. Greenberg distinguishes about 6,000 dialects or 700 languages, cultural anthropologists such as B. Davidson, H. Baumann, L. Frobenius, D. Paulme, and L. Maire, to mention some of the best known, try to analyze this wide variety with a view to reducing it to cultural zones which absorb the minor groupings. This has evidenced the fact that demographic, linguistic and geographic diversities can contain elements of unity from homogeneous systems and structures apparently divergent. The thesis, which has been demonstrated by Africanists like Cheikh Anta Diop, L. S. Senghor, Boubou Hama and others, underlines fundamental unity in African cultures and civilizations. That explains why the struggle for African independence based its strongest arguments on the need for recovering identity and building a continent not only for solidarity but even for unity. Indeed, the charter of the constitution by which the Organization of African Unity,[7] founded in 1963, stressed the motive of strengthening unity; "renforcer l'unité," implied that there was a common belief in the existence of the basic unity which was cultural. There was the belief in the "African personality," in the "African soul" and in the "African heritage." This point will be relevant for us when arguing about African philosophy and humanism.

Concretely, the Berber zone has links with the Ethiopian and Sudanese zones and hence towards the west in the Niger-Guinea groups, and to the east through the Great Lakes and Zimbabwe zones (the Azania) southwards up to the Cape Town zone including the Xhoisa and Bushmen on the Kalahari.

Thus it is that ancient civilizations of the Delta and the Berberia (200 years before Christ), and the Ethiopian ones (2000 years before Christ), are not separated from the Nubian and Nok civilizations (between 900 and 200 years before Christ). Similarly, these reach out towards the southern zone civilizations (200 years before Christ) in the area between Limpopo and the Zambezi. It is there that the Semitic-Hamitic Bantu and Bushmen line joins.

How was this possible? It happened through emigrations and immigrations (the race and tribe movements), especially of the pastoral nomads. Then there were communications and influences developing as a result of conquests and settlements. As already implicitly intimated, the Nile Valley played an important role in this process, as did the Sahara and the Rift Valley on the one hand, and, on the other, the geographic and cultural positions of Ethiopia and the Sudan.

Without overestimating Charles Seligman's view that African civilization was essentially Halitic and not Negro, it is necessary to stress that the "two African worlds," the cattle-breeder and the sedentary land-tiller, compose the entire civilization, and their interaction reduces it to unity. The cow and the land, the lance and the arrow or the hoe, the stone and the mill, the cottage and the hut, that is, the cultural symbols of the Semito-Hamitic, meet those of the Negro-Bantu and Bushmen and develop side by side into a unique cultural heritage of Africa. Hence, similar institutions overlap or integrate to complete one another. Jacques Maquet is not wrong when he notes that dividing the continent into two distinct parts (cultures, civilizations), one for the North of the Sahara and the other for the South of the Sahara, is culturally arbitrary.[8] Nevertheless a kind of subtle segregation persisted where the new arrivals of the Hamitic stock represented a large, powerful group. This is the case of the interlacustrine kingdoms (Rwanda, Burundi, BuNyoro, Ankole, and Karagwe-BuHaya) and the Peul, in the west.

A Philosophy of Life: Negritude a Philosophy

We will go back again to Leopold Senghor who defines "negritude" also as a philosophy.[9] But what philosophy?

Denying the idea that the black people of Africa were not to be called "savage" simply because their way of thinking and living was different from the Western life-style, he answered that the Negro-African way of life was an idea, a worldvision, an authentic and original conception of man, society and universe. It was a philosophy, but a philosophy built on realism, on the interpretation of living realities in the light of a proper dialectic of the African way of thinking. Without the same conceptions and categories as those of the speculative, rationalist Western mind, Negro-Africans were philosophers in their own right. They judged events and realities, they interpreted emotions and actions, they classified their own scale of values in terms close to their experience and reasoning, generally not from cause to effect but the other way around in an inductive process.

In October 1946, a simple Belgian missionary of the Franciscan Order, Placide Tempels, published his book on the "Bantu Philosophy."[10] It was an attempt to put together the result of his experience about the way the BaLuba people (Zaire) confronted life-situations in their own way of thinking. His point was that of a missionary, not by any means a professional philosopher, wishing to know his people in order to evangelize them. The "Bantu Philosophy," according to Tempels, was a philosophy of life, that is, a philosophy in which the main idea of the BaLuba, within the larger Bantu ethnic and cultural group, was a concern for living. Life was the key concept to which most of the thinking process referred.

Life was understood to be the "moving force" through which human beings attempted to gather inspiration and motivation: the desire to live, the joy to live, the need to live, all this was at the basis of aspirations, thoughts, activities in every field. From art to music, sculpture, literature and drama, it is the representation and the expression of life in one's home, within one's community, and in one's large society. The myths and legends which oral tradition communicates, as well as the taboos and behavior patterns which are prescribed, the role of religion, of skills and crafts in the village. Almost every aspect of existence is to grapple with the "mystery of life" in its reality, finally. Not least in this enumeration is the existence marked by the solemn moments of birth, puberty, marriage and death. That is the world vision centered on "living."

Tempels developed his theme on the "philosophy of life" expounding the Bantu conception of life, in the sense of a way of thinking that systematically goes to establish existence within the idea of "living force" — "force vitale or Lebenskraft." After Tempels, it has been "Africanists" who adopted and elaborated the philosophy of life extending it far beyond the populations of Central Africa. In fact, it was not Tempels who invented the theory, but he applied it, for the "concept of life" as central theme has its roots in the African vision, the spiritual vision deeply "animistic" and spiritual. Leo Frobenius had written about it when accounting for the idea of "magic force" seen by Africans in Nature and in the Universe. Teilhard de Chardin had come to recognize the same way of African vision concerning "cosmic unity." Boubou Hama gives an explanation that the African believes not only in "God," the supreme Being, but also in the participation of being which is the spiritual force in creation. If there are forces there is the spirit, and man's role is to discern the spiritual forces[11] in living things and in their symbols, i.e., material beings and man's work, namely the product of the mind and the product of the hands. In the way negritude understands things, thoughts are forces and words (Wortkunst). We shall come back to this aspect.

Philosophy of Being

To be or not to be — is the question. Negro-African philosophy is a philosophy of being. It is essentially a metaphysics. The thinking man within the African sees things beyond their visible shape, form and size; things are meant to be expressive, symbolic, in order to fulfill a function in the mind of the thinker.

To be or not to be is a principle of logic indicating identity or opposition and contradiction. To be or not to be is the question in dialectics where being and not being are contrasted and compared, to be separated or united: the principle of hypothesis, antithesis, thesis, synthesis. In the "science of being," which is ontology, to be or not to be is the key problem in order to demonstrate the nature of the true, the good, the beautiful and so on. To be or not to be is the basic principle in ethics and criteriology, the sciences of behavior and judgment. Consequently, African philosophy finds access to classical philosophy by developing the concept of being. Alexis Kagame made an attempt at this evolution in his research[12] and proposed some valid categories of person, place, time, action and potentiality.

To be, in this connection, is not to indicate the mere existential fact. To be is the initial interpretation of having within oneself the capacity to act, to do, to intervene, to represent; it means to be the subject, the agent, the center of attribution as a person. "I am there" is to be able to make one's presence active, relevant as a source of inner vitality and self-consciousness which is the attribute of beings with the life-spirit.[13]

The common status of "being" from the static condition rises to the dynamic condition in a higher status of being with or *être avec*. The connotation here is that of life together, life-participation. The perfection of "being" is made obvious and operative through the ontology of communion and participation. One is in possession of "being" in a higher degree in so far as one can communicate and create relationships and contacts. Descartes said, "cogito ergo sum." We in the African philosophy are different. We stress the capacity for communication, *loquor ergo sum*. In fact, the power of speech is an essentially distinctive quality; it is a sign of a "personality." African traditional orality and the power of the spoken word have been extolled for their sense and significance in relation to the depth and wealth of living-force. Communion with one's fellow men creates communities; communion with the cosmic forces creates harmony and balance in the universe; communion with the hierarchy of the supreme forces is the highest ideal in religion. The ontology of being is therefore measured by the capacity for participation, communication and communion.

Lastly, the philosophy of being reaches its highest point with *être plus* or *plus être* when the being, capable of communicating, can create and be productive. It is the ontology of the transcendental condition by which the person reaches the fullness of humanity and spirituality that is in his or her being. It is the measure of self-development, *dépassement de soi*, by transformation, by reproduction also in the biological sense, by attaining survival and fullness of life (eternal destiny, immortality). To possess the abundance of life (being) and to communicate it is the highest form of being. The Supreme Being, "God," being the fullness of life and abundance of force, performs the highest act which is life-giving by creation. Men and animals enter into the same ontology when they reproduce. According to Diul (large group in the Niger-Guinea-Sudan zone), being is force and the same force circulates at various levels: the supreme force that was not created is "Ata-Emit" (God); there are superior forces namely those intermediary between God and man "Boekin" (spirits); then those which carry out divine instructions "Bagum" (cosmic forces) in the forests and in the waters, and, lastly, animal and botanic forces. The pyramid holds together through the ontology of participation through the force of the life-spirit (soul), word and ritual. Examples can be multiplied from all over the continent. It is the reality and mystery together in the ontology about life-force, being-participation, reality-symbol in the worldvision of cosmic unity which the African mind perceives with extreme sensitivity. It is spiritual vision in which the visible and invisible mysteriously interact to keep life, force and harmony and help man to humanize himself and his environment.

Philosophy for Humanism

Pursuing this ontology, the hypotheses and theses of life-force-being lead to one synthesis. African philosophy is a *philosophy of man for man*. Indeed, man is at the center of the dialectical movement and the cosmic forces because of his spirit which, united with matter, transcends it to give that human touch which animates and transforms nature, art and science. If we maintain that it is the *philosophy of being*, it means "to be a man," a *being with humanity*. The Bantu concept of being is the expression of "humanity," the awareness of one's fundamental value as a human being. Being human expresses also what the philosophers of the classic age called "animal rationale." Often one will hear "what sort of man is he?" when it is intended to mean that without humanity one is not man; or referring to an old man who is not wise "he is only grey-haired and nothing else."

Again, the Aristotelian definition of philosophy which distinguishes between the nominal and real meaning of philosophy creates a wide gap between wisdom and science and between two knowledges. It seems that the exposition by Dr. E. F. Schumacher in his philosophical essay[14] is much to the point. After speaking about the Level of Being,[15] he underlines wisdom, which was so important in the old traditions, as "science for understanding" as opposed to "science for manipulation." He points out textually the spiritual nature of wisdom and the material scope in science: "the science for understanding saw *man* as made in the image of God, the crowning glory of creation. The science for manipulation, inevitably, sees *man* as nothing but an accidental product of evolution, a higher animal, a social animal."[16] The obvious conclusion is that it is wisdom that makes man by discovering and appraising man's higher level of being.

Love of Wisdom

Our children have not got our ancient sources of wisdom. Just listen when they speak. They are not concerned about that mature judgement of men which we ourselves had after a few years. They do not have the sense of life or they get a false one. They do not observe how a man lives or when they do they do not see what they ought to observe: they have no time to live. They merely pick up the ideas they get and think that they have acquired knowledge (from books). The education they receive from the White men does not form their heart; on the contrary it deforms it. If you live long enough you will tell me about Burundi's future.[17]

Thus Michel Kayoya interprets a conversation in which two old men are visibly worried as they review the old-time humanism in crisis. This is a general situation as the village civilization undergoes change. The love of wisdom in rapid decline gives way to modernity. It was a coherent lifestyle that kept the communities together, held traditions in esteem, educated families and children, formed the heart and soul to human maturity inculcating discipline and nobility.

Our conclusion is clear. If people whose chief concern is love of and search for wisdom are philosophers, then Africa had and has her philosophers, too. Yet, African philosophy in the days of yore was more radical: a philosophy of man, of being, a knowledge for understanding life and its realities and mysteries, a humanism. Indeed, there were ideas, concepts and more than these, traditions to observe, models to imitate (the old folk and the ancestors come in here), and ideals to live for, namely ethical and social values. The concept of being permeated the process of existence and development: being was higher than having — *magis esse quam habere*; being higher than knowing — *magis esse quam sapere*; being higher than commanding — *magis esse quam prae esse*.[18]

Religion and Humanism

In African tradition, it is the old persons who are generally considered to possess wisdom and humanity, for they have acquired the art of living. Old persons can teach others, by word and example, the way to observe, to think, to be counsellors and judges. By long experience they become experts in humanity.

However, a proverb reminds us "a hole in a smoking pipe is of man's doing, a hollow in a baobao tree is the effect of time, but the wisdom in an old man is God's work."[19] The elderly people's privilege is having had God's blessing for a long life with the chance of grappling with life's realities. Philosophy and humanism find their sources in *religion* from a deep sense of the sacred, which unfolds the moral and spiritual elements as basic in living and underlines the aspiration for fullness of life as the highest criterion. The elderly people are not only in long touch with the "human facts of life", but also with the ancients, and through these with the Supreme Being, the Life-giver, the Source and Fullness of living forces. Life and being are considered as gifts from above. There is the presence of the Divinity active in the Universe to maintain order and harmony, and to enforce hierarchy and authority. And this is the fundamental lesson in the art of living, namely the religious factor which permeates culture and animates civilizations with myths, beliefs, taboos, rituals. Consequently, a philosophy which investigates the ontology of being and life not only forms the heart,[20] and inspires the soul, but leads the mind towards the ultimate Cause.

Conclusion

This short paper attempts to show (a) that traditional Africa knew some kind of philosophy; (b) that today our contemporaries strive to save and preserve its specific elements for world civilization and humanism; (c) that the role of religion remains capital as a source of wisdom.

At the level of religion and culture, humanism and Christianity possess the way for the dialogue between Africa and other civilizations, especially with those of the Western culture. In this venture even philosophy can be a strong bridge for encounter and understanding, if it is presented not only as science but also as integral humanism.

Pontifical Urbanian University
Rome, Italy

NOTES

1. Hosea Jaffe, *Africa*, Ed. Mondadori (Milano, 1978), cfr I. Passato Perdu to, pp. 15-19.

2. Arnold Toynbee, *Between Niger and Nile* (London: Oxford University Press, 1965).

3. L. S. Senghor, *Interview*, in Mundo Negro, No. 161, 1974, pp. 26-30. p. 26: Hablar de la Negritud en su relacion con la modernidad, en otros terminos, presentar la negritud como un humanismo contemporaneo, es un asunto de actualidad.

4. Ibid., p. 27: "He aqui lo que es la negritud. Objectivamente, como civilizacion, es el conjuncto de los valores no solamente de los pueblos del Africa negra, sino tambien de los miborias negras de America, hasta las de Asia y de Oceania."

5. E. Mveng, *Dossier Culturel Pan-africain*, Présence Africaine 1966, p. 84: "Il faut cependant reconnaitre qu'elle (Afrique) comporte aussi des réelles qualitées positivies. Les liens culturels, constatés sur place, sont le ciment le plus solide qui noue les entités africaines et l'unité même de l'Afrique est essentielleme une unité geographique et une unité culturelle."

6. Senghor, *Discours* d'Inauguration de l'Université de Dakar, 9 Décembre 1959: "J'entends par *culture* l'esprit de la civilisation; par *civilisation*, les oeuvres et réalisations de la culture."6.

7. Mveng, p. 211, Charte de l'Unité africaine, Objecti Art. II. 1.

8. J. Macquet and H. Ganslmayer, *Die Afrikaner, Völker und Kulturen* (Munchen: Verlag Heyne, 1978), p. 25, "Den Kontinent Afrika kurturell in zwei Teile zu spalten — den einen nördlich, den andern südlich der Sahara — ist Willkürlich. In mancher Hinsicht ein Hindernis, ist die grosse Wüste doch ebenso ein Kommunikationsweg gewesen Das Niltal war ebenfalls ein Austauchweg zwischen Schwar afrika und Aegypten."

9. Senghor, p. 27: "La negritud, como civilizacion objectiva, es una idea quiero decir, una filosofia y una vida, una teoria y una practica, una moral y una arte; pero ante todo, una Idea. . . . La filosofia negro-africana, como la vivimos y como nos lo confirman los africanistas, es una ontologia; una ciencia del ser. . . ." Mveng, p. 85: "Il faut cependant souligner qu'en Afrique, toute civilisation dans ses manifestations techniques, est l'expression d'une vision du monde et d'une conception de l'homme qui lui donnent son veritable contenu. . . ."

10. F. Bontinck, *Aux origines de la Philosophie Bantoue* (Kinshasa, 1985), p. 7 fin octobre 1946 parut le texte integral Bantoe-Filosofie *La Philosophie Bantoue*, par la Presence Africaine en mai 1949.

11. Boubou Hama, *Kotia-Nima, Rencontre avec l'Europe*, Présence Africaine, Paris 1969, cfr. p. 38-46 L'Afrique sur la Scene du Monde, Son Enseignement, Son Message Possible.

12. A. Kagame, *Philosophie Bantu Comparée* (Paris, 1976).

13. A proverb from Ivory Coast in the eighteenth century: "Call gold, and it is mute, call your cloth, it is mute; what matters is man, he can speak."

14. E. F. Schumacher, *A Guide for the Perplexed*, Abacus Edition (London: Harper Collins, 1978).

15. Ibid., pp. 24-35, *Levels of Being*, p. 31: "A human being can indeed strain and stretch towards the higher and induce a process of growth through adoration, awe, wonder, admiration and imitation, and by attaining a higher level expand its understanding. . . ."

16. Ibid., p. 67.

17. M. Kayoya, *Sur les Traces de mon Père*, Ed. Lavigerie (Bujumbura: 1966), p. 33.

18. Schumacher, *Levels of Being*, pp. 24-35; Boubou Hama, p. 49: "Etre," "Etre plus" suppose l'effort physique qui cultive et la perspective qui entraine "une croyance," une foi vraie au centre du courant continu du phénomène humain sur la base du dévelopement capable de conduire par

356

accroissement de notre spiritualité à notre "humanisation" susceptible de converger vers le point Omega de l'auteur.

19. cfr. *Tercer Mundo*, Octubre 1982, 30-34, "*Ser Viejo en Africa*" por Francisca Reche: Ancianida en la tradicion africana significa plenitud de vida, de esa vida que ha sido recibida de los antepasados para que no se acabe nunca . . . La idea vida que se desprende de analisis linguistico bantu es la uan realidad interior que se palpa en el aolo que aporta la fuerza, plenitud y felicidad, que permite atraversar la duracion del tiempo y evitar la muerte, que debe ser trasmitida por procreacion; esta es el objecto ultimo del hombre. . . .

El africano no piensa que los años confieran la sabiduria automaticamente. Un proverbio minyanka lo dice muy bien: "El agujero en la pipa es trabajo del hombre, el hueco del arbol es trabajo de los años; pero la sabiduria en el viejo es el trabajo de Dios."

20. The "heart," especially for the Bantu groups, is the seat of intelligence, conscience and wisdom. Having a heart means to be kind, meek, generous, courageous and to be humane and human. Having no "heart" means to be worthless and hopeless.

DIALOGUE OF CHRISTIANITY WITH CULTURES IN CHINA OF YESTERDAY AND TODAY

Matthias Lu

The dialogue of Christianity with cultures in China of yesterday and today has been the center of my attention and study for many years. The long history of intercultural relations provides fruit for much thought and discussion. To better explore this topic, I will define the term "culture" and indicate culture's properties; then, I will point out its basic condition; finally, I will review two significant historical works as examples for our analysis.

A Definition of Culture

First of all, the term "culture" is ambiguous and often equivocal. For the sake of orientation, let us simply say that it is the human spirit's creativity. As we observe culture around us, it is human creativity acting, through communication in a community, for development. More fully, human culture is the mind's creative way of using what is given in nature and reality for the development of the human person in society, through the sharing of discovery and the production of value.

Many terms are used co-extensively to mean human culture, even if they are not all synonymous. Understood in this way, i.e., as products of human reason and art, "culture" and "civilization" can be used interchangeably. Metaphysically, human culture is the human being actively in search of human values. Coinciding with education, it requires man's self-cultivation of moral virtues as essential to human goodness and dignity. Human culture's value consists in making man and his universe humanly good, rather than inhumanly rich or mighty. For this reason, genuine human culture is not an aimless evolution of styles or fashions; rather, it is a progression guided by the principle of human goodness or rationality itself.

Apart from this principle, culture becomes irrational. As such, it becomes self-contradictory and self-destructive, producing that monstrous phenomenon "civilized savages," more capable even than uncivilized savages of worsening the human condition. In order to prevent this phenomenon, the principle of human goodness must be recognized and honored. However, this latter is precisely the problem, a most pressing problem since the beginning of history.

Christianity solved this problem by throwing light on human culture's essence through revealing the deeper essence of human nature itself. Through evangelization we have come to see that human culture, while it is the human spirit's creativity, is more profoundly a manifestation of the Holy Spirit of God's creativity. As the first cause of all causes, God is the creator of all things, the prime mover of all activities. He does all things through the power of the Divine Word, the Divine Logos.

Human spirit as human creativity is the second cause. According to the ontological principle of causality, in a given chain of causes, the first cause is more intimate to the ultimate effect than all other causes, each in its own way and order contributing to the effect; nothing causes unless it is caused by the first cause to be and to move. Since the higher a cause is, the more intimate it is to the effect; the lower and more proximate the cause is, the less intimate it is to the effect. Nevertheless, in any given chain of causes the highest cause produces no effect without the required lower causes. Thus, it is true to say that the ultimate effect is totally an effect of the First Cause, and, at the same time, is totally an effect of the more proximate secondary cause or causes.

According to this principle of causality, human culture or civilization is an effect totally of God and totally of man, with God being more intimate to it than man. It then follows by essence and by definition that human culture, in order to be a creativity of the human spirit, must also be from beginning to end a creativity of God in the Divine Trinity. Further, it follows that, in order to be what it is and should be, human culture must take on the character of an epiphany, that is, a manifestation of two realities — the divine and the human — in the one theandric reality of the Holy Infant — True Man and True God—in the manger of Bethlehem.

The first Epiphany, the Adoration of the Holy Infant by the Magi, was the first encounter of Christianity with the cultures of Gentile nations from the East. The Magi were the Wise Men of royal dignity from the Orient. The word "Orient" means the place of sunrise. On hearing of it, Japanese Christians thought of Japan, which in Chinese means the place of the sunrise's origin. Some Chinese Christians and historians went as far as to identify the Biblical Sinim (Is. 49:12) with China (regio Sinarum), and imagined the possibility of the Magi having had some Chinese sage in their company.

In any case, the expression "Orient" is broad enough to signify the eastern regions under Heaven. What the Magi adored in the first Epiphany is the Light of all Gentile nations, the common object of love and hope for all nations and cultures.

For me, the word "epiphany" is the true name of human culture because Confucius and his disciples always admired the glories of Heaven-and-Earth in the achievement of culture and art. Culture is a manifestation of God's glory rather than a gratification of man's pride. Therefore, the epiphany of the divine in the human and of the human in the divine is another name for culture and art. It is actually a common denominator of all that is qualifiable as human and good. In this light, from the Epiphany, human art is no longer merely "an imitation of nature," as the Greeks and Aristotle used to say, but it is also "an imitation of Christ," since Christ's epiphany was a theophany and an anthropophany joined into one.

Accordingly, a cultural product or work of art is not beautiful unless it manifests itself as both human and divine. This mirrors the thoughts expressed by Dr. Hsu Pei Hung in Peking (Christmas, 1946) about a "Madonna and Child" in Chinese liturgical printing. Although Dr. Hsu was not a baptized Christian, his aesthetic perception recognized that an art work needs something divine in the human in order to be beautiful. From the nature of culture as an epiphany, we may go further then to see its basic condition and necessary properties, both in its making and in its circulation.

The Basic Condition of Human Culture

Although the essential cause of human culture is the spirit of man and his God, its basic condition, by contrast, is materiality. Man needs materiality as an instrument and vehicle to embody and sustain the cultural values realized in cultural products. Cultural values, at the first moment, are spiritual ideas and intentions existing subjectively inside the human mind, i.e., within the realm of consciousness. And, at the second moment, they need materiality to gain existence, individuation, identity, and expression in cultural products existing objectively outside the human mind, i.e., within the domain of objective reality, either in the form of substance or, at least, in some physical effect.

Cultural values and products may be further divided into the spiritual and the material. The spiritual ones can be moral and intellectual, such as virtues, knowledge and wisdom. The material ones can be physical products of all kinds, such as machines, craft products, art, and architecture, although even the material products always express some spiritual values, including idea, design, purpose, intention, and beauty. Nevertheless, without exception, both the spiritual and the material products of culture need materiality for instrument and support.

Among all the cultural products of man, the most fundamental and creative one is language. In language, every word is a composite of two elements: meaning and sound, spoken or written. Meaning, as intelligible, is spiritual, without materiality. But in language, in which meaning is spiritual, materiality is required as a necessary condition for its existence and expression.

Ontologically, language is made by man through the powers of his reason and art. In turn, through education, man is made by language to be specifically human, different from other creatures. Cultural progress is made possible by language, and it is by the cultural process that man makes progress in his development. Language exercised its civilizing power more efficiently when it began to be written and printed. When we think of Gutenberg in the West, we are reminded by history that China began printing its books years before him.

Culturally speaking, written language is the beginning and sign of civilization. The ancient Chinese scholars identify written language with civilization itself. For them, savages without civilization are identical to savages without letters. Written language is so important that all other cultural products can be considered secondary and auxiliary. For, even works of art, architecture, and the like are made to aid language in expressing ideas which were first formulated in written form. Without written language, human culture becomes extremely tenuous, if not totally impossible.

Language is so important and powerful because it has the mysterious and marvelous power of what is now called "symbolism." As a symbol, each word of the human language can express many levels and kinds of ideas above and beyond the basic concrete reality that it was originally made to stand for. If the human spirit is creative, it is because it has the power of language with which to create and use symbols. Curiously enough, the making of each human word, especially in its written form, is an imitation of the epiphany in the incarnation of the Divine Word. The human idea is made letter as the Divine Word made flesh.

With the progress of writing and printing, human culture begins to grow and spread and, if properly guided, will save the world from its miseries. Under this humanitarian impulse, all cultural workers are ministers of the Written Word, analogous to missionaries as ministers of the Divine Word Incarnate. Despite all human motives which were other than moral or cultural, Western Civilization, through the zeal of the missionaries, came to China with the Bible before all else. Some political historians may wish to reverse the chronological and ideological order, saying that the Bible followed the gunboats or cargo boats. But theology and philosophy would like to suggest, rather, that cultural vitality was the primary and fundamental motive in comparison with the political ambition and commercial greed of seventeenth century Europe.

Universality of Culture

Once culture is understood as the human spirit's creative sharing of messages and goods, one can easily see that human culture requires certain properties for its being and circulation. These properties are numerous. For the sake of brevity, we will concentrate our attention on one property under which all other properties can be subsumed. Even this one property, having many aspects in itself, can be signified in one word - "universality."

By intent and by effect, culture is universal in space, time, and content, aiming at total self-actualization of each human person. It radiates from person to person until it fills up the whole space-time continuum, no limits, no barriers of any kind. Culture, like light, radiates in all directions in order to be, to produce results, and to grow. Through shared messages and values, culture unites all human beings and all things into one kingdom. It sometimes presents itself, after the Confucian and Ciceronian model of society, in the form of a great family with inner hierarchy of relationships of consanguinity, affinity, and friendship; it sometimes appears as a community of mutual love and benefit on the basis of equality, according to the ideals of mutuality and cooperation. Unfortunately, it sometimes also appears in the merciless guise of totally selfish enterprises in which each one seeks every advantage for himself, giving nothing to anyone else.

Paradoxically, true self-love eventually ends up in altruistic love of all neighbors. The love of neighbors is a new and evangelical concept, operative within space-time coordination as a creative spirit in the image of God in which self-love and love of all creatures, once freely elected, are one love. This one love, like a fire or light, warms and enlightens the self-giving. In the mystery of evangelical love, which is the essence of true love, to give is to receive a fulfillment, but not vice versa. Therefore, it is better to give than to receive, and this truth also expresses the true essence of cultural creativity. The consequence of this love of neighbor is complete self-giving to everybody, everywhere and forever. This consequence is necessary. It is the law of cultural creativity. It is its property, the law of universality.

In practice, culture is universal in space. It radiates from the heart of one person to the hearts of all persons in all places. No one seems to me to have emphasized this point as much as the Confucians. They repeat tirelessly that what is accomplished in one's heart is crystallized in the sincerity of one's intention and then made manifest. Thus, step by step, it leads to good order in one's family, nation, and the whole universe under Heaven. This is why what you say or do to your wife and children, like the undulation of a wave, will never stop until it reaches the ends of space.

According to recent research, cultural exchange between China and other countries, either through direct contact or through indirect or intermediate repercussions, was more widely spread than can be documented in history. And traces are not lacking in archaeology in all parts of the world, including Latin America. Not only in space, but also in time, culture is universal. Cultural exchange is perpetual and ceaseless. Its messages and values are transmitted from antiquity to posterity. Its benefits spread for cultural progress.

In both space and time, the circulation of cultural products is universal because it is continuous, accumulative, and creative. It is creative in the sense that accumulation of the old gives rise to the new in ideas, in skills, and in products. This universality by circulation through space and time is both a consequence of culture and an antecedent condition for culture. Culture cannot exist or grow without circulation. Its circulation demands universality in space and time, tolerating no impediments or restrictions. The greatest injustice and injury man can inflict on himself is to deny freedom of cultural exchange. Universal circulation of culture in space and time is meaningful and effective only when its content is shared in authenticity and in entirety. Universality in content is the authenticity and the wholeness of any cultural product or system given in exchange.

Universality in personalism entails the total involvement of all concerned persons in the production, circulation, enjoyment, and innovation of a cultural product or system through all phases of its life. Cultural life itself is a participation of all persons in the common task of bettering the human condition. In fact, every human being, if alive in action, as such, is a creator and a bearer of culture. Universality of culture in personalism requires freedom of travel for all persons to all places, at all times, for person-to-person communication.

Intercultural exchange is complete when interchange of personal intercommunication is as unimpeded as the circulation of the bloodstream within a healthy organism. All movements of human beings in space and time have cultural significance and effects for the benefit of all persons objectively involved, even if these persons are engaged subjectively in hostile acts.

Paradoxically, the great wars, in the end, united the warriors as they emerged from painful conflict into the one community with a new cultural network. If hate thus leads to its own reverse, it follows that a civilization of love is an undeniable essence of civilized life itself; hate and war have no lasting place in human life and culture. In its total personalistic involvement, human progress is by nature a progression from novelty in the form of mutual friendship, not in the form of terrorism with mutual harm or destruction.

The universality of culture in space, time, content, and personalism is a property, a law, and a standard of culture in action, i.e., in exchange and interchange. It is a concept which is at the same time Christian and Confucian. It is Catholic!

Thomas the Apostle and "Maha-China"

The Christian cultural interchange with the Orient might have begun at the time of the first Epiphany. The possibility of the Apostles arriving thereafter in China was suggested by the Malabar Christians of India who prayed in their litany to their Apostle Thomas for the conversion of peoples in the region of Maha-China-sthana. That name is accepted by all to signify the territory of the Chin Dynasty under the historical title "Great-Chin Kingdom"; it coincided geographically with Marco Polo's

364

China, Cathay. Although historical documentation is lacking, the possibility of the Apostle's visit cannot be ruled out.

Earlier mutual interchange of cultural significance had taken place between China and the Greco-Roman World before Christ. Caesar himself, following the Greeks, used to call the Chinese people "Serici" (Silk People). There are other signs: for example, certain fruits in China may have been imported from Greece; some historians think that the Chinese word for grapes "poo-tau" sounds exactly like the Greek word for grapes "botrous." Again, traces of Antonine Emperors' Roman Legion were found in Turkestan, China after Alexander the Great conquered parts of India. The style of Greco-Indian art reached China through India and Tibet.

In the Middle Ages, at the time of the Mongolian Empire, China was visited by missionaries, merchants, diplomats, and tourists from Europe. It is enough to mention Plan Carpin, John of Montecorvina, Oderic of Pordonone, among the missionaries, Nicolo and Marco Polo among the merchants, and John de Marignolli (1339, of Florence) and Ruy Gonzalez de Clavijo (1403, in Samarkand from Spain) among the diplomats.

St. Francis Xavier and Matteo Ricci

The first really effective interchange took place about 32 years after the death (1552) of St. Francis Xavier at Sancian Island near the coast of Canton. Historians take the date of entry to Canton Province by Matteo Ricci (Sept. 10, 1583) as the historical date of the modern beginning of Catholic missions in China. The celebration of the 400th anniversary of missions in China began in 1984 and can be said to be still going on right now. For, no one is sure of the exact date when the fourth centennial should really begin and end.

From the time of Matteo Ricci (1583-1610 in China) to the death in Macao of Cardinal Tournon in 1710, we have 126 years of Christianity in China. This period also marked the first 126 years of cultural interchange between China and the Christian West. Within these 126 years, many missionaries, Jesuits, Augustinians, Franciscans, and Dominicans, from Macao, Goa, Singapore and Manila, tried to enter China. The real stronghold was established in May 1601 when an imperial decree granted Matteo Ricci and his confreres a permanent residence in the South Gate district of Peking. The first church was also built in the same place where Nan-tang, South-Church, i.e., the

Immaculate Conception Church, serves as the Cathedral for the Patriotic
Association "church" today.

The First Collection of Leo Lee

The most decisive events in this period were the baptisms of three
Chinese remembered in history as the "Three Pillars of the Catholic
Church in China": (1) Paul Hsu, Prime Minister and tutor of the Emperor
[January 15, 1603], (2) Michael Yang, [Easter 1613] and (3) Leo Lee
[March 3, 1610]. Outstanding among the many things which Lee did for
the Church is his "First Collection of Celestial Science," edited in Peking,
1629. The collection contains twenty books, divided into two sections.

The first section, entitled "Ideas," includes the following ten books:

1. *Brief Presentation of the Curriculum of the Western Schools.*
   Rhetoric, philosophy, medicine, laws (leges), canons, and
   theology presented orally by Julius Aleni and translated into
   Chinese.

2. *Stele of Grace Religion of Tang Dynasty.* "Grace Religion" was
   the name given in Chinese to the Christian religion which came
   to China from Persia during the Tang Dynasty. The stone
   inscription is a summary of the history and the doctrine of the
   Christian religion which was later identified with the Nestorian
   Church from Persia. The name was also sometimes retranslated
   as "Luminous Religion" (King-Kiao, = Jing-Jiao, 635-845 A.D.).

3. *Ten Chapters from a Foreigner.* Questions from Chinese
   scholars were answered by Matteo Ricci, showing human life as
   a pilgrimage to the true and eternal home in Heaven. Appendix:
   Eight Songs for Harpsichord.

4. *On Friendship.* Maxims narrated by Matteo Ricci, without
   reference to source.

5. *Twenty-five Maxims.* By Matteo Ricci. For cultivation of moral
   virtues to please God, also without reference to the source.

6. *The True Meaning of Celestial Science.* A compendium of theology and philosophy in response to religious questions given to Matteo Ricci in China, 2nd edition, 1601, Peking (1st edition: 1595, Nanchang).

7. *Apologetics Recorded.* A booklet in defense of Catholic teaching against the Buddhist accusations, by Matteo Ricci, and by his disciples after his death.

8. *Seven Mortifications.* An ascetical treatise of virtues against the seven capital sins, written by D. (Didacus) Diego de Pantoja, 1604.

9. *Short Treatise on the Soul.* In four parts: (a) On the Nature of the Soul; (b) On the Powers of the Soul; (c) On the Dignity of the Soul; (d) On the Desire in the Soul for the Supreme Good. The purpose of the treatise is to know man's soul and to know God for the eternal happiness of the soul resting in God. Written by Francis Sambiasi, 1624, revised edition 1919.

10. *Julius Aleni's World Atlas with Explanations*, 1623. Six fascicles showing the countries of the five continents, including America as newly discovered by Columbus. Composed under a decree of Wanli Emperor (1592-1620), to show the world outside China.

The second section of the collection, entitled "Instruments," includes the following ten books:

1. *Western Irrigation Methods.* By Sabathinus de Ursis, 1612. Six fascicles. Accepted by the Four Partite Library in Agriculture.

2. *Astronomy Illustrated.* Two fascicles; by Leo Lee. A book similar to a part of the *Astrolabium* of Christopher Clavius, S.J., showing the movements of Heaven, Earth, and the Constellations, as a basis of season and time measurements.

3. *Euclidian Geometry.* Narrated by Matteo Ricci; translated and revised by Paul Hsu. Six fascicles. Chapters selected and con-

densed from Flavius' Digest of Euclid. Accepted by Four Partite Library.

4. *Sun Dial.* One volume. Explained orally by Sabathinus de Ursis, transcribed by Tze-Yu Chow, 1612. Describes the seasons and time measurements on the basis of the shadow of a tablet or anything placed on the ground against the sun.

5. *Summary Study of Heavens.* One volume. A booklet of astronomy written by Manuel Diaz, 1616, Peking, on the 12 Heavenly Spheres. The 12th Heaven, "Caelum Immobile," is the dwelling place of the Blessed Trinity and all the Saints. It was believed literally!

6. *Calendar Method Simplified.* Explained orally by Sabathinus de Ursis, 1611, transcribed in notes by Paul Hsu, Peking.

7. *Guide of Arithmetic.* Taught by Matteo Ricci, with exercises written by Leo Lee. Printed in Peking, 1613.

8. *A Comparative Study on Roundness* (De Circulo). Taught by Matteo Ricci, written by Leo Lee, with exercises. One volume. Printed 1641, Peking.

9. *Method of Measurement* (in Geometry of Euclid). Explained orally by Matteo Ricci, transcribed by Paul Hsu. Appendix: *A Comparative Study on the Method of Measurement.*

10. *Trigonometry Explained.* Written by Matteo Ricci; transcribed with revision by Paul Hsu. 1 volume.

ANALYSIS: A FEW REMARKS

Remark #1: Architectonic Integration

The Chinese expression "Celestial Science" signifies "Catholic Science." Astonishingly enough, it includes not only theology, philosophy, ethics, and geography, but, on an equal footing, astronomy, geometry, agriculture, arithmetic, trigonometry, and the like. All of these sciences, which were learned from the missionary fathers, were identified as Catholic. Reciprocally, the fathers themselves seemed to have taught, with equal zeal, all sciences as manifestations of the Creator's Wisdom and, therefore, as an integral part of Catholic teaching. Instead of blaming them for confusing sciences with religion, we in the twentieth century should begin to wonder if our dichotomy between science and theology might not be due to our own misunderstanding, first, about the true nature of sciences and then about theology and of their mutual relationship. We must recognize that the true character of natural science must be qualified as divine, in order to avoid relegating religion and theology to the margins of learning; for the latter, even if they are not qualifiable as empirical sciences, are divine sciences, and are interconnected with empirical sciences.

Architectonic integration of all knowledge (theology, philosophy, and the sciences) into one unified structure for the common good of civilization may still require that theology assume the place of queen of all sciences, a place given by Aristotle to metaphysics. Theology would not subordinate the others epistemologically or methodologically, but would evaluate them, engineer them, and assign each of them to its proper place within the overall structure of human culture in service to the integral development of the human person, according to his ultimate finality.

The solution of the problem of disintegration and excessive compartmentalization of human knowledge is not obtained by secularizing the divine, but by restoring divine values to the sciences. The sciences have been mistaken too easily and too radically as "secular" (in the atheistic sense of anti-divine). In fact, Father Julius Aleni, in presenting the curriculum of the Western Schools, emphasized the architectonic integration of all knowledge for the good of man, in theory, by the theology of St. Thomas Aquinas and, in praxis, by the unifying authority of "the Sovereign Ruler of Religion and Civilization" in the person of the Pope.

The role of the Pope in the West was analogous to the role of the Emperor, the Son of Heaven, reigning in Peking. The Emperor was not only the Supreme Commander of the armed forces and the head of the executive apparatus of the government, but he was also the supreme teacher and head of the Academy of all Sciences and Arts. He was supposed to govern by virtue and not by force. The Four Partite Library was supervised and directed personally by the Emperor for this reason, not only incidentally, but also because an emperor happened to be a scholar.

Remark #2: Cult of Antiquity

In accepting baptism, Chinese scholars assumed the Christian duty to propagate the Faith to their Chinese co-nationals. In doing this, they used with full awareness the method of inculturation. They used cultural motives and expressions prevailing in the Chinese culture of that time to introduce the Catholic Science to the Chinese people, and vice versa, to introduce the Chinese people to Catholic Science, called "Celestial Science." Some scholars call it "Heavenly Science."

Among the cultural motives, these scholars made strong appeal to the "cult of antiquity," which equates the wise and good with everything that is ancient. At every juncture of similarity or coincidence, they tried hard to show that Catholic teachings already existed in Chinese antiquity and were as old as human nature itself. Therefore, in accepting Catholic truths, the Chinese were made to feel that they were not embracing a foreign religion, but were rediscovering what they had always had in their ancient wisdom.

Remark #3: Intellectual Apostolate

Since the State ideology of that time was Confucian Mandarin based on the learning of Confucian classics, the missionaries soon learned to identify themselves with the Mandarin-Confucian scholars, both in lifestyle and in the scholarly endeavors of learning, teaching, writing, and publishing. There was and has always been a "cult of the written word" and a "cult of the intelligentsia" in the Chinese tradition. This is true even today.

The early missionaries not only incorporated themselves into the class of Chinese "Literati," but also, as the leadership group, at least perhaps opportunistically, aligned themselves with the winning party. That was the party of Confucian Mandarins headed by the Emperor in opposition to Buddhists, Taoists, and other religions and schools which the Emperor himself downgraded as "small religious sects of low populace class."

Remark #4: The Four Tasks

The missionaries and the early Chinese Christian scholars, as represented by Leo Lee, the editor of our "First Collection of Celestial Science," were unanimous in adopting four tasks in relation to the then predominant trend of Confucianism, historically known as Neo-Confucianism. This Neo-Confucianism was a modern synthesis of Classic Confucianism with elements from Buddhism, Taoism, and other sources. The four tasks are the following:

The first task was to unite with Confucianism in whatever was true in it. To do this, an ancient Proto-Confucianism, supposed to have existed among the ancient sages honored by Confucius himself, was invoked. Traces of this could be rediscovered by analysis of the ancient documents and by comparison with Catholic teachings.

In order to facilitate this task, Matteo Ricci had the audacity to give a Catholic interpretation to all the key words of Confucian doctrinal classics: on morals, on social discipline, and on ritual practices. In doing this, he was accused of misinterpretations or forced reinterpretations.

The second task was to supplement Confucian classics in all truths that were missing. In order to do this, contact points or points of similarity were discovered and exploited to familiarize the Chinese scholars with Catholic beliefs which were alien to Chinese tradition, but could be added to it by some remote similarities.

The third task was to correct Confucianism in everything that was not found correct.

The fourth task was to transcend Confucianism, i.e., to show the superiority of the supernatural over natural truths and virtues.

Remark #5: The Five Successes

In fulfilling the above four tasks, the missionaries and the early Christian Chinese scholars cooperating with them were successful in the following areas:

(1) Their mastery of the Chinese language in speaking, writing, and publishing was equal to their task and adhered to high standards of accuracy and elegant style. Although the modernization and vernacularization of the Chinese language in attempts to close the gap between the written and the spoken Mandarin Chinese of the

nineteenth and twentieth centuries made all the missionaries' classicist writings linguistically obsolete, their writings remain, nevertheless, valuable for scholarly consultation even today.

(2) In Christianizing Confucian thought, they did not lessen their great humanist respect toward the textual integrity of the literary documents and towards the authority of the Confucian teachers of their time. They never even thought to forge, corrupt, or interpolate the Confucian classics in order to circulate Christian ideas under Confucian cover. They did, at least, show successfully by logical analysis that certain Confucian reasoning and manner of life would find greater satisfaction in opening the mind and heart to the Church teaching and to the Western Theology and Philosophy which the Church made her own and taught in all her schools.

(3) Their survey of the ancient Confucian Classics was complete and deep. Their interpretation may have been questionable and controversial, and, indeed, still is, even more so, today. However, their intention was honest, and their approach was human and friendly. They did elicit reasonable and objective response from a considerable number of the intellectual leaders in the land. This can be seen from the fact that a great number of their writings were accepted into the Four Partite Library of the Emperor, often with direct intervention of the Emperor himself. In quality, their writings deserved to be a high rank among the classic works in that authoritative Library.

(4) They understood that, for the China of their day, the only apostolate worthy of its name was the intellectual apostolate according to the nature of the mission of Christ himself, who was sent to bring light to the minds of all men born into the earthly darkness of ignorance and sin, inasmuch as the God of Christ was a Father of lights (*Pater luminum*), while Christ was hailed by Simeon as the Light of Nations. Christ is "the God and the Lord of all sciences" *Scientiarum Dominus et Deus, Jesus Christus*).

(5) They also understood the importance of the so-called "indirect apostolate," which as a term in cultural history and in missiology means to use educational and social work to serve people's temporal needs first, in order to lead them, later on, to turn their attention to the spiritual needs. In this view, intellectual activities and services are propaedeutic to the apostolate proper, which consists in preaching the gospels and distributing the sacraments.

In their integralist view, the missionaries did, however, prefer to program their activities in terms of an architectonic unification of all sciences and skills, to the effect that all sciences and arts of value were themselves viewed as integral parts of the intellectual life, which is divine no less in men than in God himself.

It is not totally wrong for us to think that they believed what they did, for instance, in agriculture for the economy and in procurement of military weapons for Chinese national defense, was no less evangelical a work than their prayers and sacraments. This problem, however, remains today: how can a Church, in caring for the integral development of the human person and society, limit herself to the so-called "direct apostolate" alone. Possibly, the apostolate itself should be redefined so as to include or to exclude certain things that are needed for man's goal in life, i.e., for the eternal fulfillment of all his needs in terms of the Messianic Kingdom.

Finally, the intellectual apostolate of the early Christian European missionaries and Chinese scholars did not last more than about 100 years, if we count only the fruitful period between 1601 and 1710: i.e., from Matteo Ricci's arrival at Peking to the death of Cardinal Tournon in Macao.

Cardinal Tournon's publication in 1707 in Nanking of "regulations" from Rome prohibiting the Confucian Rites triggered the persecution which legally was set to last forever in varied forms, which practically, however, never stopped completely the missionaries' religious activities. At the same time, it promoted even more exchanges in the fields of pure science and culture. The qualified missionaries continued to be employed in important positions in the court and in the Astronomical Observatory.

For historical reasons, the new age of "Foreign Mission-Institutes" in the eighteenth-twentieth centuries rededicated the missionaries to new fields of the so-called direct apostolate, whereas the intellectual apostolate disappeared almost completely. Recent efforts at intellectual revival

(1926-1946) have not seemed sufficient in scope nor in manpower to make an impact on the cultural life of China as a nation. To these insufficiencies must be added the paucity of Catholics: in approximate terms three million among a population of four hundred million Chinese before 1948.

Neo-Confucianism Rejects Leo Lee's Christianity

It is very important to remember that the time of the "First Collection of the Celestial Science" was also the time shortly before the Four Partite Library of the Great Ch'ing Dynasty (1644-1911) was built.

The intention of the Four Partite Library was to collect all the valuable books existing in China from antiquity to that time, and to classify them according to the Chinese Confucian authentic tradition. Those books not qualified as assimilable were classified as heterogeneous and hybrid or syncretic. These books, if too bad, were not accepted into the collection. Some of them were given only an index of their titles with a brief criticism of their unorthodox content. The whole Library took eleven years to be completed, 1772-1783.

By re-examining the place the Catholic books occupy in the Four Partite Library, we can see clearly whether the Chinese Confucian officialdom accepted or rejected them and why. This re-examination is very important for historical cultural study, in order to reorient the efforts of cultural interchange and even to redefine the nature of cultural dialogue, in general, and the nature of Christian dialogue, in particular. For the sake of brevity, let me give a four-point summary:

Point I. All the books of theology in the section "Ideas" of the "First Collection" were radically rejected for four reasons. Epistemologically, their arguments were qualified as "not investigable," i.e., not controllable by human reason based on reality: they could neither be scrutinized nor checked nor counterchecked by the method of rational investigation against evidence from human experience and rational proof.

Point II. Economically, it was observed that they did not touch the immediate needs of the daily life of the citizens or of the nation. Therefore, they were considered useless.

Point III. Politically, by exalting the position of the Pope and of the religious teachers in the name of God, the Father in Heaven, they were suspected of downgrading the Emperor and parents. Thus, they were considered to violate the inviolable Confucian principles of loyalty to the

Emperor as the Son-of-Heaven and of filial piety toward the true father and mother in the human family. These books were judged politically pernicious because they tended to undermine the public order of the "Heavenly Way of life" in each household and in the whole world under Heaven.

Point IV. Religiously speaking, they were found to contain many points repetitious of Zoroastrianism and Buddhism. The official editor of the Four Partite Library once said that Catholicism and Buddhism, in refuting each other, seemed to him like two naked swimmers each putting the other to shame by ridiculing each other's nudity. In fact, he said both are guilty of the same shameful absurdities. Furthermore, their teachings find no evidence in the Confucian classics, although they claim it by their distorted and forced interpretations.

The last remark is important for history. The particular emphasis on the "distorted and forced interpretations" of the Confucian classics by the missionaries to suit their apologetic and proselytizing purpose shows that the leading members of the Confucian officialdom saw with clarity in these efforts not only misinterpretation of the Confucian classics, but also an insidious manipulation of the Confucian texts. They were quite aware that these efforts were not intended to promote Confucianism, but to replace it with Catholic theology according to the version given by Matteo Ricci and his confreres.

They had reason, as they said, to fear a total subversion of the Chinese world order, through the efforts of Leo Lee and others, at amalgamating Catholicism and Confucianism in order to defeat all other religions in China along with the power of the Confucian-minded Emperors, as if pursuing a cunning political intrigue to establish the Catholic Church as the sole religion in China. For this reason, there is no wonder we read that in his criticisms the official editor of the Four Partite Library made a particular point of declaring Leo Lee guilty of intellectual treason against the Empire for compiling and printing his *"First Collection of the Celestial Science."*

For these and similar reasons, all the books of religion and theology in the section "Ideas" were condemned and rejected. Only one book from that section has been retained: the World Atlas by Julius Aleni. It was a mystery why a geographical book was placed in the section of ideas except for the religious purpose of showing the power of the Church and the Pope over the whole world, with the newly discovered America among the five continents.

On the contrary, all the books of sciences, mathematics, geometry and the like in the section "Instruments" were accepted, with the exception of their theological and religious expressions, which were despised as impure mixtures, and placed in the prefaces of the books, where they should not enter at all.

Comparison With Today

By comparison, the situation today is strikingly identical to what it was in the time of Matteo Ricci and Leo Lee. True freedom of religion is curtailed. All believers are mobilized for the Four Modernization Projects in the fields of industry, agriculture, education, and defense.

Catholic priests and religious persons are admitted not as religious workers, but as teachers of approved subjects, from which evangelization under the direction of the Pope's authority is totally excluded. Union with the sovereign authority of the Pope is a crime punishable by law. All those who are actively loyal to the Pope are either put in prison or placed under other forms of restriction.

Of all the contributions that the Church can make to the development of China, the Chinese officialdom in Peking today agreed to accept only useful sciences and technology; it rejects what are most precious: theology and religion. One authoritative historian of the Catholic religion in China said that such an attitude is similar to that of a jeweler who bought a box of pearls, paid for it, and kept the box but returned the pearls to the owner.

The Communists of Peking are doing today the identical thing that the Confucians of Peking did yesterday. The reason for this lies in that fact that the Chinese are Chinese, whether Confucian, Buddhist, or Communist. Incidentally, the modern world seems to be becoming a bit Chinese in its attitude favoring science and technology over theology, philosophy, religion, and the like.

After the First Collection

The First Collection of Leo Lee (1629) is an example of the early efforts toward a Chinese Catholic synthesis between Confucian China and the Christian West. In the century that followed, many events took place rapidly: Rome's prohibition of Confucian rites, as promulgated by Cardinal Tournon in Nanking, 1707; various forms of persecution following it, up to Yung Chen Emperor's persecution (1723-1733); the Four Partite Library (1783), particularly its citing of Lee as guilty of intellectual treason; and other events. All of these converge to show that efforts to Christianize Confucianism were not acceptable to the officialdom of orthodox Confucians in China, and vice versa; efforts to Confucianize Christianity were equally unacceptable to the Church authorities. The case is similar to the episode of Judaizing Christians or Christianizing Judaist Jews in Peter and Paul's time.

It is useful to note that the Confucians' opposition to these efforts was not provoked by the Roman prohibition of the Confucian Rites, because the opposition preceded it by many years, and because the Confucians even opposed Matteo Ricci himself shortly before his death in 1611. There is evidence of this in Leo Lee's "First Collection," as well as in many other publications. Even among the Jesuits themselves, opinion was neither unanimous, nor constant. For instance, Father Nicolas Longobardi, the immediate successor to Matteo Ricci, questioned many points of Matteo Ricci's orientation, and in his Latin publications clearly identified both classical Confucianism and contemporary Neo-Confucianism basically with Materialism, or Sensism.

In order to gain respectability from Confucian Chinese, the missionary strategy needed to make recourse to the so-called Predecessors of Confucius, supposed to be rediscoverable in the form of a Proto-Confucianism here and there in the classical books of antiquity, which were quoted and revered by Confucius. All the Jesuits have had this in common: they invoked this Proto-Confucianism of antiquity to refute the classical Confucianism and the Neo-Confucianism of their day as deviating from the truth, because they were incapable of overcoming the errors of Materialism (understood in the vulgar sense as "an inability to go beyond senses").

The Papal prohibition of 1707 restrained Catholics from active participation in certain Confucian rites. It did not, however, condemn non-Catholics for participating in those rites, since it did not consider it the Church's business to approve or disapprove, given the unsolvable controversies of that time.

In 1938, the Holy See issued a new decree upon the request of the new Emperor of Manchoukuo, Henry P'u-i. It did not revoke the 1707 prohibition, but it did accept the new Emperor's interpretation. Accordingly, it declared that Catholics were free to participate actively in

Confucian rites, on the condition that these rites be intended as civil rites of social respect, without connotation of religious worship.

The basic assumption is that these rites are civil and not religious rites. This assumption was stated by both the state and Church authorities of the Manchoukuo, which is a name of the phantom Manchurian Empire restored in Manchuria by Japan, against the protests from China in 1932.

Because of this condition, future history will consider it an incongruent phenomenon: the insertion of civil Confucian-like ceremonies into the highly religious liturgy of the Catholic Mass. It is incongruous both in its nature and style. It betrays the Confucian mental habit of those Catholics who have made such insertions, in so far as they love Confucian rites as religious rites, at least subconsciously. In retrospect, the whole episode shows itself as historical irony and revenge from all sides.

To supplement evidence supplied by the "First Collection," it is historically important to recall that within some 233 years, between the first arrival of Jesuits in China in 1581 and the death of the last Jesuit, Father Louis de Poirot, at Peking in 1814 after the suppression of the Jesuit order, there were 69 Jesuit authors who published 212 books. Thirty-five of these books were of the highest quality in astronomy, science, machinery, agriculture, and technology, by the standards of the Academia of Lincei in Rome, whose members included Galileo, Kepler, Leonardo da Vinci, Christopher Clavius (teacher of Matteo Ricci and Joannes Torrenz) and others. Fifteen books belong to philosophy and theology proper, including parts of the *"Cursus Coimbricensis"* of Coimbra University, Portugal, and Saint Thomas Aquinas' *Summa Theologiae*, under the title of *"Summary of Supernatural Science."* The remaining 162 books were strictly religious, dealing with selected readings from Sacred Scripture, catechisms, maxims, liturgy, hagiographics, prayers, and devotions.

Besides this, a huge library of seven thousand Latin books was brought to Peking from Europe by Father Nicolaus Trigault, a Belgian Jesuit scholar, author, and provincial superior in China. In 1620, the books were presented by him to the Emperor as a donation from Pope Paul V. The Pope granted Father Trigault's request to translate liturgical books into Chinese and to allow celebration of Masses, Sacraments, and other rites, and recitation of the divine office (the Breviary) in the Chinese language. These authorizations were given in 1614. However,

378

they were never carried out because of practical difficulties and unfavorable historical circumstances during the Manchurian Dynasty.

The seven thousand oversize books were bound with deluxe binding in red covers which bore the Pontifical Seal and the Papal Coat of Arms in gold. They are kept in the Peitang Cathedral Library. We hope they are still intact today. Leo Lee and others had in mind that these books would be translated, but that could not be realized, and it does not appear that there will be a demand for translation in the foreseeable future.

The Age of Reason

In summing up the 400-year history (1581-1986) of Chinese-Christian cultural interchange, historians have not failed to point out that more Chinese books have been translated into Western languages than Western books into Chinese. This means that by trying to bring Christianity from West to East, the Christian missionaries, themselves Sinologists, succeeded much more than they had originally planned in bringing human culture from East to West. Some historians have gone so far as to say that the Age of Reason, which bracketed the Renaissance and the Enlightenment, was an Age of Chinese Thought in Europe, either by real influence or by coincidence.

In fact, if we take Matteo Ricci's death in 1610 at Peking and Giordano Bruno's burning to death at the stake in Rome in 1600 as the end of the Renaissance and the beginning of the Enlightenment, and take a survey of the historical scene of European philosophy and art, we realize that Europe in the maturing of its Enlightenment ideals, at least in the early stage, owed much more influence and inspiration to its knowledge of Chinese culture than was acknowledged by the historians of the Western civilization before World War II (1938-1946), or before UNESCO's founding.

Time does not allow us to go into details. It is, however, enough to call to mind a few authors in France, Italy, and Germany, in order to recognize the impressive coincidence of the spirit of Enlightenment with the spirit of Chinese civilization in the Chinese Neo-Confucian model. This model tried to integrate and synthesize all knowledge and art into the system of the orthodox Confucian tradition. This tradition, as represented by the Four Partite Library, gives value exclusively to reality and utility, in so far as they are controllable by the power of human rationality, thus, systematically rejecting theologies, metaphysics, mythologies, and all ideas which find no basis in ordinary human experience.

In France, among the Cartesians, Nicolas de Malebranche, no less than Pierre Bayle, struggling through the Jesuit missionary writing, could not stop short of asserting, contrary to what the Jesuits pretended, that Chinese civilization and Chinese thought as a whole are materialistic and atheistic. The Chinese "good heavenly order of morality and government" is based rather on naturalism than on divine commandments. Such observations indirectly encouraged the Encyclopedists (Diderot, D'Alembert, Holbach, early Voltaire and others), the French Revolutionaries including the Jacobins (Taine, Robespierre, and Herbert), and the promoters of Reason and Human Rights (understood as emancipation from the Divine Rights).

In Germany, the Chinese culture was well-known to Leibniz, Christian Wolff, Immanuel Kant, Fichte, Schelling, Schopenhauer, Hegel, Spinoza, and others. Excepting Leibniz, who saw his "Characteristica or Mathesis Universalis" in the binary counting system of the Book of Changes and accepted the Chinese legend that that system was divinely revealed on a miraculous turtle back from the Yellow River, all authors mentioned above saw naturalism and rationalism in the Chinese way of thinking. It pleased the Neo-Confucians to hear Kant restrict the rational categories to the organization of sense experiences — phenomena — and dismiss the "ideas" of God, Soul, and Cosmos as transcendental illusions (from which Confucius himself advised his disciples to keep themselves at a reasonable distance). The accurate insight of Hegel touched the heart of Neo-Confucianism in identifying Heaven or God with nature rather than with the Christian Creator or Trinity. Spinoza's theory "Deus Sive Natura," equating God with Nature, sounds like a dictionary explanation of the Confucian usage which, at both the Academic and popular levels, uses "Heaven-made" and "Nature-produced" interchangeably.

In short, if the European Enlightenment was rightly qualified by Saint Simon as anti-theology, and by Voltaire as anti-Christian, then its spirit, at least by coincidence, if not by learning, is Neo-Confucian. Neo-Confucianism, naturally, claimed to be the orthodox and authentic teaching of Confucius and the ancient sages honored by him.

The consequences of the combined Renaissance and Enlightenment impetus, in both of its branches, right and left, in so far as Roman Catholicism is concerned, are anti-theological at heart, and point to cultural de-Christianization. The right branch is Hegelian Idealism, which

380

leads to State Socialism. The left is Marxism, which through Leninism leads to Proletarian Socialism. Both the right and the left lead to nihilism by their theories of evolution and revolution. From a Catholic viewpoint, the net result from all this is a re-paganizing of the West in alliance with a basically Neo-Confucian ideology, unknowingly propagated by Jesuit Missionary Fathers returning from their "Christian Expedition to the Regions of China" (Cf. Nicolas Trigault, S.J., De Expeditione Christiana Apud Sinas Suscepta a Societate Jesu, Romae, 1615).

Ironically, the characteristic book widely circulated among the Encyclopedists, *Théologie Portative au Dictionnaire Abrêge de la Réligion Chretienne (Portable Theology, namely, Abridged Dictionary of the Christian Religion)*, authored by one of the leading Encyclopedists, Paul Henri Dietrich Baron d'Holbach, has been recently translated into Chinese and published in Peking by the Communist authorities, evidently in order to "enlighten" the Chinese readers about the significance of Christianity, as understood by the Encyclopedists, themselves former Catholics and animators of the Enlightenment cultural movement. This movement, let us recall, was at least partially animated by the spirit of Chinese culture through the works of the Jesuit Missionary Fathers. Thus, we see that with the appearance of Holbach's Dictionary in Peking, the spirit of the Enlightenment, after touring around the globe, returned without the Jesuits to where it started with the Jesuits.

This irony clarifies Lao-Tzu's paradoxical saying, "There is no going away that is not a coming back." Etymologically, "Enlightenment" insinuates nominal affinity with "Lucifer" (Lightbearer). By association of ideas, this leads us to recall the fact that missionaries, whether Jesuit or not, often said: "The obstacles of bringing Christ to China are so strangely difficult as to be satanical, including the difficulty of language itself." It seems clear that, metaphorically, Lucifer, prince of this world, with the power of Enlightenment secularism, succeeded in "hijacking" the Company of Jesus in order to secularize Europe through Sinological products. According to some historians, this fact illustrates the vain toil of Matteo Ricci and his colleagues in trying to perform the "Magnificent Substitution," namely, to replace the Confucian soul by a Christian soul within the body of Chinese culture, on one side by reviving a Proto-Confucianism which probably never existed, and, on the other side, by striking an opportunistic alliance with the Son of Heaven, in the powerful person of the Emperor, for the political purpose of putting down all other religions or sects which the Emperor detested.

Some observers have remarked, however, that merciless history registered Matteo's failure on both counts. The substitution was rejected internally by the Confucians themselves and externally by Buddhists and others who were expert in Confucian classical learning. The strategic alliance with the Imperial power proved to be a facade of peace resting on mutual deception of Matteo dreaming of the Emperor as Christianized, and of the Emperor dreaming of Matteo as Confucianized. In reality, both satisfied themselves by the fact that the Emperor got the sciences which he wanted from Matteo, and Matteo got from the Emperor the friendship and protection which he and his confreres needed for their tenure in the court.

In any case, despite all, Catholicity established its roots in Chinese soil and continuously grew stronger, numerically and spiritually. But many questions remain unanswered. Disputes about the compatibility or incompatibility of Christianity and Confucianism, in particular, and of the spirit of the Gospel and the spirit of Chinese civilization, in general, will continue, probably forever, in varied forms.

In the meantime, the present authorities in power in Peking (Beijing) are doing analogically, but more radically, what the Imperial dynasties in the past did to Christianity, namely, enrolling all Christian material and human resources for the secular purposes of making China a materially powerful and modernized country, while restraining the Christians from Christianizing in the authentic sense of evangelization. The effect is calculated to yield complete instrumentalization of the Church in service to the state and the socialist revolution.

Human political calculations, however, often produce results contrary to expectations. Human hearts remain restless in disputes about vital questions. This is why, despite or rather because of the modern persecutions, the Catholic faith among the Chinese people is growing steadily. In some areas, the old disputes have been revived. Pro-Confucian Christians as well as anti-Confucian Christians continue to grow in number among others who are indifferent or wish to remain aloof. Similar situations are occurring in other religions or cultural groups, in relation to Christianity.

The Miniature Chinas

The miniature Chinas, diasporas including the Pacific Islands, such as Taiwan, Hong Kong, Macao, and Singapore, and Chinese communities all over the world, are progressing rapidly to make up in thirty years what the missionaries could not accomplish in four centuries. These miniature Chinas would yield fruits of evangelization and inculturation in the "Maha-China" if only China could be opened up for it again.

In the meantime, let us remember that one useful and precious lesson we have learned from the early Jesuit experience in China is that of the four tasks that the Western Culture or any culture should perform in its encounter with the Chinese culture or with any other culture. They include, as mentioned earlier: (1) to agree in truths; (2) to supply knowledge; (3) to correct errors; (4) to transcend both the host and the guest in the encounter. However, history teaches us to apply these four tasks today not only to Confucianism, but equally to all other religions or cultures. Cultural conflicts can yield to reconciliation through adoption of new attitudes and methods of dialogue.

Reviewing what we have considered so far, I would like to draw attention to the phenomenon of five dimensions of cultural exchange and to the law of universality in each dimension. A cultural exchange, which is the life of culture itself, must be universal in time, space, content, and development of the human person - and, furthermore, in transcendence.

Transcendence is the last dimension that gives a sense of direction to the universal dialogue of all cultures for progress in creativity. The immanent source of the standards of evaluation within the realm of consciousness and intentionality is human subjectivity, endowed with its powers of reason and freedom. It is, paradoxically, an immanent transcendence, otherwise called the Principle of Human Rationality. To guarantee the transcendental validity of this principle, another transcendence is needed. It is the truth of all truths, the value of all values with existence in the objective reality, understood as a transcendence of the aforementioned immanent transcendence. This supreme truth and value is the Absolute per se Truth, which is God.

Therefore, any cultural dialogue is a dialogue between culture and culture, it is true, but at the same time, it is also a dialogue between culture and God. God, Himself, is the initiator of this dialogue in us men, since He has created us to be creative according to His image, with unlimited power of knowing, loving, and expressing. Because of this, it is indispensable to realize that the proper locus of dialogue with God is the manger of Bethlehem where God talks through His own Word-made-man from Mary.

This Divine Word Incarnate perpetuates its dialogical presence in the Communion of all Saints in heaven and on earth. It is broadcast by its speakers, the Apostles. The Apostles, united as one, have only one mouth with which to speak: the mouth of Peter. Saint John Chrysostom once said: "Petrus, Os Apostolorum" (Peter, the mouthpiece of the Apostles). When the Apostles through Peter speak the Word of God to humanity, it is the Spirit of Christ and of God the Father, the Paraclete, who is speaking, giving evidence to the truthfulness of the divine Word itself. The dialogue with God, then, is a dialogue with Peter.

Now if exchange of cultures is a dialogue between culture and culture, then the exchange between humanity and God is not a dialogue between culture and culture, but a dialogue between man and God, and between man and Peter. But, neither God, nor Christ, nor Peter, nor the Church, nor the human person is a mere culture. They belong to the all-transcending transcendence. The ministry of Peter or the Church as a sacrament is a sign and symbol of that Truth which gives meaning to all truths in all cultures. Hence, in this dialogue, the task of all cultures is to decipher the messages given in the Word already spoken by Christ and Peter.

Now, our thinking process is returning to observe that by rejecting theologies and Peter in his successors, the spirit of the Sino-European Enlightenment (or the spirit of anti-theology) is rejecting the Paraclete, the Holy Spirit of God Himself: it is rejecting the sign and symbol, instead of deciphering them. The dialogue of Christianity with cultures in China has reached this moment, which is a challenge to the Chinese people, and to all humanity. Christianity is not a culture, but it is the source of light and life to all cultures. The Church is the sign and symbol of the Transcendence which all cultures are called to decipher.

The Spirit of Chinese Civilization

Let me conclude this discussion with an optimistic remark. Suppose the real spirit of Chinese civilization is not exclusively the rationality of scientism, rationalism, and utilitarianism, but, more than this, it is also a rationality of feeling and gentleness. The role of rationality, then, is not confined to an ordering of sense experiences for knowing, as envisioned by Kant and Hegel or Husserl, but it is also, and more fundamentally, an ordering of feeling, affection, emotion, and psychic tension for love, as explained by Confucius and Mencius. From this, there is hope that we can manage our human relations, all possible conflicts, and cultural encounters, not only with the rigor of truth, but also with gentle civility. This attitude will open the human heart, if not the mind, to a new culture and a new civilization based on the noble gentleness of human love and honor. Then, further on, we may promote and intensify cultural interchanges in all dimensions with the serenity of Truth, Justice, Freedom, and Love. This final tetragram is the epithet of the Divine Logos incarnate.

Let us be friendly to each other always, and share with each other all we have. In love and hope we must face today's peoples and future generations internationally only through culturally civilizing ways.

St. Mary's College
Moraga, California, USA

THE CHRISTIAN DIALOGUE WITH ASIAN CULTURES AND RELIGIONS

S. Baliah Naidu

Since World War II, the East and the West have come once and for all into intimate contact on a vast scale. Each feels the necessity for mutual understanding and even for assimilating whatever in the other is true and useful. This need to understand each other more profoundly is no longer a matter of mere intellectual curiosity but of survival.[1]

If twentieth century barbarism has taught us nothing else, it should have taught us that there is an element in man other than reason, and that if this element is neglected, it is liable to fester and to erupt into something monstrously evil.[2] This element is called the religious impulse. Each religion provides the basis of the society within which it is dominant. It is then both dangerous and foolish to disregard the religious foundations on which any given culture or civilization is built.[3]

Modern man is threatened by a world created by himself. He is faced with the conversion of mind to naturalism, a dogmatic secularism, and an opposition to a belief in the transcendent. Confronted with the question of meaning, he is summoned to rediscover and scrutinize the immutable and the permanent which constitute the dynamic, unifying aspect of life as well as the principle of differentiation, to reconcile identity and diversity, immutability and unrest.

Thus man is faced with the metaphysical question of the truth of religion,[4] while he encounters the empirical question of its effects on the life of humanity and its meaning for society. The basic and poignant concern of every religion is, therefore, to point to, and overcome, the crisis in our apocalyptic epoch, the crisis of man's separation from man and of man's separation from God.

Culture and Society

Culture simply means a whole way of life of a people.[5] It is the name which has been given to man's social inheritance. It, therefore, involves all that man has and is. Even very simple people and primitive people can recognize intuitively the diversity of cultures and the importance for each people of its own way of life.

It is the cultural process that creates the society. Culture and society are interdependent aspects of a single reality, neither of which can exist without the other. In Aristotelian terms,[6] every culture is the form of a society and every society is the matter of culture.

A culture is a very fragile thing, and the delicate balance of its social structure is overthrown as soon as its spiritual limits are broken and its individual members lose their faith in the validity and efficacy of its moral order.

World cultures and civilizations[7] are the great beaten highways on which mankind has travelled through history, and in every case men believed that they were following a divinely appointed path. They all possess a corpus of sacred scriptures; each has its own sacred language and its sacred order of teachers, who are trained in the study or interpretation of the sacred writings and rites and rituals: Confucians in China, Brahmins in India, Ulemas in Islam, Jewish Rabbis and Christian Priests. Thus there has been a close relationship between the world civilizations and the world religions which has endured for ages, which we must explore if we are to understand the spiritual ideals that have inspired these great cultural unities which far transcend the national and political entities.[8]

Culture and Religion

In all his works, Professor Dawson sees religion as the dynamic element of culture. He shares with Toynbee the idea of a universal spiritual society as the goal of history; but whereas Toynbee sees this as to be achieved by a consensus of the great World Religions, East and West, Dawson sees it as coming from the working out of Catholic principles.

There is no doubt that faith looks beyond the world of man and his works. It introduces man to a higher and a more universal range of reality than the finite and temporal world to which the state and the economic order belong. Thus it brings into human life an element of spiritual freedom which may have a creative and transforming influence on social culture and historical destiny as well as on personal experience.

The Right Approach to Cultures and Religions

Our approach to cultures must be one of learning from them at the existential level. It is an approach which is less comparative than imperative, i.e., "imparare" in Latin meaning "to learn."[9] The comparative study of cultures means studying their similarities and differences, then learning from them with discernment through an active and committed listening.[10]

Learning from other cultures at the existential level consists in adopting an attitude which will help us listen to the other, not so much at the conceptual level of mere information as at the deeper level of our own lives and beliefs, and by which we allow ourselves to be challenged at the level of our deepest convictions and of our being. In short, it consists in opening up to another so that we might speak and reveal our own myth, that is, what we cannot know by ourselves. Thus, one enters into a relationship of trust and considers the other cultures as a truly potential source of inward renewal.[11]

A culture can only give itself over existentially to someone who, in a certain way, believes in it. There is true encounter only at the personal level of the heart, understood as existential openness and listening with one's whole being, with all the risks of personal transformation that this implies. Cultures are not mere individual or collective realities, but personal and communitarian realities.

If what is said above is true in the case of cultures, it is much more so in the case of religions. As Professor Smart points out, "Now for the first time in human history it is possible for members of the various religions, East and West, to speak to one another in an informed and sympathetic manner. No one can understand mankind without understanding the faiths of humanity."[12]

In a similar vein, T. W. Organ comments, "In a sense, no foreigner has ever understood any people so long as he must conceptualize their culture in his own categories .... Part of the difficulty with respect to Indian religions and philosophies is that they have been so often surveyed and examined within the context of the nature and function of Western philosophies and religions."[13]

The very concept of the philosophy of religion is largely a Western creation, as are the concepts of God, freedom, and immortality. "This selection of major ideas reveals the fact that Western culture has mainly understood religion in terms of the Judaeo-Christian tradition. But religion, of course, has a wider and deeper spread. It ill benefits the philosopher to attend merely to the concepts of his own culture."[14]

Meaning of Dialogue

Dialogue is a conversation of a common subject between two or more persons or groups of persons with different views, the primary purpose being to learn from each other. Dialogue is not a debate. In dialogue each partner must listen as openly and as sympathetically as possible in an attempt to understand the other's point of view as precisely and as much as possible.

Sine-qua-non condition: Self-criticism

Any interreligious dialogue presupposes at least some sort of self-criticism of one's own religious and philosophical tradition.[15] A lack of such self-criticism implies that one's own tradition has all the correct answers. Such an attitude not only makes dialogue unnecessary, but even impossible, because the "raison d'etre" of the dialogue is to learn, which is impossible if one's tradition has all the answers.

Surely, in interreligious dialogue one must stand within a religious tradition with integrity and conviction, but such integrity and conviction must include, not exclude, healthy self-criticism. Without it, there can be no dialogue and, indeed, no integrity.[16]

The Raging Temper of Free Enquiry in Nineteenth Century Europe

In the nineteenth century, liberal opinion in Europe was raging like wildfire. It was thought that Christianity had had its day.[17]

The spirit of free enquiry welcomed the discovery of the Eastern religions which were then becoming increasingly well-known. The first of these to impinge on the European consciousness was Confucianism. The reasonableness of the Confucian doctrines was immediately hailed by such distinguished leaders of the Enlightenment as Leibnitz, Spinoza, Voltaire, and Malebranche; and when the sacred books of the Hindus and Buddhists were in their turn translated into the main European languages, their reception was no less enthusiastic.[18]

Here at last it seemed were religions which were in accord with human reason,[19] for they seemed to have much more in common with philosophy than with "religion" as it had hitherto been understood in Europe. Here were religions which knew nothing of a "jealous" God or of the harsh spirit of intolerance which had plagued Europe since Augustine first turned his fury against Donatists and Pelagians. Neither Hinduism nor Buddhism was an intolerant creed since prophecy played no part in their more gentle view of life.

The Various Aspects of Deabsoluted "Truth"

The momentum of free enquiry, begun in the nineteenth century, hastened the movement towards the deabsolutizing of truth. Thus, truth began to be perceived from different points of view.[20]

The Historical View of Truth

In the nineteenth century, many scholars began to perceive every statement about the truth of the meaning of something as partially the product of historical circumstances. Those concrete circumstances helped determine that the statement under study was called forth (for example, abstract Platonic, or concrete legal language) particular literary forms (for example, mythic or metaphysical language) and particular psychological settings (for example, a polemic response to a specific attack). Those scholars argued that only by placing the true statements in their historical "*Sitz im Leben*" could they be properly understood (understanding of the text could be found only in context), and that to express the same original meaning in a later "*Sitz im Leben*" one would require a proportionately different statement. Thus, time deabsolutized all statements about the meaning of things.

The Perspectival View of Truth: Sociology of Knowledge

As the statements of the truth about the meaning of things were seen by some thinkers to be historically deabsolutized in time, starting in this century such statements were also seen to be deabsolutized by the cultural "standpoint" of the thinker-speaker, regardless of time. This kind of statement about the true meaning of things will be particularly determined by the worldview of the thinker-speaker. All reality was said to be perceived from the cultural, class, sexual, etc., perspective of the perceiver. Therefore, any statement of the truth of the meaning of something was seen to be perspectival, "standortgebunden," as Karl Mannheim put it, and thus deabsolutized.[21]

Limitations of Language

Many thinkers, following Ludwig Wittenstein and others, have come to understand that no statement about the truth of things can be more than a partial description of the reality it is trying to describe. It is so because, although reality can be seen from an almost limitless number of perspectives, human language can express things from only one, or perhaps a very few, perspectives at once. This is now also seen to be true of our so-called scientific truth. "A fortiori" it is the case concerning statements about the truth of the meaning of things. The very fact of dealing with the truth of the "meaning" of something indicates that the knower is essentially involved and thereby reflects the perspectival character of all such statements.[22]

The Interpretative View of Truth

All knowledge of a text is also an interpretation of the text, thereby still further deabsolutizing all claims about the "true" meaning of the text. But this basic insight goes beyond the knowledge of a text and applies to all knowledge. Hans-George Gadamer and Paul Riceur have led the way in developing the science of hermeneutics.[23] This is an interpretative view of truth, pervaded by relationality.

The Dialogic View of Truth

A further development of the basic insight about truth is that I learn by dialogue, i.e., not only by being open to, receptive of, extramental reality in a passive sense, but by having a dialogue with it. I not only "hear," but also "speak," to reality.[24] That is, I ask questions, I stimulate it to speak back to me, to answer my questions. Furthermore, I give reality the specific categories, the language, with which, in which, to respond to me. I can "speak" to me, really communicate to my mind, only in a language, in categories, that I understand. When the speaking, the responding, becomes more and more nonunderstandable to me, I slowly become aware that there is a new language being developed and that I must learn it if I am to make sense out of what reality is saying to me. This might be called a dialogic view of truth, whose very name reflects its relationality.[25]

The Pronouncements of Vatican Council II

St. Paul seems to have taken for granted that God had revealed himself outside Jewry. Vatican Council II follows him in this; but it needed a John XXIII to reaffirm what the early Church has always understood, namely, that all truth, wherever we find it, must proceed from God. The Council laid down categorically that "the Catholic Church rejects nothing which is true and holy in other religions."[26] It looks with sincere respect upon those ways of conduct and of life, those rules and teachings which, though differing in many particulars from what it holds and sets forth, nevertheless often reflect a ray of Truth which enlightens all men.

The Council did not merely declare that the Catholic Church rejected nothing which is true and holy in other religions. It spoke about each of the major non-Christian religions and the contribution that each made to the symphony of faiths to which all were invited to join their voices.

"In Hinduism," it declared, "men contemplate the divine mystery and express it through an unspent fruitfulness of myths and through searching philosophical inquiry. They seek release from the anguish of our condition through ascetical practices or deep meditation or a loving, trusting flight towards God."

"Buddhism," it declared, "in its multiple forms acknowledges the radical insufficiency of this shifting world. It teaches a path by which men, in a devout and confident spirit, can either reach a state of absolute freedom or attain supreme enlightenment by their own efforts or by higher assistance."[27]

The Religious-Philosophical teachings of Buddhism have left their mark on much of Asian civilization. Buddhism has permeated the cultures in Sri Lanka, Burma, Cambodia, Thailand, Laos, Tibet, China, Korea, Japan, and Vietnam. The distinctive Buddhist cultural traits are: an emphasis on human dignity, an attitude of nonattachment, tolerance, a spirit of compassion and nonviolence, and an inclination to meditation.[28] "Thus the age of anathemas indeed seems to have passed away. No approach to the non-Christian religions could be more conciliatory than this."[29]

The Need for Interreligious Dialogues in the Modern World

Our search for the truth of the meaning of things makes it a necessity for us as human beings to engage in dialogue. But the need for dialogue in religion is intensified in the modern world because slowly, through the impact of mass communications and the high level of mobility of contemporary society, we more and more experience "others as living not only holistic but also 'holy' lives, that is, integrated human lives related to an Ultimate Concern, not in spite of, but because of their religion. To be concrete, when I as a Christian come to know Buddhists/Hindus as religious persons who are leading whole, holy human lives out of the fullness of their Buddhism/Hinduism, I am immediately confronted with question: What is the source of this holiness? It obviously is not Christianity."[30]

Clearly, then, the only possible answer is that the source of the holiness of the Hindu/Buddhist/Moslem/Jew is the Hindu/Buddhist/Islamic/Jewish religion. Christianity is a religion that believes that God reveals himself to mankind through persons and events, and that to learn God's message, good news, Gospel, Christians must seek to listen to God wherever and through whomever He speaks, i.e., we must be in dialogue with persons of other religions to learn what God is saying to us through them.

Names and Expression of God

The intriguing question is whether the names and expressions rooted in the Judaeo-Christian tradition of Western culture are the only meaningful ways of expressing God. At this point we need to consider the relative character of human language.

The Word which became flesh was final and definite, but no word about Him is absolute. Language is not static, but goes through a process of growth, decay, and new life. Words can lose their meaning and die, or change character and be replaced by other words. No language is absolute, not even religious language. This means, for instance, that no religious expression is absolute in the sense of being unique. All over the world people use similar symbols of God, without having been in contact with each other. In the other cases, we share our religious language with other faiths as a result of continuous intercourse with other cultures. God was never worshipped in culture isolation.

Theological Terminology

In biblical history, rejection of heathen worship took place in a process which, at the same time, incorporated alien practices and ideas.[31] In Christianity, unique message of salvation was proclaimed in close contact with surrounding faiths and cults, and thereby Christian theology received its classical expression in the encounter with Greek philosophy, which provided its orthodox language, although it reflected a universe quite different from the world of Jesus the Jew.

It would be nothing but cultural provincialism to hold that the dogma expressed by the European spirit via the Greek and Latin languages is the only adequate framework for true theology. This does not mean that classical theology has lost its meaning or should be discarded. But it must be recognized that no language is indispensable. And it should be possible to accept the idea, at least theoretically, that new concepts and expression may enrich the Christian understanding.

As Dr. N. R. Thelle points out, the Japanese Christians seem to feel a sort of religious alienation in their faith. They find themselves in a constant tension between what they experience as opposite poles: being a Christian and being a Japanese. The Catholic author, Endo Shusaku, has again and again described the tension between his Christian self and his Japanese self. "There was always a feeling in my heart that it (Christianity) was something borrowed."[32]

It is true that the Church has spent much effort in defining the great mysteries of the Incarnation and the Holy Trinity. In the process it has caused much rancor and dissensions, and since these truths in any case pass all rational comprehension, non-Christians and post-Christians may be forgiven for wondering what it is all about and for losing patience at what seems to be an exercise, both futile and impious, in trying to pin down and pigeonhole the infinite and its inscrutable relationship to the finite. Alan Watts writes: "Christianity therefore impresses the modern Western as the most impossibly complicated amalgamation of odd ideas, and though it is his spiritual birthright and the faith of his fathers, it is very much easier to make him understand Buddhism or Vedanta."[33]

Person

Western Christians tend to regard it as indispensable that God is a person. Their expressions are thoroughly anthropomorphic and personal, and their faith would indeed be poor without this personal language, but it is extremely bewildering to the Eastern mind. Eastern religions have preferred to develop non-personal language concerning the Absolute, such as universal truth, dharma, brahman-atman, tao, light, life, suchness, nothingness, emptiness, etc. These are all mere symbolic expressions of a reality which belongs to a totally transpersonal sphere.

Christians are certainly aware that anthropomorphic expressions are symbols pointing toward the reality of God, who transcends all human categories. We know that God is not a person in the same sense as we are persons, but it is hard for Eastern people to understand why Christians stubbornly maintain that God is a person or at least personal. Although the Christian in the West does not feel God's personhood as a limitation, the equivocal Eastern reaction shows that the emphasis on God's personhood presents an important barrier to their understanding.[34]

In the oriental context, the question arises whether the reality of God is adequately expressed through a one-sided stress on the personal. Westerners experience non-personal categories as a diffuse world where not only personal community with God is negated, but also the human personality seems to be swallowed up by a vague universal identity. Or, even worse, the divine becomes just a cold, impersonal principle governing the world with merciless universality.

Eastern people, however, do not seem to experience a rejection of personal categories as cold impersonalism or nebulous vagueness. Impersonal language is experienced, rather, as a dynamic means of expressing the inexplicable mystery of the divine. On the depth level, of course, not only personal categories, but also non-personal expressions, are discarded. Nevertheless, Eastern religions find the impersonal expressions more suitable for conveying the mystery of the absolute.[35]

Transcendence

In a similar way we could reconsider the limitations and potentialities of our concept of God's transcendence. In the Judeo-Christian tradition, transcendence is a precondition for God's presence in the world.

In the East, however, a radical stress on transcendence tends to create an image of a God who is totally apart from this world, governing from outside through arbitrary decisions and interventions in history. Along with impersonal categories, Eastern people prefer to understand the divine as an immanent reality, a life-force, and all-pervading power that sustains everything, or as a divine principle, a universal law, the true nature behind all phenomena.

Thus, the divine belongs to a different, deeper level, but is not totally separated from the human realm. The supernatural does not represent a radical break with the natural, but is rather a mysterious extension of the immanent. Perhaps it could be characterized as an immanence with a depth dimension that Westerners have tended to ignore.

Immanence

Is it possible for Christians to speak more boldly about God in immanent categories? Even though we believed in God's continuous creation, his life-giving presence, etc., we are often so afraid of pantheism and immanent categories that it is difficult to grasp the presence of God in the creative powers that pervade the entire cosmos and flow through every particle of the universe. And even if we recognize God's presence, it is certainly difficult to convey it meaningfully in a culture where Western categories of transcendence do not seem to function very well.[36]

The search for the One Reality behind and beyond all phenomenal existence preoccupied the ancient Indians from a very early period; and the first metaphysical question they asked was: "How did the universe come into existence?" On this subject there are a series of hymns in the tenth and last book of the Rig-Veda which set the tone for all later speculation. St. Paul might have had the ancient Hindus in mind when he said that God created the whole human race: that all nations might seek the deity and, by feeling their way towards him, succeed in finding him (Acts 17:27).[37]

Christ

Vatican II declared: "In Hinduism men contemplate the divine mystery and express it through an unspent fruitfulness of myths and through searching philosophical inquiry. They seek release from the anguish of our condition through ascetical practices or deep meditation or a loving, trusting, flight towards God."[38] All this is true enough, but is it not a little strange that the Council should omit to tell us that Hinduism contained at its very center the belief in an incarnate God? Surely, this is, for Christian, a matter of the deepest significance, for where else in the history of religion do we find a belief in God made man except in Christianity itself?

To the Jews the very idea was intolerable, and Jesus' claim to be the Son of God was, for the Jews of his time, utter blasphemy, and Caiphas only symbolized the general feeling by rending his clothes. No Hindu of the time of Christ would have dreamt of doing so, and the difficulty with which Christian missionaries have all along been faced has been so great that their assertion that Jesus of Nazareth was the Son of God, was considered blasphemous or even incredible that they should be so naive as to suppose that he was the *only* incarnation of God. To the Hindus this looked rather like a narrow provincialism. Yet, in their acceptance of the possibility of divine incarnation, they stood and stand much nearer to Christianity than the Old Testament ever did.

The Bhagavad-Gita is the great divine book in Hinduism, and through the Bhagavad-Gita Hinduism becomes the "*via media*" between the "atheistic" mysticism of early Buddhism and the theistic mysticism that grew up in the religions of Semitic origin. It represents as radical a break with the past as does Christianity with the older prophetic Judaism.[39]

In Christianity it is the transcendent Lord of history who becomes man; in the Bhagavad-Gita it is the immanent principle of the universe. God transcendent and God immanent meet in man, the middle point between the "greater than the great" and the "more minute than the minute." This is not the "causeway which holds apart the world of time and eternity lest they should split asunder" of which the Chandogya Upanished speaks (8:4:1); rather it is the laying of the foundations of the bridge that may come to unite and bring into concord the apparently irreconcilable poles of total immanence and total transcendence, however discordant these may appear to be.[40]

The Idea of Salvation

The transmigration of souls is one of the most important needs of Hindus and Buddhists alike. It is accepted not merely as a dogma but as a self-evident fact: and salvation means final release from the world of *samsara*, the unending round of births and deaths from which there appears to be no escape. It is very difficult, indeed, for a Westerners even to imagine such a position. To them it seems preposterous that the whole conduct of one's life, and even one's social system, should be based on an unprovable hypothesis. Yet, when a Hindu or Buddhist speaks of moksha, "release," or "salvation," he is not thinking of sin, he is thinking of release from transmigration; and the achievement of it is the aim and purpose of this religion. For Buddha it was the sole purpose. Thus to maintain that all religions are paths leading to the same goal, as is so frequently done today, is to maintain something that is not true.

"All people, whatever their cult, station, or way of life, who are inwardly at peace attain to the same truth, as rivers (flowing into) the sea." So says the Anugita. And this is what the Hindus, in their large tolerance, genuinely believe and want all men of good-

398

will would like to believe; for the diversity of religions is a very
real stumbling-block for all who are interested in finding one that
is true. Were this diversity merely one of emphasis, it would
matter little. Unfortunately it is not; it is one of principle.[41]

The Human in the Universe

It seems necessary to raise the question of what is genuinely Christian
and what is merely a Western development in the image of the Christian
as a self-assertive individualist who perhaps can lead people, but finds it
difficult to function as a part of traditional society.[42]

It seems difficult to understand why faith should estrange people from
their society. Individualism is not a biblical ideal, but rather a late
development in Western culture. Jesus himself did not aim at creating
individualists. He knew that faith could mean a break with friends and
family, but basically he saw each person as a part of the people. The
kingdom he proclaimed was a community, not a gathering of individuals.

The one-sided cultivation of individualism is a Western invention
which, in spite of its deep influence, certainly does not fit into most
Eastern cultures. One should not take for granted that Western
individualism is closer to the biblical ideal than the Eastern stress on the
solidarity of the group.

According to Christian conviction, the human person is the center and
head of creation.

The centrality of creation and the solidarity of all created things
are vital issues in the Bible. The fall resulted in the curse of the
soil and brought death into the world (Gen. 3). The great flood
destroyed all life on earth because of the sin of humanity (Gen.
6:7). Not only human beings, but animals, and even the fields
need a sabbatical rest (Exodus 23:10-12). In the Psalms nature
is not only a passive testimony of God's glory but is actively
participating in the universe praise of God.[43]

Hence the focus of theology becomes the relation between the human and
God. The world tends to be only of secondary importance as the stage
of the interaction between God and humanity. In contrast to this, Eastern

spirituality understands the human more as an integral part of the cosmos. Humankind is not the lord of creation, but should find its place in harmony with nature.

There is no need for Christians to conceal the primary importance of humanity of God's creation, but the Eastern stress on the human as a part of the cosmos could be a valuable reminder that creation as a whole is central to biblical faith. Human beings are not only socially related, but their lives are bound to the entire creation in a deep solidarity, whether they realize this or not.

With our Western stress on the salvation of the individual soul, it is puzzling and almost incomprehensible that "the creation itself will be set free from bondage to decay and obtain the glorious freedom of the children of God" (Rom. 8:21). A somewhat artificial distinction is also often made between the order of creation and the order of salvation. According to the Bible, however, the God who saves is none but the creator of the universe, who saves by restoring and recreating his world.

The Christian theology of creation seems limited and tends to bring about an isolation of the human from the rest of God's creation. Solidarity has been lost. The Asian view of the human as an integral part of the entire cosmos is somewhat different from the Christian way of thinking, but it may inspire us to a new appreciation of a central biblical concern.[44]

The question of solidarity on the human level is of utmost importance, because the Buddhist view of interdependence challenges Christians to consider whether or not they failed to grasp the depth of human interdependence and solidarity. The most articulate repudiation of Western individualism is found in Mahayana Buddhism, which rejects every effort to grasp the essence of the human person as an isolated individual.[45]

The reluctant acceptance of causality in Western theology had ambiguous implications. It could serve as evidence of God's existence as Creator, or "First Cause." But it also created problems for a proper theology. Where the law of causality was accepted unconditionally, God was easily reduced to pale, unbiblical *prima cause*, an immovable mover, a deistic God bound by the laws of nature. And human beings seemed to lose their free will, determined by a merciless causality. The Asian version of causality is developed in a somewhat different direction; not as a linear development of cause and effect, but rather as an immense net in which all the meshes are directly related to each other by innumerable lines in all directions of time and space.

The theological implications of this Eastern causality, with its unlimited universal interdependence, makes the Christians aware that a serious theological grappling with the problems may lead to far-reaching and unforeseeable consequences with regard to the understanding of God and humanity. Theology has somewhat failed to relate Christianity to a vital part of Asian cultures, Hindu, Japanese or Chinese.[46]

The Irreconcilable Differences

To understand the non-Christian religions, one must study their main texts in their historical development, and to study them, so far as is possible, from inside, and having so studied them to try to correlate them with aspects of Christianity.[47]

Since Vatican II, the Catholic Church has not only entered into fruitful conversations with non-Catholic religions, it has also taken cognizance of the fact that non-Christian religions are also repositories of truth in one or more of its manifold aspects. This is not entirely new, since for some time now Catholic theologians have been seeking to reconcile Indian philosophy with Thomism. Yet this does not seem to be a very fruitful approach, for however important philosophy may be as an "explanation" of a given religion, and it is undoubtedly very important in Hinduism, it can never coincide with the religion itself. All too often its clarifications rob that religion of the essential mystery at its heart: by explaining overmuch and by explaining away, theologians eviscerate the very thing they are supposed to be investigating.

In religion one very much doubts whether it is possible to be accurate or objective; for if it is true that it is the Infinite which is the subject of the religious studies, what has this to do with the various objects of scientific inquiry which, of their very nature, are concerned with the finite and definable? If we are to "revive the religious sciences," as Al-Ghazali claimed to have done for Islam in the eleventh century, we must go beyond philosophy to those texts which the great religions themselves hold most sacred, for it is through these writings that "all nations" must obviously "seek the deity and, by feeling their way towards him, succeed in finding him" (Acts 17:27).

However, we have to confront with some real, irreconcilable problems. Thus, for example, such phrases as: "release from the anguish of our condition," "a state of absolute freedom", "supreme enlightenment," etc., indeed reflect Hindu and Buddhist attitudes clearly and accurately enough; and they are noble ideals. But are they in any way compatible with the ideals of Catholic Christianity? For, God did not assume our human condition in order to win release from the anguish of it: that would make nonsense of Gethsemane and the Cross itself. Rather he "consented to partake of our humanity in order that we might share in his divinity," as the Catholic Church declares itself in its daily liturgy.

If the central doctrine of Christianity is that God becomes man in order that man may become God, then Hinduism can be seen as very much more of a *"praeparatio evangelica"* than can the Old Testament for which such an idea is blasphemous.[48]

The same, however, cannot be said for Buddhism.[49] For it, in its earliest form, does not admit of a personal God and condemns material Nature out of hand because, being transient, it can only be a source of sorrow. Since this is so, there can be no redemption for it; it can only be transcended. That there is truth in this basic Buddhist assumption there is no doubt, but it is a truth that is very different from the basic assumptions of Christianity as usually understood.

Thus, Christianity, in the strongest possible terms, urges that there is a personal Creator who reveals Himself in human history, while Buddhism, specially Theravada Buddhism, rejects belief in such a Creator. The Ultimate Reality of Advaita, Brahman, is not to be equated in spirit with the dynamic God of the Judaeo-Christian tradition.

While Hinduism believes in many incarnations, Christianity affirms that God became man in Christ Jesus only once, and that is it.

The Hindu believes he is intrinsically possessed of an immortal soul, while the Christian holds that immortality, if it occurs, is granted by God. The resurrection of the body has been a more normal expression of future hope than the imperishability of an immortal soul. Further, both Hinduism and Buddhism believe in reincarnation or rebirth,[50] while Christianity does not.

These vital differences that we find in Hinduism and Buddhism are undoubtedly contrary to the Christian beliefs, and yet they should not deter Christians from having a meaningful dialogue. Surely, there can exist a concordant discord, leaving enough room for the Holy Spirit to do his quiet work.

Conclusion

No one can understand mankind without understanding the faiths of humanity. Sometimes naive, sometimes penetratingly noble, sometimes crude, sometimes subtle, sometimes cruel, sometimes suffused by an overpowering gentleness and love, sometimes world-affirming, sometimes negating the world, sometimes inward-looking, sometimes universalistic and missionary-minded, sometimes shallow, and often profound - religion has permeated human life since obscure and early times.[51]

Christianity, it seems, has gotten into a legalistic and theological rut. But at the same time, one must be aware of modern theology with its ridiculous labels (crisis theology, dialectical theology, religionless Christianity, death of God theology, and heaven knows what else), with its fraudulent introduction of obsolete words mascarading as something new in order to convince the simple-minded that these words clothe a new idea ("kerygma" for preaching, "hermeneutics" for exegesis). Theology has become the passionate pastime of the few, a ponderous game that leaves the many absolutely cold.

But I venture to think that there is much in Eastern religions[52] that is still valid, and that Christianity has much to learn from them, much indeed it must learn from them, if it is ever to become not in name only but in truth the Catholic Church, whose very name, as Augustine saw, implies that it was designed by its Founder to become the religion of the whole human race.

"May they all be one, Father, may they be one in us, as you are in me and I am in you" (John 17:21). How often has this been quoted, and not least by the protagonists of Hindu religion, for whom unity tends to be everything. For Christians too, unity has been the guideline of their spirituality.[53]

Besides, the mystical prayer of the early church has much in common with the mystical insights of the Hindus and Buddhists. They would agree that any approach to unity between the great religions must be conducted on a mystical or contemplative plane.

All great thinkers have made useful suggestions because they have dared to try something completely different. They have studied the basic assumptions of the old systems and asked: "What if we made some other assumptions?" All creation has to be courageous enough to do just this. We have to understand that loyalty goes first to life itself and not to our received ideas about life. The Angel of the Resurrection reminds us not to seek "the living" among the dead.

Although vigorous protests against old structures and antiquated ideas and traditions that limit or violate the dignity of the human person are certainly in order, what is better is simply to turn away from them wherever possible and prudent, and set about creating and demonstrating new ones. This is the call of the future: "Let us go where we have never been before." "If we are truly children of God, this is surely a most appropriate thing for us to do as our inheritance from the God who says: *"Behold, I make all things new."*[54]

University of Cape Breton
Sydney, Nova Scotia, Canada

NOTES

1. Robert C. Zaehner, *Concordant Discord* (Oxford: Clarendon, 1970), pp. 1-20.

2. Gabriel Marcel, *Tragic Wisdom and Beyond,* tr. by S. Jolin and P. McCormick (Evanston: Northwestern University Press, 1973), pp. xxxi-xxxv.

3. Christopher Dawson, *Religion and the Rise of Western Culture* (London: Sheed & Ward, 1951), pp. 21-44; Sri Aurobindo, *The Foundations of Indian Culture* (New York: Auromere, 1953).

404

4. Religion is here distinguished from Theology and its doctrinal forms and is intended to denote the feelings, aspirations, and acts of men, as they relate to total reality. See Zaehner, *The Convergent Spirit* (1963), pp. 130-156; pp. 183-210; also Ninian Smart, *The Religious Experience of Mankind*, 3rd. ed. (New York: Macmillan, 1984), p. 23.

5. Ralph Linton, *The Study of Man* (1936), pp. 326-377; Edward B. Taylor, *Primitive Culture* (London: Murray, 1871); Alfred Kroeber and Clyde Kluckhohn, *Culture: A Critical Review of Concepts and Definitions* (1963); Ruth Benedict, *Patterns of Culture* (Boston: Houghton Mifflin, 1934).

6. C. Dawson, *The Formation of Christendom* (1969), Ch. III; The Nature of Culture, pp. 30-48.

7. Dawson, Ibid., Ch. IV, The Growth and Diffusion of Culture, pp. 49-66.

8. E. W. Tomlin, *The Oriental Philosophies* (1963), p. 15: "The history of India, for example, sheds a flood of light upon the problem of what it is that constitutes a civilization or culture: for while India has been conquered and dominated again and again, its distinctive philosophy or metaphysics has survived not as a curiosity or a 'cultural heritage' (as the classical Western philosophy has survived within our own civilization), but rather as the means whereby a vast community has preserved its conscious identity. The resulting unity, to quote that remarkable Orientalist, Rene Guenon, is a 'doctrinal unity.' Now that Western political authority has receded, it is incumbent upon us to treat with respect that which we tended formerly to regard with aloof patronage. In short, we have ceased to teach; it is time that we should learn."

9. Robert Vachon, *Interculture*, Vol. XIX, No. 2, April, 1986, pp. 7-13; Ninian Smart, *The Religious Experience of Mankind*, 3rd ed. (New York), p. 23; Trevor Ling, *Buddha, Marx and God* (New York: Macmillan, 1966), Ch. 14, "Religion in the Modern World," pp. 206-217; R. Spaeman, "Mysticism and Enlightenment," *Concilium*, Vol. 5, No. 9, 1973.

10. B. Bruteau, "Global Spirituality and the Integration of East and West," *Cross Currents*, Vol. XXXXIV No. 2-3, 1985, pp. 190-205.

11. The lack of understanding and harmony among our cultures does not come so much from our conceptual differences, but from our existential attitudes, particularly from a lack of will to dialogue or relate at the level of the beliefs and existential attitudes we hold regarding the ultimate concerns of our existence.

12. Smart, op. cit.

13. Troy Wilson Organ, *The Hindu Quest for the Perfection of Man* (Athens, OH: Ohio University Press, 1970), p. 35; see also Tomlin, op. cit. p. 313.

14. Ninian Smart, *The Philosophy of Religion* (New York: Random House, 1970) p. 4; see also John M. Koller, *Oriental Philosophies*, 2nd ed. (New York: Macmillan, 1985), p. x. "But why should we force Western definitions of philosophy on the Orient? So far as I know, no one has ever demonstrated the superiority of Western concepts of philosophy over Oriental. And until this is done (if, indeed, it were possible!) Eastern thought should be studied within its own terms."

15. Leonard Swidler, "Interreligious Dialogue: A Christian Necessity," *Cross Currents*, Vol. XXXV No. 2-3, Summer/Fall, 1955, pp. 129-147.

16. Smart,16. "The Religions in Dialogue," pp. 22-23.

17. Dawson, *The Formation of Christiandom*, p. 46.

18. Zaehner, *Concordant Discord*, pp. 428-443.

19. Smart, 3rd ed., Ch. 12, "The Humanistic Experience," pp. 557-575; J.M. Domenach, The Attack on Humanism in Contemporary Culture, *Concilium*, Vol. 6, No. 9, 1973.

20. Swidler, op. cit.

21. Ibid.

22. Swidler, op. cit., pp. 129-142; M. L. Raposa, "Faith and Certainty," *Thomist*, Vol. 50, No. 1, Jan. 1986, pp. 85-119; G. Baum, "Faith and Culture," *The Ecumenist*, Vol. 24, No. 1, Nov-Dec., 1985.

23. Swidler, op. cit.

24. Vachon, pp. 7-8; Panikkar, "On Dialogical Dialogue" in Frank Whalings, ed., *The World's Religious Traditions*, (Edinburgh: Tod and Tod Clark Ltd. 1986), pp. 201-221; Panikkar," Myth, Faith, and Hermeneutics," *Cross Currents*.

25. Swidler. We should look to others and therefore to different "standpoints" of view to complement our points of view. That means, we need to engage in dialogue with those who have differing cultural, philosophical, theological, social, and religious viewpoints so as to strive toward an ever fuller perception of the truth of the meaning of things.

26. Vatican II, *Nostra Aetate*, Art. 2; M. Vorgrimler, ed., *Commentary of Vatican II*, 1968; C. B. Papli, "Excursus on Hinduism," pp. 132-144; H. Dumoulin, "Excursus on Buddhism," pp. 145-150.

27. Vatican II, op. cit.; N. R. Thelle deals about Buddhism in the light of Japanese culture in the article "Christianity in a Buddhist Environment," *Cross Currents*, Vol. XXXV, Nos. 2-3, 1985, pp. 173-189.

28. Koller, op. cit., " Basic Characteristics of Buddhist Culture," pp. 238-244.

29. R. Siebert, *"Religion in the Perspective of Critical Sociology,"* *Concilium*, Vol. I, No. 10, Jan. 1979, pp. 56-69.

30. Thelle, op. cit. See also H. Fries, "Unity in View: Twenty Years After the Council," *Theology Digest*, Vol. 33, No. 1, 1986, pp. 107-111.

31. Ling, op. cit., Ch. 12 and 13, pp. 175-205.

32. Thelle, op. cit. p. 173.

33. Alan Watts, *Beyond Theology*, N.P., p. 88,

34. Smart, op. cit. p. v.

35. The encounter with Eastern thought may help us to a recognition of a truer meaning of personal language. In a discussion of Christianity and Buddhism, H. Dumoulin states that "all that can be predicted of God in human speech must be complemented by a radical negation of the finite and an elevation to the unspeakable dimension of the absolute" (*Christianity Meets Buddhism*, Illinois: Open Court, 1974, p. 167). With this background, both personal and impersonal language may become meaningful ways of expressing faith in God, because both are functioning as dynamic expressions of a reality we now "see in a mirror dimly" (I Cr. 13:12).

36. There are possible pitfalls in the understanding of God as an immanent reality. God may fade away in a shallow belief in immanence. On the other hand, it is difficult to see that the misconceptions created by a one-sided stress on God's transcendence are much preferable to distorted belief in his immanence. If Eastern thought does not always grasp the transcendent presence of the divine, our categories are often unable to express the transcendent presence in a meaningful way.

Perhaps we should accept a complementary way of thinking, in which transcendence and immanence, personal and impersonal categories together, give a more valid picture of reality.

Why should we not complement the belief in the Creator who governs the world with an understanding of God as present in the creative powers of the universe? The former (Western mind) will tend to be expressed in personal categories, such as father, king, creator, and lord; the later (Eastern mind) in more impersonal terms, such as creative powers, life, light, nature, ground of being, creative presence, etc. Both sets of language are relative and represent two symbolic models of the world, each with inherent limitations and potentialities. I believe that they do not refer to two separate worlds, but are poles of the same reality. Held together, our understanding of God's presence can be more complete.

37. P. J. Johanns, S. J., *New Catholic Encyclopedia* (1967), Vol. 6, pp. 1135-1136: "Hinduism is the most searching quest in the natural order for the Divine that the world has know. In common with Christianity, it has its own ideas of Trinity and Incarnation, of sin, and salvation, of revelation and inspirations, of sacrifice and sacrament, of law and morality, of the ascetic and mystical life, of grace and love, and of man's ultimate goal of union with God. It is impossible not to admire the

408

profundity of this conception of God as *saccidananda*, being, knowledge, and bliss, and the degree of intimacy with God to which it declares that the soul is called."

38. H. Nakamura, *Ways of Thinking of Eastern Peoples: India-China-Tibet-Japan* (Hawaii: East-West Centre Press, 1964). R. Panikkar, *The Unknown Christ of Hinduism* (New York: Maryknoll).

39. Zaehner, *Concordant Discord.*

40. Ibid. The idea of a Divine incarnation and a Divine mediator in Eastern religions arises as a later development and it is not in accordance with, but in opposition to, the whole sense and tenor of all the non-Christian sacred books. Similarity, then, there is; but the similarity is between Christian orthodoxy and non-Christian heterodoxy. What similarity there is proves not that there is an inner sense underlying all the religions, but that there is in man a craving for an incarnate God strong enough to force its way into the most unpromising religious systems. This idea is the cornerstone of Christian belief; essentially it is at variance with all the non-Christian orthodoxies. Its constant reappearance demonstrated the truth of Tertullian's great saying, *O testimonium animae naturaliter Christianae*. See also: F. S. Northrop, *The Meeting of East & West* (Macmillan, 1946), Panikkar, *The Interreligious Dialogue* (Asian Trading Co., 1984).

41. Direct Quote. *The Anugita.*

42. G. R. Malkani, "Spirituality: Eastern and Western," *The Philosophical Quarterly*, Vol. 37, No. 2, July, 1964, pp. 103-110.

43. Thelle, op. cit.

44. In Buddhism there is no permanent substance which can be called ego, soul, or self; every person like all other things in the universe, is an integral part of a whole which comes into being and changes in a process of interdependence. There is no unchanging essence apart from, or independent of, others.

45. Panikkar, "Global Perspectives: Spirituality in Interaction," *Journal of Dharma*, Vol. X, No. 1, Jan-March, 1985, pp. 6-17. J. M. Pohier, *One Dimensional Christianity, Concilium*, Vol. 5, No. 7, May 1921, pp. 27-38.

46. As Christians, too, we are aware of the solidarity of humanity. Our lives are created and molded in the encounter with thousands of people, situations and happenings. And we ourselves have a hand in shaping an creating the lives of people we meet, for better or worse. We are bound to each other in an unbreakable relationship of solidarity. Perhaps the Mahayana Buddhist vision of suffering and salvation ought to be taken more seriously. (Thelle). See A. Peiris, S. J., "Inculturation in Non-Semitic Asia," *The Month*, Vol. 19, March 1986, pp. 83-87.

47. Organ, *Hinduism as an Integrating Culture*, pp. 89-92.

48. The Vedantin monism (the theory that Reality is one and that all multiplicity is therefore illusory, being no more than an appearance) was the ultimate Truth, and that all the religions were thus simply empirical paths leading towards this same Truth.

Such a position can, of course be substantiated by carefully selected quotations from other religious systems and the philosophies allied to them, but such support (if you can call it support) will then be apparent and fictitious, for it leaves wholly out of account the core and center of the other religions from the scriptures of which these quotations are violently wrenched. This kind of method leads in the long run not to understanding, harmony, and friendship, but to misunderstanding and discord. As pointed out by Zaehner: "We must force nothing; we must not try to achieve a 'harmony' of religions at all costs when all we can see is a 'concordant discord'".

49. H. Dumoulin, *Christianity Meets Buddhism* (Peru, Il: Open Court Publishing, 1976); H. deLubac, *La Rencontre du Buddhism et de l'Occident* (Aubein, 1952).

50. S. Cranston & C. Williams, *Re-Incarnation* (Julian, CA: Julian Press, 1984), pp. 157-258; P. D. Devanandom, *Christian Concerns in Hinduism* (Bangalore, 1961).

51. Smart, *The Religious Experience of Mankind*, p. 23.

410

52. J. M. Kitagawa, ed., *The History of Religions: Retrospect and Prospect* (New York: Macmillan, 1985); J. Scheuer, S.J., "Buddhists and Christians Towards a Closer Encounter," *Lumen Vitae*, Vol. XXXIX, No. 1, 1984, pp. 11-22.

53. A. S. Wesley, "Hindu Spirituality: An Invitation to Dialogue," The Ecumenical Review, Vol. 38, No. 1, Jan., 1986, pp. 75-81. Zaehner, op. cit. Ch 5, pp. 130-156 and Ch. 7, pp. 183-210.

54. Bruteau, op. cit. See also E. Cornelis, "Valeurs Chretiennes des religions non-Chretiennes," CERF. 1985; Thomas F. Stransky, C.S.P., "Attitudes to non-Christian Religions," *The Month*, Vol. 19, No. 5, May 1986, pp. 164-169; J. P. FitzPatrick, S.J., "The Unity of the Human Family; The Lord's Promise and the Contemporary Quest," *Catholic Mind*, Vol. LXXVI, No. 1328, pp. 11-14; J. C. Winslow, *The Christian Approach to the Hindu* (London, 1950); Zaehner, *Mysticism: Sacred and Profane* (New York: Oxford University Press, Inc. 1961); D. T. Suzuki, *Mysticism: Christian and Buddhist* (London: Allen and Zemvin, 1957); K. Koyama, "Asian Spirituality," *The Westminster Dictionary of Christian Spirituality*, pp. 29-32.

JOSEPH KENTENICH: SOCIAL, MORAL INTEGRATION OF THE PERSON

Elena Lugo

Contemporary ethical theory seems inclined to move away from an emphasis on individualism and self-centered ethics of rights, from conflicting or contradictory pluralisms, and from stressing autonomy and contractual relations as the basis for human action. But there is likewise caution in avoiding the opposite extreme of collectivism and dogmatic imposition of duties. The trend in ethical theory is rather toward a new conception of the communitarian person committed to an ethics of responsibility that enables him or her to establish interpersonal bonds and mutual obligations in terms of love as well as duties.

Here we ask some critical questions regarding each trend, the individualistic and its challenger, the communitarian. Neither trend satisfies the intrinsic requirement of moral experience and hence an ethical theory capable of integrating both trends becomes necessary.

Joseph Kentenich's organic approach to the question of contemporary interest, his ability to examine all issues from many perspectives, theological, philosophical, psychological, and pedagogical, just to mention the main ones, enables him to contribute key concepts to the above trend as well as to add further clarity and consistency to its propositions. We only have to recall his conception of the new man and a new community living according to a covenant of love to realize in advance the relevance of his teachings for contemporary ethics.

Predominant in today's ethics are individual rights, interests, autonomy, and contractual relationships, which are inadequate. This can be corrected by an ethics of responsibility, of command, obligation, and covenanted relationship. Though this type of ethics will still prove inadequate, it serves as a point of contact for Father Kentenich's special way of integrating rights and duties, the autonomous individual and communal obligation, justice and love in human relationships.

Accordingly, Teilhard de Chardin, in his *Man's Place in Nature*, described the current phase of history as "socialization" which he in turn divided into two contrasting periods. He called the first period the "socialization of expansion," and the second the "socialization of compression." Accompanying the expansion period of socialization was a growing sense of the importance of the *individual* and the development of human *rights*. The eighteenth and nineteenth centuries were the "age of individualism" and Chardin saw it as being filled with "pluralisms" of all sorts.

> This was the age of rights of man (i.e., of the citizen) against the community: the age of democracy, naively conceived as a system in which everything is for the individual and the individual is everything: the age of the superman, envisaged and awaited as, standing out in isolation above the common herd.[1]

This peaked around World War II with its rash of petty nationalisms and autonomous movements. Promises of utopia requiring a centralization of power and control emerged before World War II and led to the yet undreamed of forces of totalism. That is, the pendulum oscillated from individualism and pluralism to collectivism and totalitarianism. In moderation, Kentenich favored neither extreme, while advocating that a person, with inner freedom, bind oneself in a covenant of love to form a federative community. But the times were not yet responsive to him.

The reason for the end of the phase of pluralism with its emphasis on human rights, said Chardin, was the fact that the terrestrial globe is of limited size, and mankind, after reaching its limits, turns in on itself and attains ever more complexly-organized units with greater and greater psychic energy, striving toward a more progressive stage of evolution. Shortage of space and limits on natural resources dictate that man must organize in order to survive. Thus, the experience of contingency, as Kentenich could express it, points in the direction of social cohesiveness. But what Chardin had in mind was a whole world turned into a sort of superorganism by way of a process of continuing cerebralization, which meant that the whole world had to develop one intellectual center.

Chardin observed the economical and geographical limitations of the growing population, enlarged in number and complexity, and postulated the evolutionary trend toward unity, centralization and supranational order. Mankind was envisioned as able to transcend individualism and pluralism for the sake of survival. But, as we shall later see, there are other incentives, beyond the vital need for survival, inducing mankind toward further unity and order at a *moral* and not merely political or economical level.

Moreover, for Chardin, the key to survival in the new stage of "compressive socialization" is science, for only through science and its application in technology can man learn how to control his own fate. We could easily appreciate the need to complement scientific-technical know-how with cultural values that enlighten the *why* or the *what-for* of the need for "compressive socialization." Contemporary man realizes that science and technology without philosophical and theological wisdom can be destructive of humanity at worst, and/or at least inducive of an assertive form of individualism. An integrative or a holistic approach, in which science, technology, social sciences, philosophy and theology, each as separate and autonomous, that complement the other with certain priorities, has now become urgent. A valid technological knowledge must secure not only what is technologically possible, but also what is socially desirable, avoiding detrimental long-range consequences to those parts of nature indispensable for man's well-being. Kentenich formulated such a new humanistic technology which will be guided by overall social and human concerns. Founded on an ethics of responsibility for future generations, it blends the private and the public, the individual and the communal sense of the good.

Thus, according to Chardin, individualism and pluralism threaten human survival in an overpopulated world where geographical and economical limitations are most acute. The evolutionary trend, aided by science and technology, is toward communal life and world unity culminating in Christ. Though relevant, this fails to touch upon the moral code of the economic crisis.

Accordingly, Daniel Callahan, questioning the adequacy of individualism and its supportive ethics of rights/autonomy for "economic hard times," demands a different ethics of the common good and responsibility.

As we move into what will most likely be chronically hard economic times, how can our society muster the moral resources necessary to endure as a viable human culture? Three assumptions underlie the question: 1) economic strength and military power have no necessary ethical connection with the internal human and moral viability of a culture — they can only help assure its mere existence, 2) the era of sustained economic growth is over, and with it the perennially optimistic psychology of affluence and 3) *the kind of morality that was able to flourish during times of affluence will, if carried over unchanged into hard times, lead to moral chaos or even worse.*[2]

Callahan's "morality of affluence" immediately equates with a "minimalistic ethics," so prevalent in our own time.

The morality of affluence is one that stresses the transcendence of the individual over the community, the need to compromise and tolerate all moral viewpoints (moral pluralism), the autonomy of the self as the highest human good, and the voluntary informed-consent contract as the model of human relationships. The central core of this morality, or rather the ethical theory that sustains it, revolves around the principles of individual liberty or autonomy, self-realization, liberation from cultural and economic restraints and freedom to find one's own truth and way of life. Indeed these ethical principles are rooted in man's own dignity as a person, and as such cannot be easily ignored or subordinated to any other principles. They must be somehow retained while transcending their exclusivity.

The morality of affluent times, the exclusivity of its ethical principles, can lead to a *minimalist* ethics, rooted in John Stuart Mill's conception of personal freedom. Its unsuitability for any time, not merely for economic hard times, can be shown. *Minimalist* ethics can be characterized in terms of two main propositions and by seven other features: 1) one may morally act in any way one chooses so far as one does not do harm to others; its sole test (minimum) is whether it avoids harm to others; 2) there is no further basis for judging personal or communal goods and goals, for praising or blaming others, or for educating others about higher moral obligations to self or to the community. These two principles lead to the following features: 1) *minimalist* ethics confuses utility and rules with moral norms; 2) it sharpens the distinction between the private and the public rights; 3) it limits obligation to the consented or freely chosen; 4) it reduces life and personal relations to contractual agreements; 5) it pays no attention to the inherently or the intrinsically good and has no way to judge the behavior of others except by the principle of maleficence; 6) it reduces moral problems to psychological, social or political issues; and 7) it only stresses the morality of justice and autonomy. The value of close community life, transcendental values, and duties over and above self-realization are thus tactically overlooked.

Thus far we have seen how Teilhard de Chardin advocated a new concern for communal bonds and duties in view of the political and economical difficulties of individualism, while Daniel Callahan pointed to the moral inadequacy of an ethics of individualism in view of similar difficulties, but also in terms of the inherent limitation of an ethics that overlooks communal obligations. Let us now clarify the ethical significance of concepts like individualism, autonomy, and pluralism in order to reveal how certain interpretations of these concepts can be morally misleading. They can nevertheless be properly understood in order to form part of an ethical theory as presented later in this study.

Josiah Royce spoke of "individualism" as an attempt to extend and enrich that core of uniqueness by pursuing the goal of a "separate happy self." Such an attempt can be equated with "possessive individualism" as described by political theory. Possessive individualism as understood by C. B. McPherson is supported by seven premises: 1) what makes a person human is his/her freedom from dependance on the will of others; 2) freedom *from* means freedom from any relations with others except those that the individual enters into voluntarily with a view to his/her own interest; 3) individuals are essentially proprietors of their own person and capacities, for which they owe nothing to society; 4) although an individual cannot alienate the whole of his property in his person, he may alienate his capacity to labor; 5) human society consists in a series of marked relations; 6) since freedom from the will of others is what makes us human, each individual's freedom can rightfully be limited only by such obligations and rules as are necessary to secure the same freedom to others; 7) *political society is a human contrivance* for the protection of property in person and goods.[3]

The first premise, i.e., "what makes a person human is his/her freedom from dependence on the will of others . . ." as well as the second premise, i.e., "freedom from any relations . . ." single out the principle of autonomy and acknowledge its predominance over other moral principles' clear understanding of what autonomy entails. This is required if we are to attempt to overcome individualism in favor of the communal person and speak of autonomy in harmony with communal obligation.

Moreover, "autonomy" entails *self-rule* and *independence* as common denominators. Autonomy is not a matter of what the agent does but rather a matter of *why* he does it. Piaget points out that autonomy, in a manner, follows upon heteronomy: the rules of a game appear to the child no longer as an external law, sacred in so far as they have been laid down by adults, but as a matter of a free decision and worthy of respect in the measure that it has enlisted mutual consent. Thus, just as Gerald Dworkin so clearly explains autonomy in relation to independence, so also we may explain behavior via upbringing, social class, culture, glands, genes, and religion.[4] But autonomy concerns the relationship (the *why* of the agent's behavior) between the self and these explanatory factors. One may neither presuppose a self pre-existing independently from these factors, in isolation from their influence, nor a self passively molded by these factors. The autonomous individual is one that is able to step back and formulate an attitude towards the factors that influence one's behavior.

Autonomy depends on the attitude a person takes toward the influence motivating him or her, which in turn determines whether or not the rules of conduct or any influences are authentically accepted as personal convictions. This autonomy, which is more than mere independence, is then a question of *authenticity* resulting from effective deliberation and moral reflection.

In summary, we can distinguish four basic meanings of autonomy: 1) autonomy as free action — action that is voluntary and intentional, i.e., not the result of coercion, duress or undue influence; 2) autonomy as authencity — an action that is consistent with the person's attitudes, values, disposition, or life plans; 3) autonomy as effective deliberation — action taken where a person believed that he was in a situation calling for a decision, was aware of the alternatives, evaluated both, and chose an action based on that evaluation; and 4) autonomy as moral reflection — acceptance of the moral values . . . this meaning is the deepest and most demanding when it is conceived as reflection founded on complete sets of values, attitudes and life plans. It requires vigorous self-analysis, awareness of alternative sets of values, commitment to a method for assessing them, and an ability to put them in place.

In view of the above exposition of what autonomy entails, one can recognize the incorrectness of the narrow conception of autonomy or freedom as associated with possessive individualism, a conception which perhaps can only be identified with the first and possibly the second above meanings of autonomy. That is, autonomy as free-action or independence might be compatible with only a morality that does not aspire beyond the minimum. While, in contrast, an autonomous person, in the first and fourth meanings of autonomy, can be an integral part of an ethics of responsibility and of communal involvement.

According to the narrow conception of autonomy, as mere independence, the only moral obligations one has toward others are those one voluntarily undertakes, and the only moral obligation that others have toward one are those that autonomously one allows them to have. All that is owed by others is respect for one's autonomy.

The above interpretation of moral obligation is hazardous to moral relationships and can hardly form a moral community. It buys our freedom to be ourselves, and to be free of undue influence by others, at too high a price. This mode of autonomy can become, as Callahan warns, a justification for selfishness.[5] It establishes contractual relationships as the principal and highest form of relationships. It elevates isolation and separation as the necessary starting point of human commitments. It presumes that the moral life can be made a wholly voluntary matter (for the consenting adult), by attempting to deny the validity of many uninvited moral obligations that ordinary life, with other people, usually casts before us. It will inevitably diminish the sense of obligation that others may feel toward us, and reduce our sense of obligation toward others. A mere juxtaposition of individuals with no mutual bonds of obligation cannot constitute a community, because the recognition of duties and obligations can morally bind humans to their fellows in ways to which they have not explicitly consented. Such obligations originate simply in the sorts of reciprocal relatedness, beyond the contractual, that constitute being a human in the pursuit of the common objective good of man-as-man, as persons, as substances of a rational nature, who receive their existence from and thus participate in the order of being. That is, the individual person is not a cause of his/her existence and does not exhaust the order of being.

Only a theory of the common good, whose truth and propriety is independent of whether it is chosen or not, points in a direction beyond the predominance of an ethics of rights, based on the priority of the principle of autonomy. The concept of the common good, as a normative standard for morality, envisions society in a way which is neither liberal nor utilitarian, nor pluralistic in the narrow sense. Before we explore the new ethics of duties for a new communal person, the modern trend of *pluralism* must be now connected with individualism and autonomy as both concepts were just described.

Possessive individualism and the predominance of the principle of autonomy in the moral life, and as a defining quality of being human, foment a pluralistic society. Political as well as moral "pluralism" in turn depend on compromise and toleration as ways to secure social cohesiveness. Are the above viable ways for the modern man in "hard times" now or at any time in the future?

The four main postulates of pluralism that support the ethics of rights (liberalism-individualism) are: 1) society consists essentially of a variety of groups organized around what they conceive to be their particular interests; 2) in order to promote and defend their interests, groups use their resources to influence public officials and politicians, hoping thereby to shape public laws, decisions and policies; 3) conflict and competition among groups is restrained by a tacit consensus among the groups that they will observe the "rules of the game" as embodied in the relevant constitutional and public laws; 4) if group politics is to be kept within socially desirable limits, public officials and group leaders must accept a "politics" of *negotiation* in which *bargaining and compromise* are the primary forms of political action and the substantive determinants of public policies.

Pluralism is thus the dissolvent of the idea of *the people* and hence of any claim that *the people* can act or can will. But if that is the case, we possess a form of politics that has no theory or legitimacy to accompany it and to clothe its results in *rights*, but only compromise and tolerance with no guarantee of moral unity.

Although the value of compromise seems obvious and a natural complement to the politics of pluralism, when economic or material issues are at stake, an extrapolation of compromise to morality is a poor foundation for ethical thinking. That is, when pluralism takes the form of ethical, religious, ethnic or cultural diversities, it seems less appropriate, even wrong, to install *compromise* as the primary value.

But toleration does not seem to overcome the deficiencies of compromise. *Toleration* is the value that seems more appropriate to these forms of pluralism. Toleration is often treated like compromise, as the natural ethical complement to pluralism. Tolerance is a necessary condition of social peace in a society which, in fact, is pluralistic in that it proclaims that all groups should be allowed the freedom to act as they see fit, provided they do not harm other groups, interfere with their freedom or upset public order. That is, tolerance stipulates that public authority should be neutral toward the various groups.

But, neither compromise nor tolerance provides much in the way of guidance for resolving public controversies, nor for establishing moral legitimacy. While compromise suggests a counsel of prudence that advises against pushing one's power or claims to the extreme, tolerance seems mainly a negative ethic. There seems to be a need for a political ethic that would serve in guiding action toward what is *right* in circumstances where claims, values, and powers are in conflict, i.e., for public norms to which there can be appeal in order to reconcile the inevitable conflicts among diverse groups. A theory of moral obligation is simply lacking.

For real obligatory affirmation, the concept of the *good* is needed, which is not identical with the concept of value, which signifies the distinction between the objective and subjective status of value (value in itself and valuation by someone). And it is the relationship between goodness and being (*bonum* and *esse*) which a theory of value must clarify, if it can hope to ground the binding force of values. By grounding the good in being, a theory of values gains objectivity. Only hence can it be argued that *Nature*, in adhering to values, also has authority (natural law) to sanction them and to demand their acknowledgment by us and by every knowing, willful being. The justification of an objective order of being, as grounds for the ethical right, remains as ever a vital, permanent and fundamental philosophical issue, neither to be dismissed as a pseudo-speculation nor affirmed with dogmatic certitude.

We now return to our main question of the study. How are we to foster community life, to blend private right and public duty while respecting the creative tension between the two? We cannot retreat to a mere Hobbesian societal model where individual rights are totally subordinated to society and where the organized community is the source of all authority and legitimacy. As Kentenich would insist, collectivism and totalitarianism depersonalize and brutalize the human individual.

Societies based on notions of man as a citizen by nature, the polis as the natural state of man, or based on divine decree, a theocracy, that makes duty to God the principal source of law and social institutions, may be more cohesive, nurture finer human qualities and promote more dutiful and virtuous citizens. Nevertheless, in some of them, it would make no sense to speak of the natural rights of the people. In some of these societies, a citizen is granted permission to act only as far as necessary to perform his duties to state and/or church.

The above societies often seek to achieve a sense of public duty through indoctrination, patriotism, inculcation of love for the fatherland through a teaching of the national, racial or religious superiority of the nation, tribe, sect, or city. A strong cohesion is thus developed by a sense of a common aspiration, a common danger, a shared superiority, or some ideology to set this group off from all others as distinctive and exclusive. A strong disapproval of concern for individual benefit at the expense of others in the group, and a strong approval of group loyalty and personal sacrifice for the sake of the group are fostered.

But the societies just described and the methods they have used to inculcate communal cohesion have all too often appeared in history as dictatorships responsible for violating the dignity and the personal freedom of the individual human being. Marxist dictatorships, military dictatorships, racist regimes, and theocratic tyrannies are evidence of their failure to blend community and individual rights.

One begins to suspect that neither a liberal democracy nor any form of a Marxist dictatorship can inculcate a real willingness to subordinate private to public ends. A theocracy might be neither liberal nor dictatorial but it would be unthinkable in a modern secularized civilization. But still, the self-denial of some people, their self-discipline or disciplined obedience to others, their selflessness, devotion to a cause, and readiness to sacrifice their means and even their lives, impress us and win our admiration as well as awaken hope regarding a new community constituted by free personalities. What type of communal living and social structure can such be?

Against excessive individualism, we need to seek or create an open community where there is a "wholesome" relationship between community and member-individuals based on a creative tension and a continuous search for a balance, but not domination of one by the other. Both individuals and the community are twin essential elements and need to have the same status and are to be kept in balance. Can the balance be secured by an ethics that stresses responsibility? Seemingly yes, provided we retain the essential contribution of an ethics of rights. We anticipate an integral view of man as a unique being of intrinsic value, but who, precisely as such, also limitedly participates in the order of being. This demands a recognition of his or her necessary relations and bonds with other beings as a complement of being and as the basis for communal responsibility.

We now need to reaffirm an ethics of responsibility in response to "hard times," to acknowledge the inseparable character of man and community in a relation of mutual responsibility, and to identify the special role of family and woman in securing a vital basis for ethics. Within this context, we might then appreciate Kentenich's insights regarding human nature, community life, a covenanted ethics, linking rights and duties in terms of the common good of the integral person.

Callahan reminds us that the hard times require a new morality for which an ethics of mere right is not an adequate rational foundation. How is this morality described? It is a morality of self-sacrifice and altruism which an ethics of moral autonomy, in the narrow sense already described, does not sustain or nourish. It is a morality which emphasizes a sense of community and of the common good, in the pursuit of which all are bound, while the ethics of rights is primarily directed toward the cultivation of independent selfhood. It is a morality of restraint in blaming others for one's misfortunes, while the ethics of autonomy/rights tends to make more people blameworthy for the harms they supposedly do others. The new morality fosters a new sense of duty toward others, especially those out of sight, while the ethics of autonomy/rights stresses responsibility only for one's freely chosen consenting adult relations.[6]

When one's perceived and culturally supported *primary* duty is to others rather than to self, to the transcendental rather than to private values, to future needs rather than to present attachments, then there can be a solid moral foundation to survive pain, to endure turmoil, to overcome evil and "prepare the way for the church and society at the new shores" according to Kentenich. We seek a foundation for a morality beyond individualism-liberalism-pluralism, and toward a morality of responsibility, which incorporates the natural rights of man, as a fully integrated person of nature and supernature. This responsibility acquires at this time of immense technological power a special urgency. We have a special responsibility for future generations. Hans Jonas points out that:

> Gratitude, piety and respect are ingredients of an ethic called upon to stand guard over the future in the technological tempest of the present. Concrete duties toward the well-being of the future humans may well be derived from an ethic of solidarity, of sympathy, of equitableness, indeed, even of compassion, by whose standards and through a transference from our own hopes and fears, joys and sorrows, we accord to those future individuals, in a kind of fictive

contemporaneity, the same right which this ethic also accords to those living now.[7]

Before centering upon Kentenich's view of man and community in a mutual bond of responsibility, we must inquire regarding the type of community the ethics of responsibility envisions, and the role it ascribes to women's thinking in fostering this new moral way.

As we have already seen, our modern Western culture is not so inclined to foster community. Our culture has systematically tried to forswear communal goals, tried to replace ultimate ends with procedural safeguards, and worked to abolish the most profound question of human meaning. But there can be no valid community unless the members have some sense of common good, one that transcends the sharing of procedural protections (liberal democracy), and is qualitatively different from an aggregate of individual goods. There can be no community without a powerful sense that my neighbor is my obligation, quite apart from whether I choose that obligation or not. Community requires constraints, limits and taboos, just as it requires shared ideals, common dreams, and a vision of the self that is an integral part of the organic whole. Thus, a society of any kind can achieve the cohesion that makes individuals into a society only if there is a widely shared concern regarding what is good or harmful for the community as a whole. There can be no community if the drive for a *just* society cannot, in principle, encompass an effort to define the nature of a *good* society.

The new morality of responsibility and self-renunciation presents itself as committed to foster an ideal of community, that is, it strives to bring about a community in which the potentials of all individuals *and* their interrelations are maximally supported. This ideal, even if not reachable, is indeed approachable. The family in its traditional sense with its emphasis on covenant, or in contemporary language, on contract beyond the contractual in interpersonal relationships, approximates this ideal.

The goal of the family is to become an entity whose adult members have come together to create a mutual ethical order, who acknowledge and accept the new identities that this coming together forges, making them social beings of a particular kind, and who commit themselves to responsibility for the future, either through rearing their own children, or through other generative activities that link them not only to the past, but most significantly to future beings. Family life fosters responsibility for the future, an ever so important dimension of ethical concern at a time of technological innovations that threaten the future of mankind.

But the family cannot grow within a world founded by the sovereign self, founded on the primacy of rights and *contractual obligation* as the only acceptable form of obligation. A *contract*, or what Callahan identifies as *compact bonds*, is urgently needed for the family to survive. The self in "contract"/"compact" is a historically oriented person who acknowledges that he/she has a variety of debts, inheritances, rightful expectations, and obligations, and who realizes that these links constitute the "given" in one's life, or the "moral starting point." The concept of the compact points at an ideal that bears within it an intrinsic notion of "good" as not reducible to the functional requisites of some undefined "higher order" without proper basis in being or reality conceived in metaphysical terms.

As we shall see, in the *contract* model for human relations, the family gets bracketed and/or severed, and hence woman's traditional identities and roles within a family are, and have been, devalued. Within the *compact* model, however, woman's identities as wife and mother, her role as community benefactor and as social instrument of cohesion in whatever her profession or occupation, are not to be devalued or ignored.

As family is said to foster a morality of contract/compact, so women are regarded by some to be capable of a morality of *attachment* (organic bindings in Kentenich's language). Both contract and attachment, as moral experiences, secure a pre-reflective or affective basis for the ethics of responsibility for the new man in a new community. Carol Gilligan speaks of the morality of attachment, in contrast to a morality of rights, as one which finds its roots in women's propensity to sacrifice themselves to others' needs and expectations, to be dependent on others, and to give priority to involvement with persons, rather than to individual development and self-assertion.[8] This description of women in traditional terms serves as a counter force to individualism and minimalistic ethics as presented earlier.

Women's unique capacity for care brings to the feminine experience and to the constitution of social reality a distinctive voice and a specific moral tone to ethical conceptions. Their perspective on the formulation and the resolution of moral dilemmas emphasizes personal concern, nurture and responsibility. Women tend to construe, understand, and judge moral conflicts in terms of tensions between self and others (perhaps between rights and duties to others or self-realization and magnanimous service to others). There is a relational bias in women's thinking that leads them to reconstruct moral dilemmas in terms of their effects on the personal dimension of the other self. The moral sensitivity of women becomes a cultural value presented to our generation as decisive for moral strengthening.[9] Thus as we blend reason and emotion in a single moral experience, the ethics of rights and the ethics of responsibility appear in their complementary relation.

How do Kentenich's teachings contribute to this integration? He explains that neither the minimalistic ethics of individualism, liberalism and pluralism, nor the new morality of communal responsibility, can be by themselves the core of ethical theory. Thus, neither an ethics of rights nor an ethics of duties/responsibilities can be self-sufficient as a rational justification for moral values. As long as each asserts its exclusivity and/or independence from the other, and as long as one either ignores the other or attempts to assimilate the other, we fall victim to the fragmentation of the moral reality as concretely experienced. This fragmentation reflects a reductivistic frame of mind, that is, an intellectual tendency to interpret the whole in terms of its parts or elements, and to assert one part as representative of the whole.

The fragmentation of reality and its reductivistic interpretation are samples of what Kentenich calls *mechanistic thinking* or worldview. A mechanistic worldview separates into distinct ontological units what in reality are aspects or dimensions of a complex whole or structured order of being. It isolates itself into self-sufficient units and stresses the static in the structure of being, to the detriment of the dynamic processes of life, growth, and of becoming in the world.

From a mechanistic perspective man can either appear in isolation from the rest of reality, as ontologically self-sufficient, ethically independent from objective values, or else as reduced to a disposable part of a collectivistic system. Mechanistic thinking has also contributed to a further reduction of man's whole interior structure into a single aspect of his person, be it to the rational, or to the irrational (emotive, biological). In any case, mechanistic thinking views man as an atom-like entity doomed to depersonalization and dehumanization, while all his bonds with self, with others, with nature and with the Transcendental are severed.

A fragmented, reductivistic or, in Kentenich's language, a mechanistic worldview is incapable of harmonizing the polaric tensions of contemporary ethical theory. It needs to be counter balanced or substituted by a worldview that secures *integration* of various dimensions of reality. Only then can we expect to go beyond mere compromise, in the attempt to cope with the poles in tension within ethical theory, and beyond toleration in solving moral conflicts. Herein *integration* has double meaning. First we single out integration as a worldview, very much favored by Kentenich when he spoke of an organic way of thinking, living and loving. Then we will speak of integration as embodied in the concept of a fully *integrated* person. The first provides a theological-philosophical basis to restore harmony between man and all the rest outside of himself, while the second provides a psycho-educational-practical model for harmony within one's own person. That is an *integral* perspective both as theological and metaphysical in its theoretical foundation, as well as psychological and educational in its application.

Within the Scholastic tradition we find two distinct but complementary sources of truth, faith and reason, revelation and human inquiry, or the affirmation of belief, and the demonstrations of logic. Faith, revelation and the affirmation of belief, constitute the theological foundation without which no full *integration*, or reliable integrating perspective of reality, is secured. The theological dimension secures, complements, and elevates, in function analogous to grace regarding nature, the knowledge which reason, by way of logical inquiry, can and indeed must demonstrate. The theological dimension of an integral world-view reveals the ultimate origin and finality of reality, the source and purpose of human life, individual and communal, and provides a transcendental justification in terms of Being, for man's sense of the good as a moral category.

The metaphysical dimension complements the theological with a rational inquiry into the distinct quality of the being of the person in its ontological identity and proper autonomy, and demonstrates how the finitude and limitation, inherent to the being-person, require for its unfolding such communitary bonds of love, particularly those of love within a family. The psychological dimension, better appreciated when speaking of the integral person, contributes to the *integral* worldview a special sensitivity for the inner processes of personal life, as it unfolds in time and space, according to the laws of human development. The educational dimension pertains to the practical order by which an integral view also leads the way toward the realization, in time and space, of the goals and ideals that the theological dimension reveals and the metaphysical dimension demonstrates. Thus theory and practice, ideas and life, must each play a role and retain their proper domain and specific laws within an integral worldview. But ultimately the primary and transcendental creative cause of reality secures the *integration*, as contrasted to the mechanistic disintegration of the structure and order of all existence. The integral perspective as exemplified in Kentenich's approach to man and community can help to harmonize the polaric tensions in contemporary ethical theory.

In contrast to the collectivistic image of man and inspired in the Pauline concept of the Christian person, Kentenich proclaimed the "new man" as "the person who is able to live in community, who is enraptured with God, and who agrees to all God-willed ties out of inner convictions. . . . The thoroughly divinized, moral, spirit-impulsed and integrated person" (North-America - Bericht II, S.212).

In true humanistic fashion the new man strives for *self-realization*, or perfection of his/her nature, but within the order of supernatural grace which calls man to become divinized, to be the child of God. A person is perfect when her/his life is marked by an ideal fundamental attitude, and when all his/her noble natural and supernatural talents have unfolded harmoniously. (Grace presupposes nature: grace does not destroy nature but elevates and perfects it.)

The new man is a spirit-imbued-person who in his/her attachments to ideals principally from the point of view of inner freedom transcends all forms of cohesion and attains the *autonomy* of *authencity* of being and of a *life lived by inner convictions*.

The new man takes joy in the individual nature of each person, as a special gift of God's wisdom and creative love, and expresses this joy in his/her reverence toward the unique traits, qualities and talents of *each* personal nature. That is a full responsibility for one's perfection as an autonomous being, conscious of one's natural and human rights, including and demanding for its exercise a personal integration into a community also called to perfection, particularly as the *family*.

In an ideal family all the members are united in love. This shows in a community of life and destiny, of ideas and hearts, and of prayer and sacrifice. Such an ideal family has not only to be understood in purely natural terms, but also supernaturally. It takes its bearings from the love that the three Persons in the Blessed Trinity give to one another, from Christ's love for his Church, and from the Holy Family at Nazareth. In this new community, the members live spiritually in one another, and feel a deep, inner sense of responsibility for one another before God and Our Lady.

But the integration of the autonomous person and community life does not eliminate the tensions. Rather, the tension existing between the free personality or the autonomous person and the community is extremely valuable. Strong personalities inject the community with new life and innovative ideas, protect it from superficiality and any disregard for the uniqueness of the person. The community, in turn, ensures that the individual persons offer their talents and capacities to the service of the common good and do not develop one-sidedly in isolation and dissipation of talent. Thus, one of the most valuable life forces of an ideal state is to be found in the tension between the person and the community.

The tension between the person and the community/family is ultimately harmonized by the power of love. Love is the basic and central drive of the human soul. As basic, love animates all the spiritual functions of the person, leading him/her to unity and integration with the *beloved you*. As central, love is connected with all the powers of the soul and therefore seizes, rules and coordinates all that the person is and can do. Love bridges the differences between people and unites them in great goals. As a strong fundamental power, it forms the individual person in an original way, thus preserving his/her individuality, but also directs him/her towards the common good of the community. Rights to self and duties to others, the private and the public, are blended by the formative power of love.

But the power of love works through structural principles which give form to the community, helps to harmonize the rights of the individual and the *duties to the community* and animates all forms of responsibility. The structural principles secure an objective basis for the interplay of love between those in authority and their followers, and vice-versa, and of love among equals.

The community requires for its identity a net of bindings and restrictions which offers a stable and permanent structure through time or through the changes in membership and circumstances. But in order to be a community of autonomous persons in pursuit of natural and supernatural perfection, the restrictions must be acknowledged and appreciated by personal inner conviction fostered in turn by a growth in supernatural outlook.

We have here a federative structure (above and beyond liberal democracy and dictatorship) which realizes law and order, secures freedom to develop one's own life, protects and coordinates the individuals uniting them as a group, and which opposes collectivistic tendencies of the leveling and equalizing centralism as well as opens the way to the workings of supernatural grace. This Kentenich called the *principle of construction*, "Restriction only as far as necessary, freedom as far as possible, spiritual formation as much as possible."

The community also requires for its functioning as such and its carrying out of its tasks and mission the presence of responsible leaders. Neither a monarchy nor democracy expresses the authority of the responsible leader who must inform and be informed, consult and be consulted, who shares in the decision but must have the final say, and who participates in the execution of the decision feeling uniquely responsible for its realization and its consequences. Kentenich called this arrangement the *principle of government*, "Authoritative in principle, democratic in application." This principle corresponds with the basic rights of each person, and a justified desire to share responsibility democratically, and also to support a legitimate authority which unites the persons as individuals and effectively guides them toward a common good.

But a community, besides responsible leaders, requires for the attainment of its goals responsible followers and co-workers seeking solidarity. The members unite for life and work, but must preserve their originality and innate autonomy for their own perfection and for the perfection of the community. Hence, it is important that each member feels responsible for an area of work, solves the problems of daily life at the level these occur with his/her own resources, while coordinated by the leader, and takes initiative to reject his/her personal originality within the aims of the common task. This Father Kentenich called the *principle of communication*. This principle regulates the relationships of the members to one another in the spirit of subsidiarity.

The heart of the community is the power of love, and as such it can be called the *principle of unity*, which in turn is complemented by the *principle of creative tensions*. For indeed love fosters the growth of life among diverse and individual persons who retain their individuality precisely by contrasting and enriching it in complementary contact with others who must also be respected in their own individuality, if we are to retain our own. Thus, as Kentenich understood it, *the principle of unity* singles out the central role of the covenant of love, which forms a community together with the *principle of creative tensions*, which preserves and increases the vitality of the community. It is precisely these two last principles which contribute the most in integrating man as communitarian, in communion with God and the rest of creation. A perfect community presupposes, then, perfect personalities who are united in love and who strive toward a common ideal recognized as an objective good.

The self-realization of the new man, integrated within the new community, presupposes as is by now evident, a *covenant of love* which is not only the *contractual bond* or the ethics of rights, nor merely the contract/compact bond advocated by the counter balancing ethics of responsibility. Beyond the language of rights and of duties is *love*, but love preserves the claims of justice and autonomy. The covenant of love fosters a communal obligation which strives to secure a real unity and does not rest in the mere accommodation of compromise and tolerance, which love tries to fill with its *spirit*. The covenant of love harmonizes the polaric tensions of self-realization and self-renunciation, or of autonomy and surrender to a person.

In essence a covenant of love is an exchange of hearts — the core of one's personality — of interest, and of goods with a beloved person. The idea of the covenant answers man's innate aptitude and longing to be complemented by another in the unique dignity, being and value of this other person. First of all, man as a spiritual being in dependence on God, needs the complement of God for his perfection. God revealed Himself as God of the covenant and appointed man to enter the covenant and thus gain salvation. In our surrender to a personal God, we gain our true self as desired by God from all eternity.

The covenant of love responds to man's fundamental power of soul, and guards us against the loss of personality. God for us is not only the spiritual God, an incomprehensible idea, but a person who loves us and who expects our love in return. It secures the worth of the individual person, the root of one's dignity and rights to autonomy. Renunciation of one's primitive nature and acceptance of God, by way of love, secures the realization of our redeemed nature.

But the covenant, besides securing the experience of a personal God, and the personality of each indivdual, also fosters the Christian community. It overcomes the loss of personality in one's fellow man. The other is not a number, not a replaceable object. God has entered into a covenant with each person in the community, thus elevating, complementing and securing his or her unique personal ideal and value. They are with us drawn into God's covenant of love with mankind, and therefore we are connected with one another and thus bear responsibility for one another. Renunciation of part of one's self, for the sake of the good of the other, also enhances the power over one's selfish nature, increases one's autonomy and realizes *one's true self* in its relational or interpersonal dimension.

At this point, our exposition of the *integral view* of reality leads to a consideration of a fully-integrated person. Within the theological dimension of the integral worldview, we discovered the person of the Blessed Mother as image of the integrated person, in full harmony with self, the model of the new man.

The Marian person within a covenant of love with Mary represents the new man entrusted with bringing into morality a new vitality, a new way of integrating right and responsibility, autonomy and self-surrender, by way of love. That is, rather than centering on woman as such in order to restore the intuitive, the affective, the personal into moral discourse, we speak of the *marian* personality independently of the categories male and female. The marian personality is ontologically and ethically, that is, according to being, attitude and life, another Christ. Since Mary is the most perfect child of the father, the permanent helpmate of the Son for the salvation of souls, as well as temple for the full indwelling of the Holy Spirit, she embodies all the virtues of the "new man" in Christ. She is the perfect Christian. She is, as the "Immaculata" embodies, the perfect harmony of spirit and matter, of reason and emotion, of justice and love.

In the image of the Immaculata we can see clearly the *whole* person, as the one healed (made whole by God), the sensitive human being who forms an entity in himself, who is not closed off in himself, who, on the contrary, is unfeignedly open to others. The whole person is an integrated person. His mind is clear, judgment prudent, will imperturbable and decisive, and emotions refined and ordered to the perfection of the whole. All mental and spiritual faculties cooperate when he enters into communication with the social, cultural, physical surroundings with which personal and vital bonds are established.[10]

In the image of the Immaculata we have discovered the fully integrated person, the microcosmos who, in creaturely dependance and openness to God, restores the order of reality within the person and in relation to the rest of the creation. Through the covenant of love with the Blessed Mother a person can hope to resemble the Immaculata, and thus strive for a religious ethics of love in terms of which the polarization of right and duties, private and public, individual and community, can find a harmony of complementarity.

Another feature of the Schoenstatt-Kentenich covenant of love which we find relevant is its *pedagogical effectiveness* regarding the *moral* education within a religious context and as oriented toward a supernatural good. A certain pluralism of style of life and a corresponding subjective appreciation of values find in Kentenich's psychology and pedagogy a link to the absolute and objectivity of values.

Kentenich was fully aware that the stimulation of the mind alone is not enough to form human nature. All man's forces, including the heart (Gemut) and will, have to be gripped in order that the movement of ideas may become a movement of life. In order to secure the correct appreciation of the subjective within the integrated person, we must have a right definition of *heart*.

Heart is not a metaphoric description of emotions and feelings. Here *heart* designates the essence of the inner life of man, the center of all mental, volitional and emotional powers to which God (Absolute) Himself turns, and from which man governs himself and becomes fully committed to the objective good or to values in their objectivity.

Just as Kentenich went beyond an "education to duty," he also encouraged us to think of morality as inclusive of duties and rights as incorporating and transcending either by way of love. Education through ideals, attachment, the covenant, trust and organic development provides a basis for *moral* education and hence a security for morality as such.

First, education through ideals aims at creating attitudes and fostering generosity and freedom. It thus counterbalances "minimalistic" disposition with its exclusive emphasis on rights, as well as transcends mere duty. Second, education through attachment overcomes the isolation, the uprootedness and illusory self-sufficiency of modern individualism. It introduces the person to a natural and supernatural organism of attachments to places, persons and ideas as well as the holy places, even as the Divine Persons and the truths of faith enable him or her to form the new community. Third, education through the Covenant aims at completing the bond of love in its height, depth, extent and duration with God and mankind. The transmission of moral knowledge (objective) as well as motivation of the will and heart (subjective) to realize it in life requires education through trust. An education of trust on the part of the educator awakens and unfolds any number of good qualities and forces in the learner. And finally, the spiritual interplay between educator and learner is further facilitated by attention to the organic development of the learner. The educator adapts to the student's receptivity for values and stage of development, and offers intellectual and spiritual goods to the student. As a result the learner is motivated to acquire these goods in an organic manner, that is, to conquer them gradually according to his or her power of comprehension by way of development.

It is in the person of the mother of God that contemporary ethical theory benefits from an incarnation or concrete realization of the theological metaphysical ideal and objective value of the integrated person, and of woman as a distinct mode of being a person. Theology points at a real embodiment of the ideal, a model or an archetype with a real content of what eternal woman is, as well as what is essential in being a person. Such a transcendental foundation is needed in order to justify woman's distinct cultural role without falling into a reductionist thinking of some feministic trends.

We find that integration as a worldview with its theological, metaphysical, psychological and educational dimensions unfolds into a universal-concrete reality, the Immaculata as a fully-integrated person, an *alter Christus*. The image of the *Immaculata* reflects a mode of being which represents the full harmony with self and with other, with God and all of nature toward which all mankind tends, thus its universal quality. But the image of the Immaculata is also realized in the person of Mary the Mother of God, and is an operative principle of transformation for all those who enter into a Covenant of Love with Her. It is a true concrete event.

This blends into a creative and harmonious unity, the polaric tension in contemporary ethical theory. The integrated person fully endowed with supernatural grace overcomes the theoretical difficulties of intellectual discourse of natural reason. The personal reality of the mother of God transcends, but also secures, a point of reference for theological-philosophical thinking.

In Her, the new man in his or her individuality finds personal identity, autonomy and a model for self-realization. In Her, the new man also finds the incentive and the correct way to find himself in contact with things, with living beings, with other persons, and with historical events. The most significant encounter with others is mediated by Her by way of the Covenant of love in its divine as well as human dimension. And in a Covenant with Her, a moral education towards a religious ethics of right as well as duty, of justice in the service of love, secures the harmony between the Absolute and the relative, between Divine Providence and the human response.

University of Puerto Rico
Mayaguez, Puerto Rico

NOTES

1. Teilhard de Chardin, *Man's Place in Nature* (New York: Harper and Brothers, 1966), pp. 94-95.

2. Daniel Callahan, *Ethics for Hard Times* (New York: Plenum Publishing Co., 1981), pp. 262-263.

3. C. B. McPherson, *The Political Theory of Possessive Individualism* (Oxford: Oxford University Press, 1963), p. 54.

4. Gerald Dworkin, *Report* (New York: Hastings Center, February, 1976).

5. Daniel Callahan, *Report* (New York: Hastings Center, October, 1963).

6. Ibid., p. 263.

7. Hans Jonas, *The Imperative of Responsibility* (Chicago: The University of Chicago Press, 1981), pp. 32, 42.

8. Carol Gilligan, *In a Different Voice* (Cambridge: Harvard University Press, 1982).

9. Sara Ruddick, "Maternal Thinking," *Feminist Studies*, Summer, 1980.

10. Sr. M. Ludowika, "Mary Immaculata — Blueprint of the New Man," Conference, October 1971.

CONCLUSION

In each of the essays, our scholars examine some distinctive aspects of Christian humanism. In Part One, Walter Artus sets up the broader conceptual basis by providing a cultural history of humanism as an intellectually solid venture operating right up to our present day, showing mostly optimistic prospects at least for the near term. He finds that Christian humanism is balanced with a validity and correct understanding of God and man. It recognizes the loftiness of human nature, the spiritual quality of the life principle and a destiny beyond our earthly existence. Interwoven as fundamentally important dimensions, elaborate different analyses are added from aesthetics, ethics, and education. From aesthetics, Richard Francis explains the wondrous intersections of religion and art, and calls for a regular, powerful, creative, even therapeutic renewal of aesthetic experience, imbued with holiness, in an often resisting, cruel and drab world. Aesthetic and religious experience are at least equivalent and blend into a vital unity in acquiring the beautiful.

From ethics, John Crosby clarifies the paradoxical quality of objective and subjective moral obligation. Conscientiously bound moral actions arbitrate the paradox by our willfully following moral imperatives in self-actualizing even autonomous ways. Subjective relativism is avoided because moral duty commands for its own sake and its value that grounds it. Alexius Bucher establishes human rights as moral entitlements that correspond to the dignity of the Christian person. These basic rights entail the obligations for existence and for material goods, combined with educational, sociological, economic and political involvements.

From education, John Fitzgibbon renews the Christian aim of learning to be a guide to the person's self-development, armed with knowledge, good judgment, and moral virtue. The gain is creative spontaneity and true spiritual freedom, conditioned by faith, love and truth. He warns against jeopardizing the liberal arts, the civilizing arts, by dangerously narrowing the curriculum to favor the professions and technologies. He insists that the practical character of liberal learning is to live well regardless of occupation. He notes that responsible learning, by restoring the central importance of Christian philosophy and theology, revitalizes the students' intellectual and moral roots. From social philosophy, James O'Leary addresses the problems of ambiguity and confusion about human nature. Such confusion, to a great extent, is caused by the technological assault of the industrial age. History and religion aim to help with our adjustment to a limited degree, with uncertain prospects.

Part Two clarifies the scientific aspects of Christian humanism, beginning with Charles Dechert's notion of models as the meeting place for the very successful scientific culture and the more abstract humanistic culture of philosophy, theology and the arts. The terms of scientific models correlate with what is directly observable and measurable with reliable, real-world testing. The multiparadigmatic social and behavioral world operates in a more complex manner with a cultural mixture of things in context. Still, everything being related to everything can be beneficially understood by means of various philosophical, theological, ideological, historical, and artistic models. Furthermore, Feodor Cruz articulates a synthesis of philosophy, of the natural, social, and behavioral sciences, and of the uniqueness of human nature. Having explained the adequacy and inadequacy of the scientific method, he distinguishes humans from all other creatures and sets the need for philosophy to study human nature correctly. By being helpful and hurtful, science confuses us and cannot define the human good. Religion can do this, but religions dispute among each other. Only philosophy can provide an understanding of human nature with the intrinsic formal essence and a correct moral theory. Science and philosophy, as separate, damage our society, but, as intimately complementary, help each other, with philosophy giving the theory and science clarifying and testing it.

Then, Richard Francis reestablishes a traditional metaphysical basis for technology wherein God, as first and final cause, shares intermediate causation with us in a regular kind of concurrence and conservation. We must use this causal power responsibly according to the biblical injunctions of law and love. Technology thus can serve human happiness beneficially within God's providence and avoid the dangers of a secular, barbaric technocracy. John Dudley follows with a critical, historical detailing of the conflict between ethics and science, and observes the ongoing problem of applying ethical standards to science. The disorientation of science and technology, a most urgent and fundamental problem today, stems from a classical notion of the superiority of scientific knowledge over ethics. Interest in God also has been dropped. But scripturally God is shown as love, not as intellect, and Jesus as the one true way of life. Ethics extends to every human activity, including the scientific, intellectual and emotional, and real reform can be made by willfully putting our religious beliefs into practice in every aspect of life.

Richard Francis concludes this part by explaining that in today's scientific technological world, ethics seems to be ambiguous, nonexistent or even suppressed. But he claims that we still must demand a fundamental ethical code for our technology. As scientific technology becomes universal, so also must its ethics. Giving examples of "doing good and avoiding evil," he concludes that the basic principles of the Christian West and of the non-Christian East are practically interchangeable. In that context, while technology is here to stay, its only moral purpose is to improve the human condition.

Part Three analyzes the more personal qualities of Christian humanism by examining human dignity, love, gratitude, and our confrontation with death. Robert Lauder begins by distinguishing between humanism as eschatological and as incarnational. The former stresses sin and salvation; the latter stresses meritorious value enfleshed by God's Son. These can be complementary, but, if extreme, each can seriously distort Christianity. Within each, nevertheless, the human person gains an inherent, transcendent dignity because therein our knowledge and love of God are fundamentally operative in shaping us. Next, David Goicoechea relates personal love and personality preference. He considers personality to be the center of preferential love and the person as the center of neighborly love. The special dignity of the person prevents our love of neighbor to be reduced to preference by personality and feelings. The person is a relational agent of loving transcendence, while personality is an individual substance of a rational nature. The person transcends personality, he argues, and grounds his or her dignity integrally in the "Eternal Thou" and also in every other "thou." The mystery of personhood is not substantial and individual but a loving interpenetration, created by God to seek the peace of divine love.

John Snyder continues with an examination of Christian marriage as a community of love, as a natural union and an intimate partnership. Conjugal love, in which the partners freely give their whole persons, even when accompanied by a romantic quality and sexual satisfaction, basically, actively and willingly seeks the good of the person loved. Such love pervades the couple's whole life and by generosity grows better and greater. Because God enters into the marriage, conjugal love is supernatural but is also eminently human. In a truly loving marriage, sexual intercourse is primarily a manifestation of the partners' personal, mutual love which simultaneously endorses their willingness to have children. The personal aspects are always overriding in the exclusive persevering marital commitment. John Davis follows by explaining the concepts of guilt and gratitude. Guilt is a hallmark of humanism outside of religion and sometimes functions as an alternative to that found in the Judeo-Christian tradition. Guilt and gratitude, as constantly fundamental to the human condition, may serve as a conjunction between religious and secular humanists. Both these conditions are central to our awareness. Guilt and gratitude feed our conscience. Guilt illuminates gratitude, as gratitude illuminates guilt. Guilt means having fallen from some norm, being thus burdened, self-enclosed and hiding from the judging self. Gratitude, however, supplies an openness that expands the norm of life unexpectedly and undeservingly, for no discernible reason. In guilt, some obligation burdensomely is never perfectly fulfilled. In gratitude, some gratuitous gesture is done for us by another. Indeed, that other may well be God.

Ken Bryson examines human value in our confrontation with death. He assumes that the Christian faithfully following Jesus in this life survives death and enjoys God's vision in the next. He also assumes the existence of the world independently of our sensing or intellectual awareness of it. Life before and after death is a continuous connection. He distinguishes between the existential perspective, the view from the living, and the ontological, the view from the dead. Existentially we do not expect to live through death. Ontologically we do. Something radical happens in reference to the temporal scheme of things. Our temporal life, together with experiencing death, sets our eternal destiny. John Dudley concludes this part by noting that, while the New Testament dualistically presupposes two ultimate realities, the material and the immaterial, based on Plato and Aristotle, such a dualism is unrealistic. Opposing the present naturalistic and materialistic threat, he corrects this by determining that "substance" must be restricted properly to living beings, especially to those possessing a soul and having a supernatural destiny.

Part Four penetrates more deeply into the more metaphysical aspects of the human person. Certainly some of the previous essays carry ontological teachings, but this group more technically conveys Christian humanistic analyses of the person. Thomas Michaud begins by exploring the mystery of the soul and holds to the notion that the person is a union of both body and soul. He deplores today's tendencies, materialistically and scientifically, to reduce the person to a complex of organic machines devoid of spiritual character and worth. Drawing from the distinction between problem and mystery, he argues that belief in the human person even as a mysterious union of soul and body can be reasonably preserved. Reductionists cannot sustain their claims. Josef Seifert then analyzes phenomenological and classical metaphysics of the person. The meaning and greatness of human nature reside in our ability to engage in metaphysical inquiry. We can even grasp being-in-itself. He gives four meanings of being-in-itself and investigates being as person. While substances possess their own being more properly than do accidents, the human substance possesses his own being in an incomparably superior way. This is by self-consciousness, cognition, and self-knowledge. Conscious self-possession links with our own being, and thus we experience and know ourselves as substance. He further asserts freedom as a new mode of self-possession, which allows for moral quality and the inalienable dignity of the person. He then advances a personalistic metaphysics and theology.

In addition, Francisco Peccorini relates the notion of human dignity to self-consciousness by noting that the possible and the agent intellects are two different active aspects of the human soul. The possible intellect, in intuiting Being as an object, becomes Being, while the agent intellect, as a subject, knows itself in the soul, which, in turn, empowers the soul to know everything. Through these means, he argues that the "I" feels its self-existence in the world, with an infinite cognitive horizon, also by knowing Being itself. He demonstrates then that the intimate activity of divine grace in the soul has correlative relationship to the Trinity. Afterwards, Heinrich Beck uses the classical ontological principles regarding the unity of being, truth and goodness to understand human nature's basic unifying structure. He still allows for real distinctions within this ontology and, analogously, among different peoples, while he advances a creative cooperation based upon the sameness and differences of humankind.

Mary O'Hara explores the human person according to our essentially bodily reality. She sees the body as a system of meanings, as a culturally created symbol, even though it is concrete. Detailing some historic references to our bodies and to our clothing, she focuses upon the category of "habitus," or human clothing or adornment, as a way of reflecting the human spirit as incarnate in the body. Usually a more favorable treatment is given to our mind or soul and harsher treatment to our body. Still, habitus, being only one of the many categories and often neglected, can mean habit of behavior or clothing, etc. She explains the various meanings of "having," like "possessing," as definitive of human nature. To a large degree, our willfully gained possessions, including our clothing, from jogging shoes to jewelry and armor, define us. They also preserve us. Elena Lugo concludes this part by examining "technological man" as a cultural category or agent. She defines person first in relation to oneself, second in relation to others, and third in relation to the Absolute. The ideal person represents a proper involvement in all three. Influenced by positivistic, natural-mechanistic and utilitarian presuppositions and also by an excessive drive for pleasure, honor and power, the technological man seriously fails the ideal. By constant experimentation, innovation and control, technological depersonalization causes severe anguish to the person. As a cultural counter- balance, she offers the role of the personhood of Mary to function as co-redemptrix and as the relevant ideal person to establish with the Christ a theocentrically based technologically advanced world.

Part Five clarifies the more theological dimensions of Christian humanism. Several previous essays necessarily entailed religious components, but the following more essentially convey theological understanding. Terry Tekippe begins by comparing the God of reason with that of revelation, insisting that the philosopher's God is not fundamentally incompatible with the God of religion. Arguing from metaphysics, epistemology, anthropology, and history, he refines that conclusion especially through convincing epistemological analysis of our unlimited human intelligence and by the historical synthesis between the God of reason and of scripture. Dominic Iorio then describes the intimations of God that exceed the usual rational demonstrations about God's existence as an abstraction. Intimate experience can certainly satisfactorily lead to a God of devotion and love. He seeks a new opening to faith based upon a return to a divine primordial encounter. Being our first response to God, intimations, as intellectual, moral, aesthetic and sensuous, engage something beyond the object contacted. That further quality is the intimation which, in its unreflective surprise and wonder, precedes any definition. Repeated intimations lead to meaning of and devotion to an immanent, not transcendent, divine presence in everything.

Heinrich Beck, using the analogy of the Holy Trinity, explains that, since all is created by God, who is the Trinity, everything necessarily, structurally, images the Trinity. Articulating the intrinsic dynamics of three persons in one God, he stipulates their constant involvement in our world in their distinct but unified functions as Father, Son and Holy Spirit. He draws examples of the Trinitarian rhythm in nature and then of a similar rhythm in culture. Nature and cultural history analogously swing rhythmically out of God and into God thus preserving an existential and spiritual dimension. Today's world's structural problem is solved thus by analogy, by dynamic differences in unity and the unity in difference, as God goes out of himself by the Word and completes himself in return by the Holy Spirit. Mary-Rose Barral then explains that metaphysics is deeply rooted in the fabric of everyday experience. Even in our humanistic culture, correct reflection moves us towards the highest possible reality, God. She finds that Christian humanism is compatible with Christian metaphysics. While there are many views of humanism in history, such as that of the Renaissance man above nature, the Sartrean "creation" of human nature in oneself, the Marxist idea of human dignity against alienation born of oppression, the pragmatist's person as the "measure of all things," and our present glorification of a human reason with no bounds, according to Christian humanism, the person is a value not in "having" but in "being." Evanghelos Moutsopoulos concludes this part by defining history as the consciously reported succession of events. In both the cyclically balanced and the recurringly unbalanced historical models, discontinuity of events, as important points, shifts the motion. Such extreme points, made significant ontologically and axiologically by the consciousness of "becoming," actualize the past and the future in the present. "Kairicity" intentionalizes the process for God providentially to work through history.

Part Six explores Christian humanism according to its dimensions of social and political philosophy. Robert O'Brien begins this section by elaborating the story of man's deliverance in the teachings of Karl Marx and comparing this with Christian eschatology. He reminds us that the attractive part of Marxism is its secular eschatology, the whole meaning of human life and destiny in the relentless, economic history of this world carrying the promise of improvement, a class-less, strife-free self-fulfillment. History's original structural misery and suffering are not human caused, but a fact of history with the current conditions being played out in the economic power struggle of the workplace. Capitalism

442

is the oppressor which alienates us from ourselves and others. In the ongoing revolution, Communism will save us. Fundamentally flawed because it is based completely in the self-sufficiency of man, Marxism cannot satisfy. Christianity inherently is the way of salvation, and must address the concrete suffering of people with the correlative hope in the ever present risen Christ. George Lavere then follows by addressing the crisis in contemporary democracy, namely the fragmentation of the body politic into various independent groups or constituencies, each demanding its asserted rights in the name of absolute freedom and equality. The unifying consensus has been replaced by the special interests of immediate claims made directly to the state rather than through the channels of the political community. Direct confrontation and judicial and administrative action, rather than legal action, have eroded majority rule. Without restoring the unity of the political community, anarchy and totalitarianism will ensue. Reform can be made by reestablishing the "common good," the best feature in the Western tradition, with its ideal, ethical, and transcendental implications as found in the Christian political order.

Robert Rweyemamu explores humanism in Africa as an integral philosophy of life. Noting the African cultural renaissance in the 1920's and the gaining of independence of the various states and their joining the world of nations, he portrays Africa as now giving not its exploitable resources, but its civilization in soul, thought and life, not so much disparate values, but the cultural context itself. African culture comprises 850 societies, with about 6,000 dialects in 700 languages, and tribal diversity within the same culture. Some convergence exists among the differences. Without the same speculative, nationalist conceptual categories of the West, Africans philosophize in their own right, judging and interpreting events, realities, emotions, and actions close to their experience, on their own scale of values, not from cause to effect, but more in an inductive way. Life, a concern for living, prevails as a moving force of desire, joy and need. It is God's magic force in a cosmic unity represented in visible and non-visible form. Life is participation, communication and creation in harmonious fashion.

Regarding Christianity's dialogue with Chinese cultures, Matthias Lu compares the Chinese character of the Imperial Dynasties and today's China as Neo-Confucianism coinciding with the European Enlightenment. Both have secularized and de-Christianized culture. Culture is human creativity, communication, shared discovery and value-making directed towards goodness and rationality. Christianity honors human goodness by the power of the Logos (Christ) and the Holy Spirit. Asian culture is an "epiphany," admiring God's manifest glory in Heaven-and-Earth achievements, and in the imitation of Christ. Even as Christian and Confucian culture is universal, both use the cult of antiquity, equating the wise and the good with everything ancient. Both identify with the cult of intelligentsia, using learning and teaching. Christianity identifies what is true in Confucianism and supplements what is missing, corrects errors, and places the supernatural over the natural. When Christian authorities forbade the Confucian rites (1707), the Church was henceforth persecuted. Recent intellectual revivals (1926-46) have been insufficient. Under Communism, religion must serve the state, except in the smaller Chinas, like Taiwan, where Christianity has some promise.

S. Baliah Naidu continues this part by more broadly explaining the Christian dialogue with Asian cultures and religions. Since the Second World War, East and West have intimately been related on a vast scale. Understanding and some assimilation are essential for survival. Cultural process creates a society. The great societies all think that they follow a divinely appointed path. Religion is the dynamic element in culture. Thereby we can learn from each other at intellectual and deeper levels in an inward renewal. Any undertaken dialogue presupposes self-criticism in the face of deabsoluted, perspectival, and dialogic truth. Still all truth proceeds from God. The Hindus seek release from worldly anguish in trusting God; the Buddhists move from worldly insufficiency towards supreme enlightenment. As do the Moslems and Jews, such people live holy lives, and not from Christianity. What is God saying to us through them? Christianity uses a Greek and Latin framework, and personalizes God; Asians use more inscrutable and non-personal references. God transcends all such categories. For the West, God is transcendent, for the East, immanent. Incarnation and salvation have Eastern expression as well as Western. But differences persist in principle. Individualism is Western, the community Eastern. In the former, man is lord of creation, in the latter, in harmony with nature. God's linear causation is Western, an interdependent causal network is Eastern. The soul's immutability and bodily separation are Western. Some Asians reject the soul, while others profess reincarnation of a soul. Some of these differences are irreconcilable, but the dialogue continues.

In conclusion, Elena Lugo asks the main question of how are we to foster community life, to blend private right and public duty, while

444

respecting the creative tension between the two. Those societies whose citizens are permitted to act dutifully only to the state or church, based on indoctrination, patriotism, or sense of national superiority, easily turn into totalitarian dictatorships. But the more democratic, excessively selfish individualism, constituted of free personalities, also falters or fails to effect a strong sense of unity, or community as such. Stressing individualism, Western cultures overall fail to promote a sense of community, and instead protect procedural safeguards rather than transcendental common goods. Proper justice, so essential for every community, begins with the mutual, ethical responsibilities within the family's roles. Therein also pervades a covenantal ethics, linking rights and duties as a responsible community. There the person self-integrates all of these features, together with contracts and compacts relating to the larger community's values, especially love. Love bridges all differences, private and public, etc. Within covenantal love, the fully integrated person is another Christ, sharing also the affective, womanly qualities of the Mother of God. Altogether this reflects the full harmony of all of nature, which is society at its best.

The spirit of all of the preceding essays is overall optimistic, carrying some hope for our future. Yet these professor-scholars almost universally, in the content of their essays, find something debilitating about today's world often in a modern perversion of traditional values. In seeing major cultural problems in very many features of modern life, they often give warning coupled with some suggested remedy. They acknowledge the ongoing vitality of a Christian Humanism that continues to give us our bearings in a world buffeted by competing philosophies and progressively more accessible to more people. Where Christ's message is misunderstood and challenged, in every case they resist doctrinal weakening, clarify the fundamentals, and call for dialogue over apparent irreconcilables. Christianity, after all, while profoundly fundamental to the West, is originally an Eastern religion and must continue to be made attractive to every culture. Philosophically it makes good sense; theologically, salvation depends on it.

Richard P. Francis

PROFILES OF CONTRIBUTORS

With a Ph.D. in Philosophy from St. John's University, New York, Walter Artus has taught in the philosophy department there since 1959. A Mediaevalist with a particular interest in the thought of Ramon Llull, he was inducted in 1976 into the ranks of *Magistri* at the International *Schola Lullistica Maioricensis* in Palma de Majorca, Spain. He has published more than thirty articles on Ramon Llull and Mediaeval Philosophy and has contributed to conferences in the United States and Mexico.

Mary-Rose Barral, B.S., M.A., Ph.D., Fordham University, NY, did post doctoral work at the Universities of Milan, Italy, of Nice and the Sorbonne in France; at Yale and Johns Hopkins as Visiting Fellow. She attained Full Professorship at Seton Hall University and distinguished Professor at Gannon University. In addition to her books, *The Body Subject, Progressive Neutralism* and *Life-Sharing for a Creative Tomorrow*, she has published over forty articles and lectures extensively in the United States, Western and Eastern Europe, Asia, Africa, and South America. A member of the International Association of Christian Thought, she is President of the International Thomas Aquinas Society and also the International Society for Philosophy and Psychotherapy whose Journal she recently published.

Heinrich Beck, M.A., University of Munich, Ph.D., University of Salzburg, is a Professor of Philosophy at Otto-Friedrich University, Bamberg, Germany. He has taught at the University of Salzburg, the Pontifical Institute for Philosophy, Salzburg-Rome, Complutense University, Madrid, the University of Salvador and John F. Kennedy University in Buenos Aires, Argentina, the Catholic University in Salta, Argentina and is a permanent Scientific Advisor at the Pontifical University of Mexico. He lectures extensively in Europe, North America, Asia and Africa. Professor Beck is the author of fourteen books and numerous articles and is published worldwide.

Kenneth A. Bryson is a Professor of Philosophy and chairs the Humanities Department at the University College of Cape Breton,

446

Sydney, Nova Scotia, Canada. His books include *Death Can Be Beautiful*, Halifax, N.S., Formac, 1981, and *Flowers and Death*, North York, Ont., The University Press of Canada, 1992. Professor Bryson's papers have been published in *Archives of the Foundation of Thanatology*, New York, and several of his book reviews in *Canadian Philosophical Reviews*, Edmonton, Alberta, in *The New Scholasticism* and in *The Thomist*. A member of the International Association for Christian Thought, Bryson's interests extend to Biomedical Ethics, STS Courses and Psychology.

Born in Herzogenaurach, Germany, Alexius Bucher received his Ph.D. in Philosophy at the University of Mainz (1975) and taught there before going to the University of Ankara, Turkey in 1977 as Guest Professor. Since 1982 he has taught Practical Philosophy and History of Philosophy in the Theology Department of the Catholic University of Eichstätt, Germany. His publications include *Metaphysikkritic als Begriffsproblematik*, Auflage, 1983, *Erkenntnisgegenstand und Gegenstandserkenntnis*, Bonn, 1980, and *Ethik-eine Hiniführung*, Bonn, 1988. Besides teaching in Germany and Turkey, he has lectured in Mexico.

John Crosby, a graduate of Georgetown University, Ph.D., University of Salzburg, Austria, is currently a Professor and Chair of the Philosophy Department at Franciscan University of Steubenville, Ohio. He has published papers in Value Theory, in the philosophy of John Henry Newman, and recently in the philosophy of the human person. He has contributed to national and international conferences. His book, *Essay on Personal Selfhood* is forthcoming.

Feodor Cruz, Ph.D. St. Louis University, Missouri, studied in Asia, Europe and the U.S. He received academic awards from the Fulbright-Hays, Ford Foundation, National Endowment for the Humanities, Danforth Foundation among others. The author of *John Dewey's Theory of Community*, Bern, Peter Lang, 1988, and *The Human Factor*, Manila, IBEX, 1993, Cruz is currently a Professor of Philosophy at Loras College, Dubuque, Iowa. His concerns focus on Ethics and Political Philosophy. He is the Founder and President of the International Foundation for the Support and Education of Indigent Children and a member of the International Association for Christian Thought.

Father John Davis, Ph.D. The Pennsylvania State University, is a priest of the Order of Preachers (Dominicans) ordained in 1966. He served as Catholic Chaplain at Princeton University, New Jersey and taught at The Catholic University, Washington, D.C. and at Providence College, Rhode Island. Presently teaching at Caldwell College in New Jersey, Father Davis has served as editor of *The Thomist* and has published reviews in *Ethics* and *Spirituality Today*.

Charles Dechert, Professor of Politics at The Catholic University of America since 1967, taught Government and Political Science at Purdue University and from 1957-1959 he was visiting Professor of Comparative Economic and Social Policy and Director of the North American Institute, International University of Social Studies Pro Deo in Rome. During the Korean War period, he was engaged in social and behavioral science research with the United States Air Force and did post-doctoral work at Johns Hopkins University's Bologna Center. He has published extensively in the areas of political theory and public policy including books on the *Ente Nazionale Idrocarburi, The Social Impact of Cybernetics, Sistemi-Paradigmi-Societa*, plus many articles.

John A. J. Dudley, M.A. in Classical Philology, University College, Dublin, Ph.D, Universität zu Köln, is a Professor at The Institut Libre Marie-Haps (Université Catholique de Louvain). He also teaches philosophy at two institutes of higher education in Germany and The Netherlands. Awarded the honorary distinction of the town of Abdera (Greece) in 1983, he was also elected a member of the Société Internationale pour l'Etude de la Philosophie Médiévale in 1986. Dudley is the author of *Gott Und Theoria bei Aristoteles, Die metaphysische Grundlage der Nikomachischen Ethik* and numerous philosophical articles published in international journals.

John F. Fitzgibbon, Ph.D., University of Notre Dame, Professor Emeritus and Chairman of the Philosophy Department at St. Ambrose University, Davenport, Iowa, where he taught for thirty-two years, also taught Philosophy at Georgetown University, Washington, D. C., and The University of Notre Dame, South Bend, Indiana. A specialist in Ethics, he was the author of three books and numerous articles and reviews. Active in the American Catholic Philosophical Association, the Iowa Philosophical Association, Metaphysical Society of America, American

Maritain Association, and Society of Medieval and Renaissance Philosophy, he received a distinguished service award in 1983 from St. Ambrose College. Professor Fitzgibbon died November 30, 1992.

Richard P. Francis, B.A., The Catholic University of America, Washington, D.C., M.A., University of Colorado, Boulder, Ph.D., University of Notre Dame, taught at Notre Dame and Purdue University before becoming Dean of the College of Arts and Sciences at the University of Colorado, Colorado Springs. He was chairman of the Philosophy Department and taught there for twenty-five years. Awarded the E.C. Harwood Chair of Philosophy at Franklin College, Switzerland, 1982-1983, he has studied and researched in Israel and Europe, published articles and numerous papers in Eastern and Western Europe, the United States and Canada. Now Professor Emeritus, he received the University of Colorado Regents' Medal, in 1992. His interests include Religion, Ethics, American Philosophy, Value Theory, Human Nature and Aesthetics. Books on Human Nature and John Dewey's Value Theory are forthcoming. Francis is founder and President of the International Association for Christian Thought.

David Goicoechea, Ph.D., Associate Professor of Philosophy at Brock University in St. Catharines, Ontario, organized a series of discussions exploring humanism sponsored by the Brock Philosophical Society. He co-edited the proceedings of these discussions, published in *The Question of Humanism* (Prometheus, Buffalo, 1990), *Joyful Wisdom*, Vol. I, *A Postmodern Ethics of Joy* and *Joyful Wisdom*, Vol. II, *Sorrow and Ethics of Joy* (Thoughthouse Publishing Group, St. Catharines, 1991, 1992). His special interests include the Philosophy of Love and Existential-Postmodern Philosophy.

Dominick A. Iorio, Ph.D., is Professor of Philosophy and Dean of the School of Liberal Arts and Sciences at Rider College. A winner of the Lindback Award for Distinguished Teaching, he is the author of several books and articles on Malebranche, Pomponazzi, McCosh, and Teilhard de Chardin. His most recent publication is *The Aristotelians of Renaissance Italy* (Mellen Press).

Robert E. Lauder, Ph.D., Marquette University, is a Professor of Philosophy at St. John's University, Jamaica, NY. Author of eight books, the most recent being *God, Death, Art and Love: The Philosophical Vision of Ingmar Bergman*, and numerous articles, Fr. Lauder is a columnist for *The Long Island Catholic* and *The Brooklyn Tablet*. A lecturer in the United States, Europe and Mexico, his writings have appeared in *American, Commonweal, New York Times Sunday Arts and Leisure, The Thomist, Cross Currents, Philosophy and Theology*, and *The American Catholic Philosophical Quarterly*. His interests include Phenomenology, Philosophy of God, Philosophy of the Person, and he has an international reputation as an authority on film.

George J. Lavere, Ph.D., Laval University, Quebec, is currently Emeritus Professor of Philosophy at Canisius College, Buffalo, NY. Prior to his appointment to Canisius, Professor Lavere taught at Villanova University. His main areas of interest are Patristic and Mediaeval Philosophy, Ethics and Political Philosophy. His publications include articles on St. Augustine's Political and Moral Philosophy, the Aesthetics of Jacques Maritain, issues in Medical Ethics and several studies of the role of the common good and Natural Law in political systems.

Matthias Lu, Ph.D., Pontifical Urbanian University in Rome, Italy, taught Philosophy and Theology at Fujen University in Peking China, taught at the University of Notre Dame, Notre Dame, IN, and came to the Bay Area as research associate at the University of California, and for the Center for Chinese Studies, a position he still holds. He taught Logic and Philosophy of Science at St. Mary's College, Moraga, CA and is the Director of the St. Thomas Aquinas Center International (Everyone's Aquinas), Oakland, and is Vicar for Chinese and Asian People, Oakland Diocese. Author of many books and articles, Fr. Lu has translated works of Aristotle and St. Thomas into Chinese and is Director of Chinese Translations at the Lublin University International Translation Center, New Britain, CT. He is a member of numerous international and national academic organizations, including American Philosophical Association, Chinese Historical Society and International Association for Christian Thought.

Elena Lugo, Ph.D., Georgetown University, is Professor of Philosophy and Director of the Center for the Philosophy and History of Sciences and Technology, University of Puerto Rico at Mayaguez. She is noted for her work in Medical Ethics and Bioethics having published

450

her own text book, *Medical Ethics* (1986) and numerous articles on the subject as well as for initiating workshops on clinical ethics at the regional hospital and for continuing education. Other books include *Philosophy and Psychology* (1984), and *Ethics and Engineering* (1985). Dr. Lugo is a member of the Secular Institute of the Schoenstatt Sisters of Mary (Wisconsin, USA Province). She has lectured in North and South America, Mexico and Canada, and has organized successful conferences on Ethics and Technology in Puerto Rico.

Evanghelos Moutsopoulos, Ph.D. University of Paris, has taught Philosophy at the University of Aix-Marseilles, the University of Thessaloniki, and the University of Athens where he served as President in 1977. A member of numerous national and international academies and societies, Moutsopoulos has taught in Europe and the United States and has presented papers at and organized international meetings. President of the Foundation for Research and Editions of Neohellenic Philosophy, director and editor of *Corpus Philosophorum Graecorum Recentiorum* and of the international philosophical review *Diotoma*, he is the author of numerous books and articles on Ontology, Axiology, Aesthetics, Philosophy of History and History of Philosophy. Known as "the philosopher of kairicity," for his theory of the *kairos*, he is also recognized for his scholarly editions of modern Greek philosophers and as the creator and founder of the Foundation for Modern Greek Philosophy.

S. Baliah Naidu, professor of Sociology and Religion at the University College of Cape Breton, Nova Scotia, Canada, has taught there for the past twenty years. He has degrees in Philosophy, Economics, Theology, and a Doctorate in Sociology from the Sorbonne, Paris, France. He has published in both French and English, topics such as religion, culture, philosophy, health and development and contributed to International Congresses in Monterrey, N.L. Mexico and the International Conference on Medical Ethics in Beijing, China, 1993.

Robert C. O'Brien, B.A., M.A., Ph.D., Fordham University is currently an Assistant Dean for Academic Planning and Associate Professor of Philosophy at Fordham University's College at Lincoln Center. He specializes in histories of modern European and American Philosophy, Personalism and Existentialism, and has presented conference papers on Marx, Royce, Peirce, Kierkegaard, and technology. He is a member of the Metaphysical Society of America, the American Catholic Philosophical Society and the International Association for Christian Thought.

Mary L. O'Hara, C.S.J., Ph.D., formerly Professor of Philosophy at the College of St. Catherine and at the College of St. Mary, Omaha, NE, as well as Visiting Professor at St. Paul Seminary and the College of St. Teresa, Winona, MN, is currently writing a book on the philosophy of the human person. Researching this subject took her to India and Monterrey, Mexico and she has published articles on the subject in the ACPA *Proceedings*, the APA Newsletter on *Philosophy and Medicine, Apeiron*, and *Philosophy Today*, as well as other periodicals and proceedings.

James F. O'Leary, Ph.D., Syracuse University, is a member of the Philosophy and Religion Department at Daemen College, Amherst, NY. He has published in a variety of journals such as *The Journal for the Scientific Study of Religion, Journal of Aesthetics and Art Criticism, Philosophy and Phenomenology, Modern Schoolman*, and others. Currently, he is completing a book on "The Failure of Socrates."

Francisco L. Peccorini, Ph.D., Pontifical University Comillas, Santander, Spain, was born in San Miguel, El Salvador and taught there at the National University as well as at the University Deusto, Bilbao, Spain, the University of San Diego, and California State University, Long Beach. As Professor Emeritus, Peccorini retired to San Salvador where he taught "his philosophy," The Personalizing "Personalization of Being" in the human self at the Academy of the Language of El Salvador, a branch of the Royal Academy of the Language of Madrid. Peccorini was a writer and editor of *Estudios Centro Americanos*. Author of *A Method of Self-Orientation to Thinking, La Voluntad del Pueblo en la Emancipación de El Salvador; From Gentile's "Actualism" to Sciacca's "Idea;" On to the World of Freedom, A Kantian Meditation on Finite Selfhood; Selfhood as Thinking Thought in the Work of Gabriel Marcel*, and numerous articles. A member of national and international associations, Dr. Peccorini died in San Salvador June 5, 1989.

Robert Rweyemamu, Ph.D. Biographical data unavailable.

452

Josef Seifert, Ph.D., University of Salzburg, habilitation from the University of Munich. He was Professor and Chair of the Department of Philosophy at the University of Dallas, TX. In 1980 he co-founded and directed the International Academy of Philosophy (IAP) in Irving, TX and has been the Rector of the IAP in Liechtenstein since 1986. He is presently Professor of Philosophy at the IAP with special emphasis in Epistemology, Metaphysics and Philosophical Anthropology. Among his most important publications are: *Back to Things in Themselves: A Phenomenological Foundation for Classical Realism; Essere e Persona: Verso una Fondazione fenomenologica di una Metafisica classica e personalistica, Schachphilosophie.*

John J. Snyder, Ph.D., University of Toronto, Ontario, Canada, teaches Philosophy and Religious Studies at King's College in London, Ontario. Author of *Marrying for Life*, published in July, 1993, Snyder has written several articles and given numerous papers in Canada, the United States, Mexico, Puerto Rico and other countries. He is a member of the International Association for Christian Thought.

Terry J. Tekippe, Ph.D. in Theology, Fordham University, NY, and in Philosophy, Tulane University, LA, retains an interest in both fields, like his mentor, Bernard Lonergan. He has taught at Notre Dame Seminary in New Orleans, the Gregorian University in Rome, Italy, and is presently enjoying the Lonergan Fellowship at Boston College. Tekippe has contributed to Philosophical Conferences in the United States and Mexico.

Jane E. Francis